CHRONICLES OF THE CURSED SWORD

Volume 14

Story by
YEO BEOP-RYONG
Art by
PARK HUI-JIN

HAMBURG // LONDON // LOS ANGELES // TOKYO

Chronicles of the Cursed Sword Vol. 14
written by Yeo Beop-Ryong
illustrated by Park Hui-Jin

Translation - Youngju Ryu
English Adaptation - Matt Varosky
Retouch and Lettering - Chris Anderson
Production Artist - Ana Lopez and Alyson Stetz
Cover Design - Kyle Plummer

Editor - Aaron Suhr
Digital Imaging Manager - Chris Buford
Production Managers - Jennifer Miller and Mutsumi Miyazaki
Managing Editor - Lindsey Johnston
VP of Production - Ron Klamert
Publisher and E.I.C. - Mike Kiley
President and C.O.O. - John Parker
C.E.O. - Stuart Levy

A  Manga

TOKYOPOP Inc.
5900 Wilshire Blvd. Suite 2000
Los Angeles, CA 90036

E-mail: info@TOKYOPOP.com
Come visit us online at www.TOKYOPOP.com

ISBN: 1-59532-646-4

First TOKYOPOP printing: January 2006
10 9 8 7 6 5 4 3 2 1
Printed in the USA

Chronicles

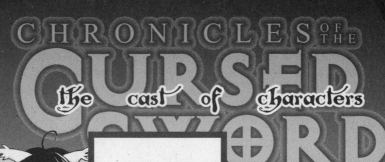

CHRONICLES OF THE CURSED SWORD

the cast of characters

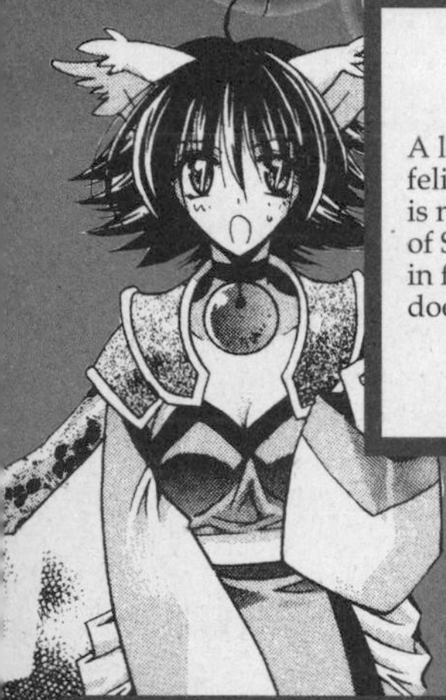

MINGLING

A lesser demon with feline qualities, Mingling is now the loyal follower of Shyao Lin. She lives in fear of Rey, who still doesn't trust her.

THE PASA SWORD

A living sword that hungers for demon blood. It grants its user incredible power, but at a great cost - it can take over the user's body and, in time, his soul.

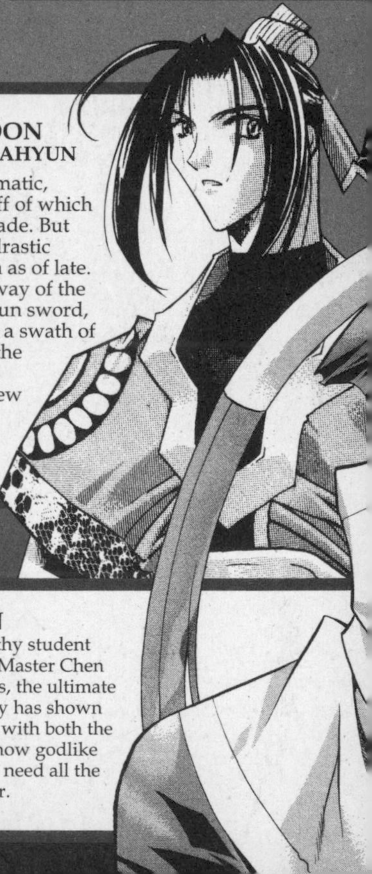

JARYOON
KING OF HAHYUN

Noble and charismatic, Jaryoon is the stuff of which great kings are made. But there has been a drastic change in Jaryoon as of late. Now under the sway of the spirit of the PaChun sword, Jaryoon is cutting a swath of humanity across the countryside as he searches for his new prey: Rey.

SHYAO LIN

A sorceress, previously Rey's traveling companion and greatest ally. Shyao has recently discovered that she is, in fact, one of the Eight Sages of the Azure Pavilion, sent to gather information in the Human Realm. Much to her dismay, she has been told that she must now kill Rey Yan.

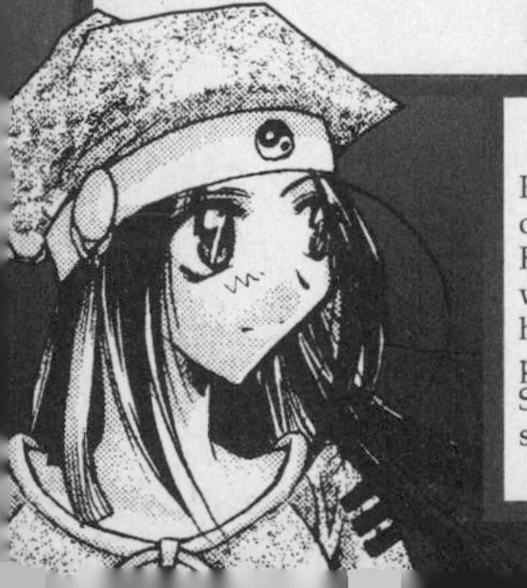

REY YAN

Rey has proven to be a worthy student of the wise and diminutive Master Chen Kaihu. At the Mujin Fortress, the ultimate warrior testing grounds, Rey has shown his martial arts mettle. And with both the possessed Jaryoon and the now godlike Shyao after his blood—he'll need all the survival skills he can muster.

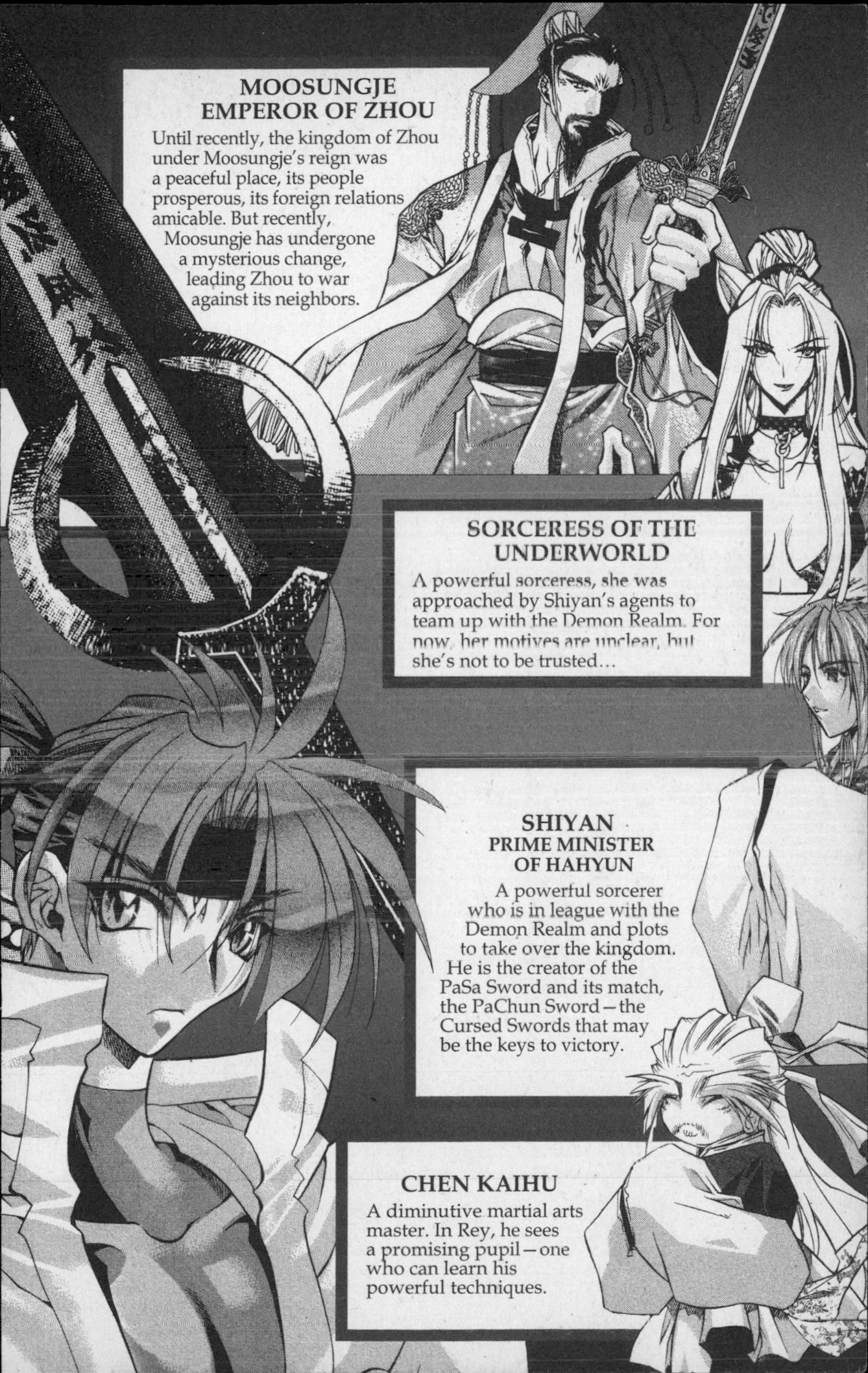

MOOSUNGJE EMPEROR OF ZHOU

Until recently, the kingdom of Zhou under Moosungje's reign was a peaceful place, its people prosperous, its foreign relations amicable. But recently, Moosungje has undergone a mysterious change, leading Zhou to war against its neighbors.

SORCERESS OF THE UNDERWORLD

A powerful sorceress, she was approached by Shiyan's agents to team up with the Demon Realm. For now, her motives are unclear, but she's not to be trusted...

SHIYAN PRIME MINISTER OF HAHYUN

A powerful sorcerer who is in league with the Demon Realm and plots to take over the kingdom. He is the creator of the PaSa Sword and its match, the PaChun Sword—the Cursed Swords that may be the keys to victory.

CHEN KAIHU

A diminutive martial arts master. In Rey, he sees a promising pupil—one who can learn his powerful techniques.

Thus Far In...

CHRONICLES OF THE
CURSED
SWORD

In an era of warring states, warlords become kings, dynasties crumble, and heroes can rise from the most unlikely places. Rey Yan was an orphan with no home no skills and no purpose. But when he comes upon the PaSa sword, a cursed blade made from the bones of the Demon Emperor, he suddenly finds himself with the power to be a great hero...

In their struggle to save Lady Hyacia, Rey and company finally succeed in shutting down the treacherous defense of the Sorcerer King's fortress...only to be faced with new challenges from within. And the final obstacle: a showdown with the Sorcerer King himself! However, the Sorcerer King's new powers are so great that he threatens all three realms. Will it be possible to defeat the corrupted King?

Chapter 55
Spellbound

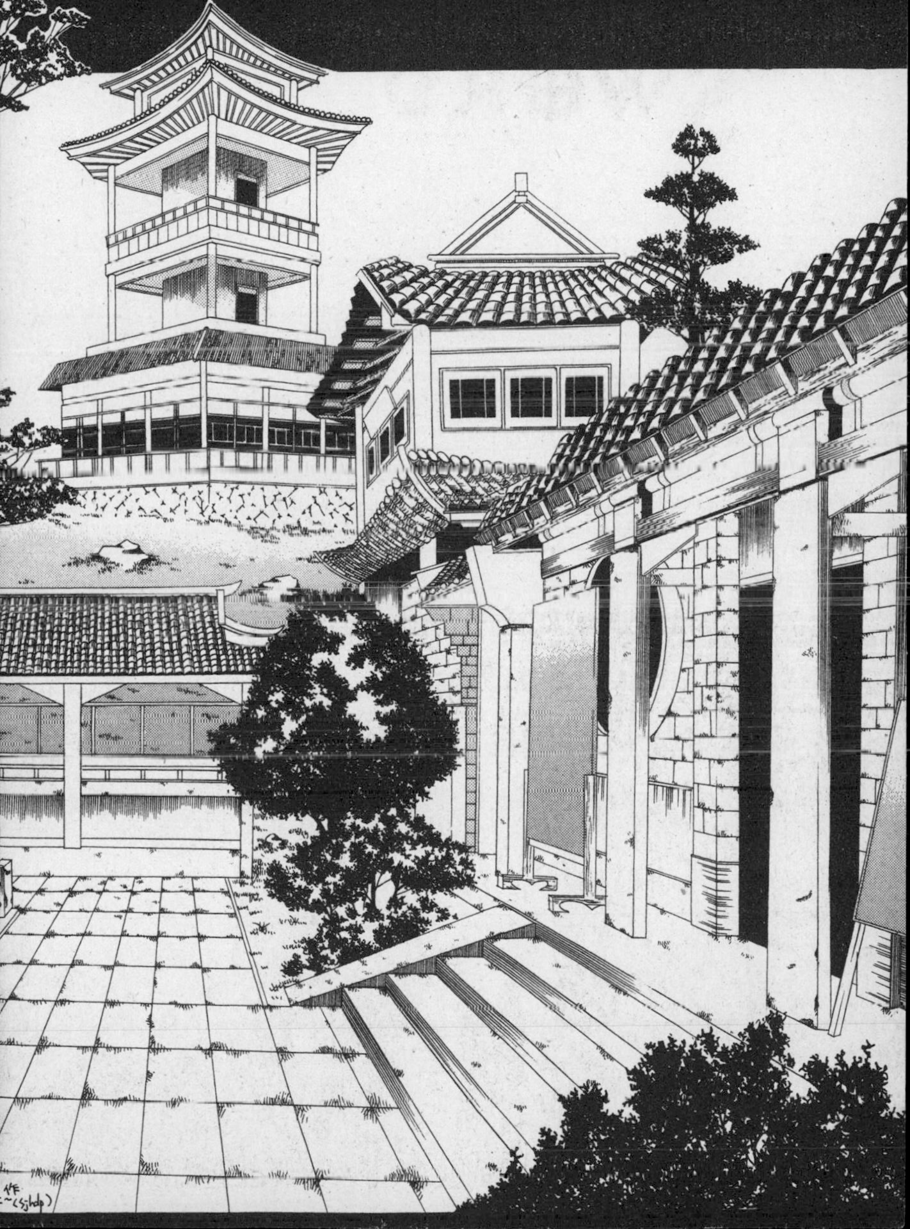

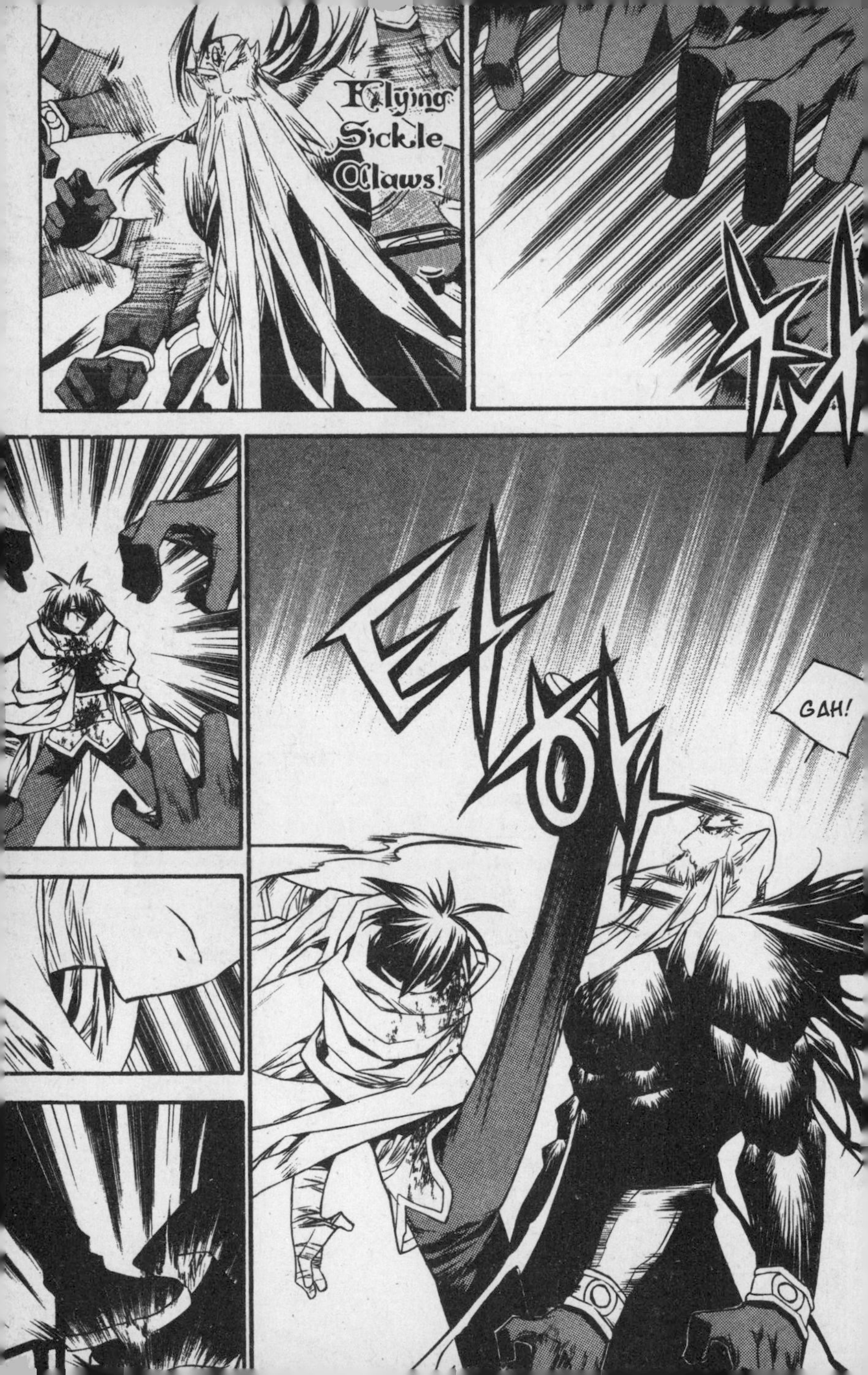
Flying Sickle Claws!
GAH!

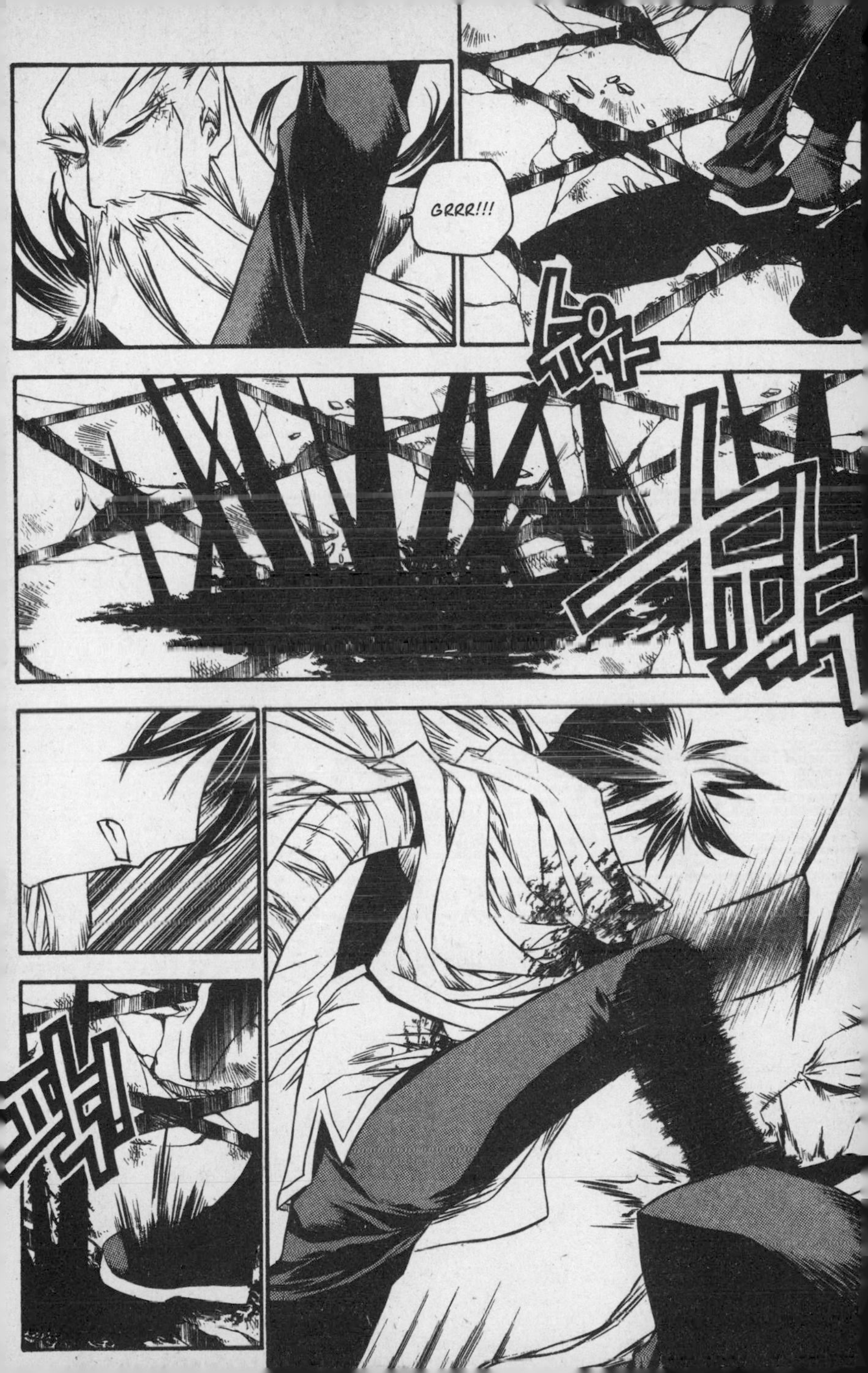
GRRR!!!

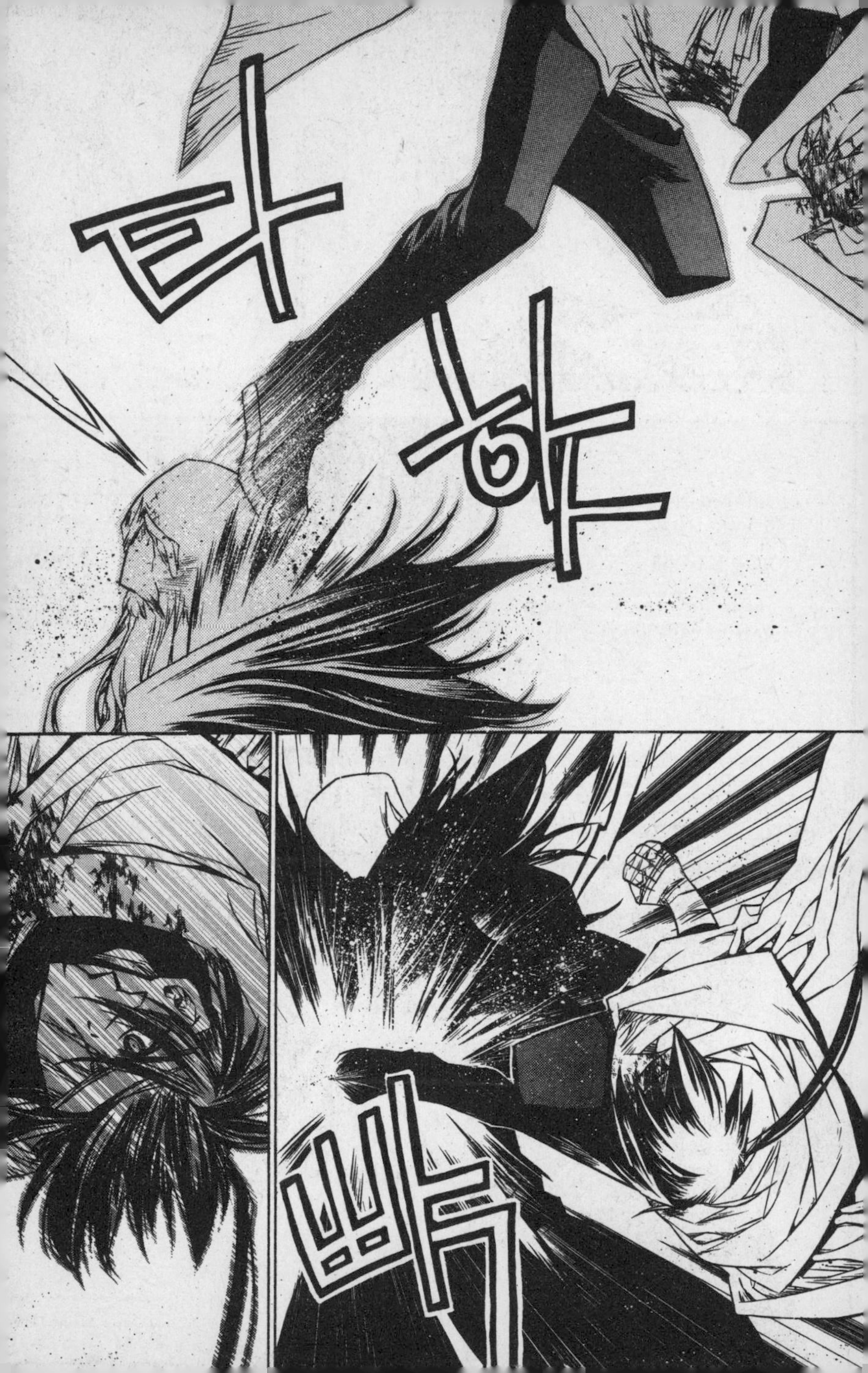

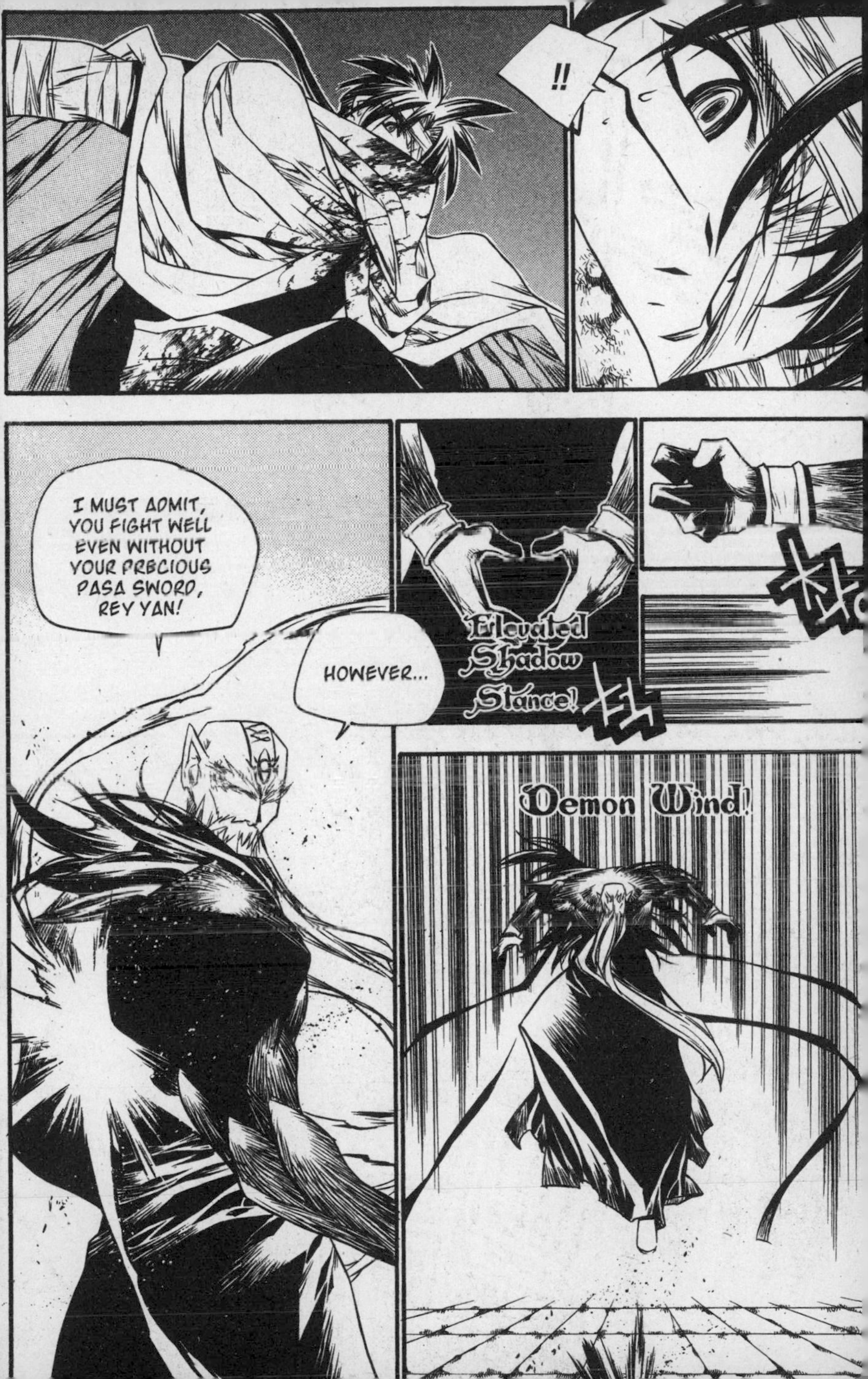
!!
I MUST ADMIT, YOU FIGHT WELL EVEN WITHOUT YOUR PRECIOUS PASA SWORD, REY YAN!
HOWEVER...
Elevated Shadow Stance!
Demon Wind!

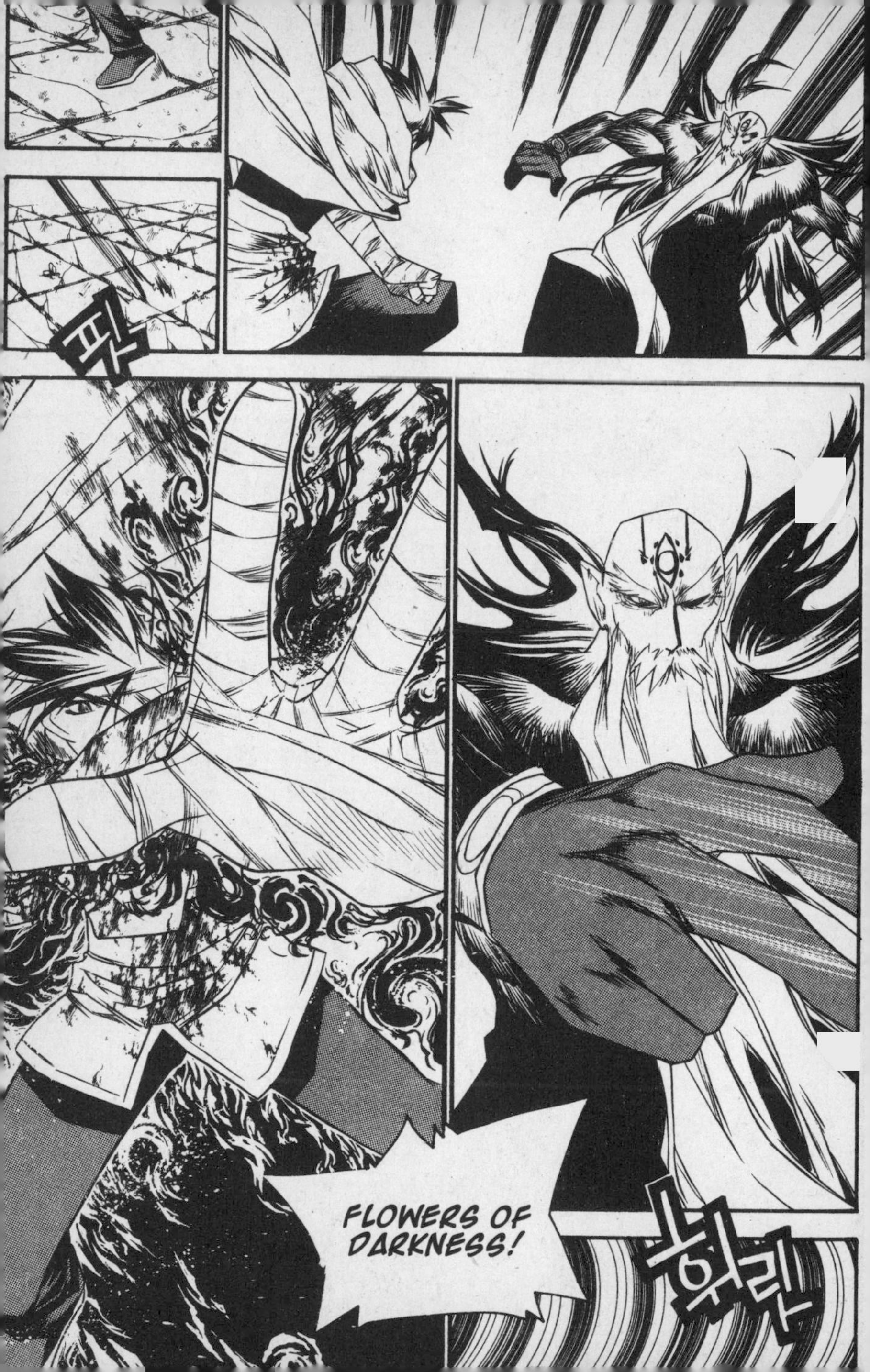
FLOWERS OF DARKNESS!

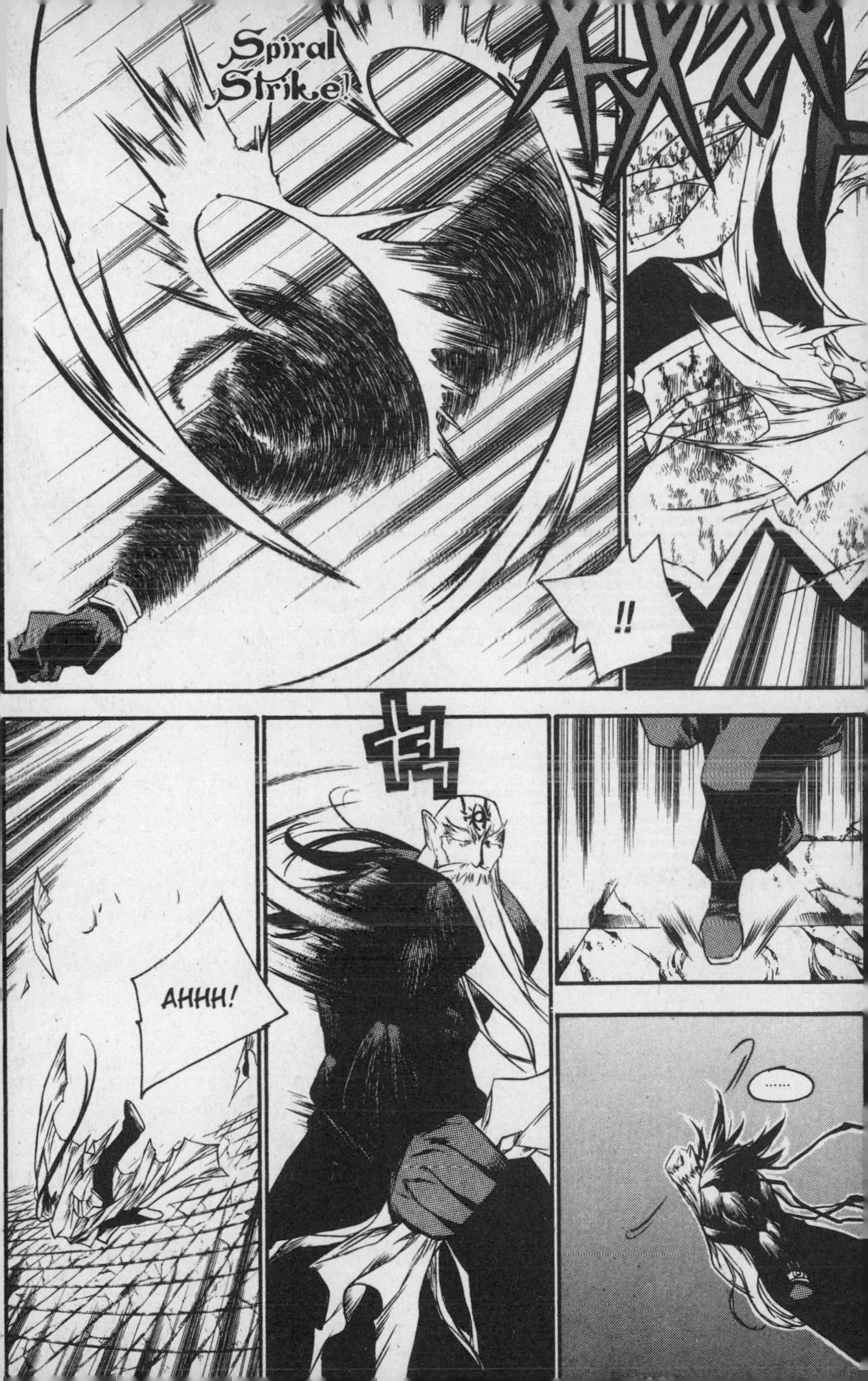
Spiral Strike!!
!!
AHHH!
......

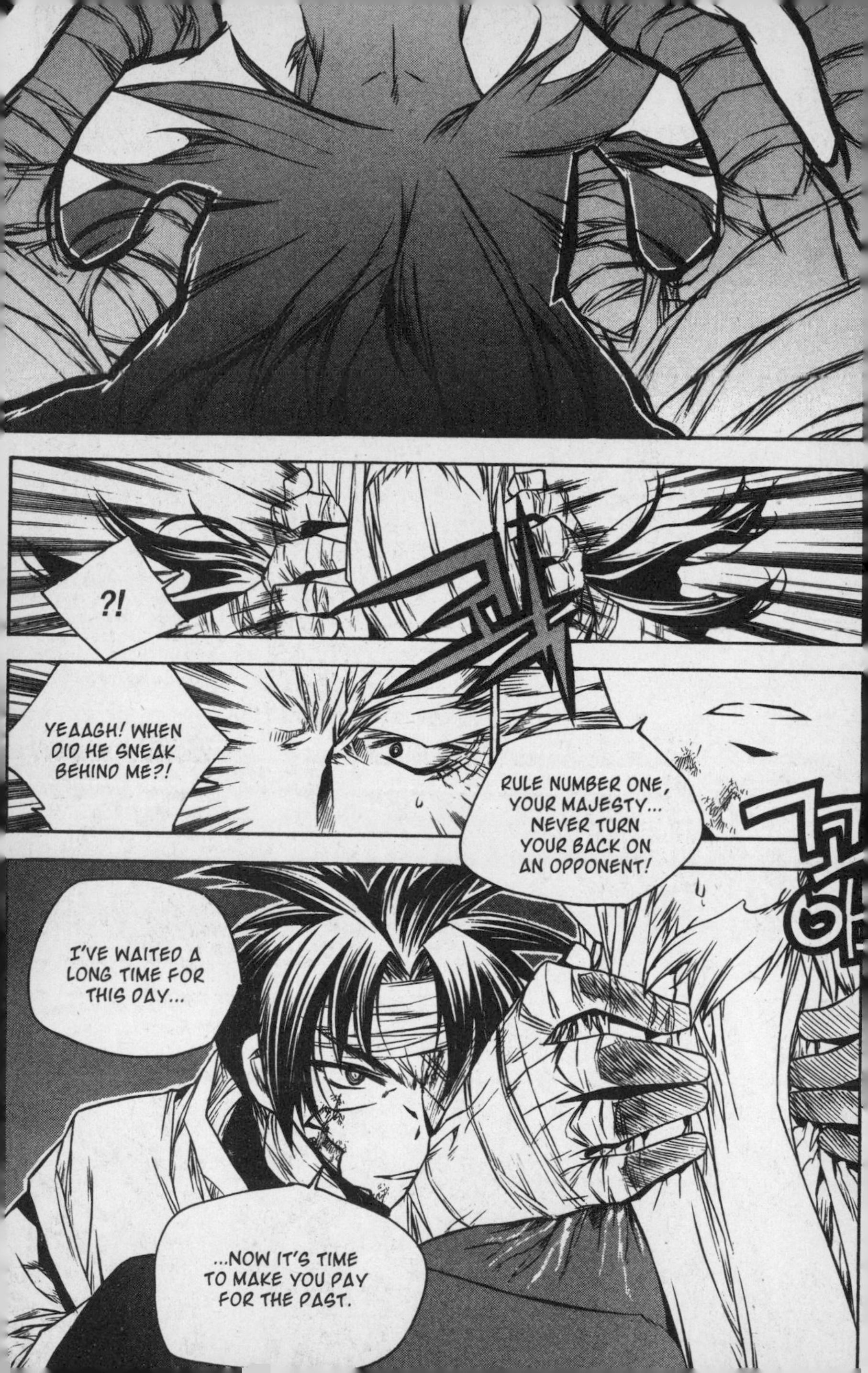
?!
YEAAGH! WHEN DID HE SNEAK BEHIND ME?!
RULE NUMBER ONE, YOUR MAJESTY... NEVER TURN YOUR BACK ON AN OPPONENT!
I'VE WAITED A LONG TIME FOR THIS DAY...
...NOW IT'S TIME TO MAKE YOU PAY FOR THE PAST.

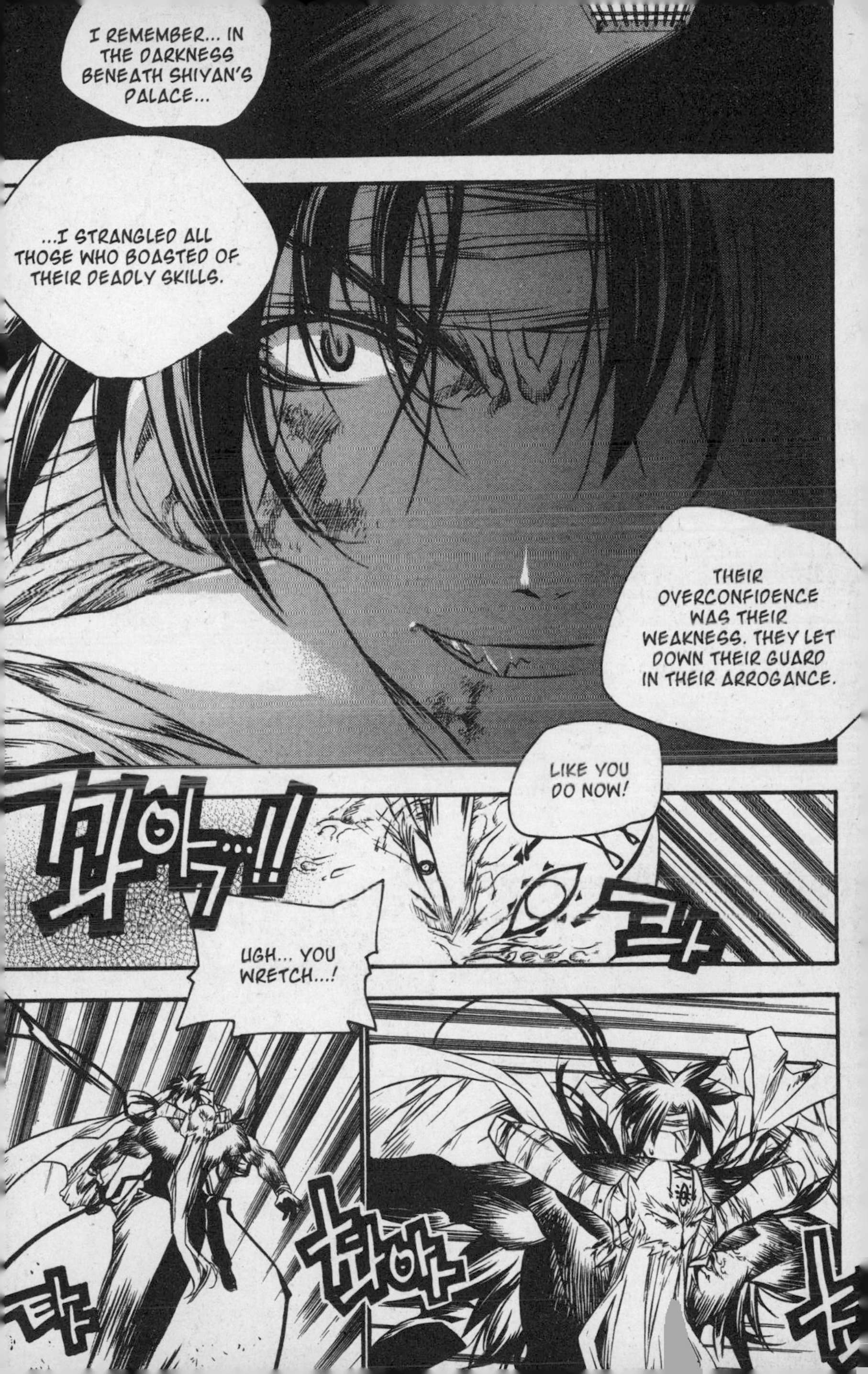
I REMEMBER... IN THE DARKNESS BENEATH SHIYAN'S PALACE...
...I STRANGLED ALL THOSE WHO BOASTED OF THEIR DEADLY SKILLS.
THEIR OVERCONFIDENCE WAS THEIR WEAKNESS. THEY LET DOWN THEIR GUARD IN THEIR ARROGANCE.
LIKE YOU DO NOW!
UGH... YOU WRETCH...!

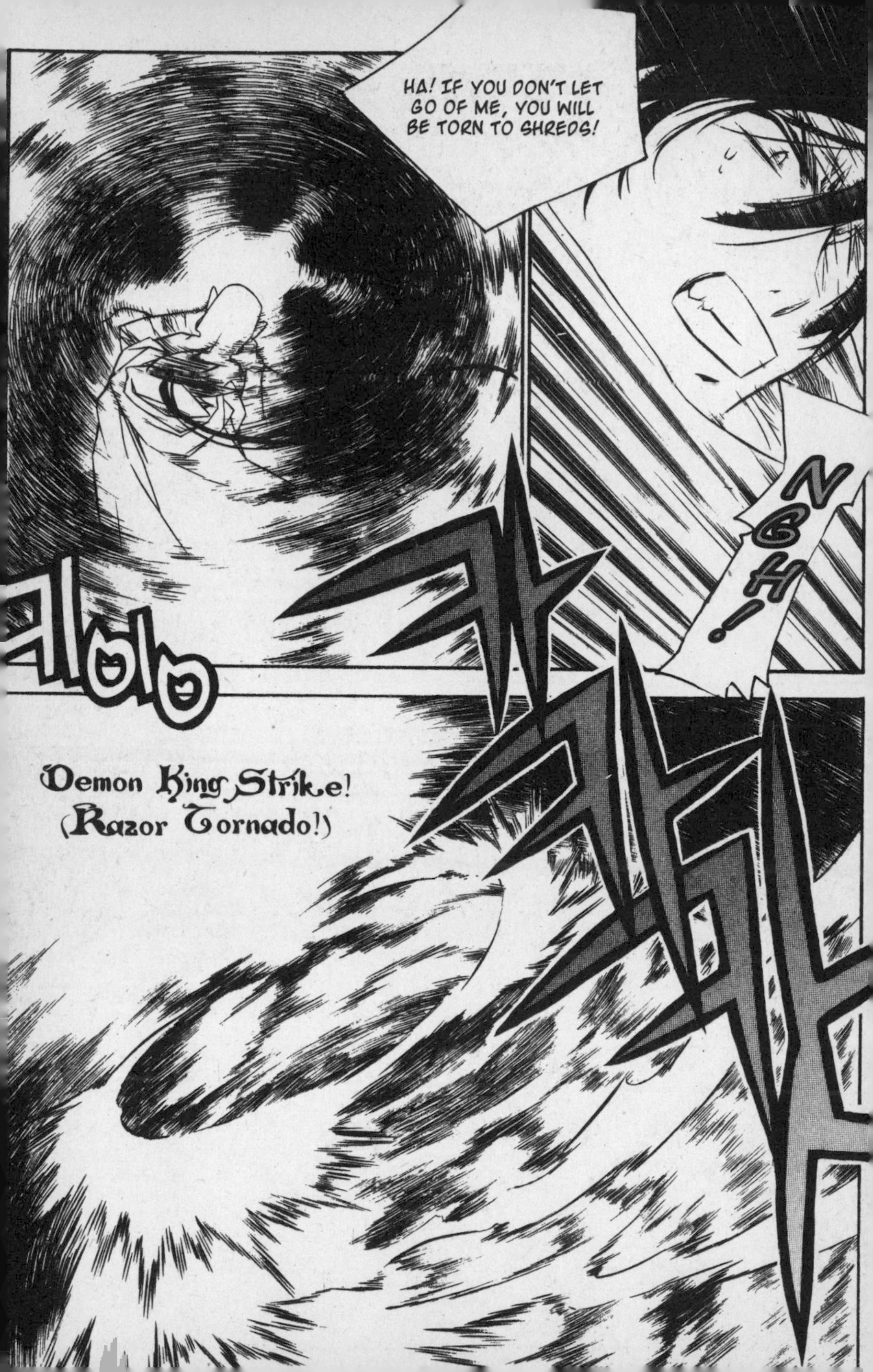
HA! IF YOU DON'T LET GO OF ME, YOU WILL BE TORN TO SHREDS!
NGH!
Demon King Strike! (Razor Tornado!)

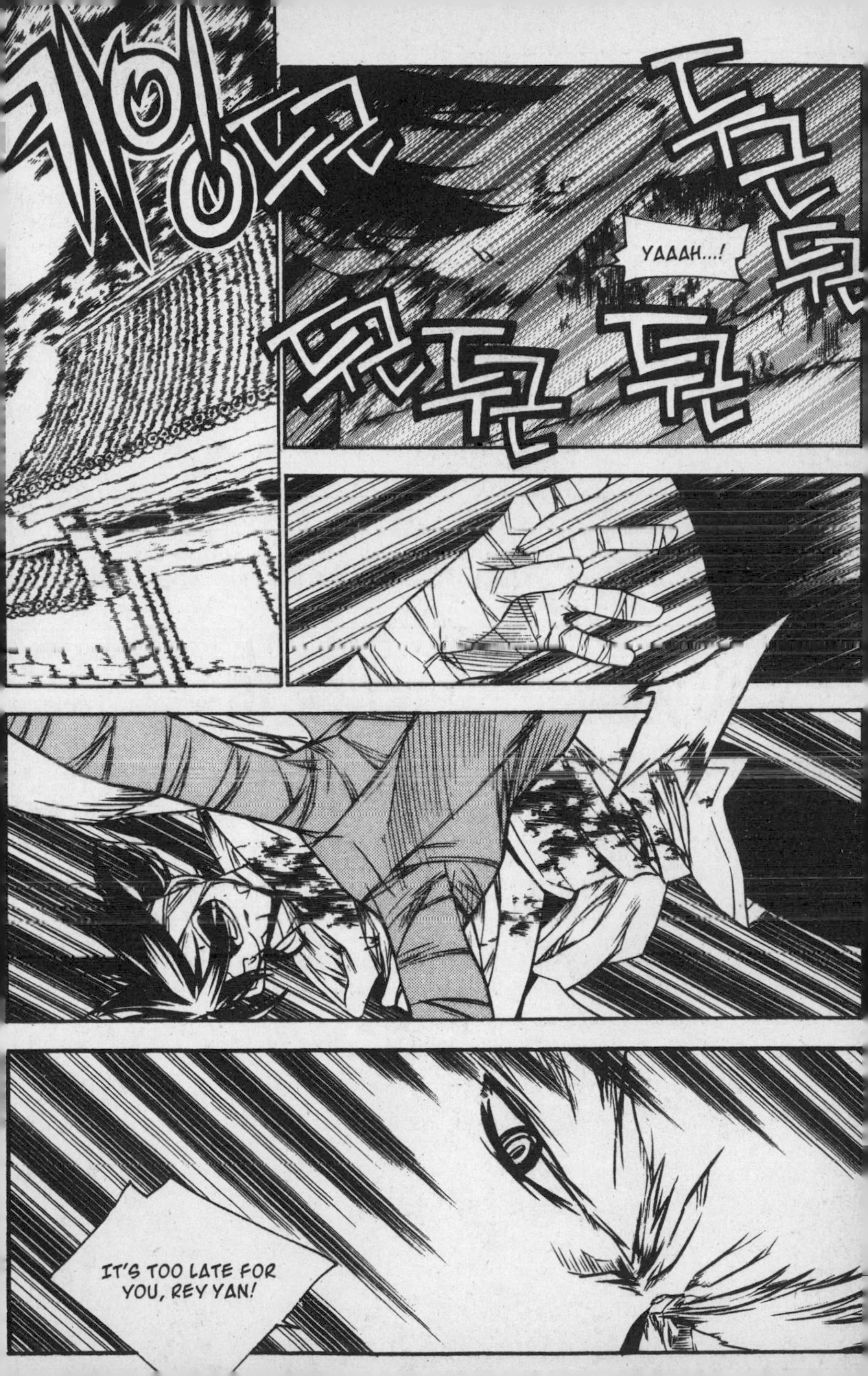
YAAAH...!
IT'S TOO LATE FOR YOU, REY YAN!

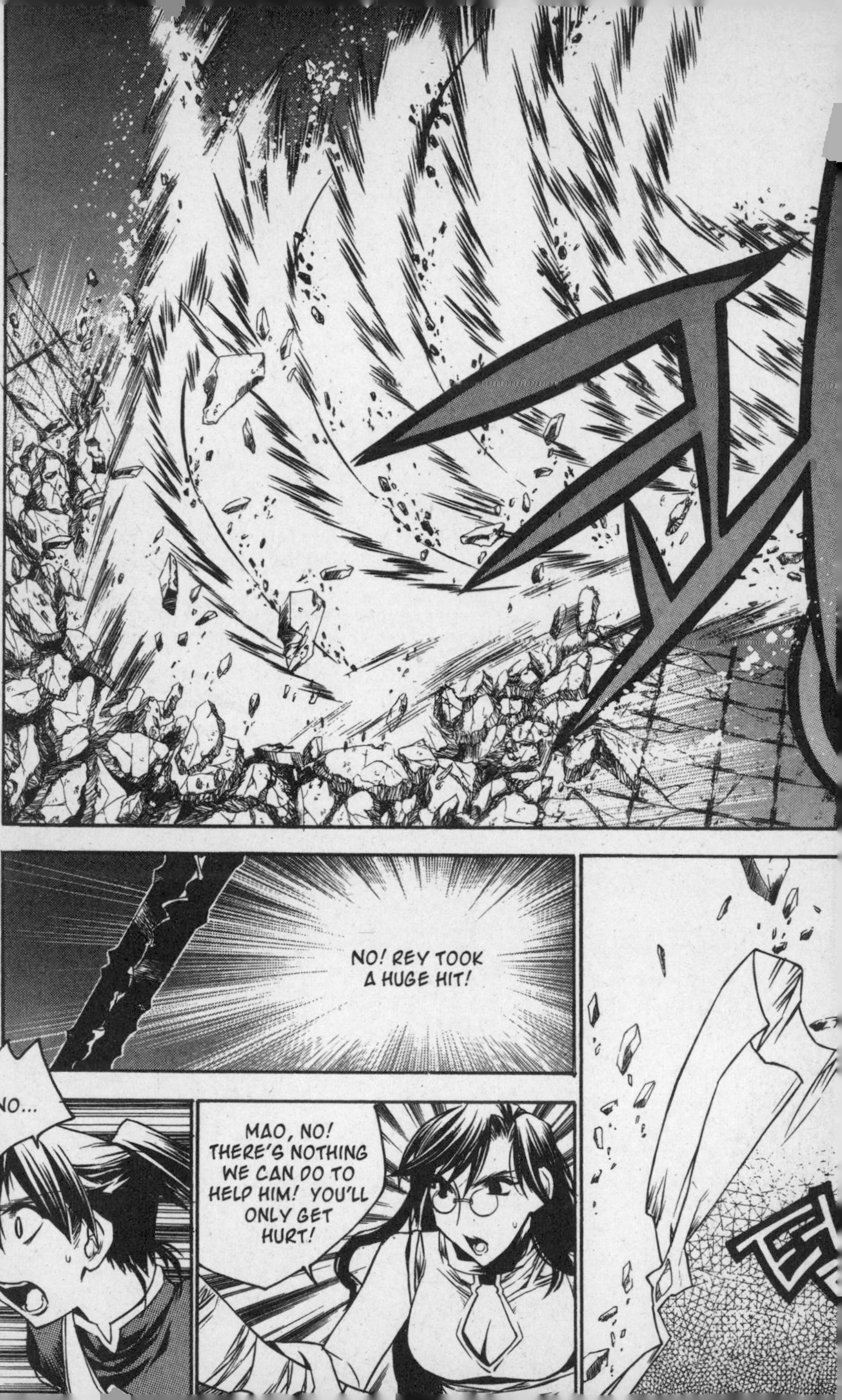
NO! REY TOOK A HUGE HIT!
NO...
MAO, NO! THERE'S NOTHING WE CAN DO TO HELP HIM! YOU'LL ONLY GET HURT!

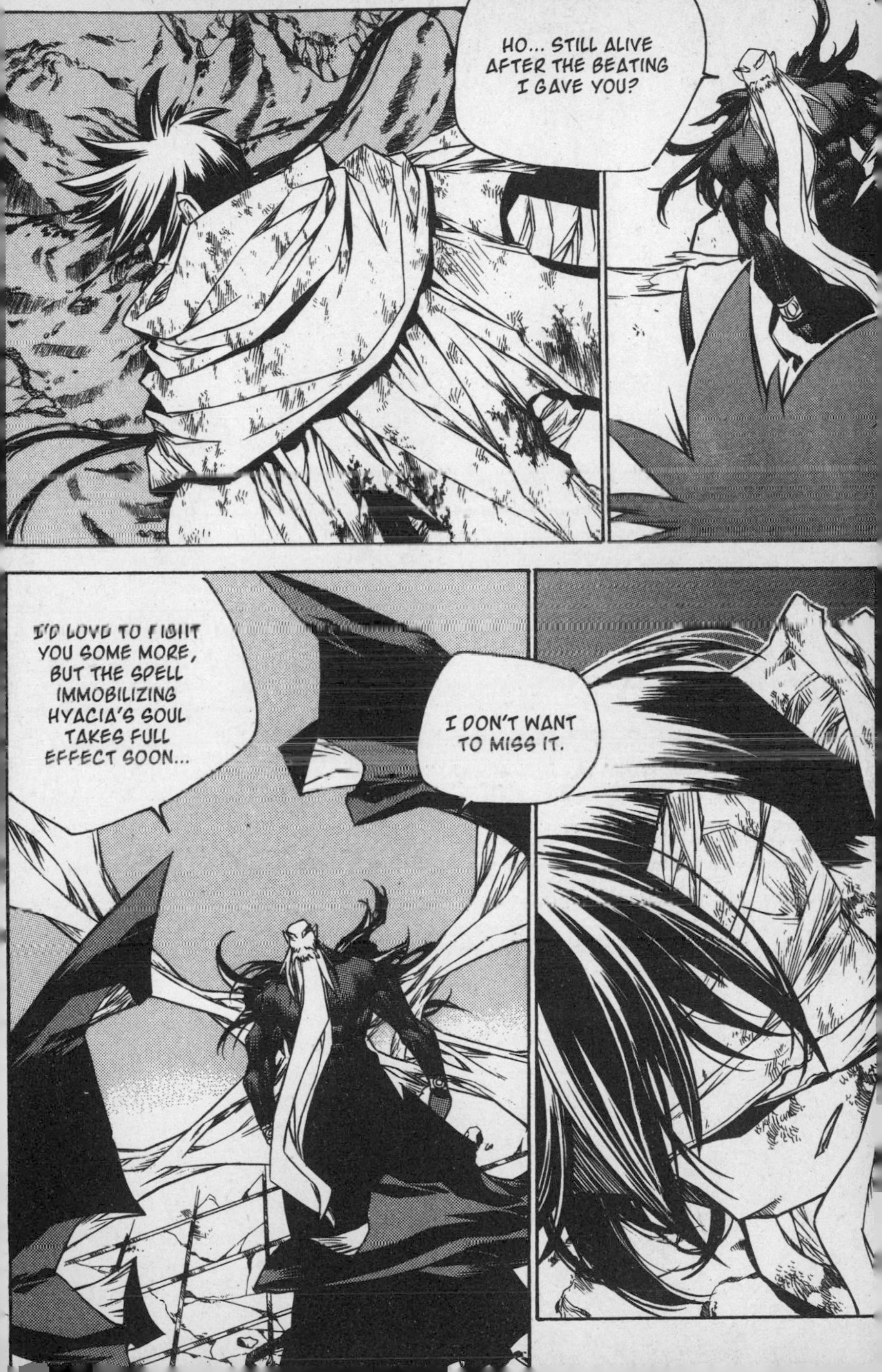
HO... STILL ALIVE AFTER THE BEATING I GAVE YOU?
I'D LOVE TO FIGHT YOU SOME MORE, BUT THE SPELL IMMOBILIZING HYACIA'S SOUL TAKES FULL EFFECT SOON...
I DON'T WANT TO MISS IT.

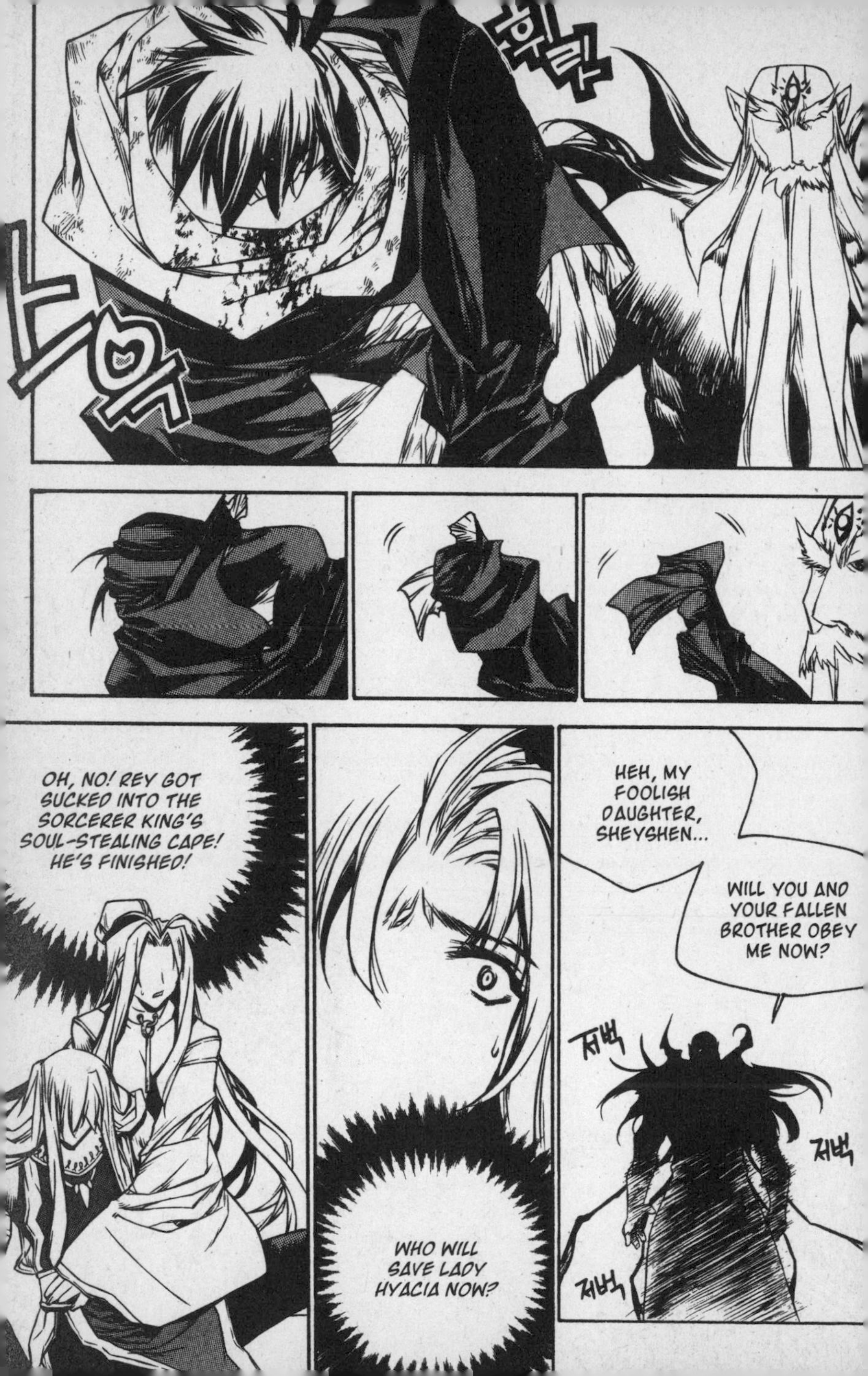
OH, NO! REY GOT SUCKED INTO THE SORCERER KING'S SOUL-STEALING CAPE! HE'S FINISHED!
WHO WILL SAVE LADY HYACIA NOW?
HEH, MY FOOLISH DAUGHTER, SHEYSHEN...
WILL YOU AND YOUR FALLEN BROTHER OBEY ME NOW?
저벅
저벅
저벅

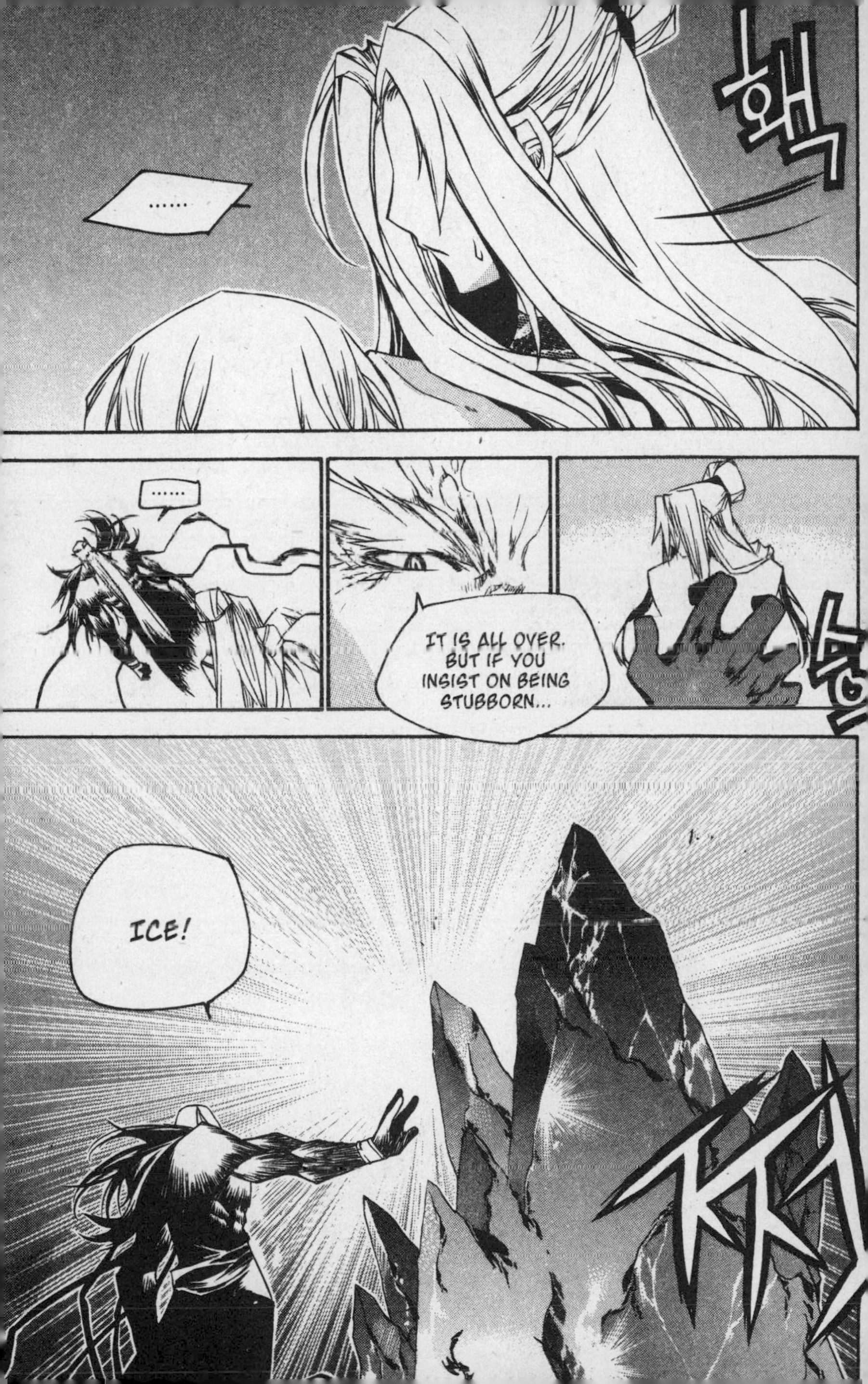

......
......
IT IS ALL OVER. BUT IF YOU INSIST ON BEING STUBBORN...
ICE!

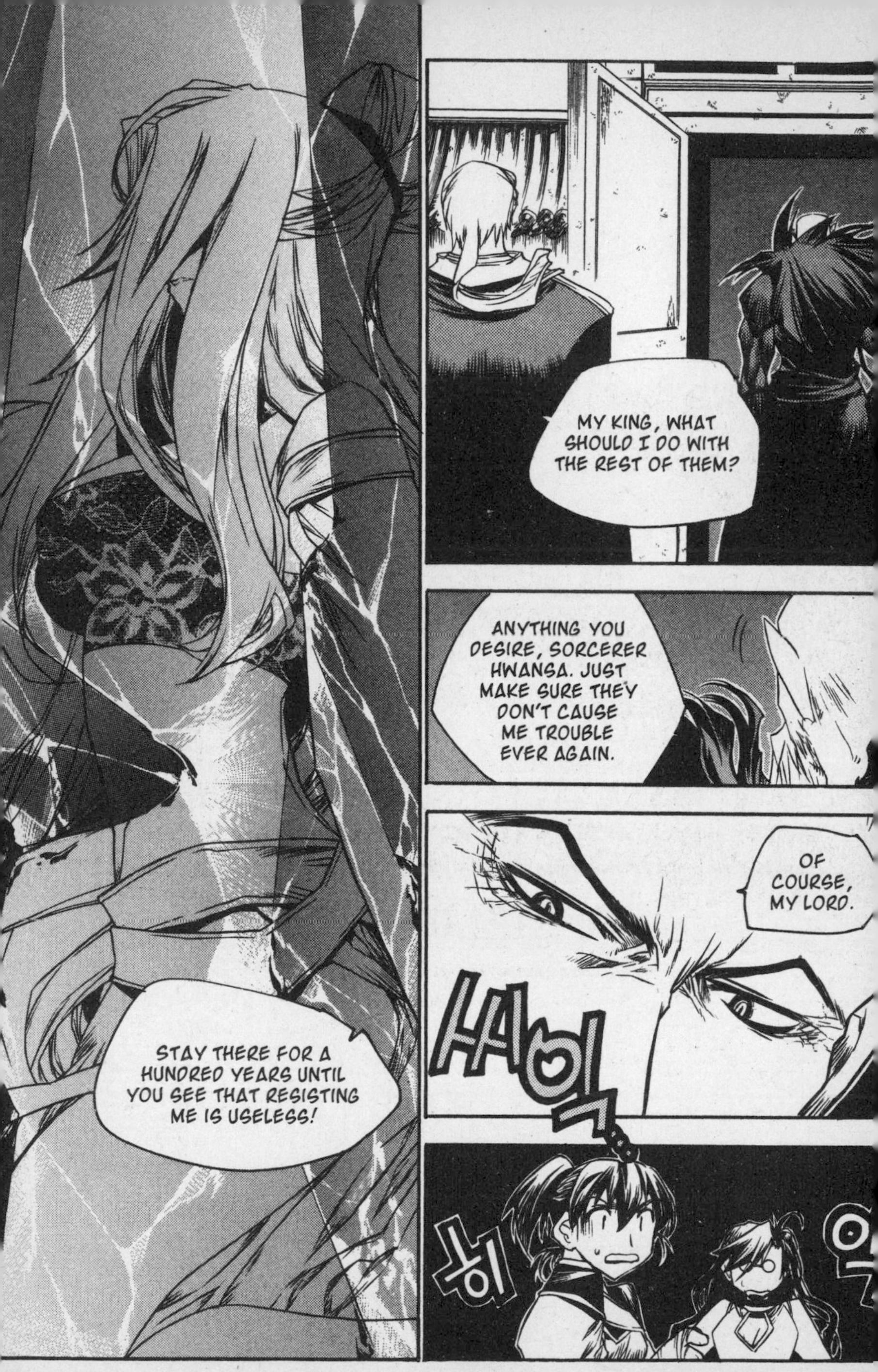
STAY THERE FOR A HUNDRED YEARS UNTIL YOU SEE THAT RESISTING ME IS USELESS!
MY KING, WHAT SHOULD I DO WITH THE REST OF THEM?
ANYTHING YOU DESIRE, SORCERER HWANSA. JUST MAKE SURE THEY DON'T CAUSE ME TROUBLE EVER AGAIN.
OF COURSE, MY LORD.

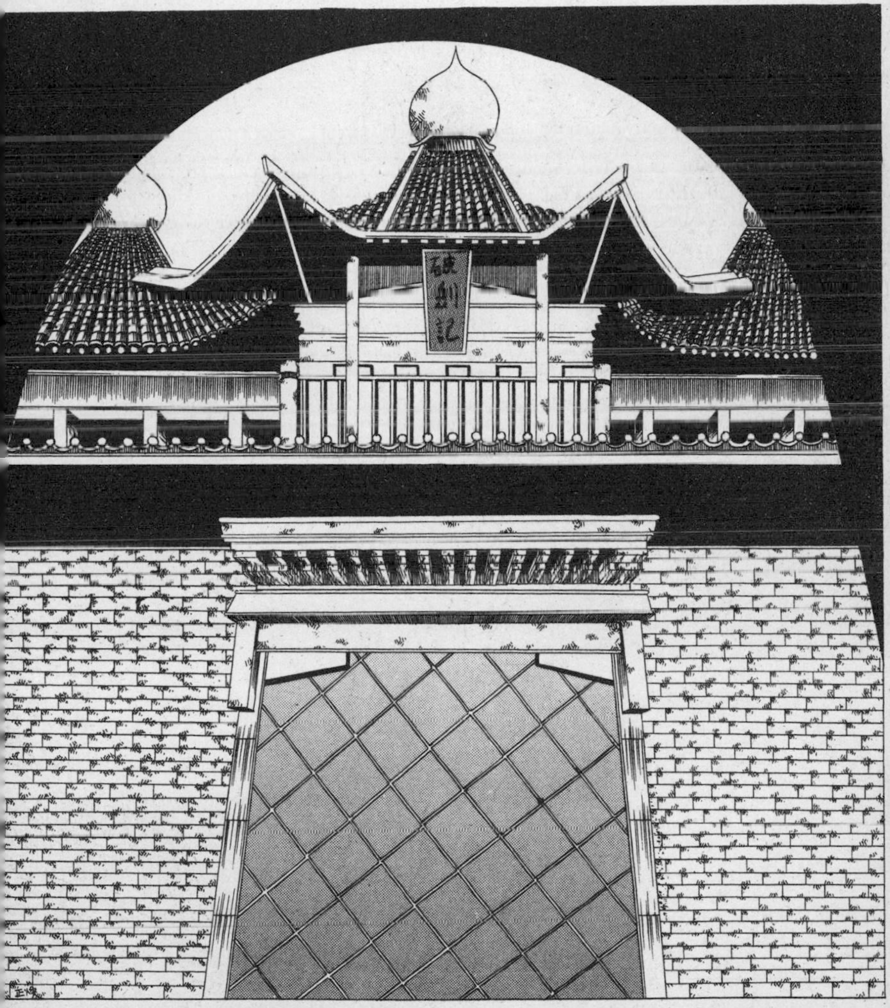

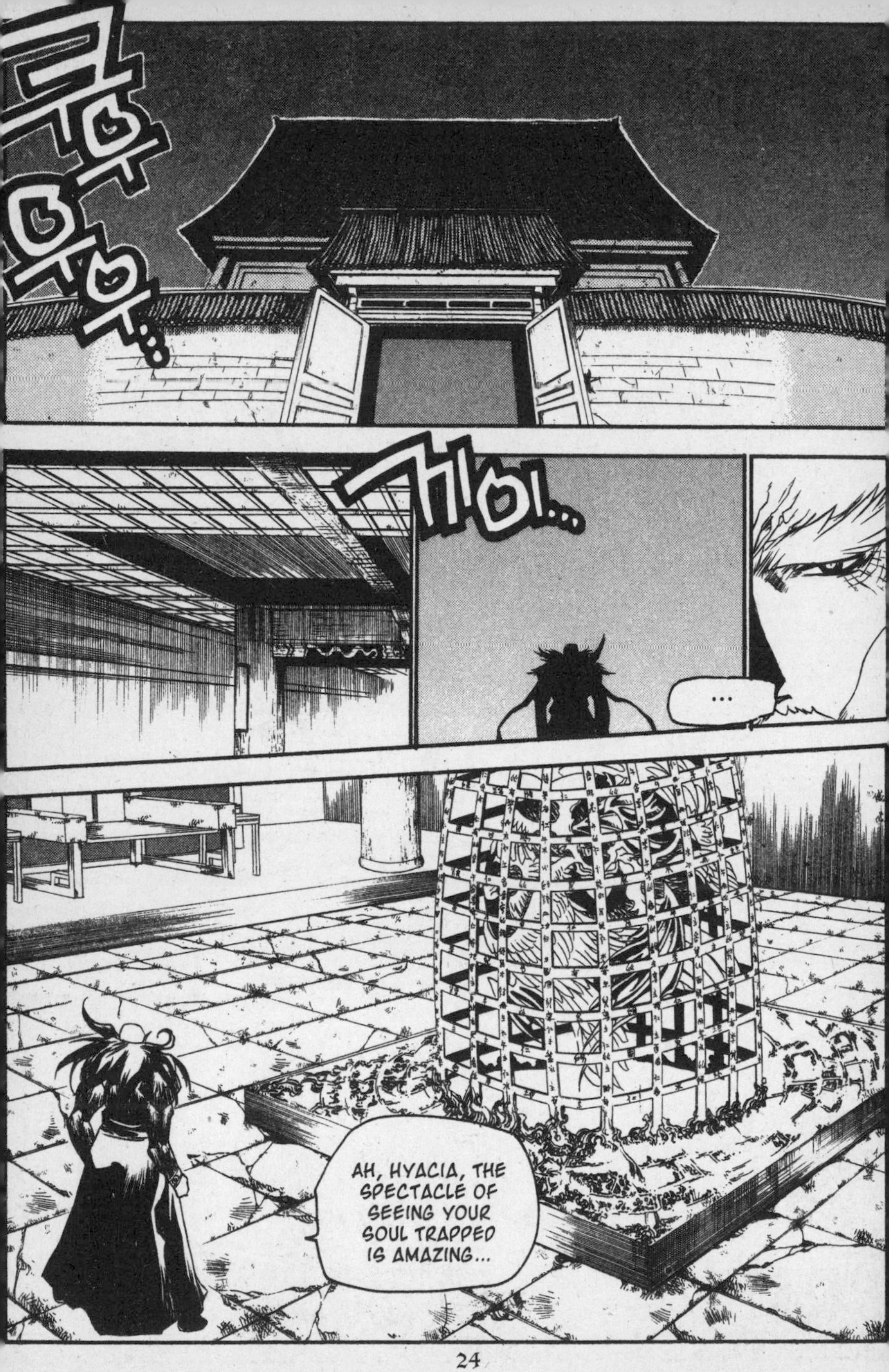
...
AH, HYACIA, THE SPECTACLE OF SEEING YOUR SOUL TRAPPED IS AMAZING...

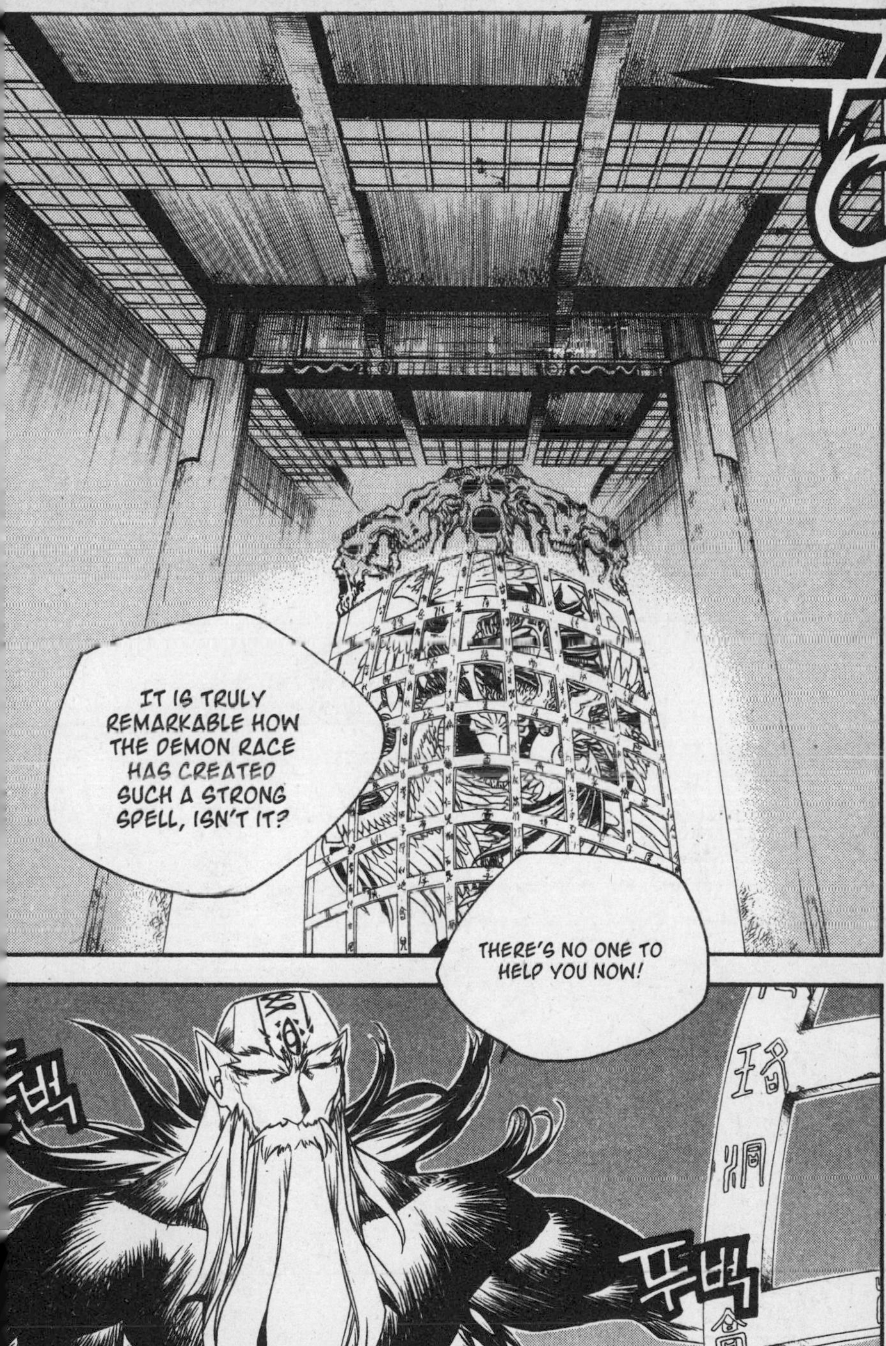
IT IS TRULY REMARKABLE HOW THE DEMON RACE HAS CREATED SUCH A STRONG SPELL, ISN'T IT?
THERE'S NO ONE TO HELP YOU NOW!

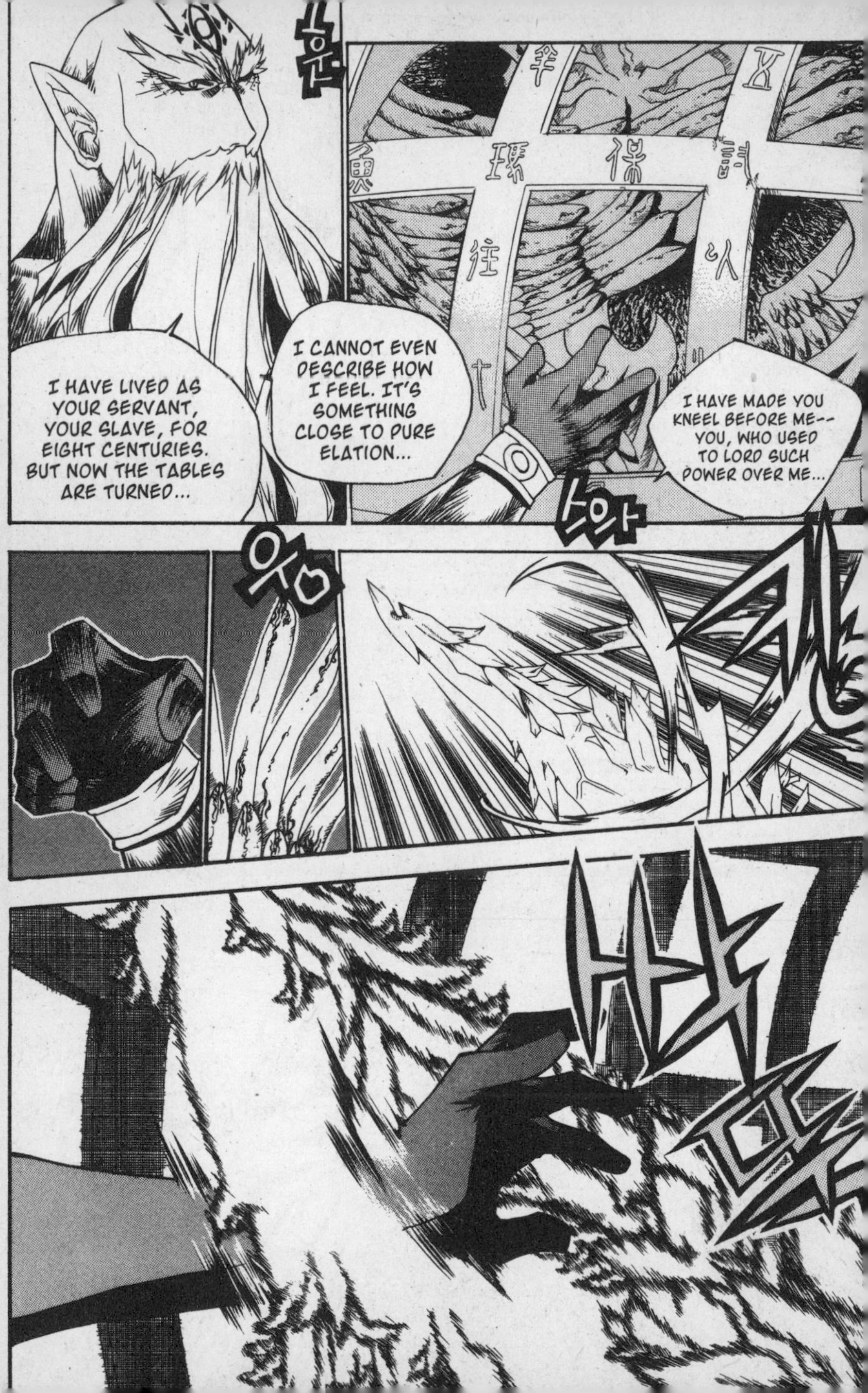
I HAVE LIVED AS YOUR SERVANT, YOUR SLAVE, FOR EIGHT CENTURIES. BUT NOW THE TABLES ARE TURNED...
I CANNOT EVEN DESCRIBE HOW I FEEL. IT'S SOMETHING CLOSE TO PURE ELATION...
I HAVE MADE YOU KNEEL BEFORE ME--YOU, WHO USED TO LORD SUCH POWER OVER ME...

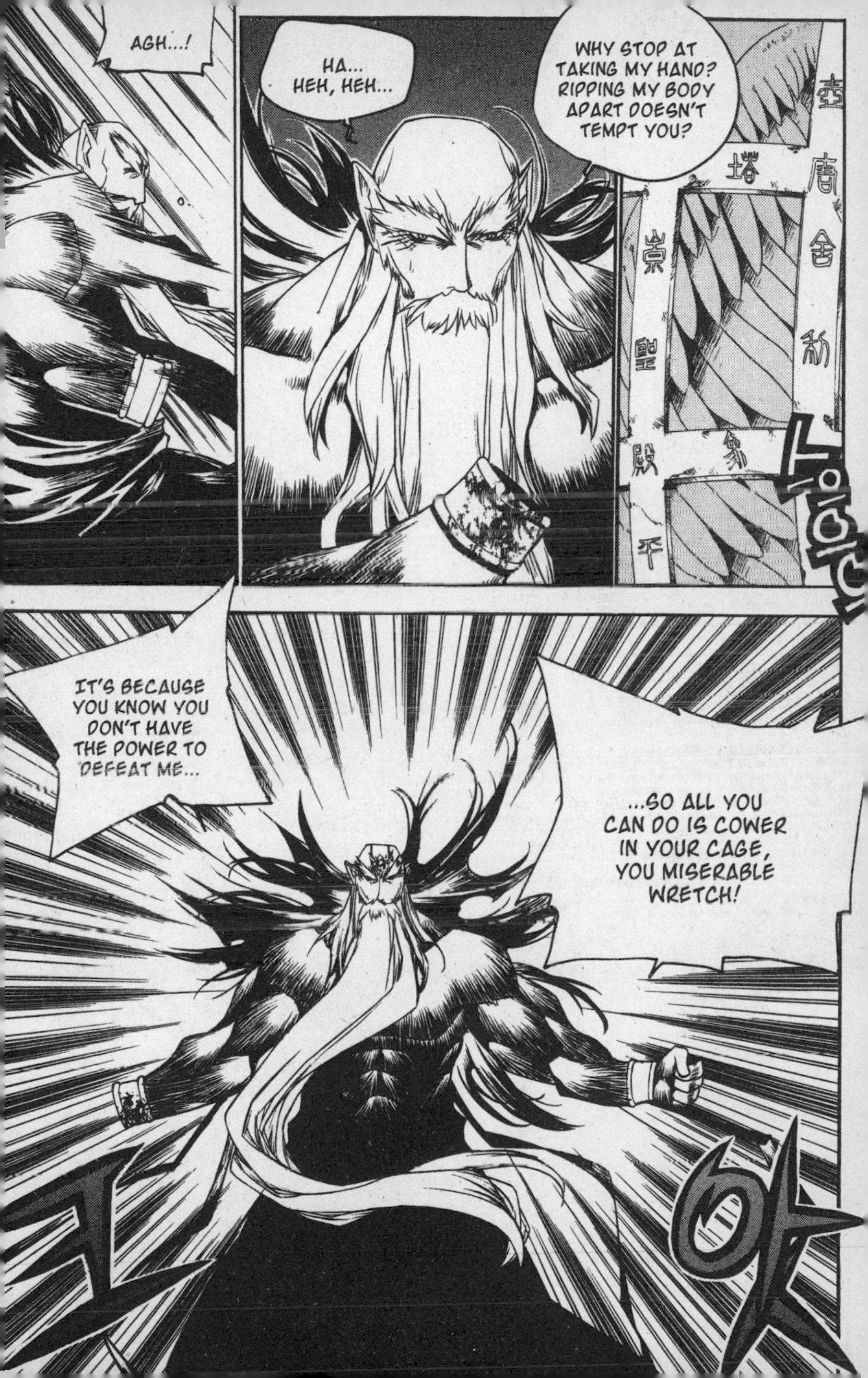
AGH...!
HA... HEH, HEH...
WHY STOP AT TAKING MY HAND? RIPPING MY BODY APART DOESN'T TEMPT YOU?
IT'S BECAUSE YOU KNOW YOU DON'T HAVE THE POWER TO DEFEAT ME...
...SO ALL YOU CAN DO IS COWER IN YOUR CAGE, YOU MISERABLE WRETCH!

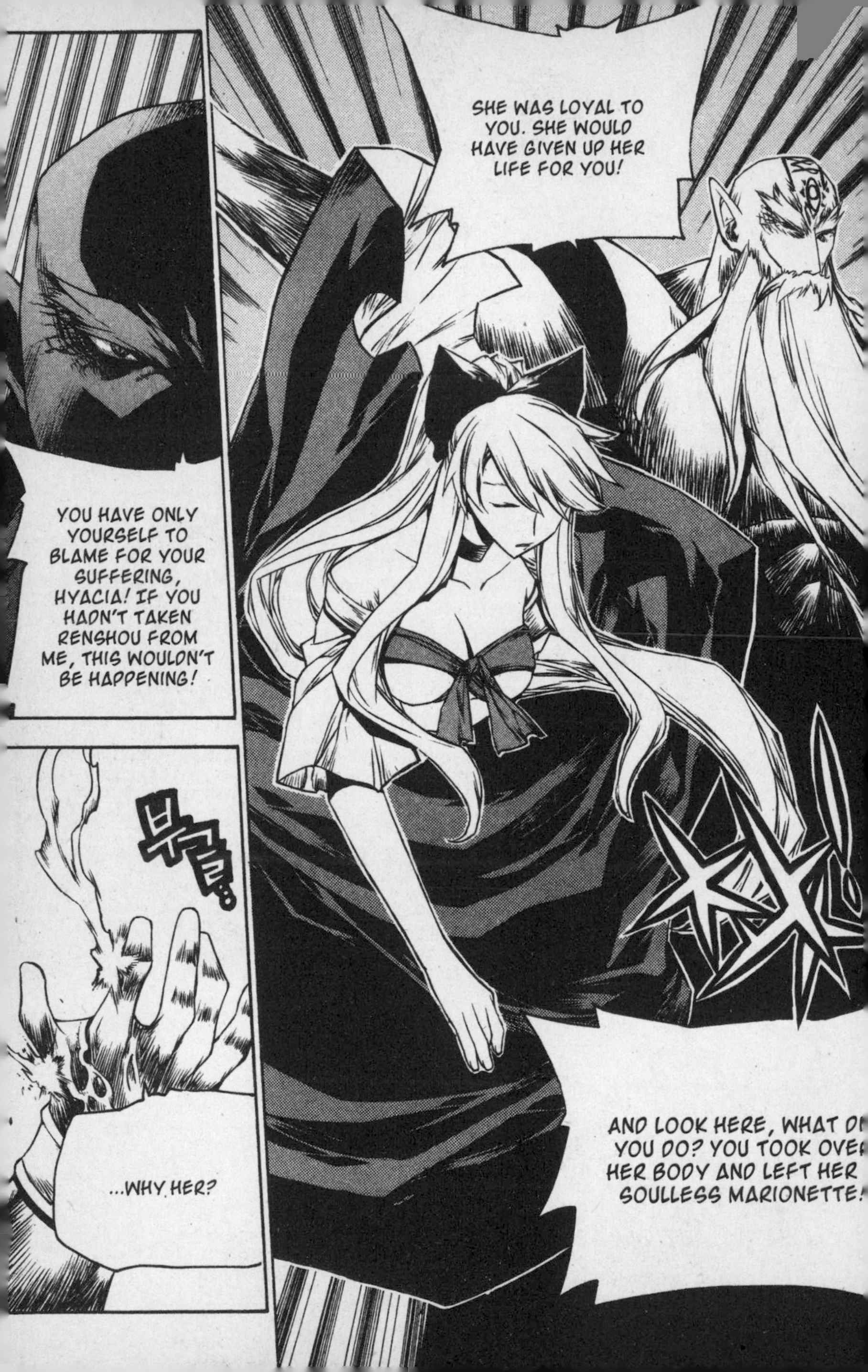
YOU HAVE ONLY YOURSELF TO BLAME FOR YOUR SUFFERING, HYACIA! IF YOU HADN'T TAKEN RENSHOU FROM ME, THIS WOULDN'T BE HAPPENING!
부글
...WHY HER?
SHE WAS LOYAL TO YOU. SHE WOULD HAVE GIVEN UP HER LIFE FOR YOU!
AND LOOK HERE, WHAT DI
YOU DO? YOU TOOK OVE
HER BODY AND LEFT HER
SOULLESS MARIONETTE!

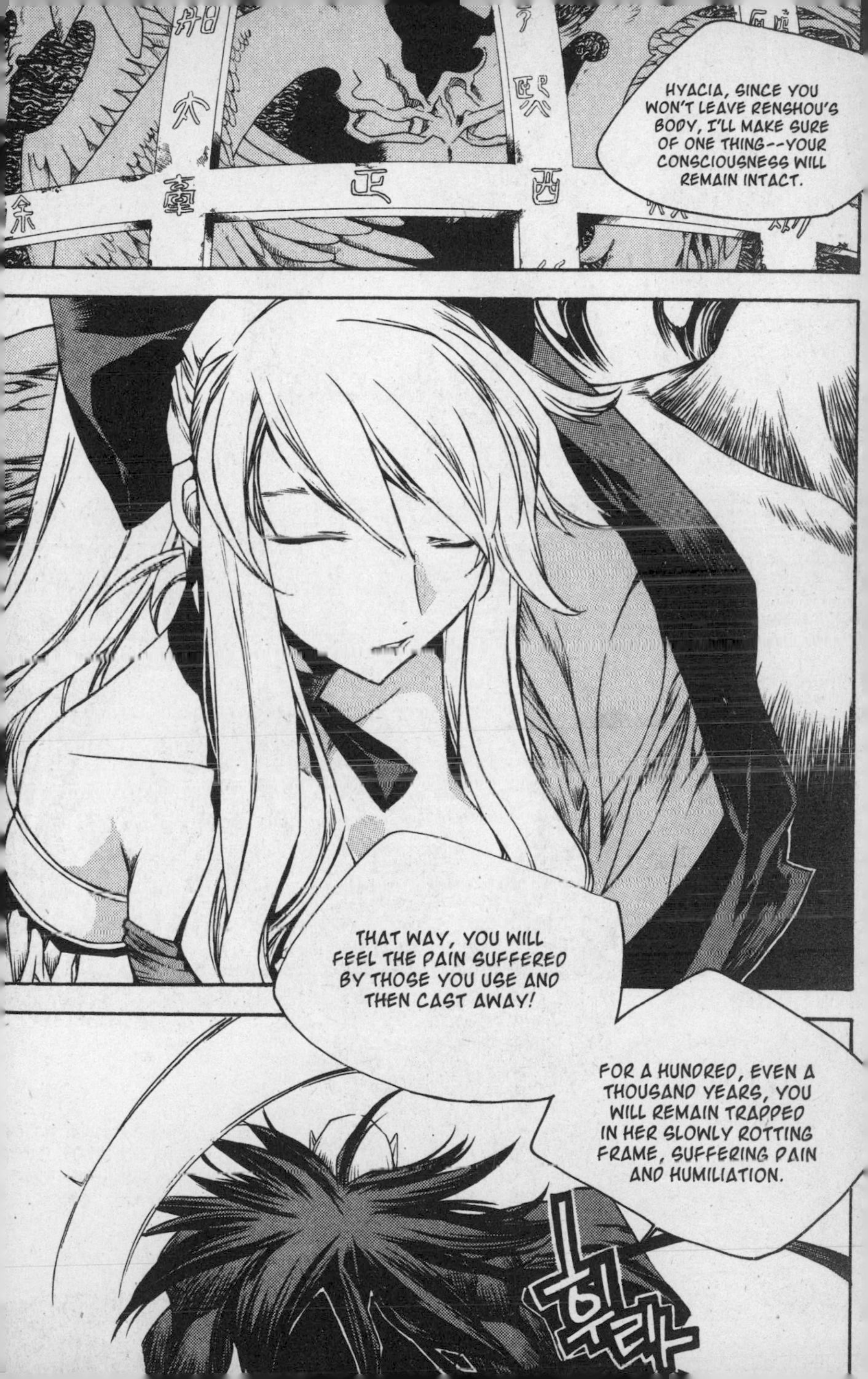
HYACIA, SINCE YOU WON'T LEAVE RENSHOU'S BODY, I'LL MAKE SURE OF ONE THING--YOUR CONSCIOUSNESS WILL REMAIN INTACT.
THAT WAY, YOU WILL FEEL THE PAIN SUFFERED BY THOSE YOU USE AND THEN CAST AWAY!
FOR A HUNDRED, EVEN A THOUSAND YEARS, YOU WILL REMAIN TRAPPED IN HER SLOWLY ROTTING FRAME, SUFFERING PAIN AND HUMILIATION.

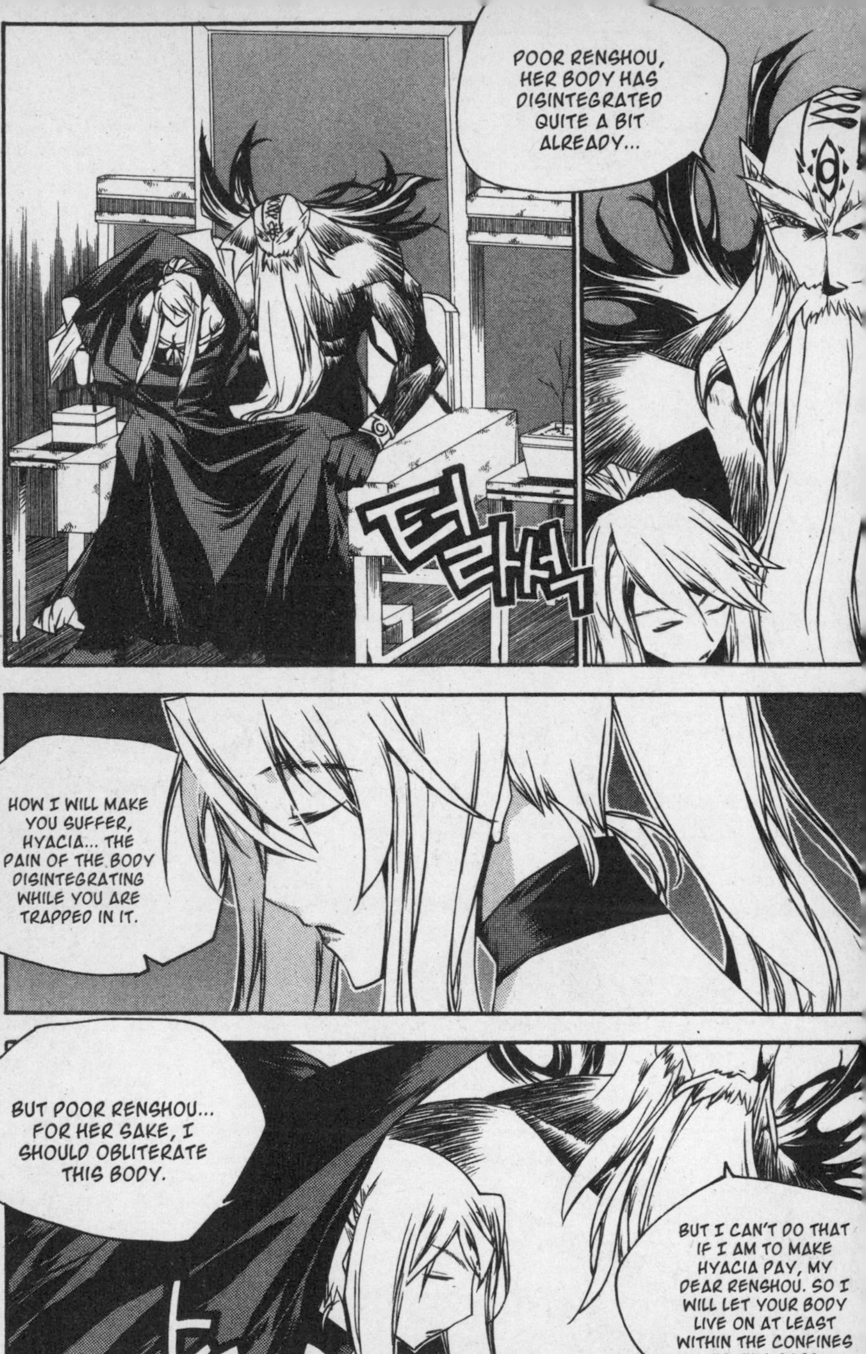
POOR RENSHOU, HER BODY HAS DISINTEGRATED QUITE A BIT ALREADY...
HOW I WILL MAKE YOU SUFFER, HYACIA... THE PAIN OF THE BODY DISINTEGRATING WHILE YOU ARE TRAPPED IN IT.
BUT POOR RENSHOU... FOR HER SAKE, I SHOULD OBLITERATE THIS BODY.
BUT I CAN'T DO THAT IF I AM TO MAKE HYACIA PAY, MY DEAR RENSHOU. SO I WILL LET YOUR BODY LIVE ON AT LEAST WITHIN THE CONFINES OF THIS CAPE.

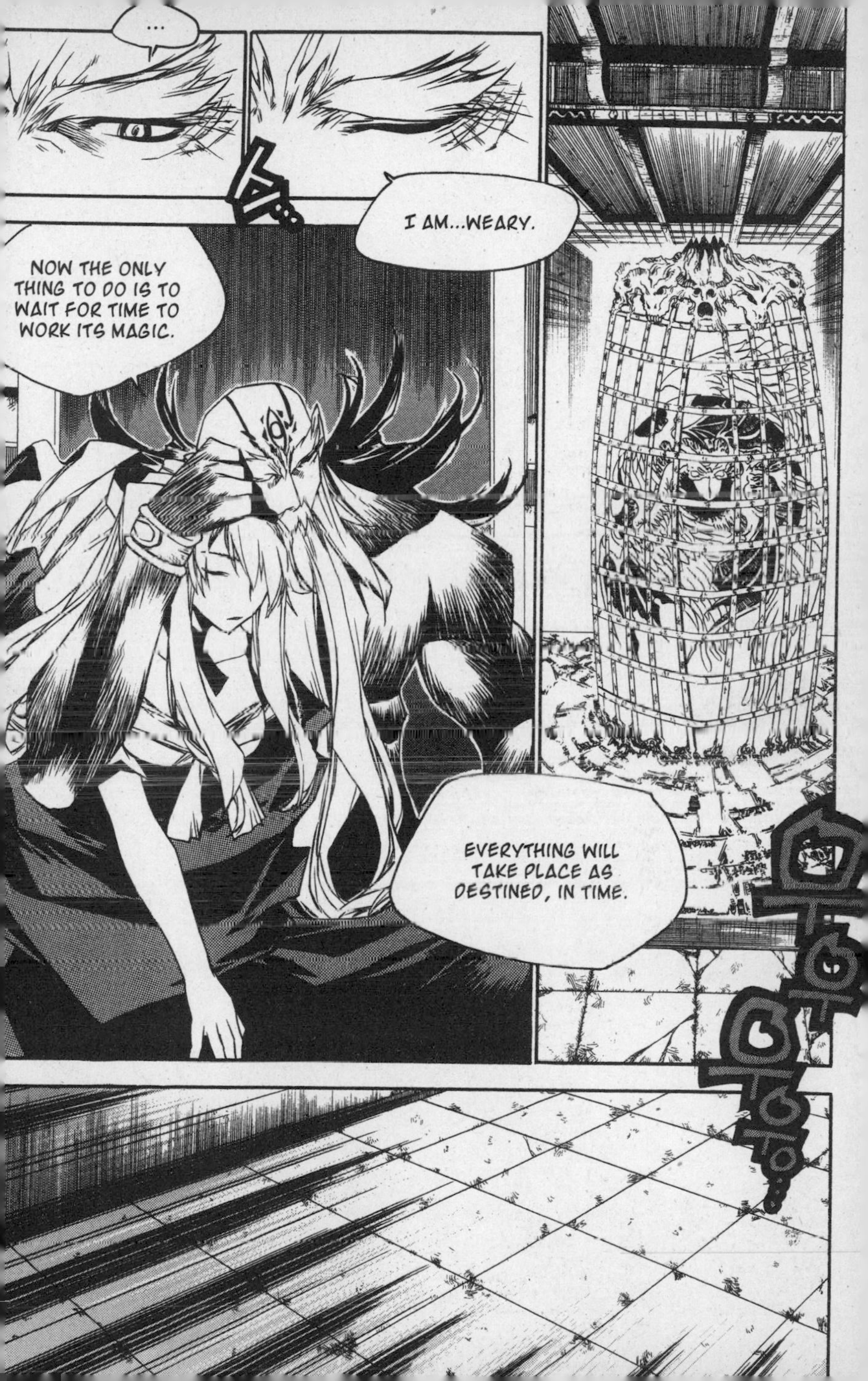
...
I AM...WEARY.
NOW THE ONLY THING TO DO IS TO WAIT FOR TIME TO WORK ITS MAGIC.
EVERYTHING WILL TAKE PLACE AS DESTINED, IN TIME.

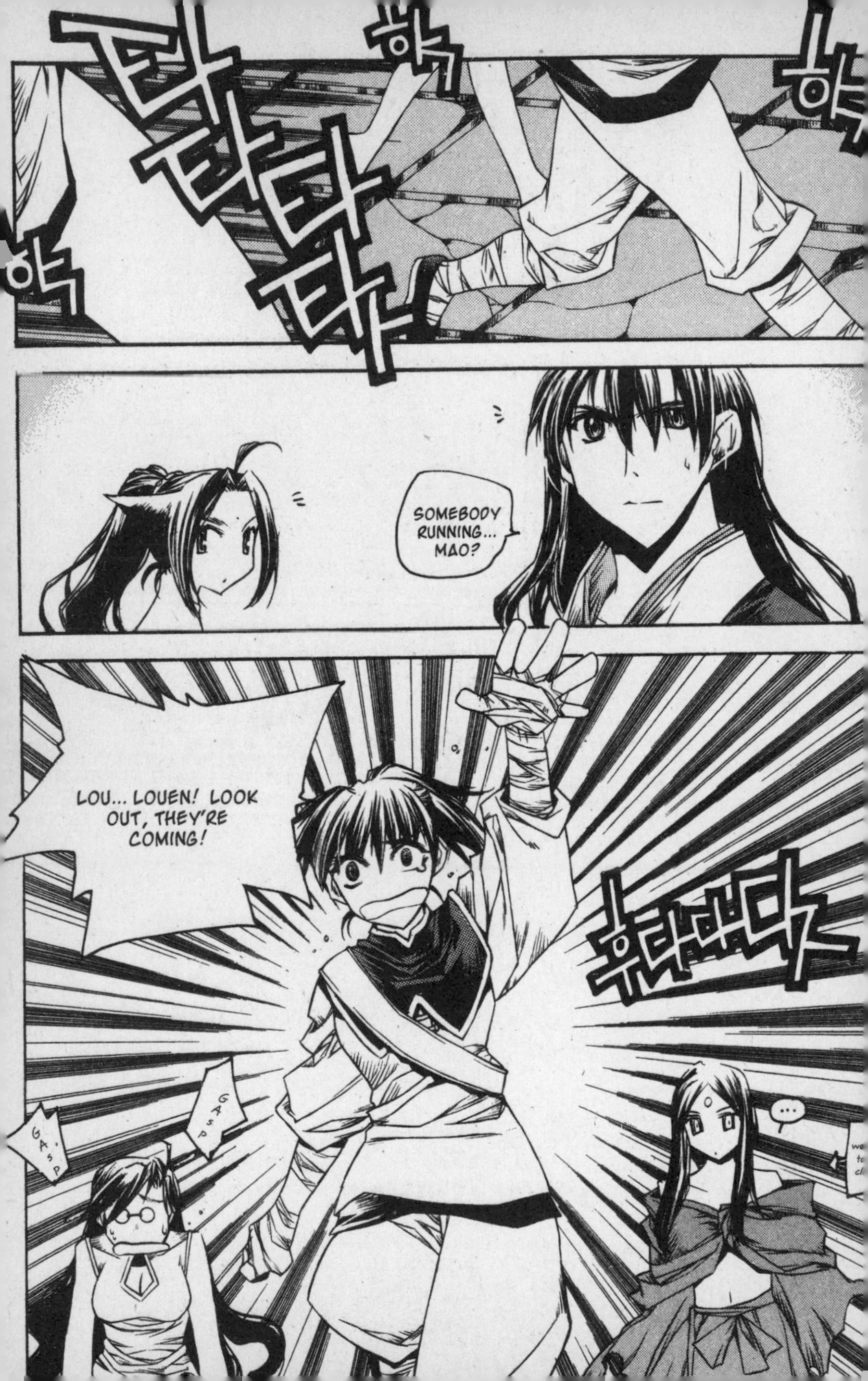

학
타타타타
학
학
SOMEBODY RUNNING... MAO?
LOU... LOUEN! LOOK OUT, THEY'RE COMING!
후다다닥
GASP
GASP
...

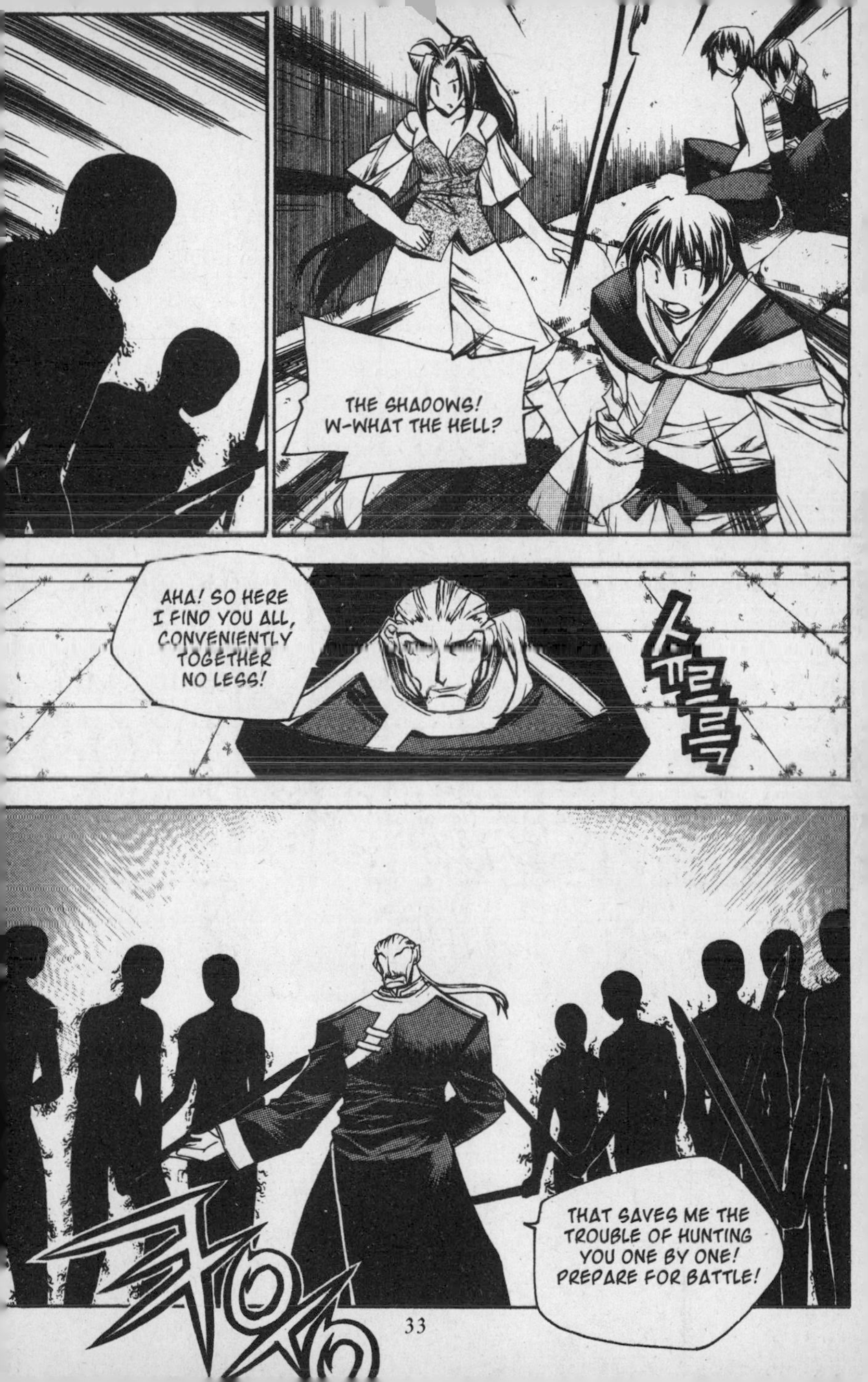
THE SHADOWS! W-WHAT THE HELL?
AHA! SO HERE I FIND YOU ALL, CONVENIENTLY TOGETHER NO LESS!
THAT SAVES ME THE TROUBLE OF HUNTING YOU ONE BY ONE!
PREPARE FOR BATTLE!

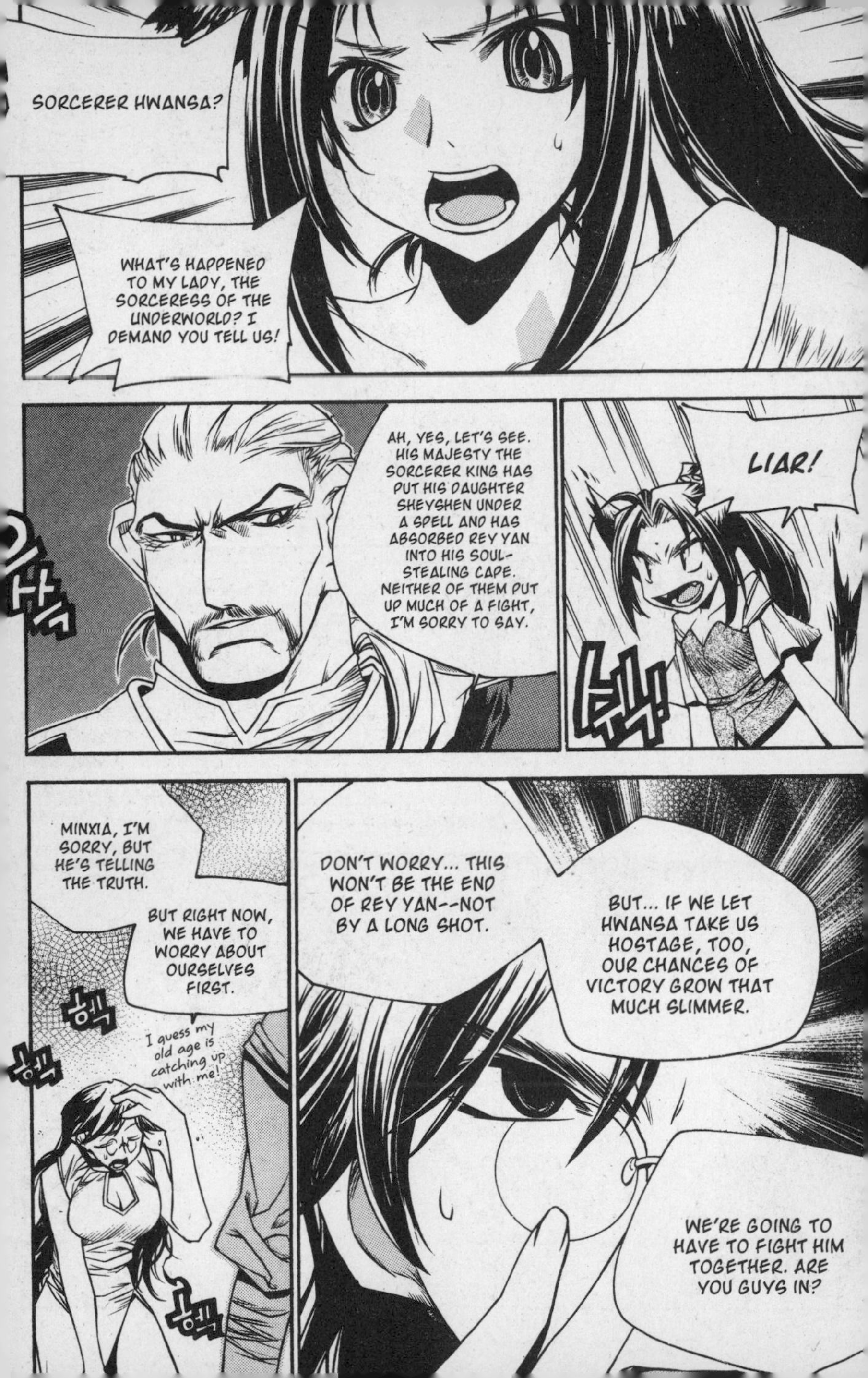
SORCERER HWANSA?
WHAT'S HAPPENED TO MY LADY, THE SORCERESS OF THE UNDERWORLD? I DEMAND YOU TELL US!
AH, YES, LET'S SEE. HIS MAJESTY THE SORCERER KING HAS PUT HIS DAUGHTER SHEYSHEN UNDER A SPELL AND HAS ABSORBED REY YAN INTO HIS SOUL-STEALING CAPE. NEITHER OF THEM PUT UP MUCH OF A FIGHT, I'M SORRY TO SAY.
LIAR!
MINXIA, I'M SORRY, BUT HE'S TELLING THE TRUTH.
BUT RIGHT NOW, WE HAVE TO WORRY ABOUT OURSELVES FIRST.
헉
I guess my old age is catching up with me!
헉
헉
DON'T WORRY... THIS WON'T BE THE END OF REY YAN--NOT BY A LONG SHOT.
BUT... IF WE LET HWANSA TAKE US HOSTAGE, TOO, OUR CHANCES OF VICTORY GROW THAT MUCH SLIMMER.
WE'RE GOING TO HAVE TO FIGHT HIM TOGETHER. ARE YOU GUYS IN?

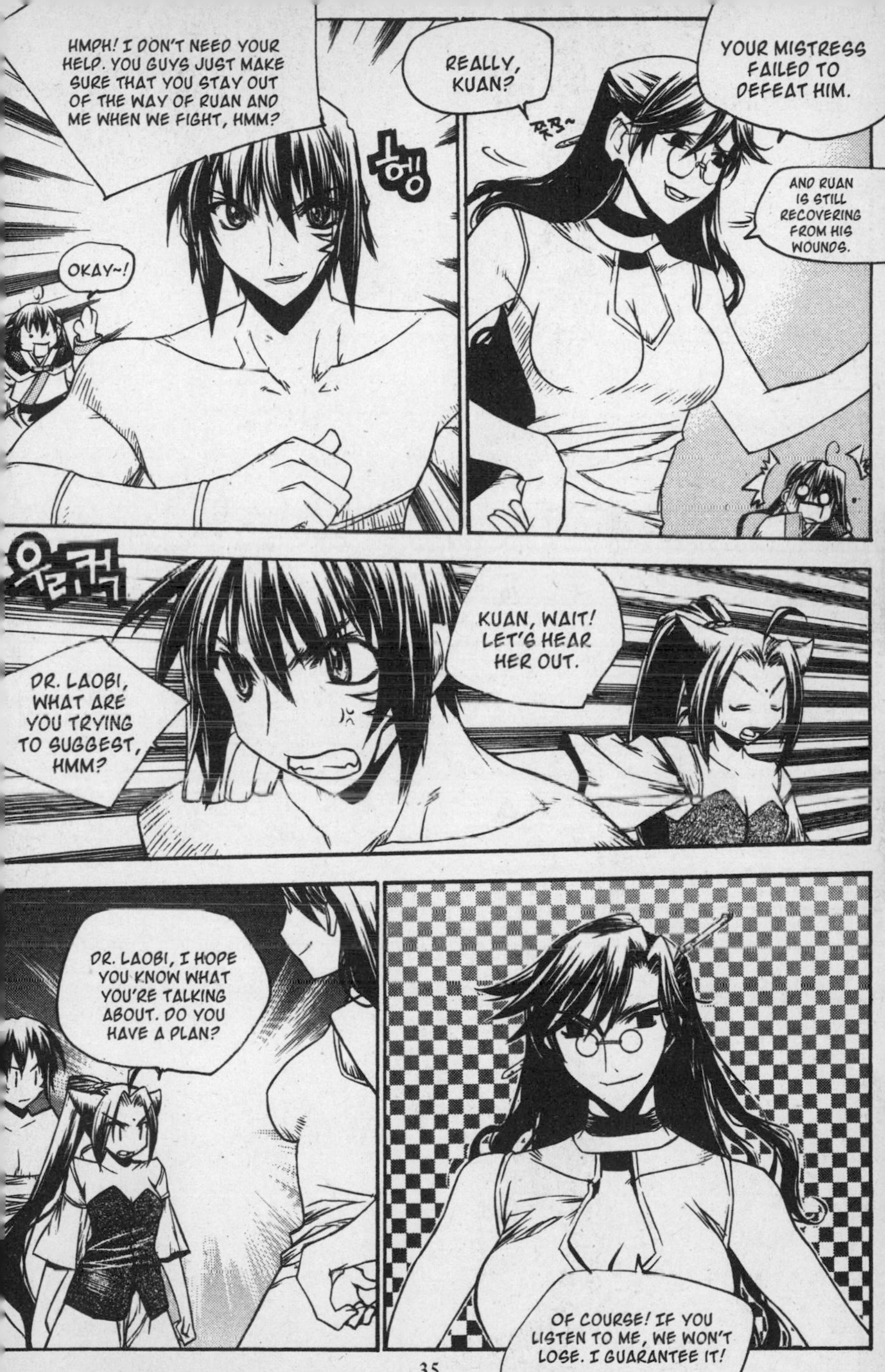
HMPH! I DON'T NEED YOUR HELP. YOU GUYS JUST MAKE SURE THAT YOU STAY OUT OF THE WAY OF RUAN AND ME WHEN WE FIGHT, HMM?
흥
OKAY~!
REALLY, KUAN?
YOUR MISTRESS FAILED TO DEFEAT HIM.
AND RUAN IS STILL RECOVERING FROM HIS WOUNDS.
울컥
DR. LAOBI, WHAT ARE YOU TRYING TO SUGGEST, HMM?
KUAN, WAIT! LET'S HEAR HER OUT.
DR. LAOBI, I HOPE YOU KNOW WHAT YOU'RE TALKING ABOUT. DO YOU HAVE A PLAN?
OF COURSE! IF YOU LISTEN TO ME, WE WON'T LOSE. I GUARANTEE IT!

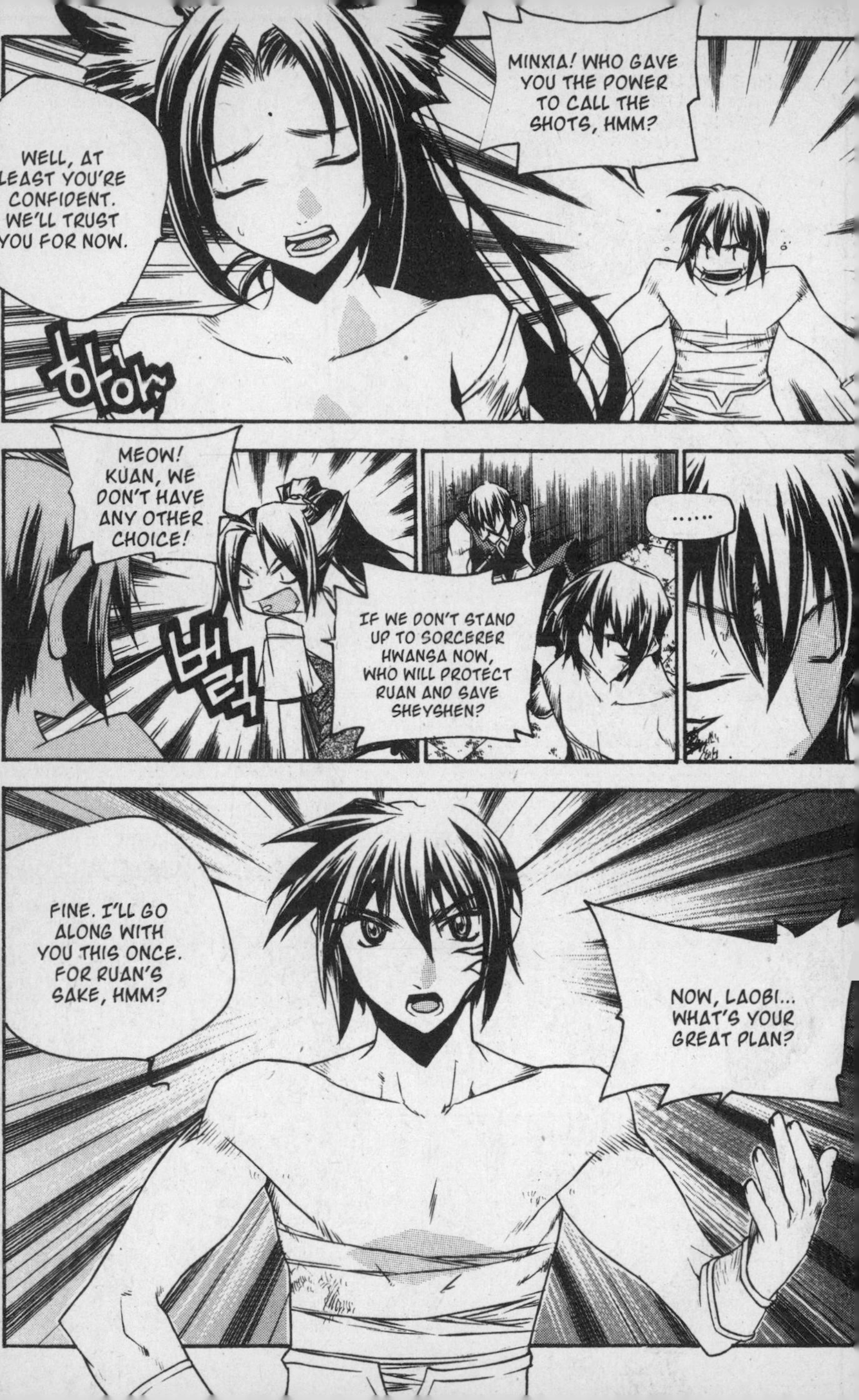
WELL, AT LEAST YOU'RE CONFIDENT. WE'LL TRUST YOU FOR NOW.
하아
MINXIA! WHO GAVE YOU THE POWER TO CALL THE SHOTS, HMM?
MEOW! KUAN, WE DON'T HAVE ANY OTHER CHOICE!
버럭
IF WE DON'T STAND UP TO SORCERER HWANSA NOW, WHO WILL PROTECT RUAN AND SAVE SHEYSHEN?
......
FINE. I'LL GO ALONG WITH YOU THIS ONCE. FOR RUAN'S SAKE, HMM?
NOW, LAOBI... WHAT'S YOUR GREAT PLAN?

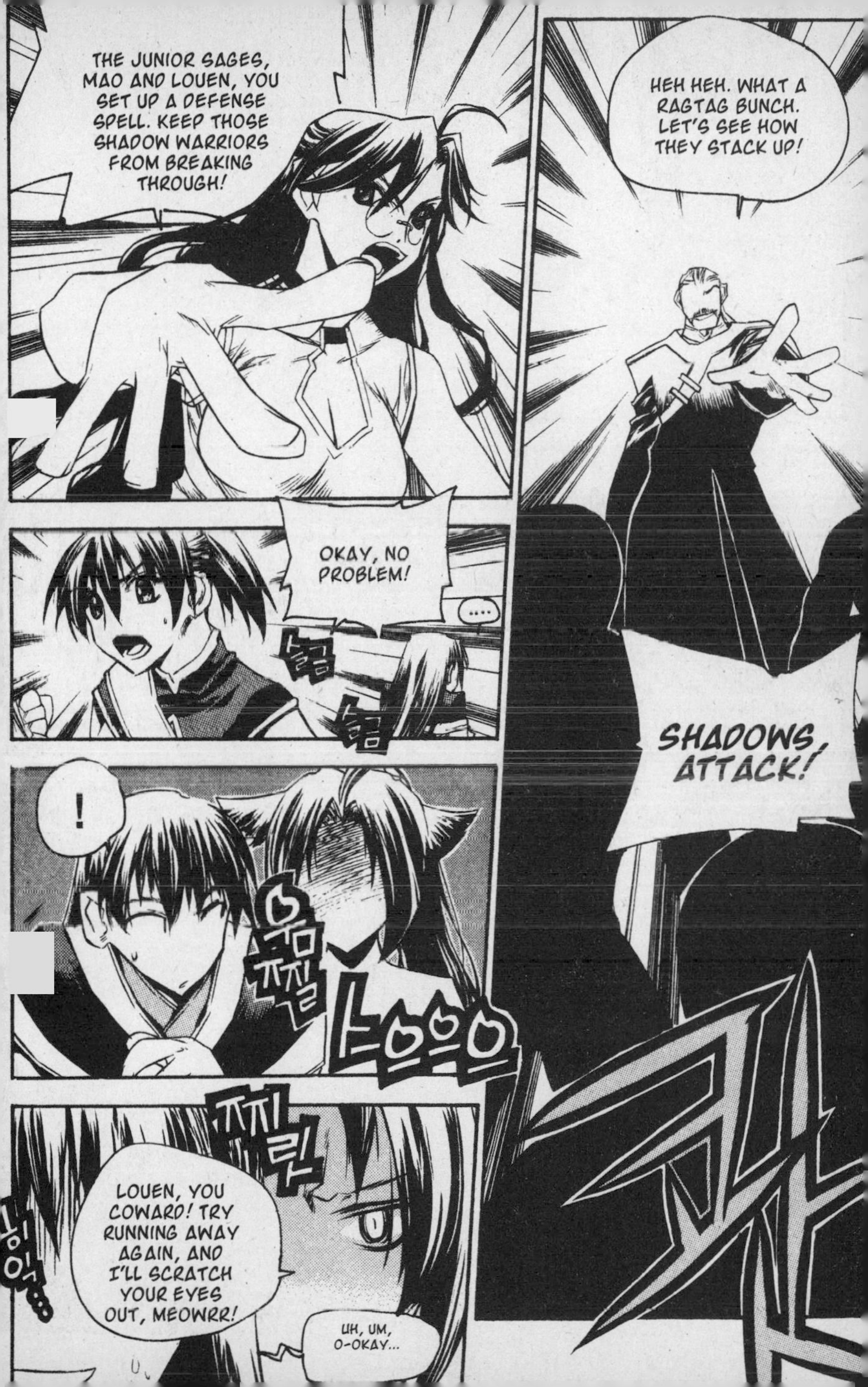
THE JUNIOR SAGES, MAO AND LOUEN, YOU SET UP A DEFENSE SPELL. KEEP THOSE SHADOW WARRIORS FROM BREAKING THROUGH!
OKAY, NO PROBLEM!
....
!
LOUEN, YOU COWARD! TRY RUNNING AWAY AGAIN, AND I'LL SCRATCH YOUR EYES OUT, MEOWRR!
UH, UM, O-OKAY...
HEH HEH. WHAT A RAGTAG BUNCH. LET'S SEE HOW THEY STACK UP!
SHADOWS, ATTACK!

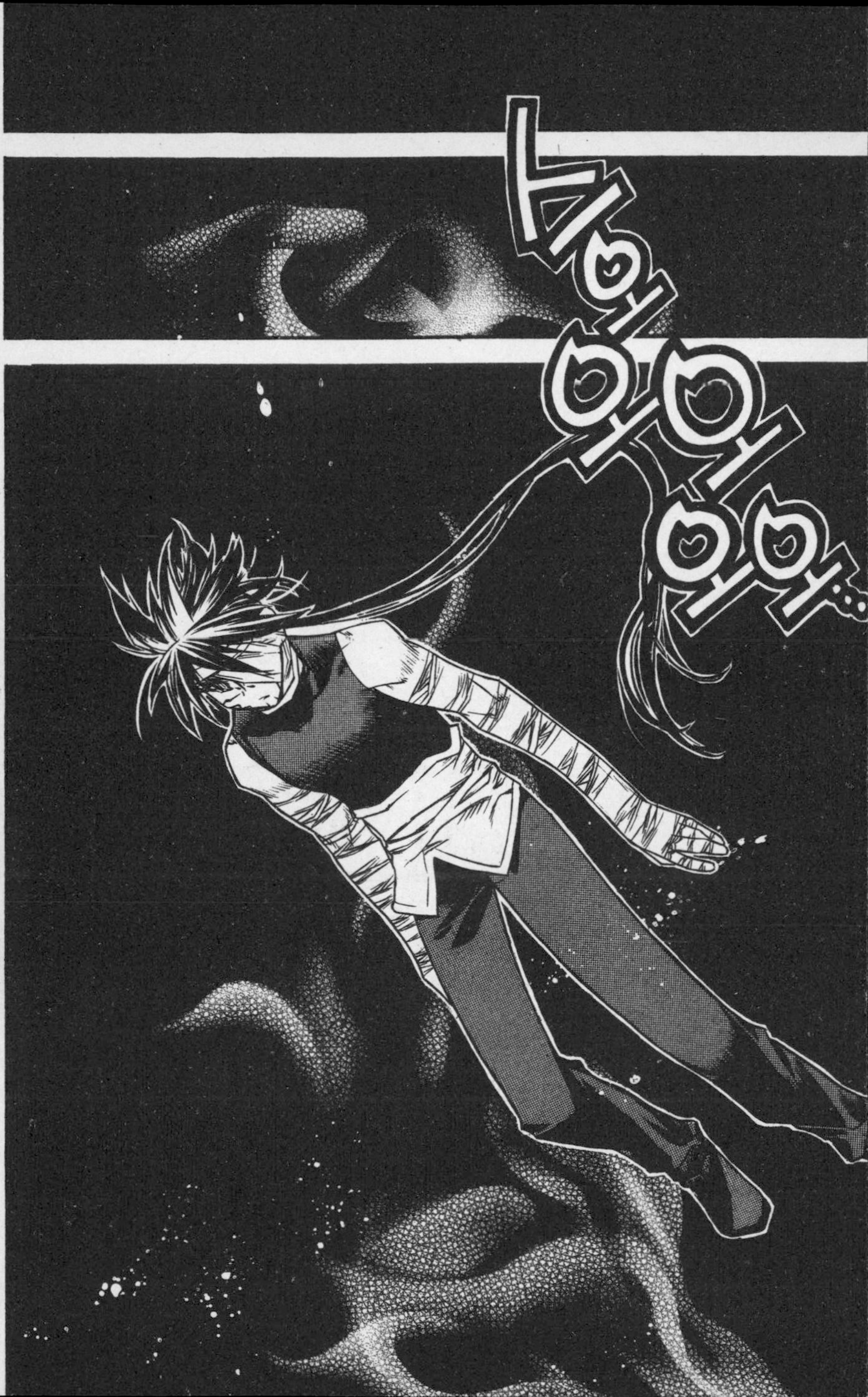
Aaaaaah...

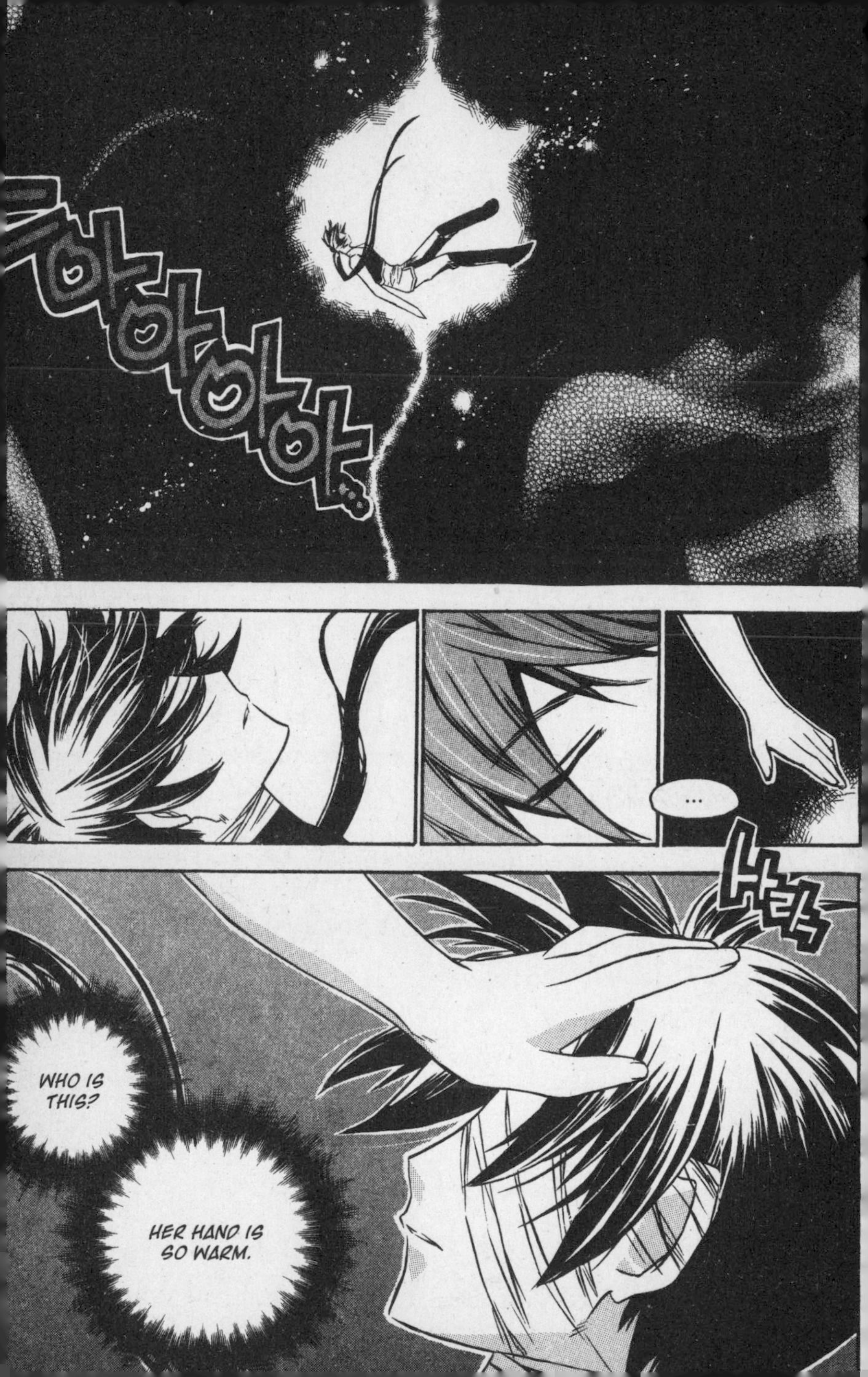
...
WHO IS THIS?
HER HAND IS SO WARM.

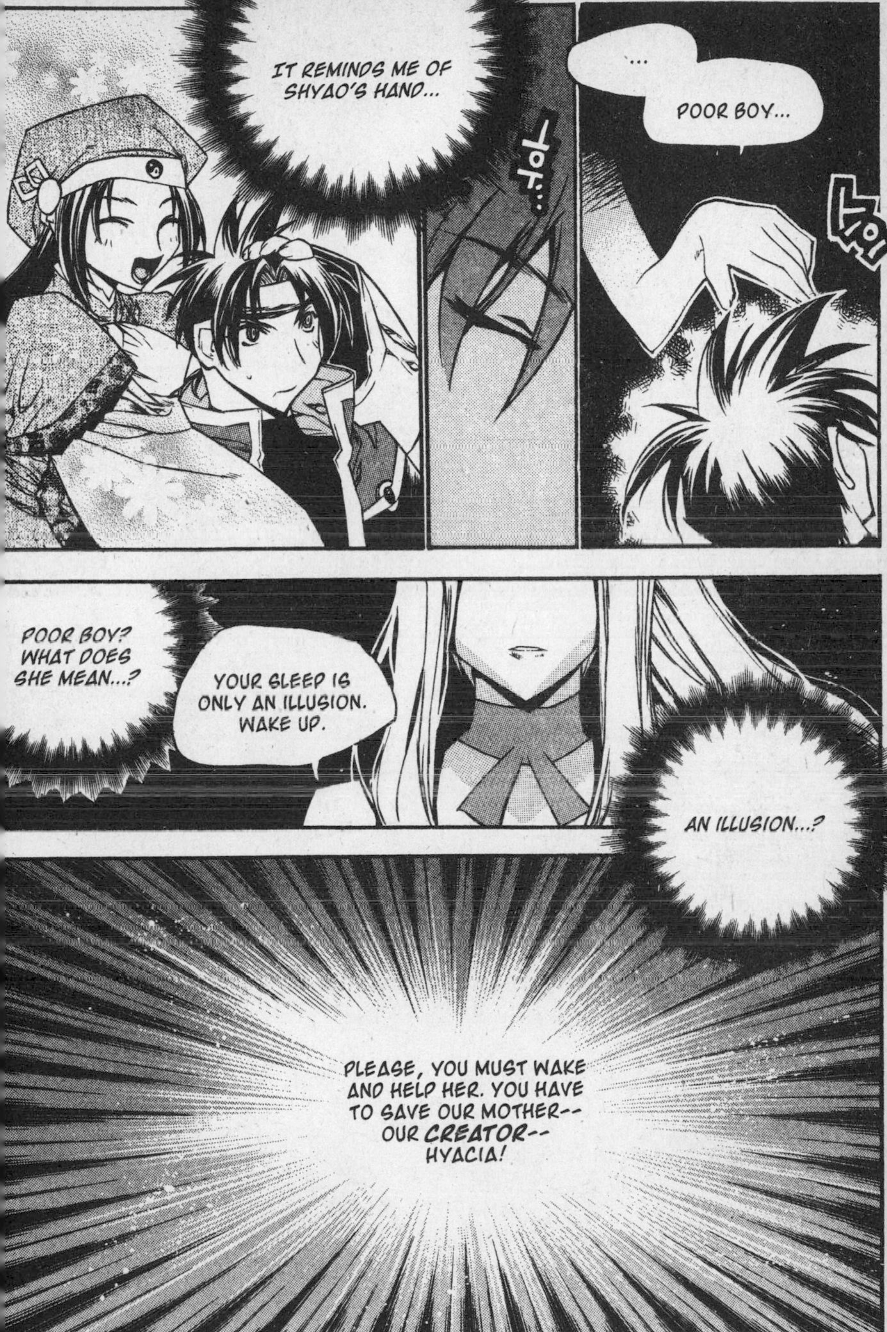
IT REMINDS ME OF SHYAO'S HAND...
TOK...
...
POOR BOY...
TOK!
POOR BOY? WHAT DOES SHE MEAN...?
YOUR SLEEP IS ONLY AN ILLUSION. WAKE UP.
AN ILLUSION...?
PLEASE, YOU MUST WAKE AND HELP HER. YOU HAVE TO SAVE OUR MOTHER-- OUR CREATOR-- HYACIA!

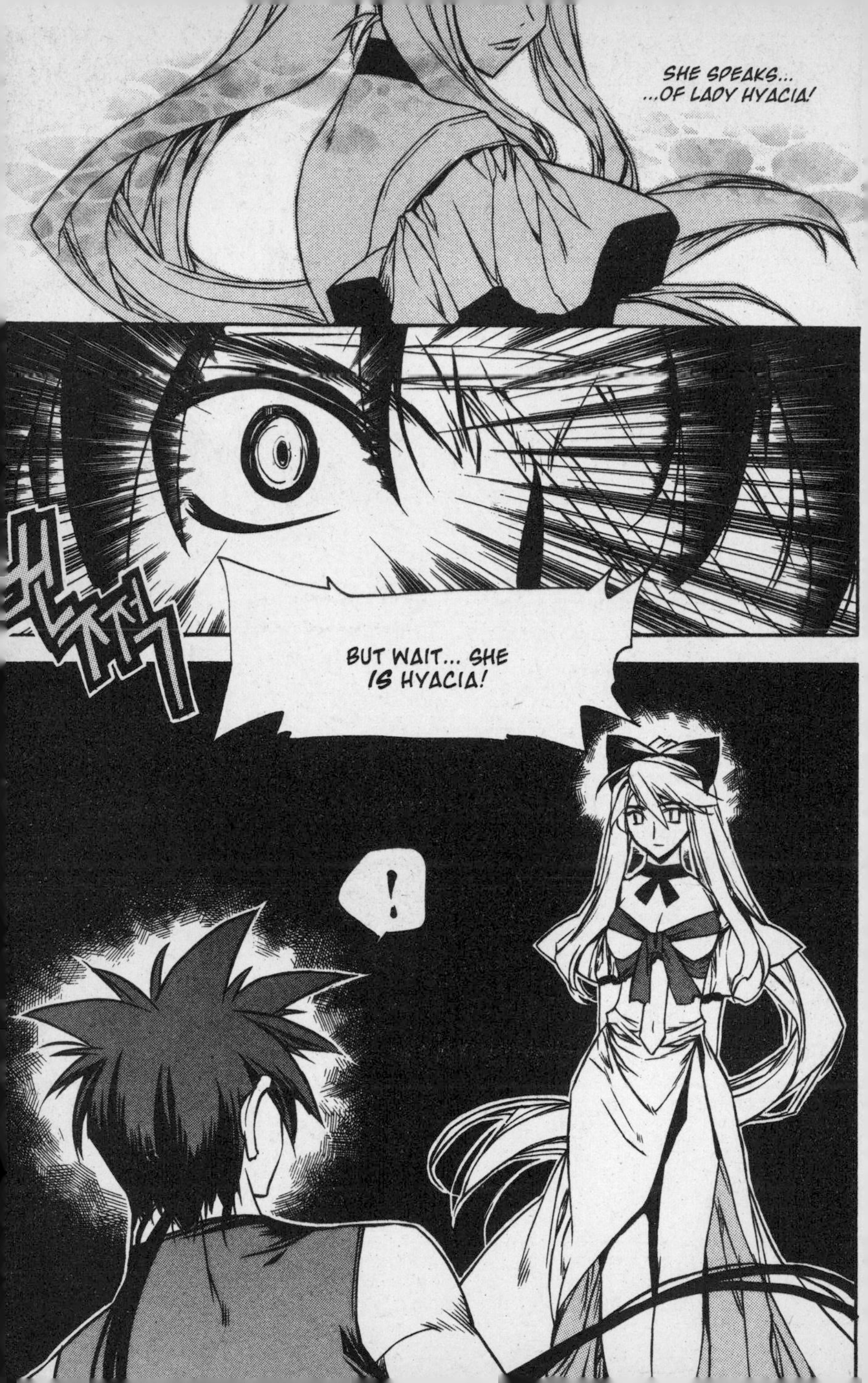
SHE SPEAKS...
...OF LADY HYACIA!
BUT WAIT... SHE *IS* HYACIA!
!

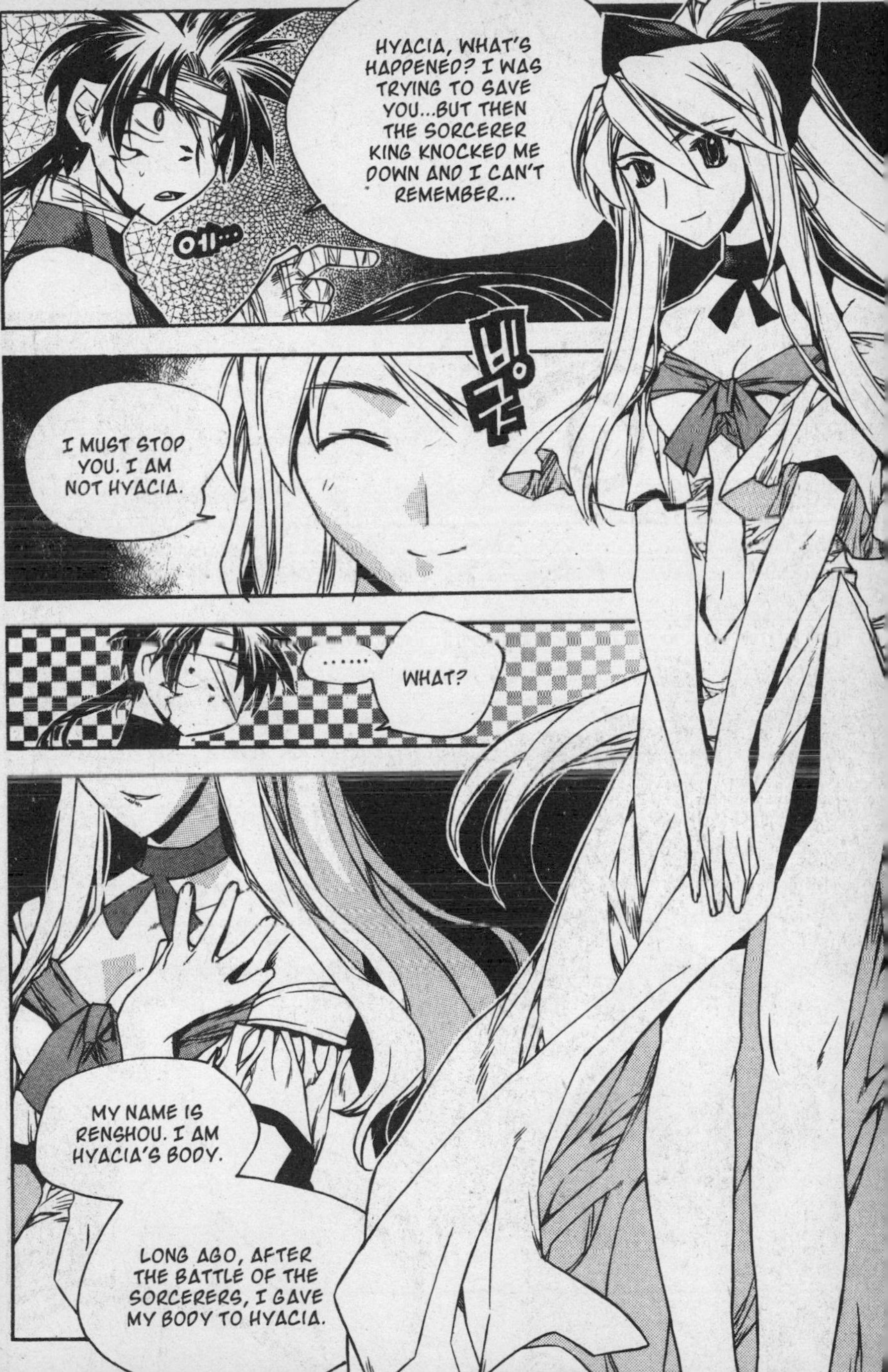
에…
HYACIA, WHAT'S HAPPENED? I WAS TRYING TO SAVE YOU...BUT THEN THE SORCERER KING KNOCKED ME DOWN AND I CAN'T REMEMBER...
I MUST STOP YOU. I AM NOT HYACIA.
빙긋
....
WHAT?
MY NAME IS RENSHOU. I AM HYACIA'S BODY.
LONG AGO, AFTER THE BATTLE OF THE SORCERERS, I GAVE MY BODY TO HYACIA.

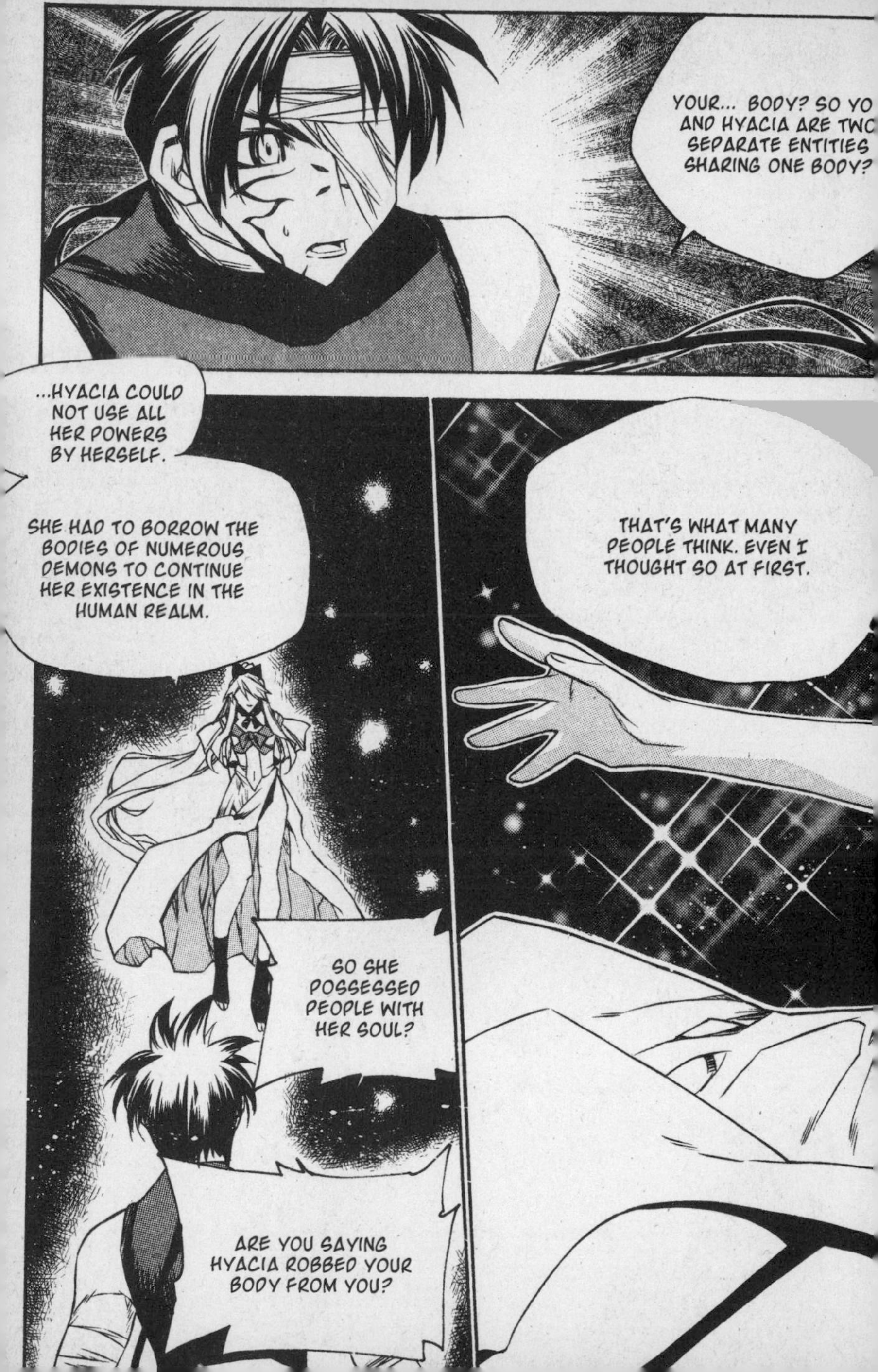
YOUR... BODY? SO YO AND HYACIA ARE TWO SEPARATE ENTITIES SHARING ONE BODY?
...HYACIA COULD NOT USE ALL HER POWERS BY HERSELF.
SHE HAD TO BORROW THE BODIES OF NUMEROUS DEMONS TO CONTINUE HER EXISTENCE IN THE HUMAN REALM.
SO SHE POSSESSED PEOPLE WITH HER SOUL?
ARE YOU SAYING HYACIA ROBBED YOUR BODY FROM YOU?
THAT'S WHAT MANY PEOPLE THINK. EVEN I THOUGHT SO AT FIRST.

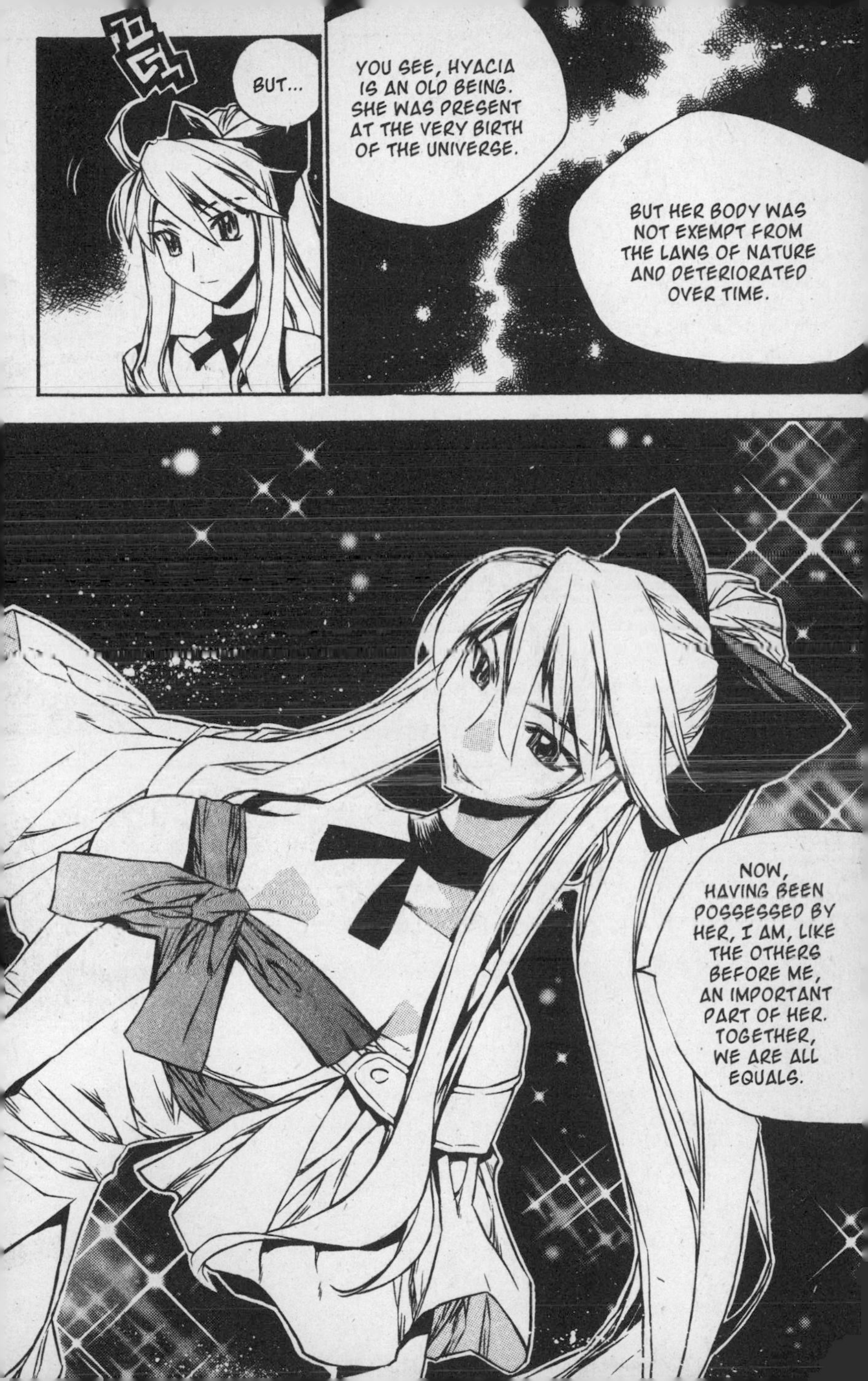
BUT...
YOU SEE, HYACIA IS AN OLD BEING. SHE WAS PRESENT AT THE VERY BIRTH OF THE UNIVERSE.
BUT HER BODY WAS NOT EXEMPT FROM THE LAWS OF NATURE AND DETERIORATED OVER TIME.
NOW, HAVING BEEN POSSESSED BY HER, I AM, LIKE THE OTHERS BEFORE ME, AN IMPORTANT PART OF HER. TOGETHER, WE ARE ALL EQUALS.

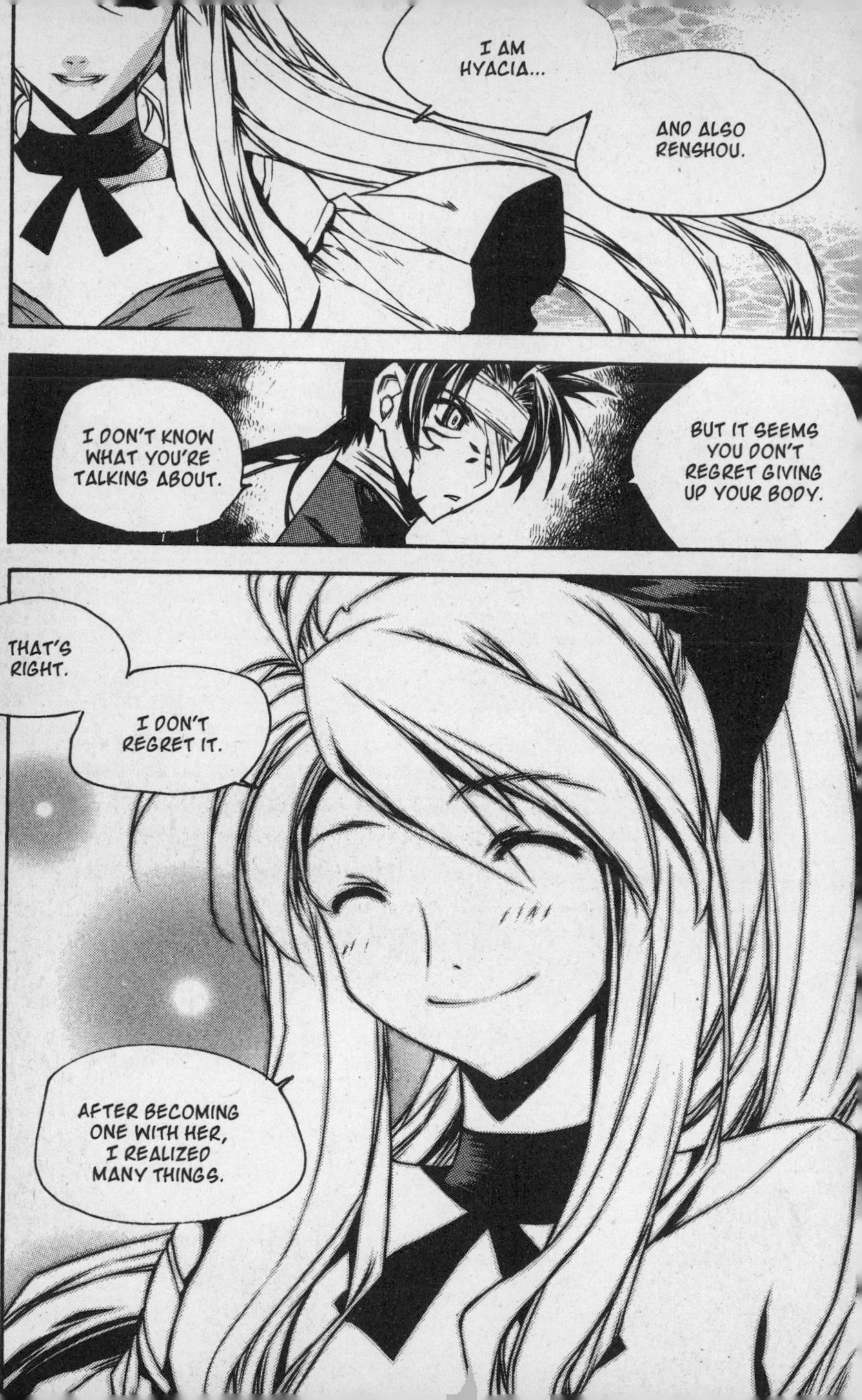
I AM HYACIA...
AND ALSO RENSHOU.
I DON'T KNOW WHAT YOU'RE TALKING ABOUT.
BUT IT SEEMS YOU DON'T REGRET GIVING UP YOUR BODY.
THAT'S RIGHT.
I DON'T REGRET IT.
AFTER BECOMING ONE WITH HER, I REALIZED MANY THINGS.

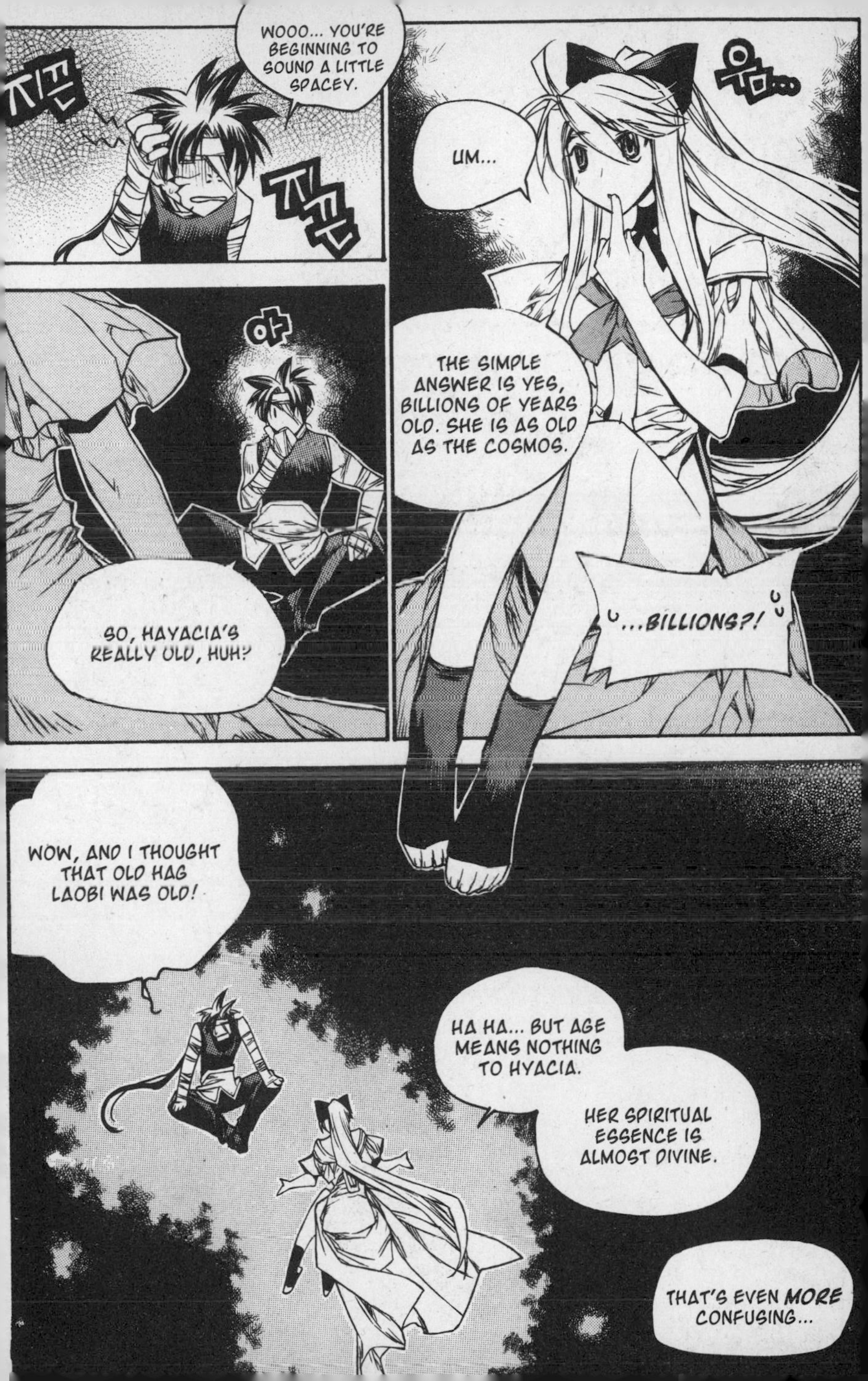
지끈
WOOO... YOU'RE BEGINNING TO SOUND A LITTLE SPACEY.
지끈
야
SO, HAYACIA'S REALLY OLD, HUH?
움...
UM...
THE SIMPLE ANSWER IS YES, BILLIONS OF YEARS OLD. SHE IS AS OLD AS THE COSMOS.
...BILLIONS?!
WOW, AND I THOUGHT THAT OLD HAG LAOBI WAS OLD!
HA HA... BUT AGE MEANS NOTHING TO HYACIA.
HER SPIRITUAL ESSENCE IS ALMOST DIVINE.
THAT'S EVEN MORE CONFUSING...

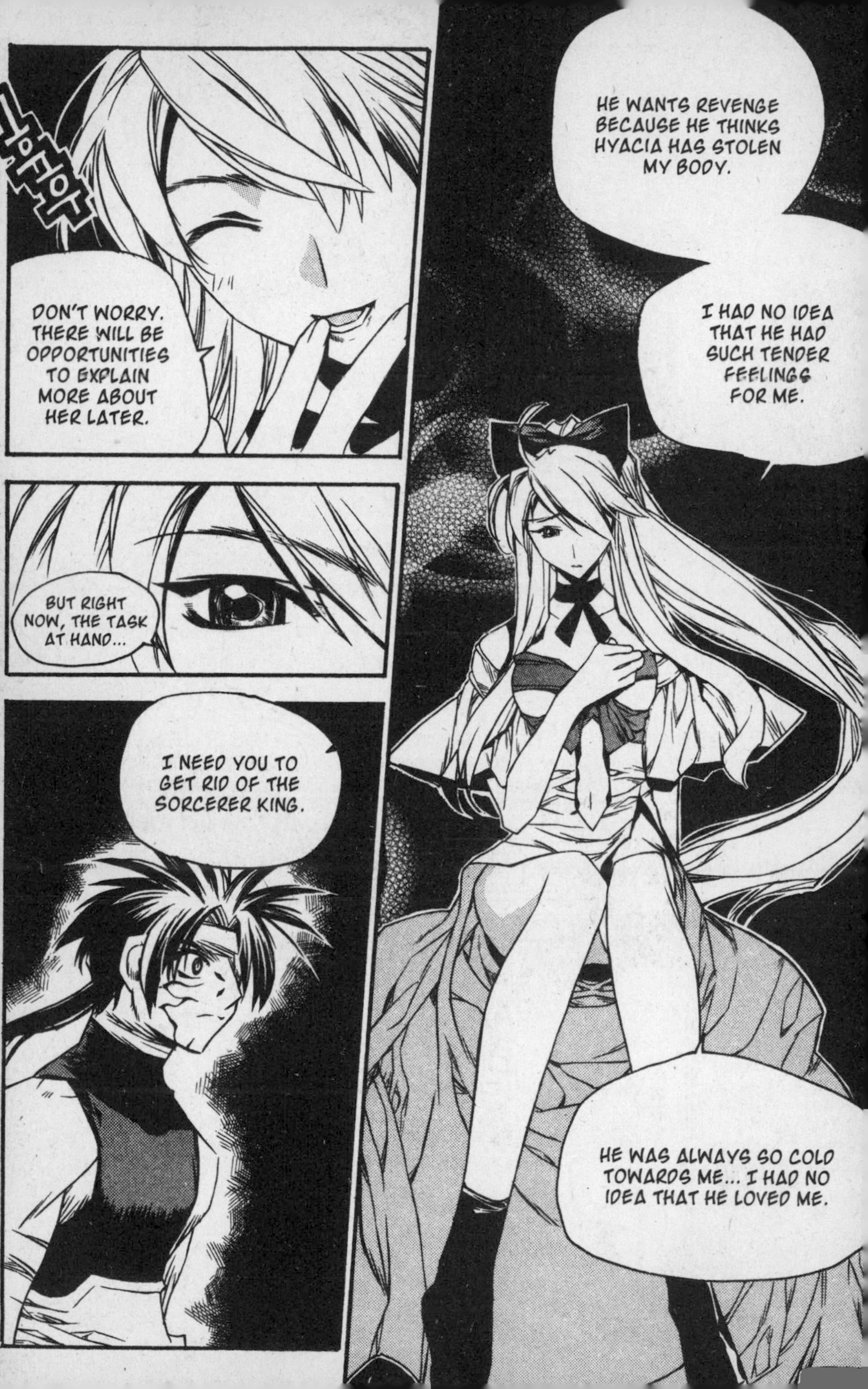
DON'T WORRY. THERE WILL BE OPPORTUNITIES TO EXPLAIN MORE ABOUT HER LATER.
BUT RIGHT NOW, THE TASK AT HAND...
I NEED YOU TO GET RID OF THE SORCERER KING.
HE WANTS REVENGE BECAUSE HE THINKS HYACIA HAS STOLEN MY BODY.
I HAD NO IDEA THAT HE HAD SUCH TENDER FEELINGS FOR ME.
HE WAS ALWAYS SO COLD TOWARDS ME... I HAD NO IDEA THAT HE LOVED ME.

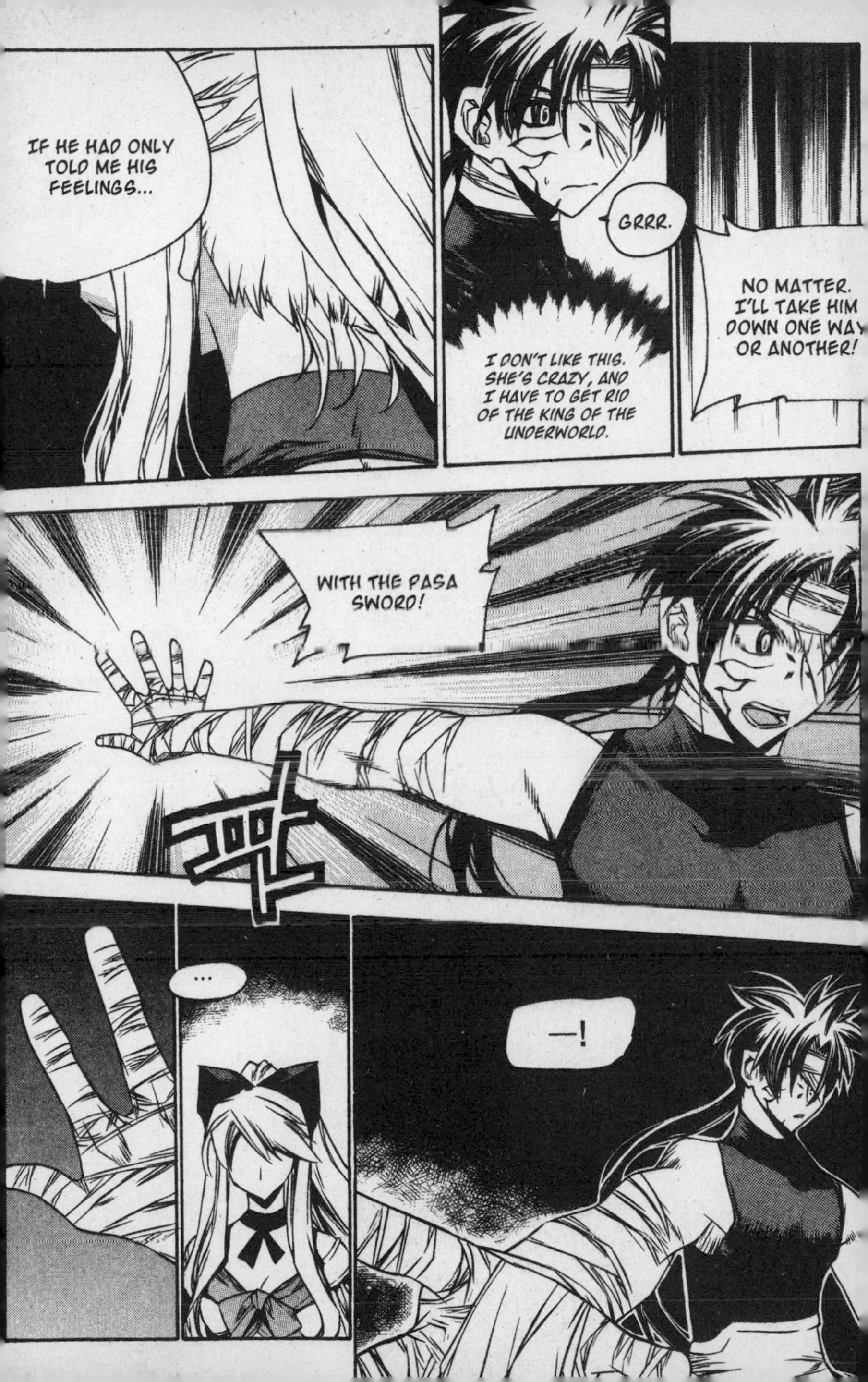
IF HE HAD ONLY TOLD ME HIS FEELINGS...
GRRR.
I DON'T LIKE THIS. SHE'S CRAZY, AND I HAVE TO GET RID OF THE KING OF THE UNDERWORLD.
NO MATTER. I'LL TAKE HIM DOWN ONE WAY OR ANOTHER!
WITH THE PASA SWORD!
...
—!

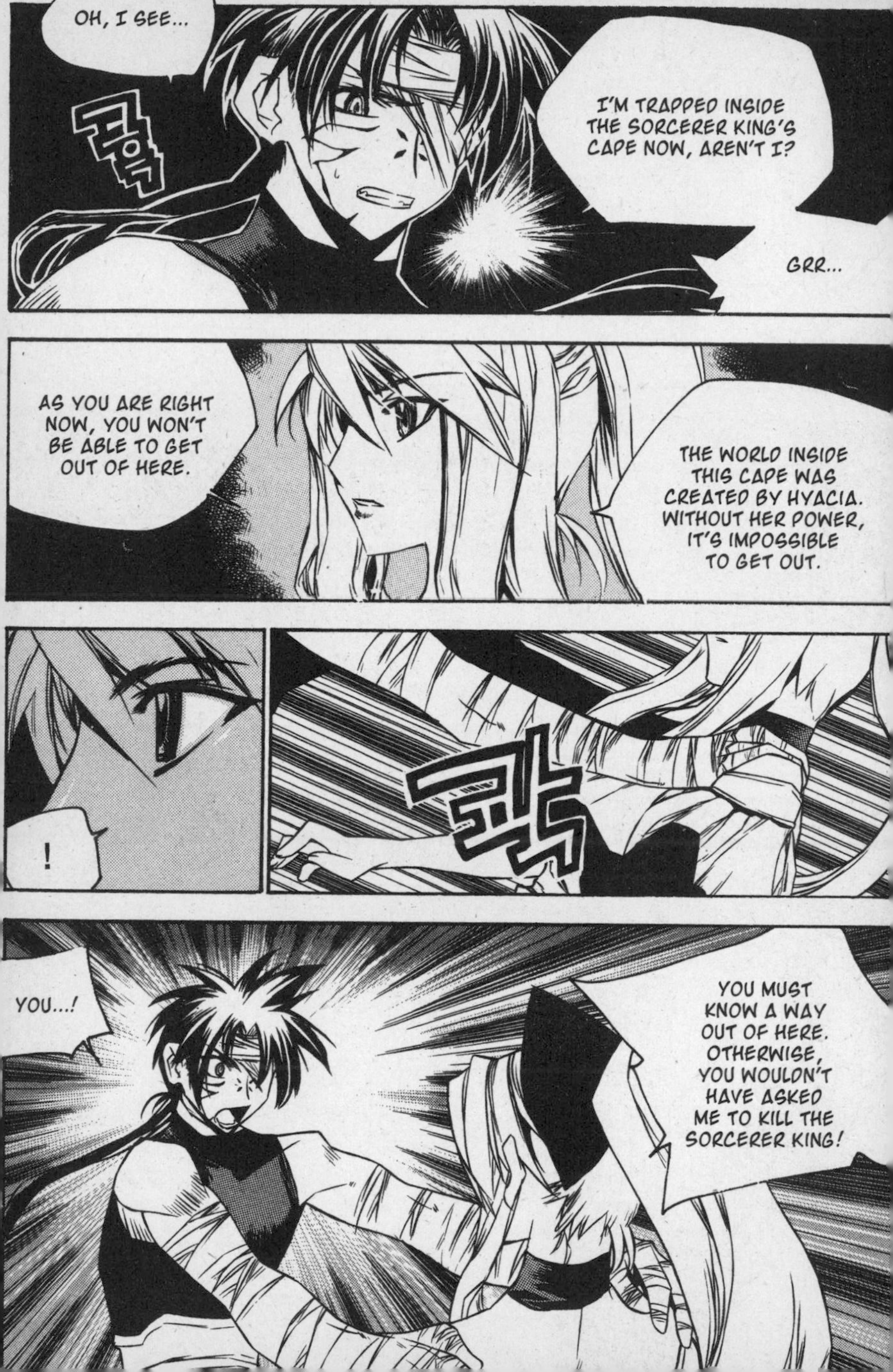
OH, I SEE...
I'M TRAPPED INSIDE THE SORCERER KING'S CAPE NOW, AREN'T I?
GRR...
AS YOU ARE RIGHT NOW, YOU WON'T BE ABLE TO GET OUT OF HERE.
THE WORLD INSIDE THIS CAPE WAS CREATED BY HYACIA. WITHOUT HER POWER, IT'S IMPOSSIBLE TO GET OUT.
!
YOU...!
YOU MUST KNOW A WAY OUT OF HERE. OTHERWISE, YOU WOULDN'T HAVE ASKED ME TO KILL THE SORCERER KING!

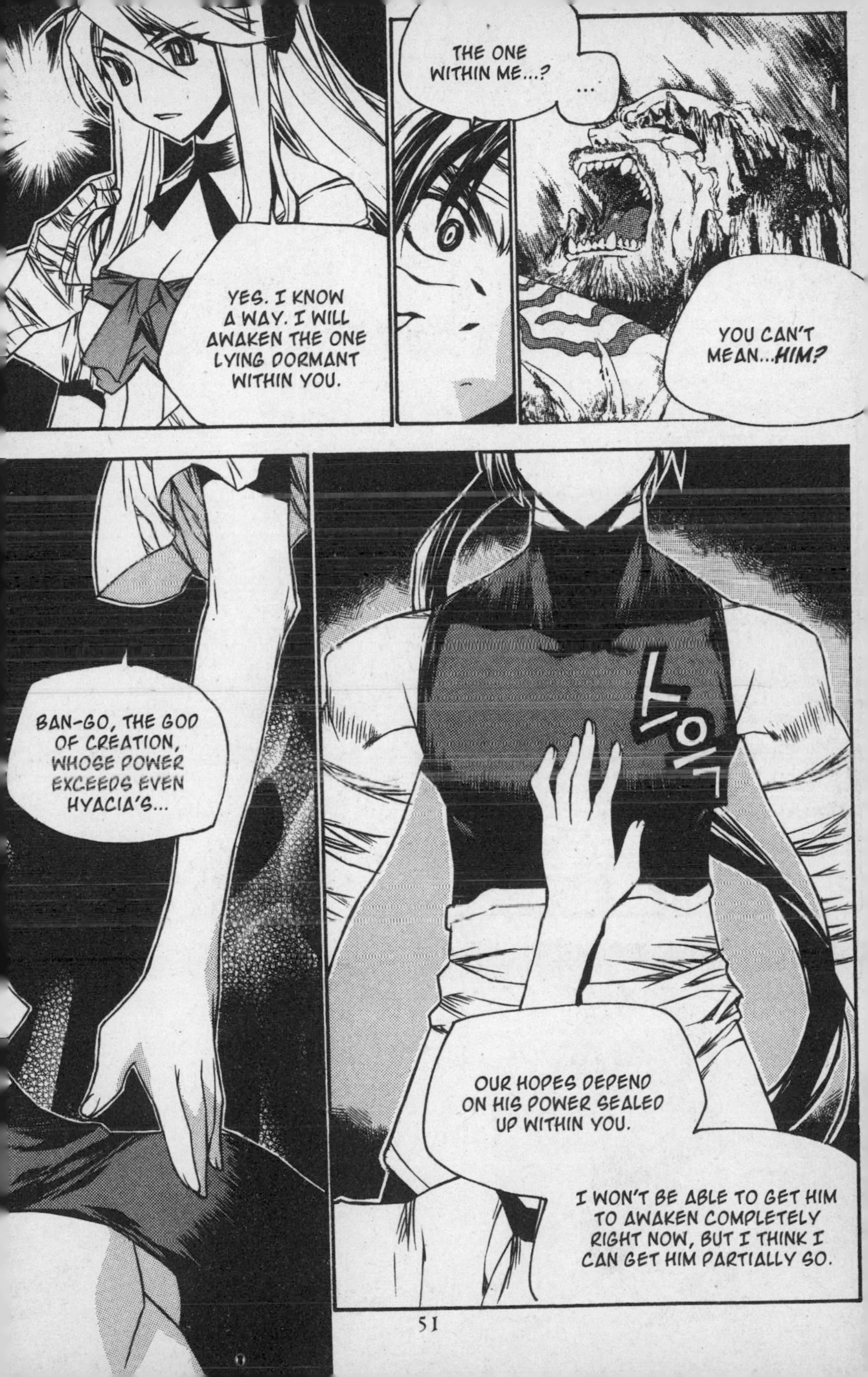
YES. I KNOW A WAY. I WILL AWAKEN THE ONE LYING DORMANT WITHIN YOU.
THE ONE WITHIN ME...?
...
YOU CAN'T MEAN...**HIM?**
BAN-GO, THE GOD OF CREATION, WHOSE POWER EXCEEDS EVEN HYACIA'S...
OUR HOPES DEPEND ON HIS POWER SEALED UP WITHIN YOU.
I WON'T BE ABLE TO GET HIM TO AWAKEN COMPLETELY RIGHT NOW, BUT I THINK I CAN GET HIM PARTIALLY SO.

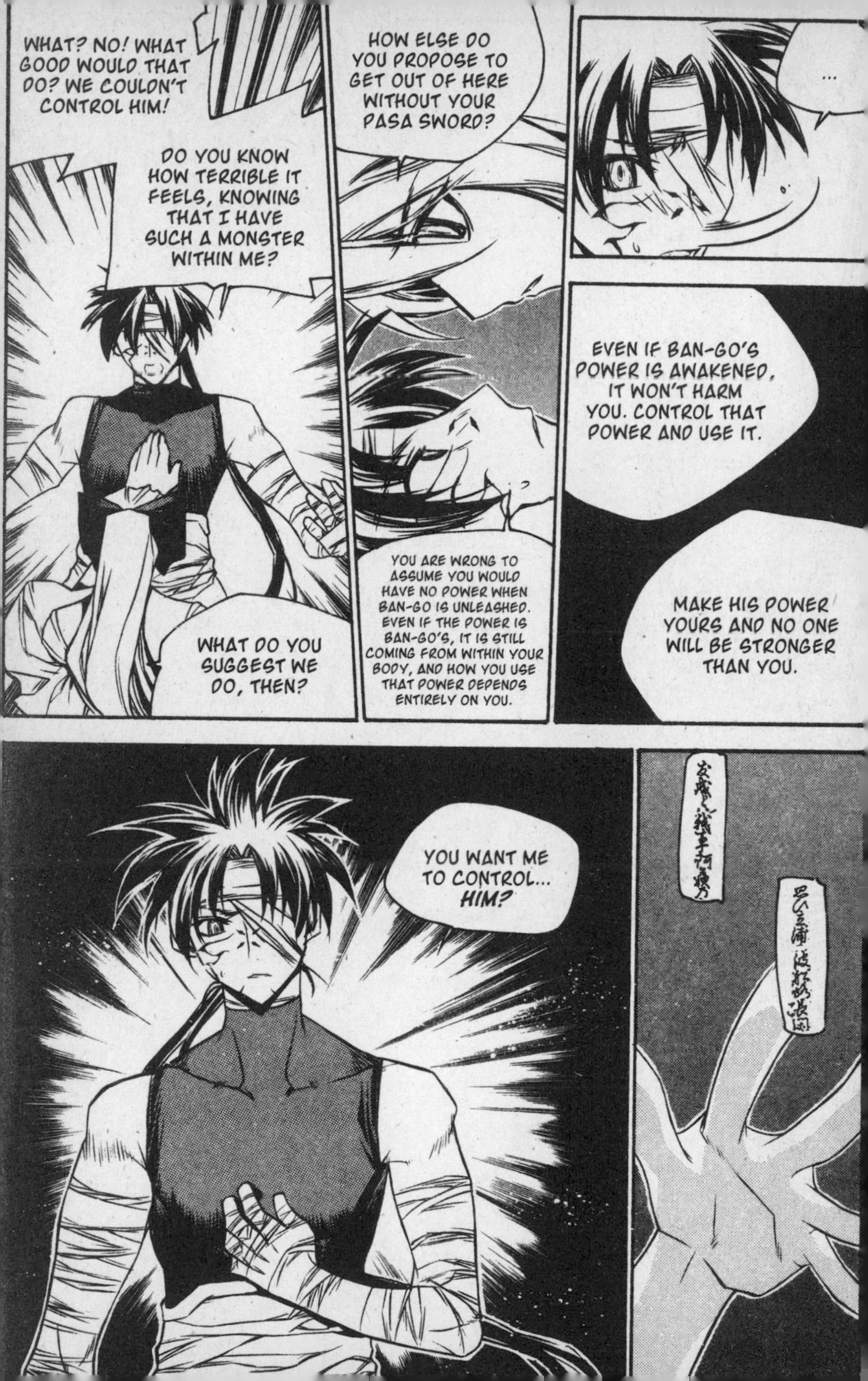
WHAT? NO! WHAT GOOD WOULD THAT DO? WE COULDN'T CONTROL HIM!
DO YOU KNOW HOW TERRIBLE IT FEELS, KNOWING THAT I HAVE SUCH A MONSTER WITHIN ME?
WHAT DO YOU SUGGEST WE DO, THEN?
HOW ELSE DO YOU PROPOSE TO GET OUT OF HERE WITHOUT YOUR PASA SWORD?
YOU ARE WRONG TO ASSUME YOU WOULD HAVE NO POWER WHEN BAN-GO IS UNLEASHED. EVEN IF THE POWER IS BAN-GO'S, IT IS STILL COMING FROM WITHIN YOUR BODY, AND HOW YOU USE THAT POWER DEPENDS ENTIRELY ON YOU.
...
EVEN IF BAN-GO'S POWER IS AWAKENED, IT WON'T HARM YOU. CONTROL THAT POWER AND USE IT.
MAKE HIS POWER YOURS AND NO ONE WILL BE STRONGER THAN YOU.
YOU WANT ME TO CONTROL... **HIM?**

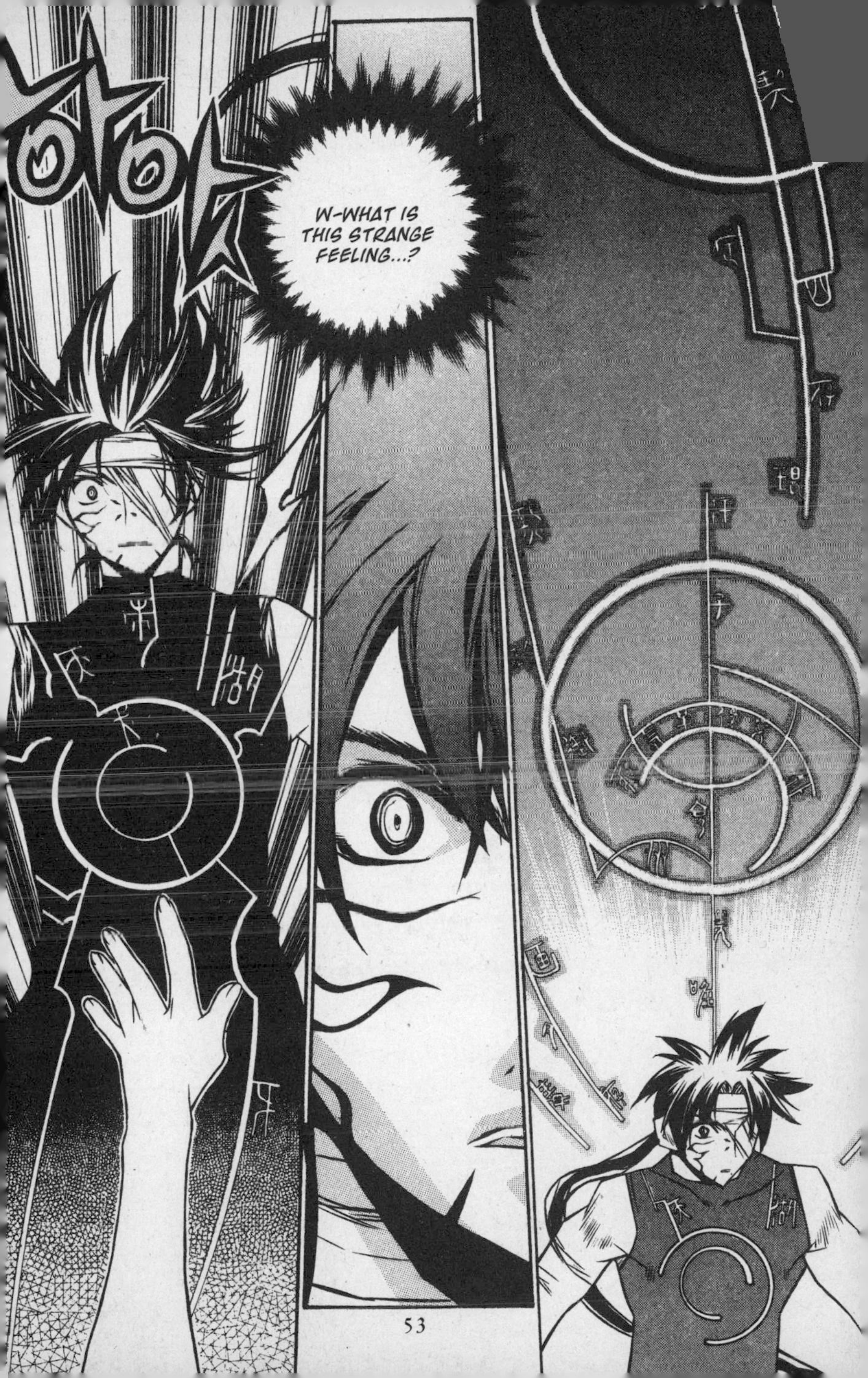
W-WHAT IS
THIS STRANGE
FEELING...?

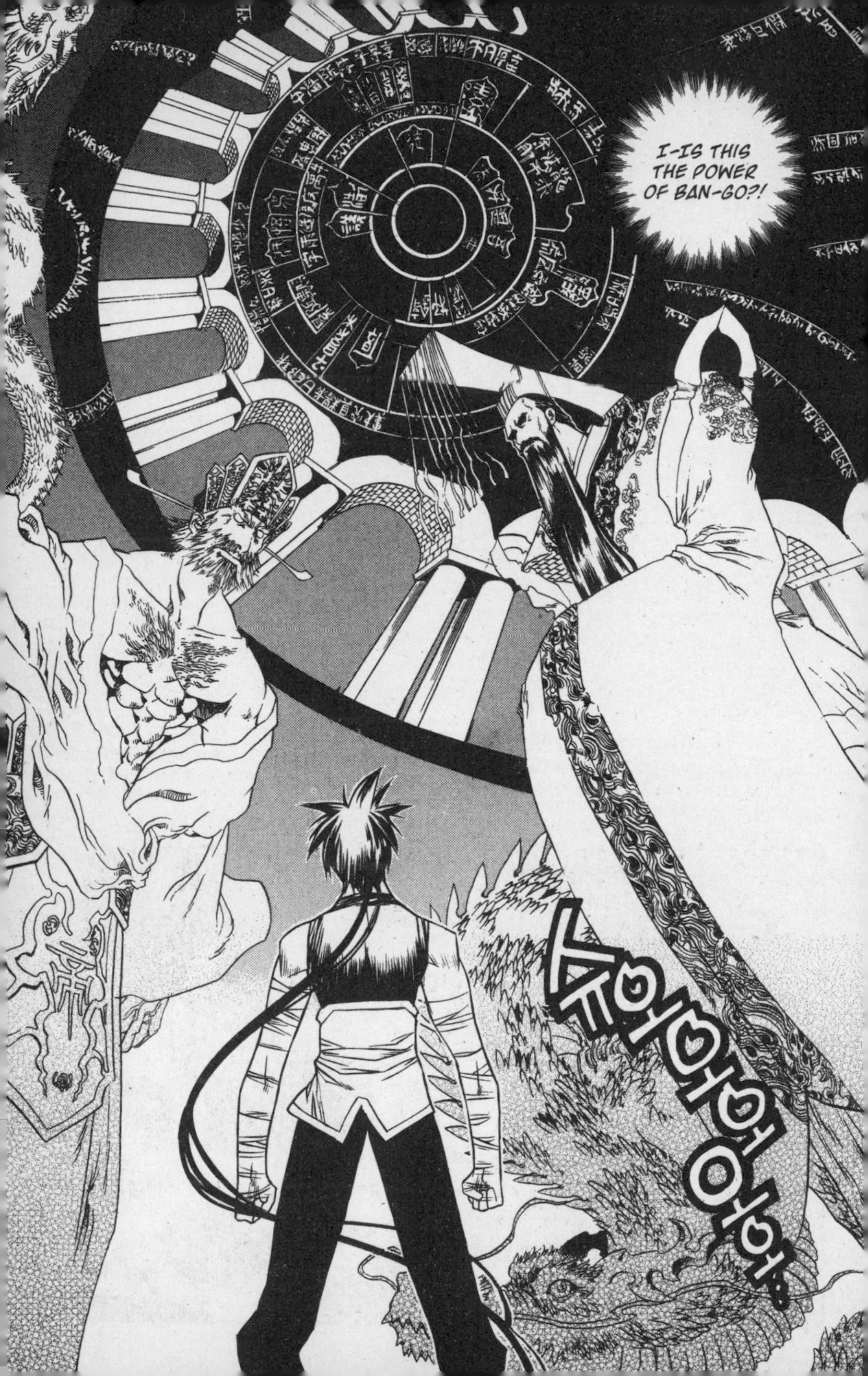
I-IS THIS THE POWER OF BAN-GO?!

Chapter 56
The Escape

—!!

AДДH... AHHH...

아악뜨

...

...

56

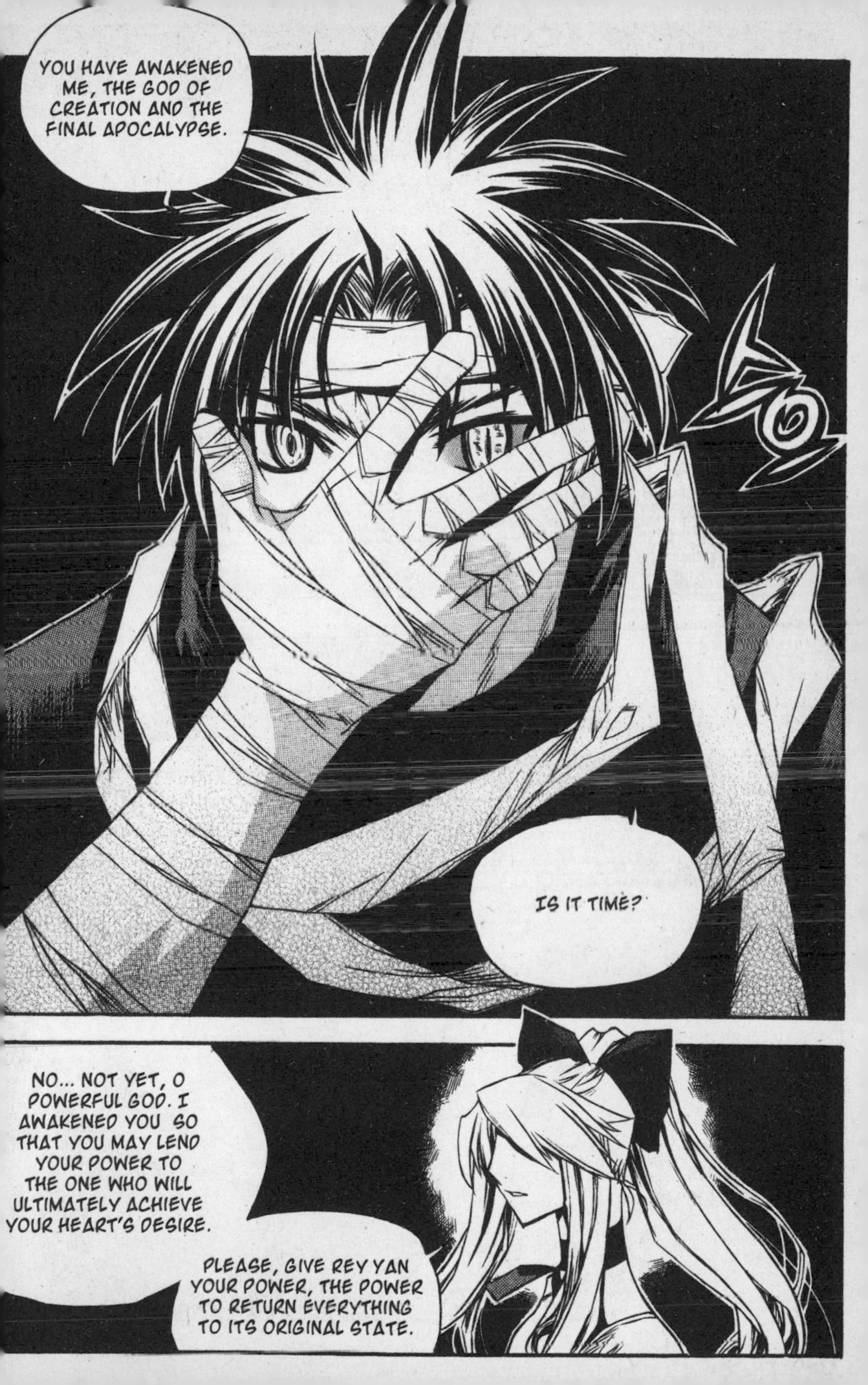
YOU HAVE AWAKENED ME, THE GOD OF CREATION AND THE FINAL APOCALYPSE.
IS IT TIME?
NO... NOT YET, O POWERFUL GOD. I AWAKENED YOU SO THAT YOU MAY LEND YOUR POWER TO THE ONE WHO WILL ULTIMATELY ACHIEVE YOUR HEART'S DESIRE.
PLEASE, GIVE REY YAN YOUR POWER, THE POWER TO RETURN EVERYTHING TO ITS ORIGINAL STATE.

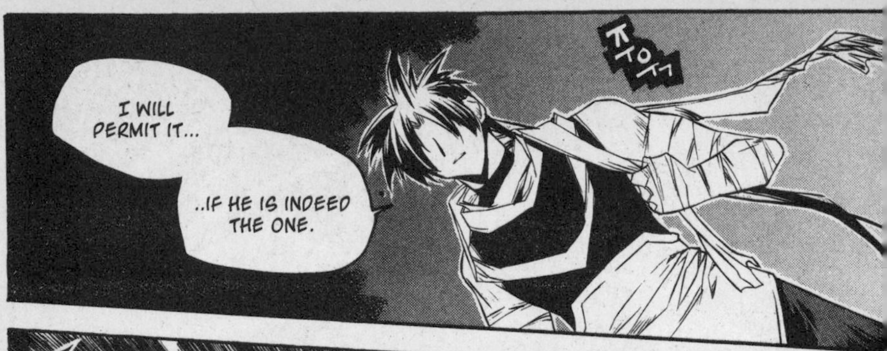
I WILL PERMIT IT...
..IF HE IS INDEED THE ONE.

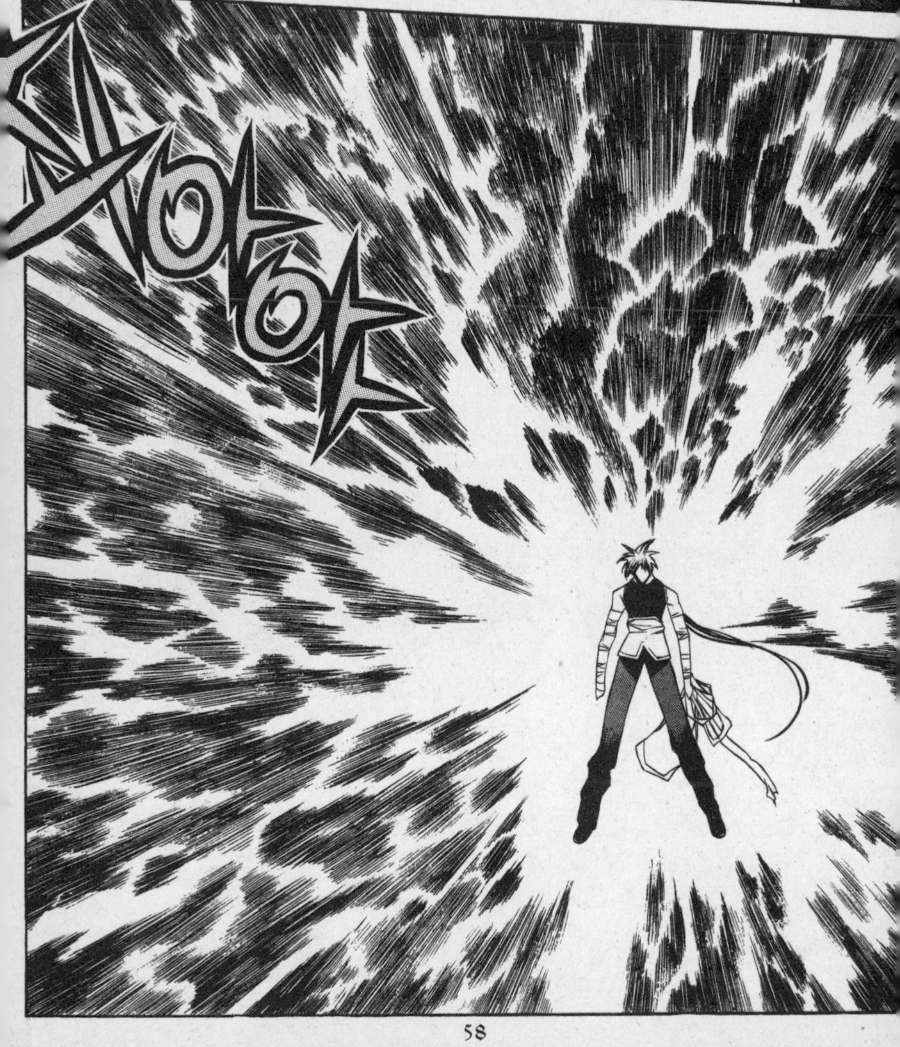

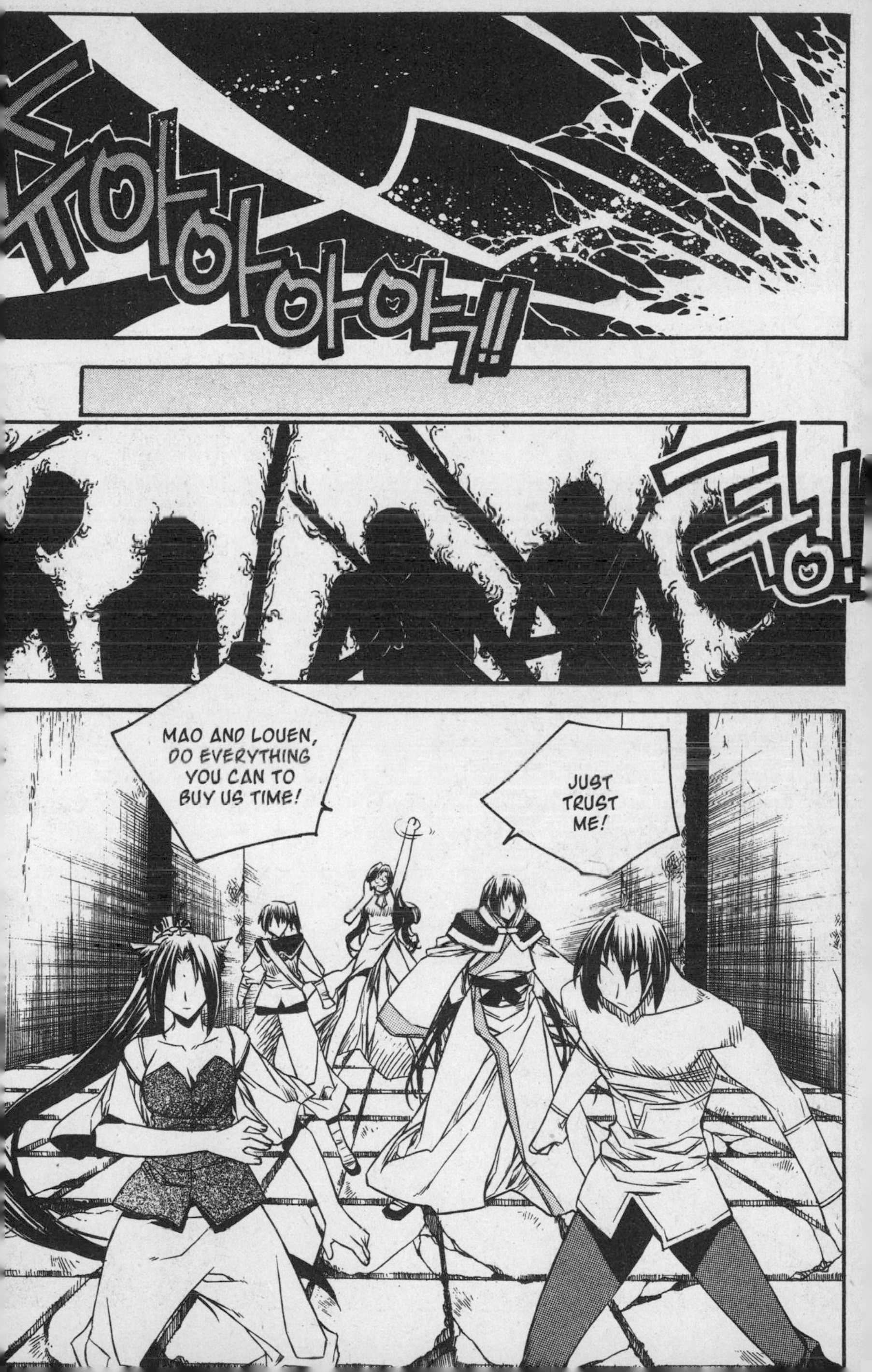
MAO AND LOUEN, DO EVERYTHING YOU CAN TO BUY US TIME!
JUST TRUST ME!

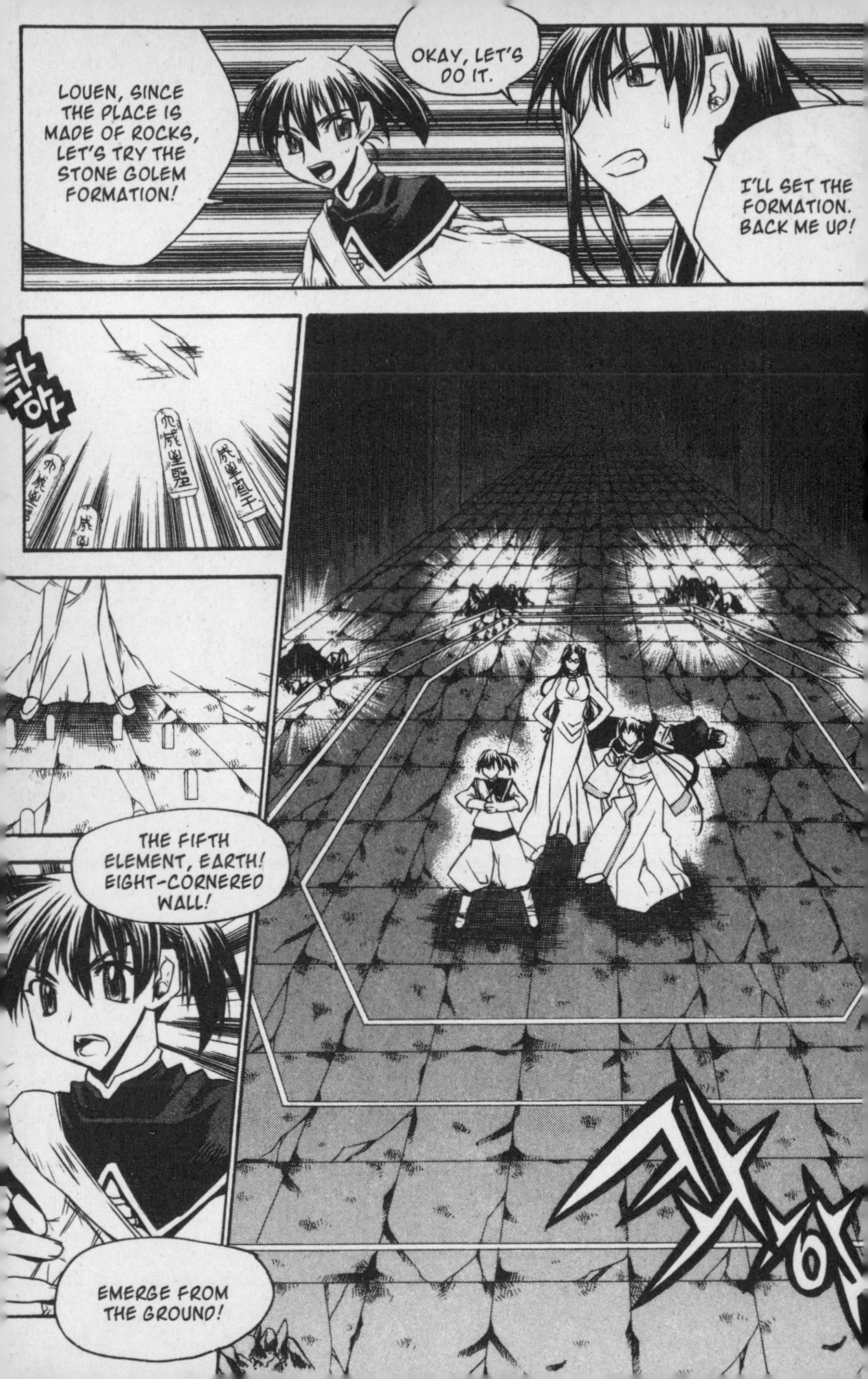
LOUEN, SINCE THE PLACE IS MADE OF ROCKS, LET'S TRY THE STONE GOLEM FORMATION!
OKAY, LET'S DO IT.
I'LL SET THE FORMATION. BACK ME UP!
THE FIFTH ELEMENT, EARTH! EIGHT-CORNERED WALL!
EMERGE FROM THE GROUND!

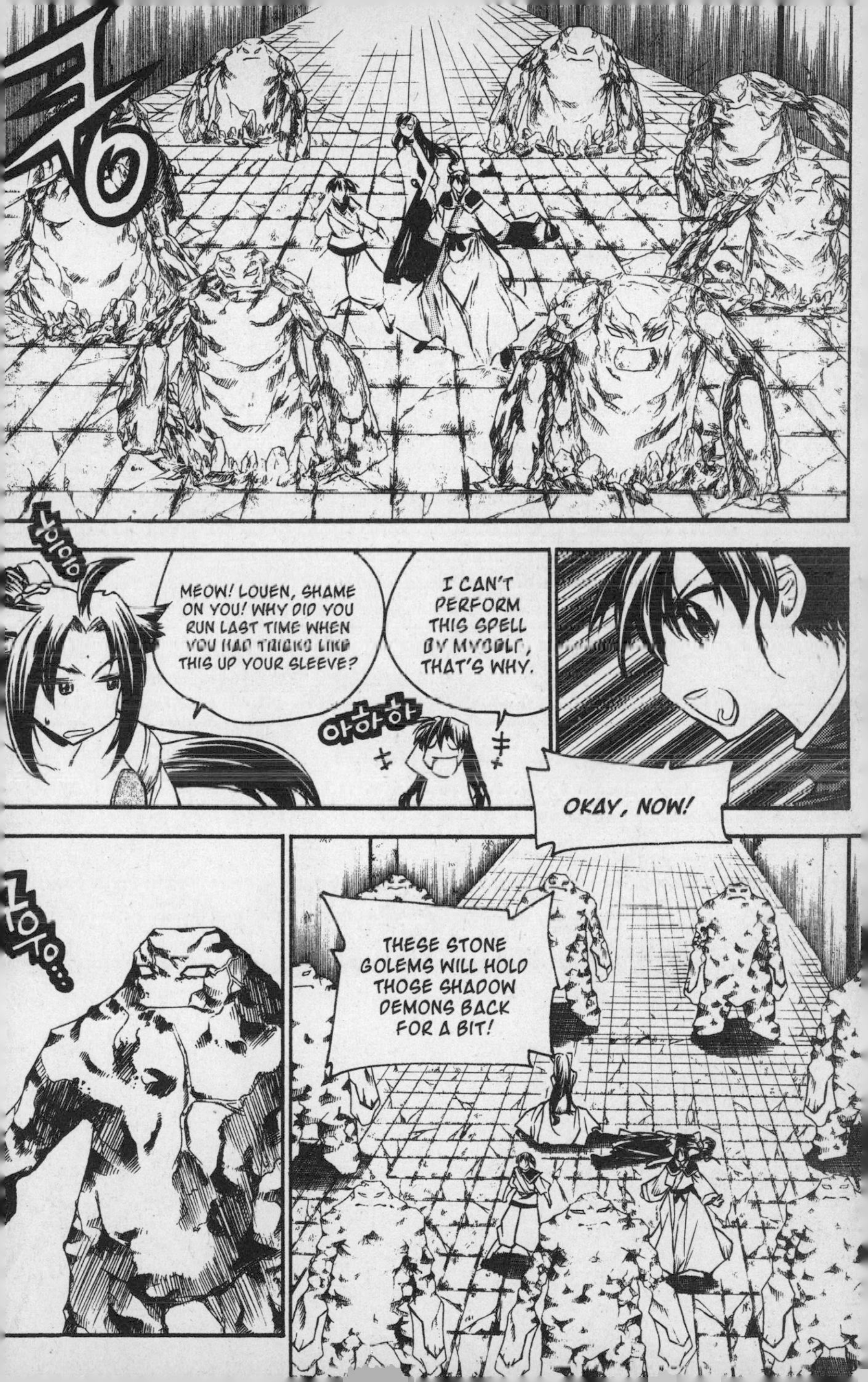
냐아아
MEOW! LOUEN, SHAME ON YOU! WHY DID YOU RUN LAST TIME WHEN YOU HAD TRICKS LIKE THIS UP YOUR SLEEVE?
I CAN'T PERFORM THIS SPELL BY MYSELF, THAT'S WHY.
아하하
OKAY, NOW!
고오오...
THESE STONE GOLEMS WILL HOLD THOSE SHADOW DEMONS BACK FOR A BIT!

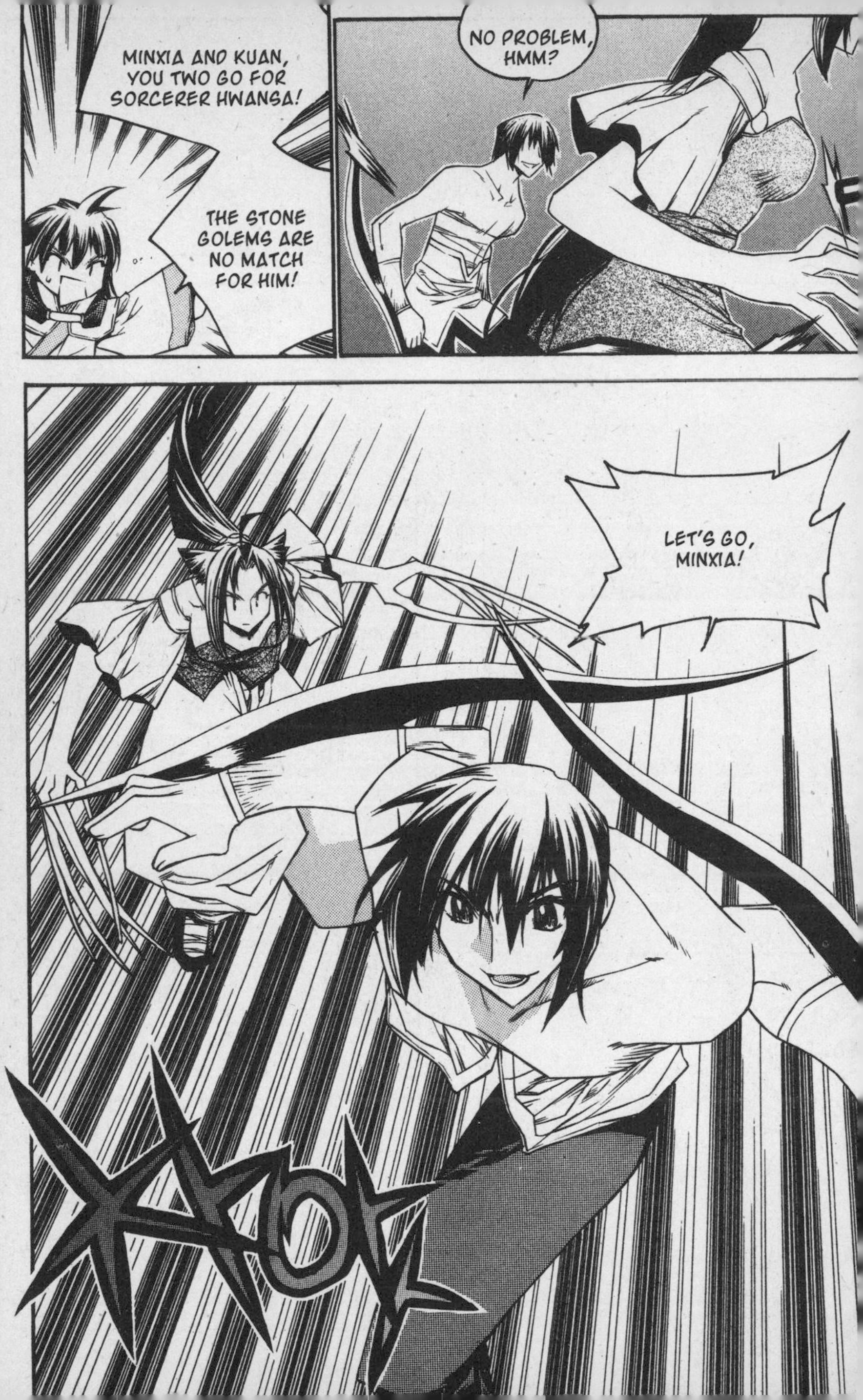
MINXIA AND KUAN, YOU TWO GO FOR SORCERER HWANSA!
THE STONE GOLEMS ARE NO MATCH FOR HIM!
NO PROBLEM, HMM?
LET'S GO, MINXIA!

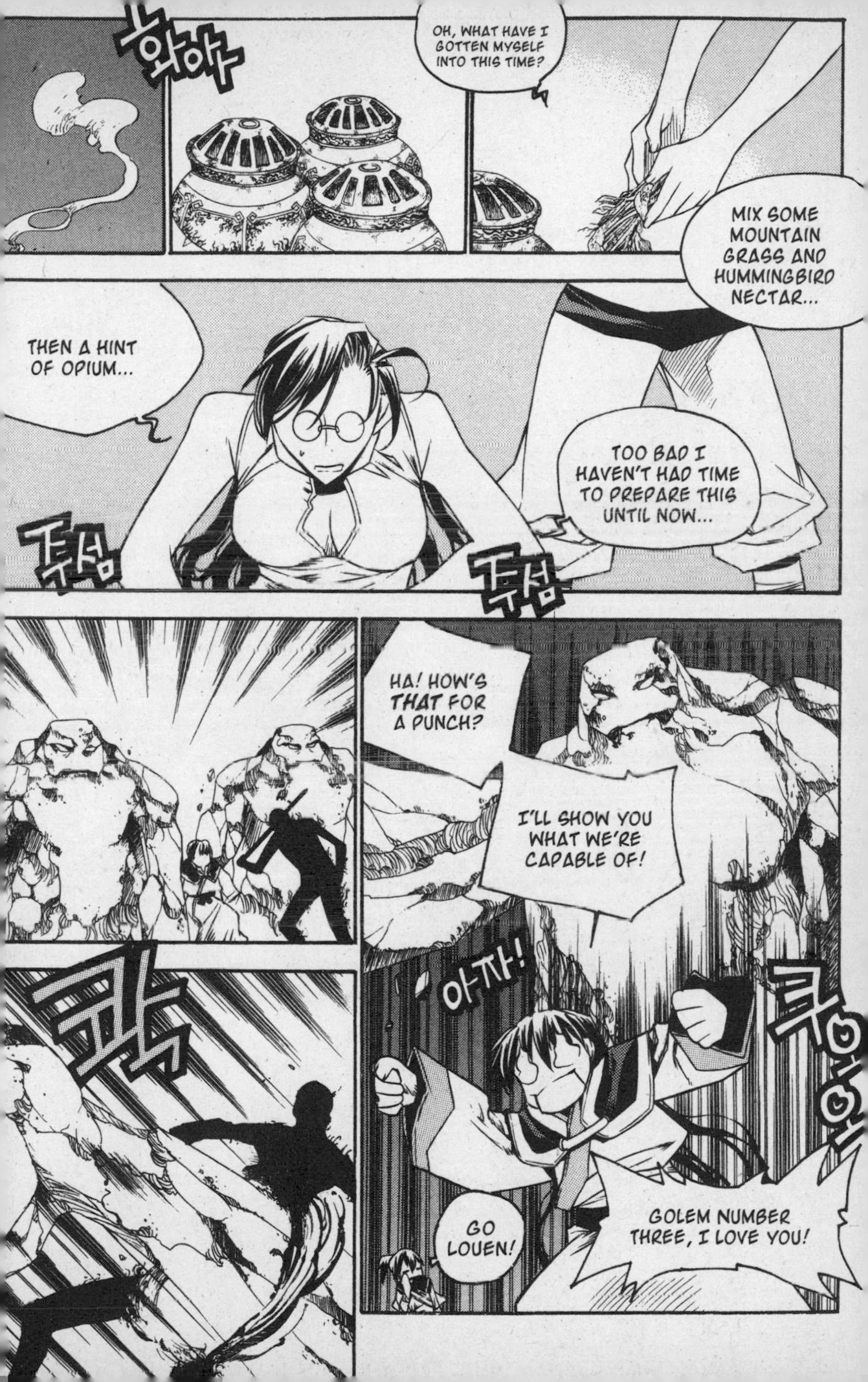
OH, WHAT HAVE I GOTTEN MYSELF INTO THIS TIME?
MIX SOME MOUNTAIN GRASS AND HUMMINGBIRD NECTAR...
THEN A HINT OF OPIUM...
TOO BAD I HAVEN'T HAD TIME TO PREPARE THIS UNTIL NOW...
HA! HOW'S THAT FOR A PUNCH?
I'LL SHOW YOU WHAT WE'RE CAPABLE OF!
아자!
GO LOUEN!
GOLEM NUMBER THREE, I LOVE YOU!

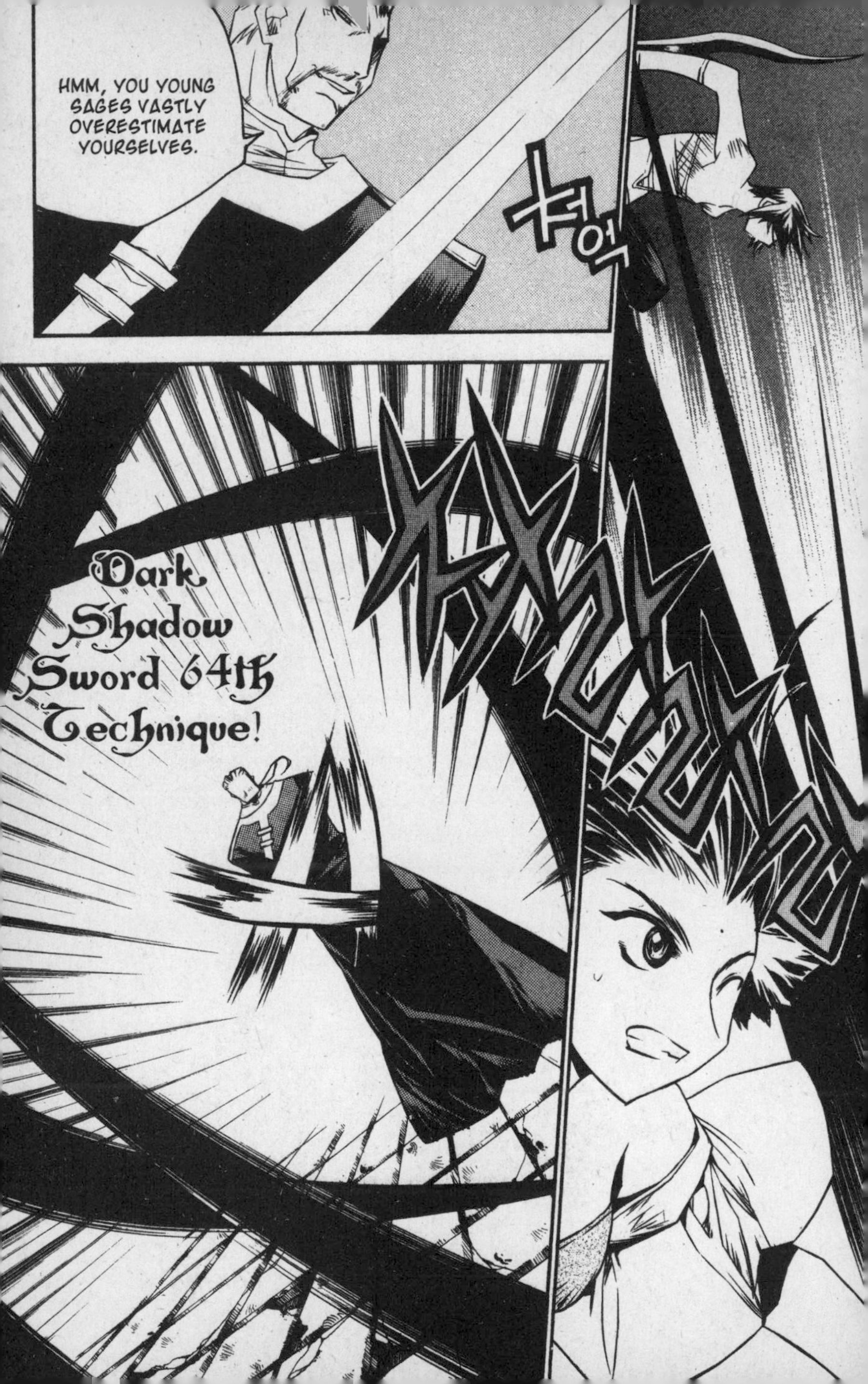
HMM, YOU YOUNG SAGES VASTLY OVERESTIMATE YOURSELVES.
Dark Shadow Sword 64th Technique!

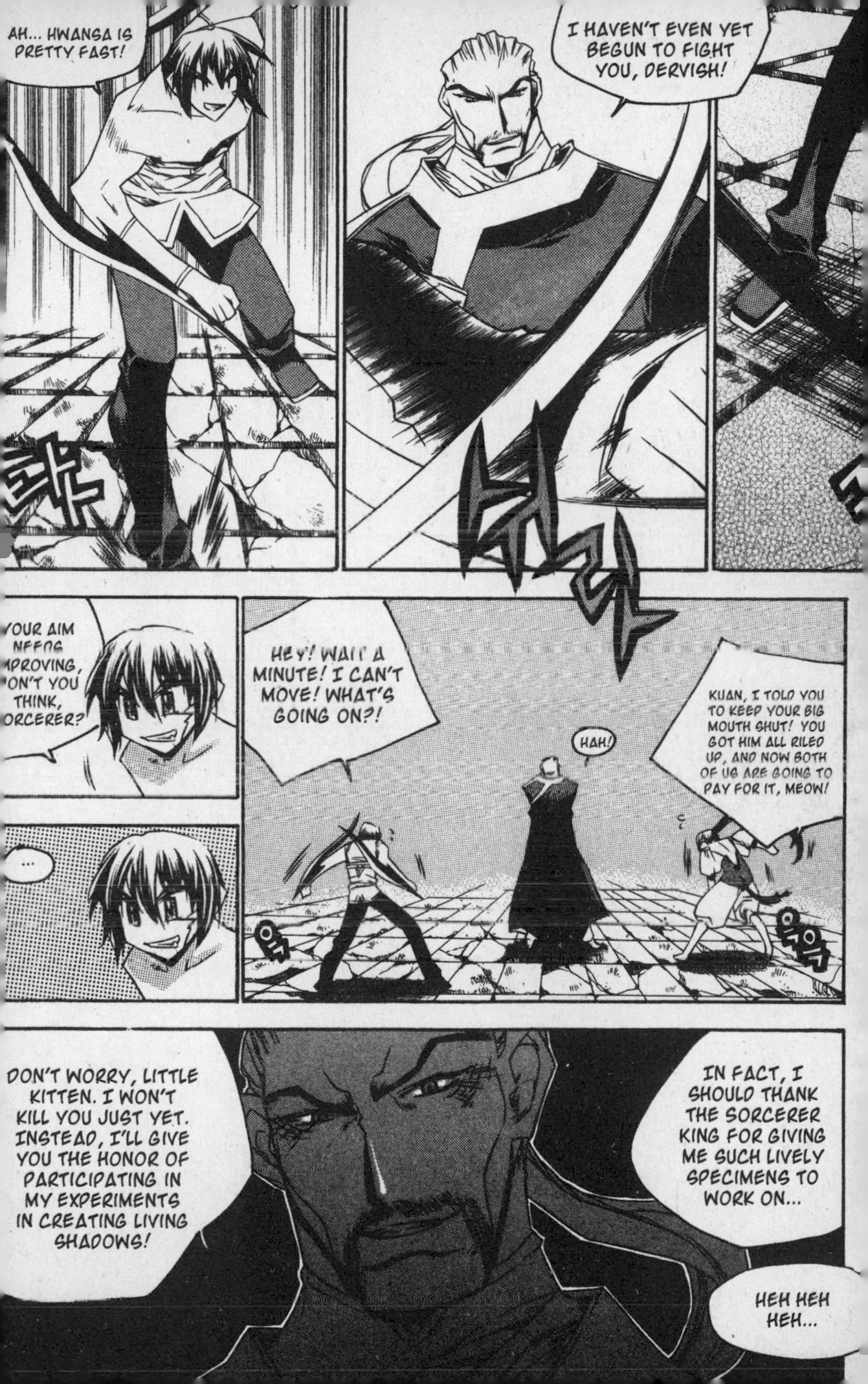
AH... HWANSA IS PRETTY FAST!
I HAVEN'T EVEN YET BEGUN TO FIGHT YOU, DERVISH!
YOUR AIM NEEDS MPROVING, ON'T YOU THINK, ORCERER?
...
HEY! WAIT A MINUTE! I CAN'T MOVE! WHAT'S GOING ON?!
HAH!
KUAN, I TOLD YOU TO KEEP YOUR BIG MOUTH SHUT! YOU GOT HIM ALL RILED UP, AND NOW BOTH OF US ARE GOING TO PAY FOR IT, MEOW!
DON'T WORRY, LITTLE KITTEN. I WON'T KILL YOU JUST YET. INSTEAD, I'LL GIVE YOU THE HONOR OF PARTICIPATING IN MY EXPERIMENTS IN CREATING LIVING SHADOWS!
IN FACT, I SHOULD THANK THE SORCERER KING FOR GIVING ME SUCH LIVELY SPECIMENS TO WORK ON...
HEH HEH HEH...

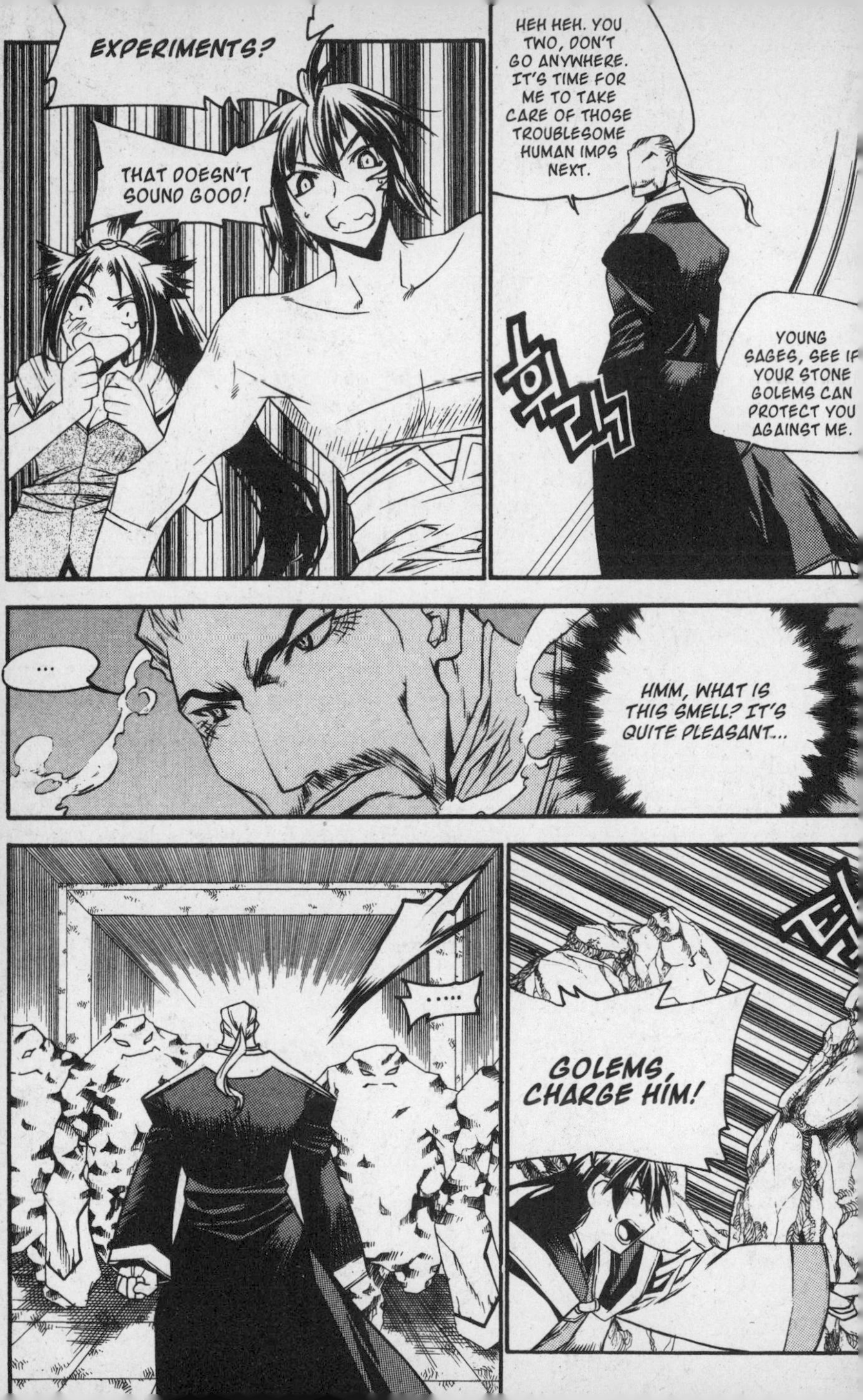
EXPERIMENTS?
THAT DOESN'T SOUND GOOD!
HEH HEH. YOU TWO, DON'T GO ANYWHERE. IT'S TIME FOR ME TO TAKE CARE OF THOSE TROUBLESOME HUMAN IMPS NEXT.
YOUNG SAGES, SEE IF YOUR STONE GOLEMS CAN PROTECT YOU AGAINST ME.
...
HMM, WHAT IS THIS SMELL? IT'S QUITE PLEASANT...
.....
GOLEMS, CHARGE HIM!

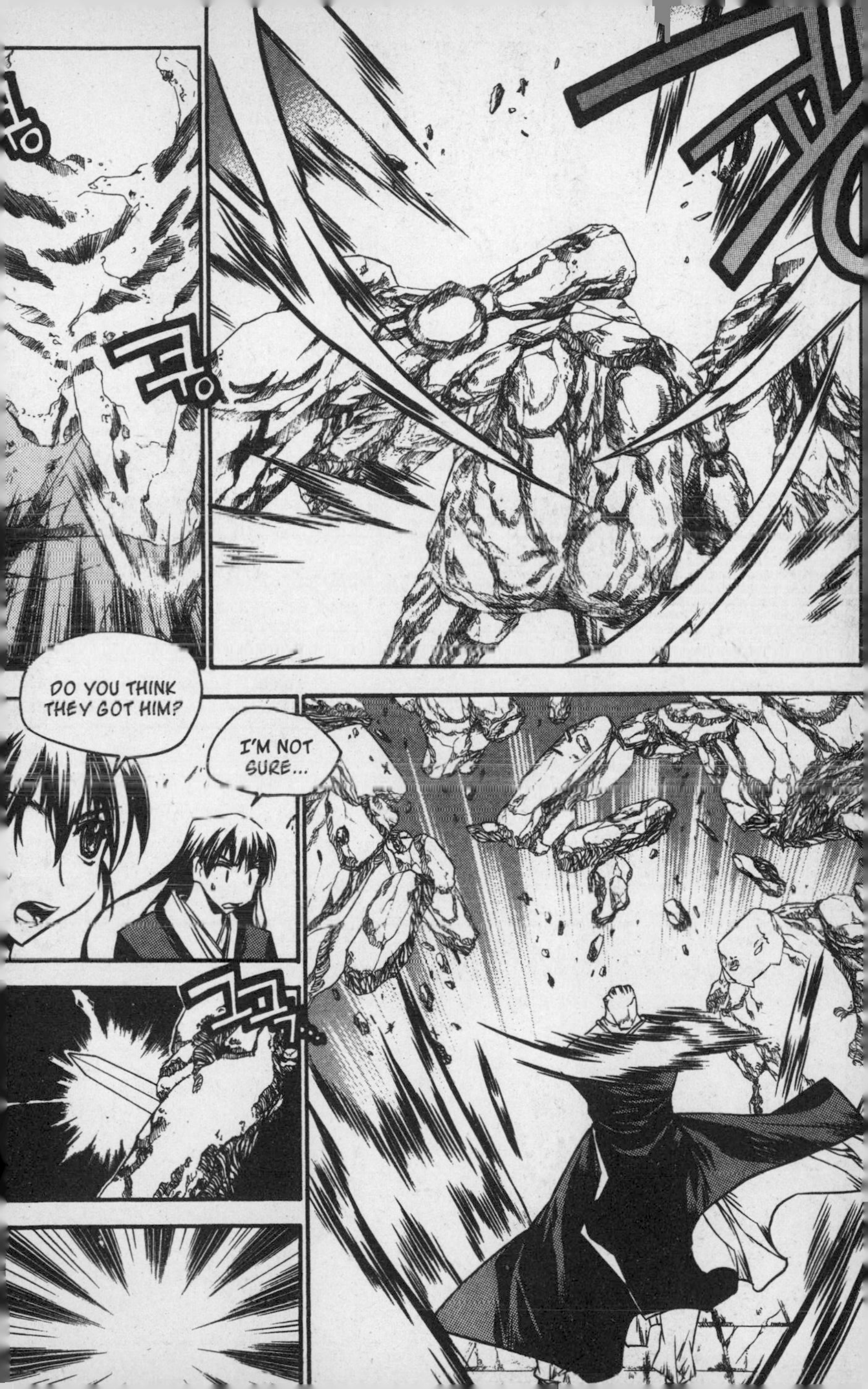
DO YOU THINK THEY GOT HIM?
I'M NOT SURE...

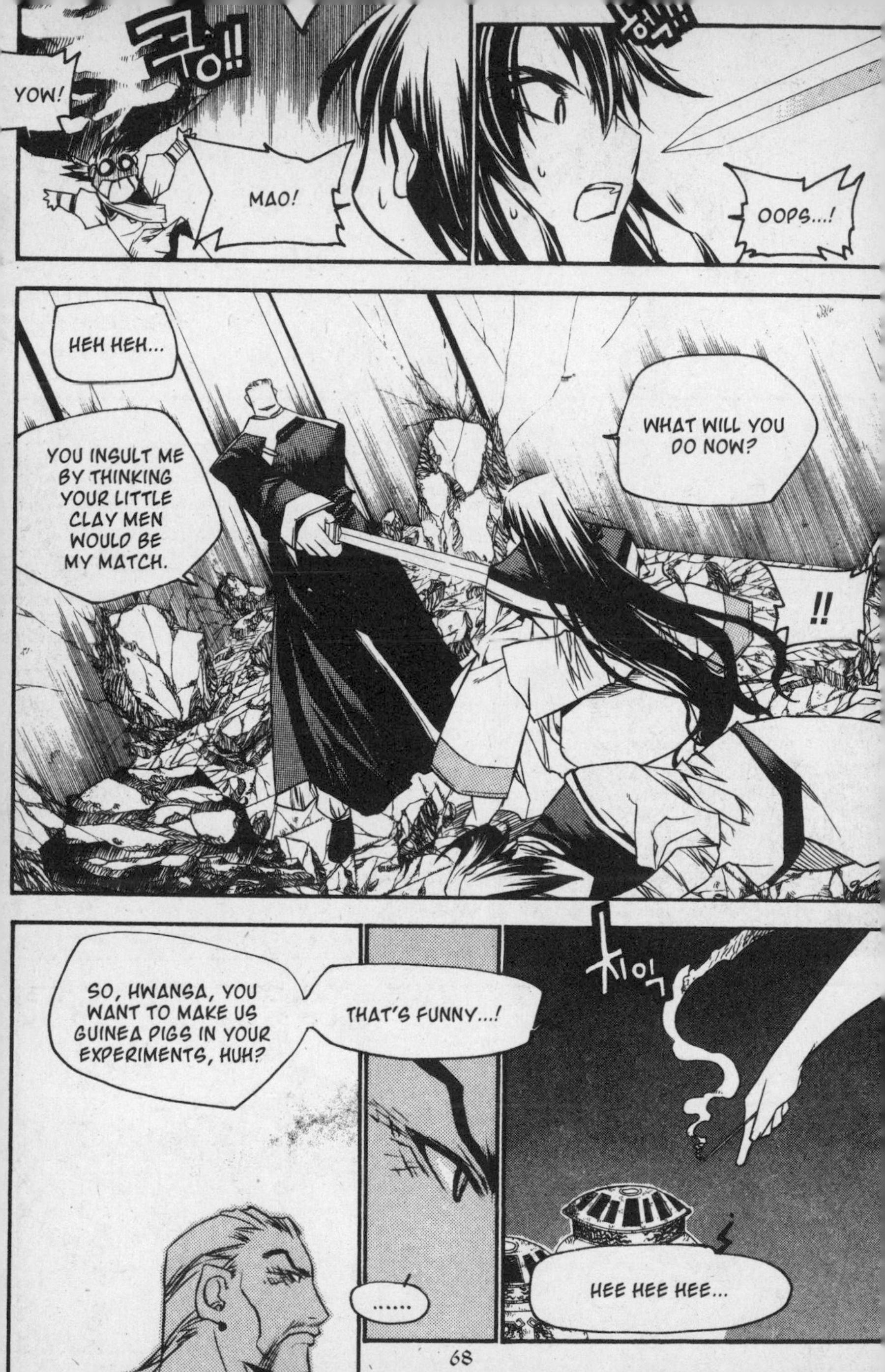
YOW!
MAO!
OOPS...!
HEH HEH...
YOU INSULT ME BY THINKING YOUR LITTLE CLAY MEN WOULD BE MY MATCH.
WHAT WILL YOU DO NOW?
!!
SO, HWANSA, YOU WANT TO MAKE US GUINEA PIGS IN YOUR EXPERIMENTS, HUH?
THAT'S FUNNY...!
......
HEE HEE HEE...

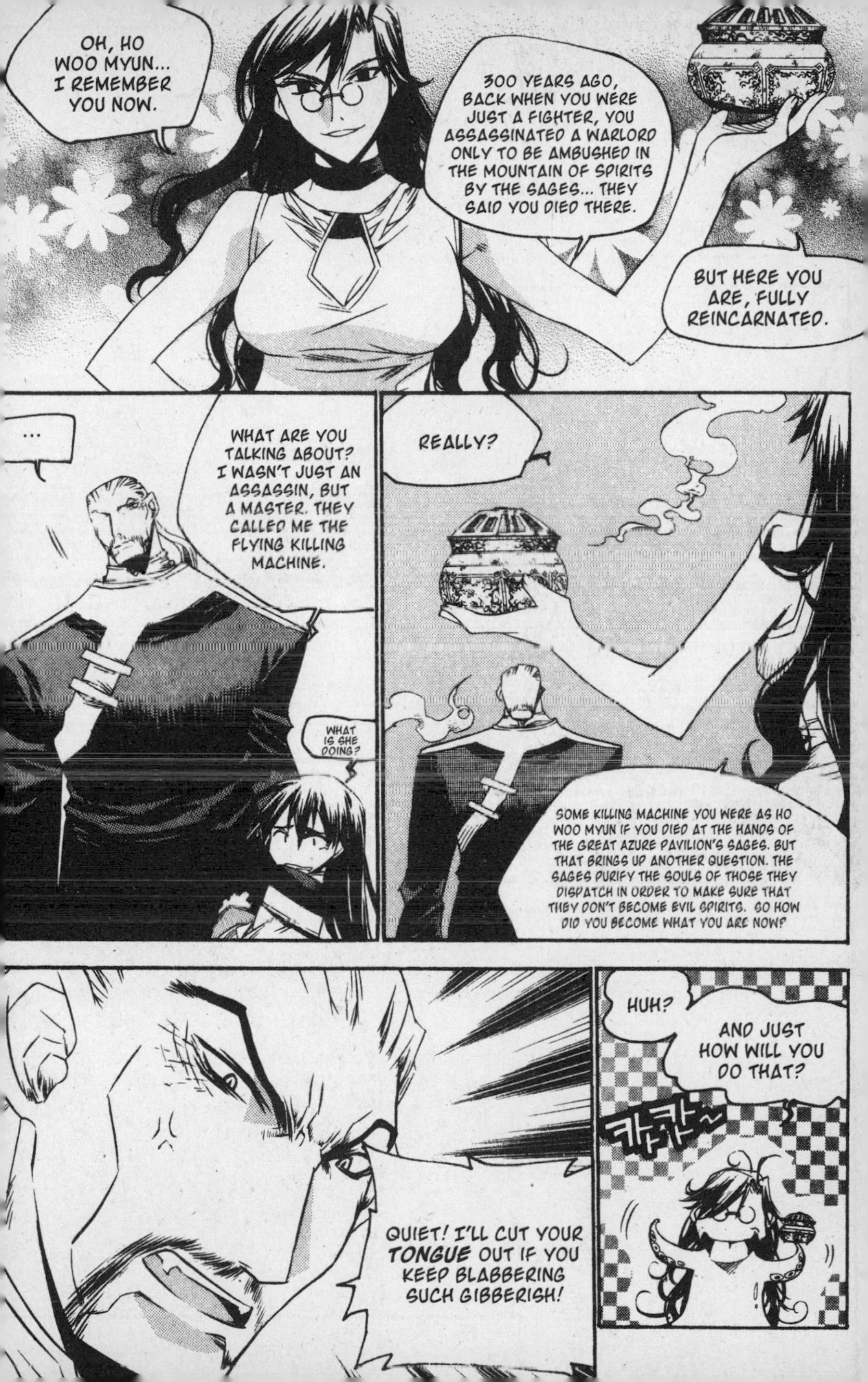
OH, HO WOO MYUN... I REMEMBER YOU NOW.
300 YEARS AGO, BACK WHEN YOU WERE JUST A FIGHTER, YOU ASSASSINATED A WARLORD ONLY TO BE AMBUSHED IN THE MOUNTAIN OF SPIRITS BY THE SAGES... THEY SAID YOU DIED THERE.
BUT HERE YOU ARE, FULLY REINCARNATED.
...
WHAT ARE YOU TALKING ABOUT? I WASN'T JUST AN ASSASSIN, BUT A MASTER. THEY CALLED ME THE FLYING KILLING MACHINE.
WHAT IS SHE DOING?
REALLY?
SOME KILLING MACHINE YOU WERE AS HO WOO MYUN IF YOU DIED AT THE HANDS OF THE GREAT AZURE PAVILION'S SAGES. BUT THAT BRINGS UP ANOTHER QUESTION. THE SAGES PURIFY THE SOULS OF THOSE THEY DISPATCH IN ORDER TO MAKE SURE THAT THEY DON'T BECOME EVIL SPIRITS. SO HOW DID YOU BECOME WHAT YOU ARE NOW?
QUIET! I'LL CUT YOUR *TONGUE* OUT IF YOU KEEP BLABBERING SUCH GIBBERISH!
HUH?
AND JUST HOW WILL YOU DO THAT?
카카~

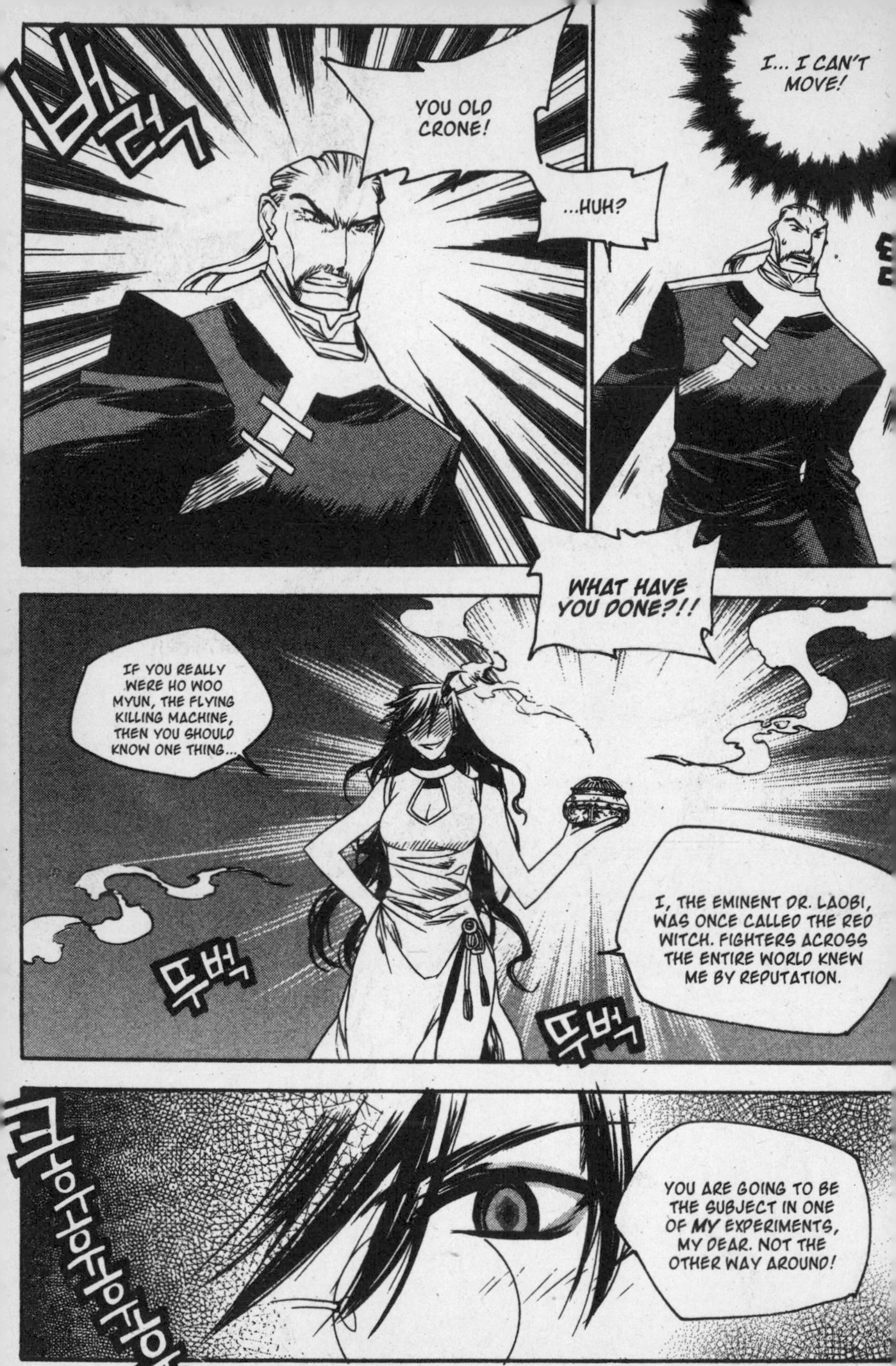

벌컥
YOU OLD CRONE!
...HUH?
I... I CAN'T MOVE!
WHAT HAVE YOU DONE?!!
IF YOU REALLY WERE HO WOO MYUN, THE FLYING KILLING MACHINE, THEN YOU SHOULD KNOW ONE THING...
I, THE EMINENT DR. LAOBI, WAS ONCE CALLED THE RED WITCH. FIGHTERS ACROSS THE ENTIRE WORLD KNEW ME BY REPUTATION.
뚜벅
뚜벅
YOU ARE GOING TO BE THE SUBJECT IN ONE OF *MY* EXPERIMENTS, MY DEAR. NOT THE OTHER WAY AROUND!

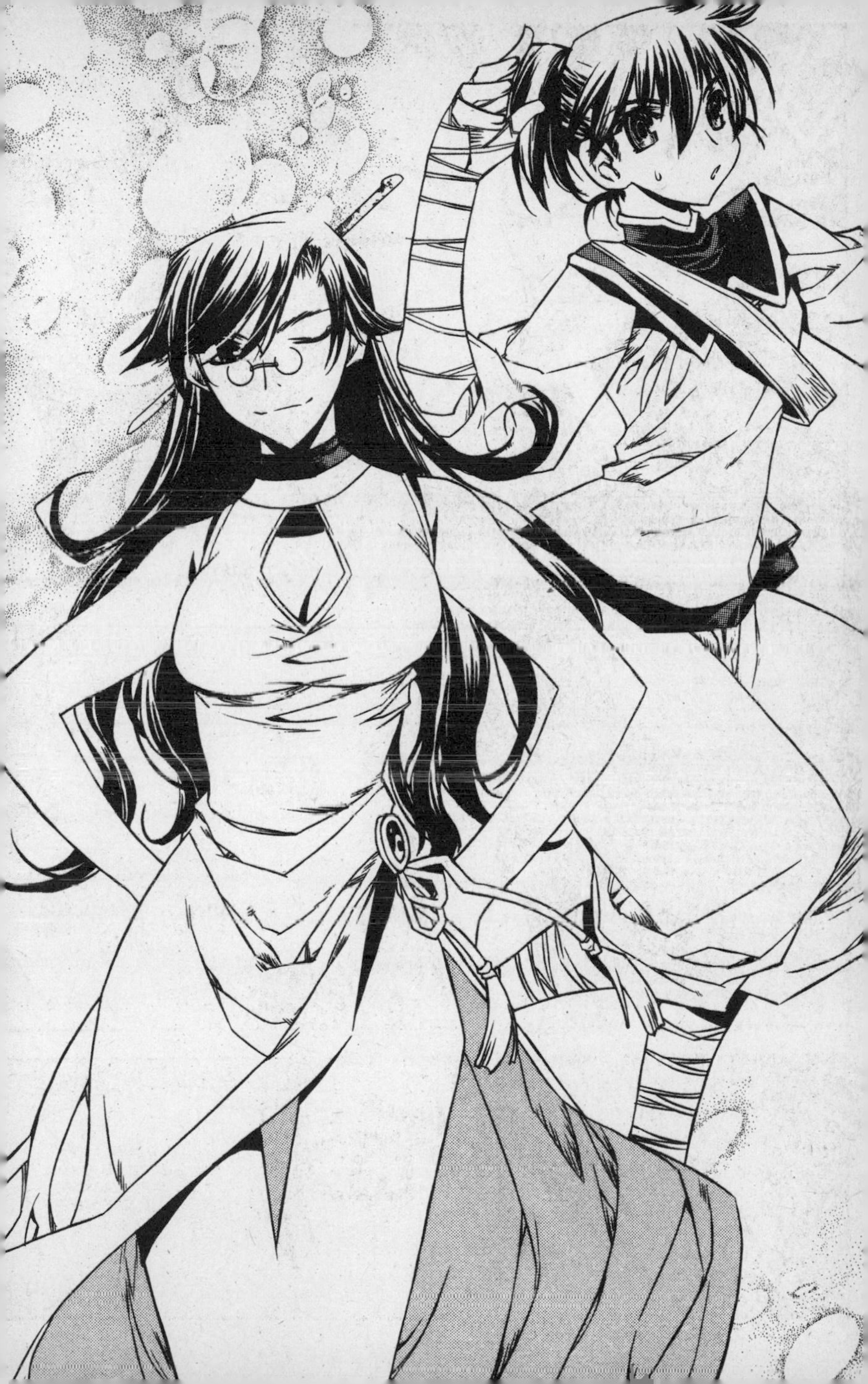

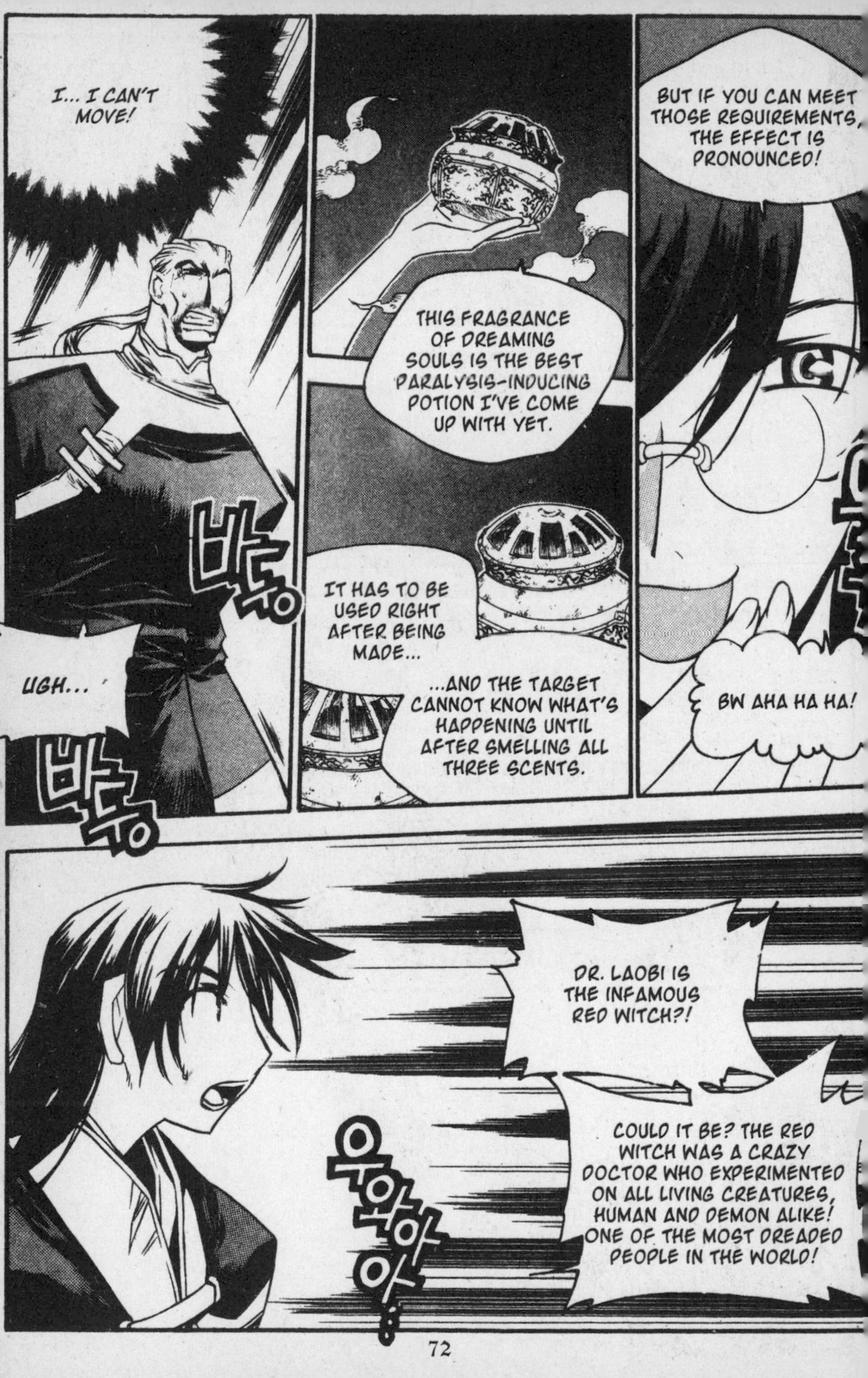
I... I CAN'T MOVE!
UGH...
THIS FRAGRANCE OF DREAMING SOULS IS THE BEST PARALYSIS-INDUCING POTION I'VE COME UP WITH YET.
IT HAS TO BE USED RIGHT AFTER BEING MADE...
...AND THE TARGET CANNOT KNOW WHAT'S HAPPENING UNTIL AFTER SMELLING ALL THREE SCENTS.
BUT IF YOU CAN MEET THOSE REQUIREMENTS, THE EFFECT IS PRONOUNCED!
BW AHA HA HA!
DR. LAOBI IS THE INFAMOUS RED WITCH?!
COULD IT BE? THE RED WITCH WAS A CRAZY DOCTOR WHO EXPERIMENTED ON ALL LIVING CREATURES, HUMAN AND DEMON ALIKE! ONE OF THE MOST DREADED PEOPLE IN THE WORLD!

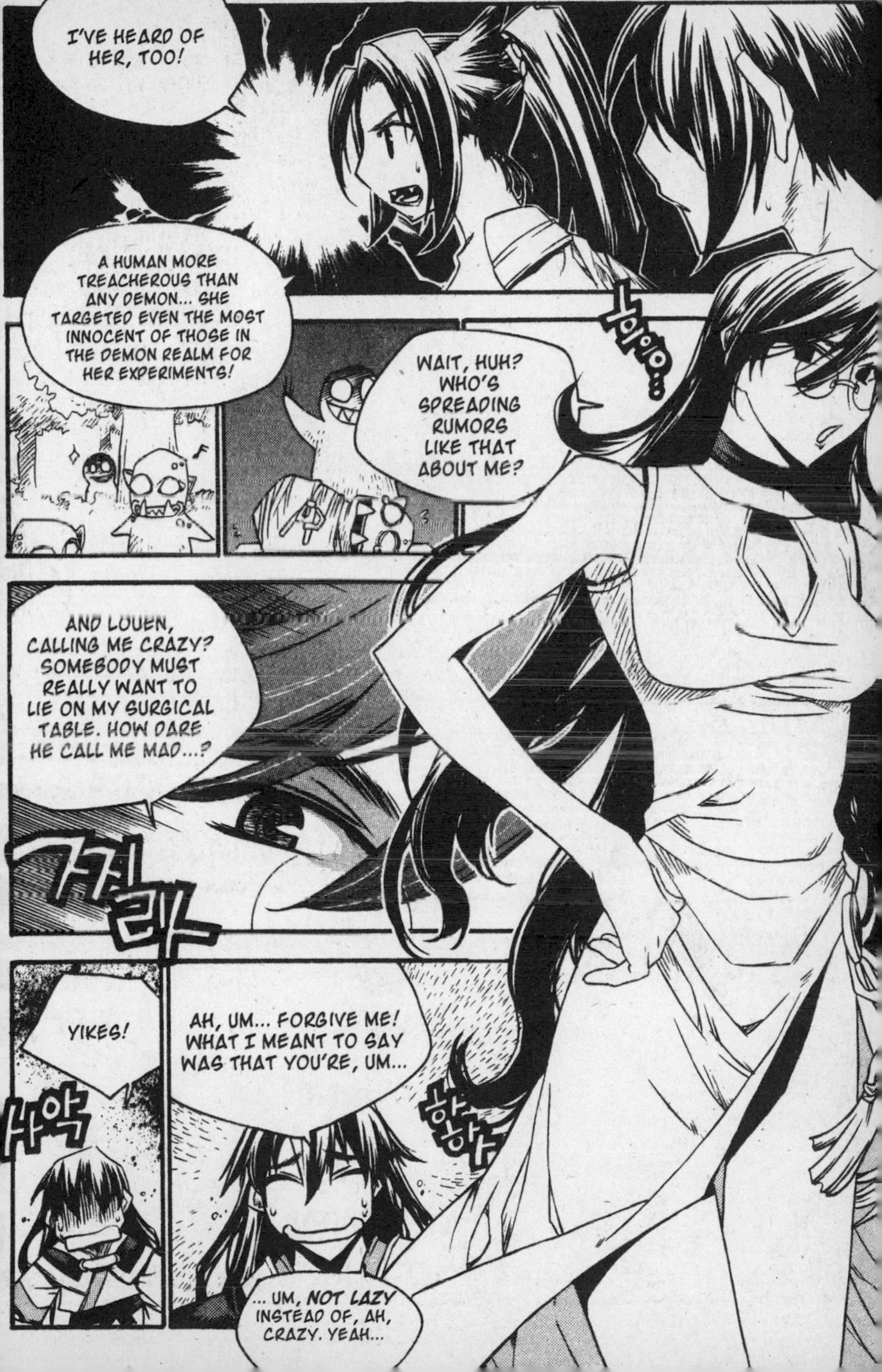
I'VE HEARD OF HER, TOO!
A HUMAN MORE TREACHEROUS THAN ANY DEMON... SHE TARGETED EVEN THE MOST INNOCENT OF THOSE IN THE DEMON REALM FOR HER EXPERIMENTS!
WAIT, HUH? WHO'S SPREADING RUMORS LIKE THAT ABOUT ME?
AND LOUEN, CALLING ME CRAZY? SOMEBODY MUST REALLY WANT TO LIE ON MY SURGICAL TABLE. HOW DARE HE CALL ME MAD...?
YIKES!
AH, UM... FORGIVE ME! WHAT I MEANT TO SAY WAS THAT YOU'RE, UM...
... UM, *NOT LAZY* INSTEAD OF, AH, CRAZY. YEAH...

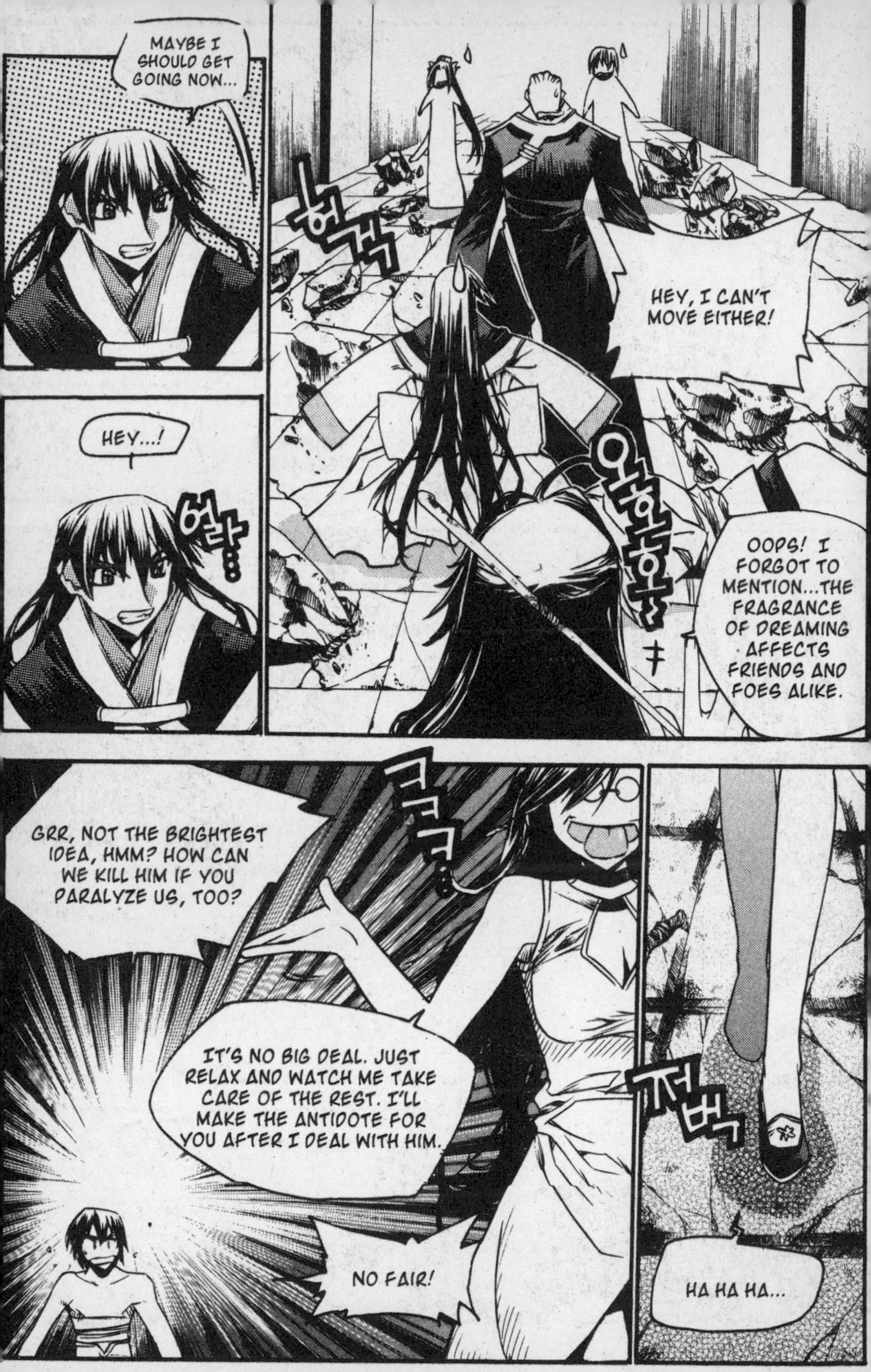

MAYBE I SHOULD GET GOING NOW...
HEY...!
허걱
HEY, I CAN'T MOVE EITHER!
오호호호
OOPS! I FORGOT TO MENTION...THE FRAGRANCE OF DREAMING AFFECTS FRIENDS AND FOES ALIKE.
GRR, NOT THE BRIGHTEST IDEA, HMM? HOW CAN WE KILL HIM IF YOU PARALYZE US, TOO?
크크크
IT'S NO BIG DEAL. JUST RELAX AND WATCH ME TAKE CARE OF THE REST. I'LL MAKE THE ANTIDOTE FOR YOU AFTER I DEAL WITH HIM.
NO FAIR!
저벅
HA HA HA...

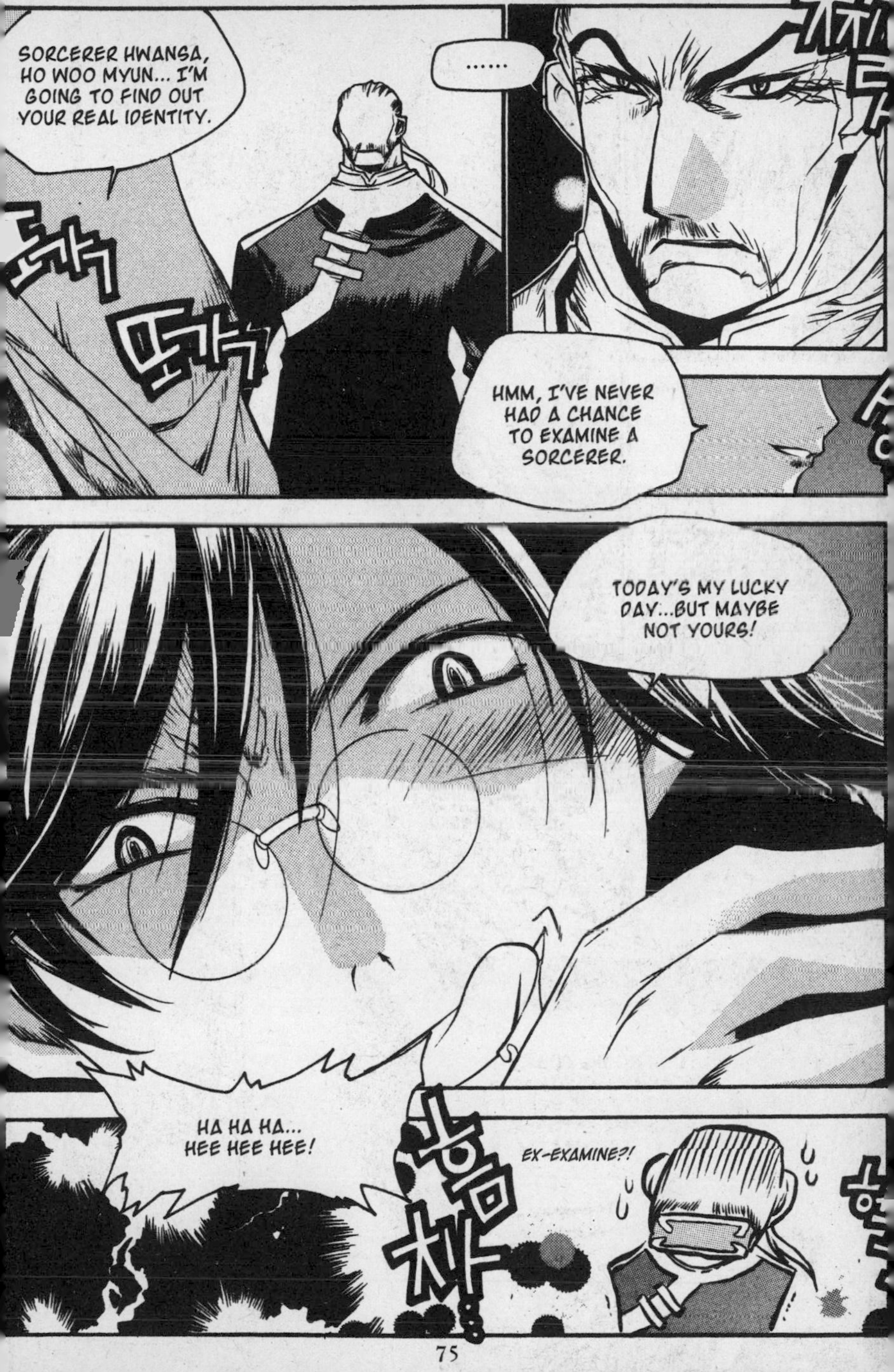
SORCERER HWANSA, HO WOO MYUN... I'M GOING TO FIND OUT YOUR REAL IDENTITY.
....
HMM, I'VE NEVER HAD A CHANCE TO EXAMINE A SORCERER.
TODAY'S MY LUCKY DAY...BUT MAYBE NOT YOURS!
HA HA HA... HEE HEE HEE!
EX-EXAMINE?!

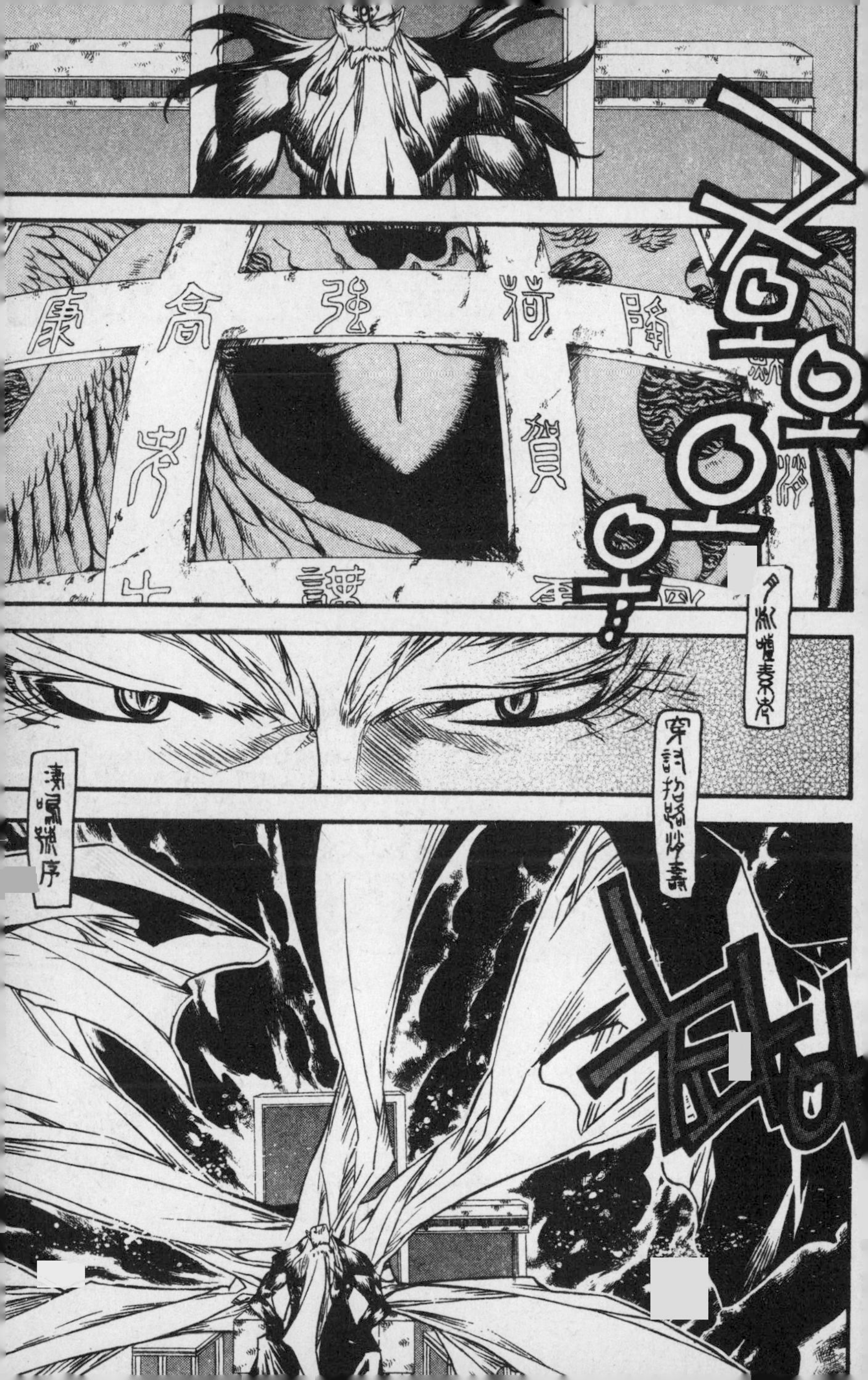

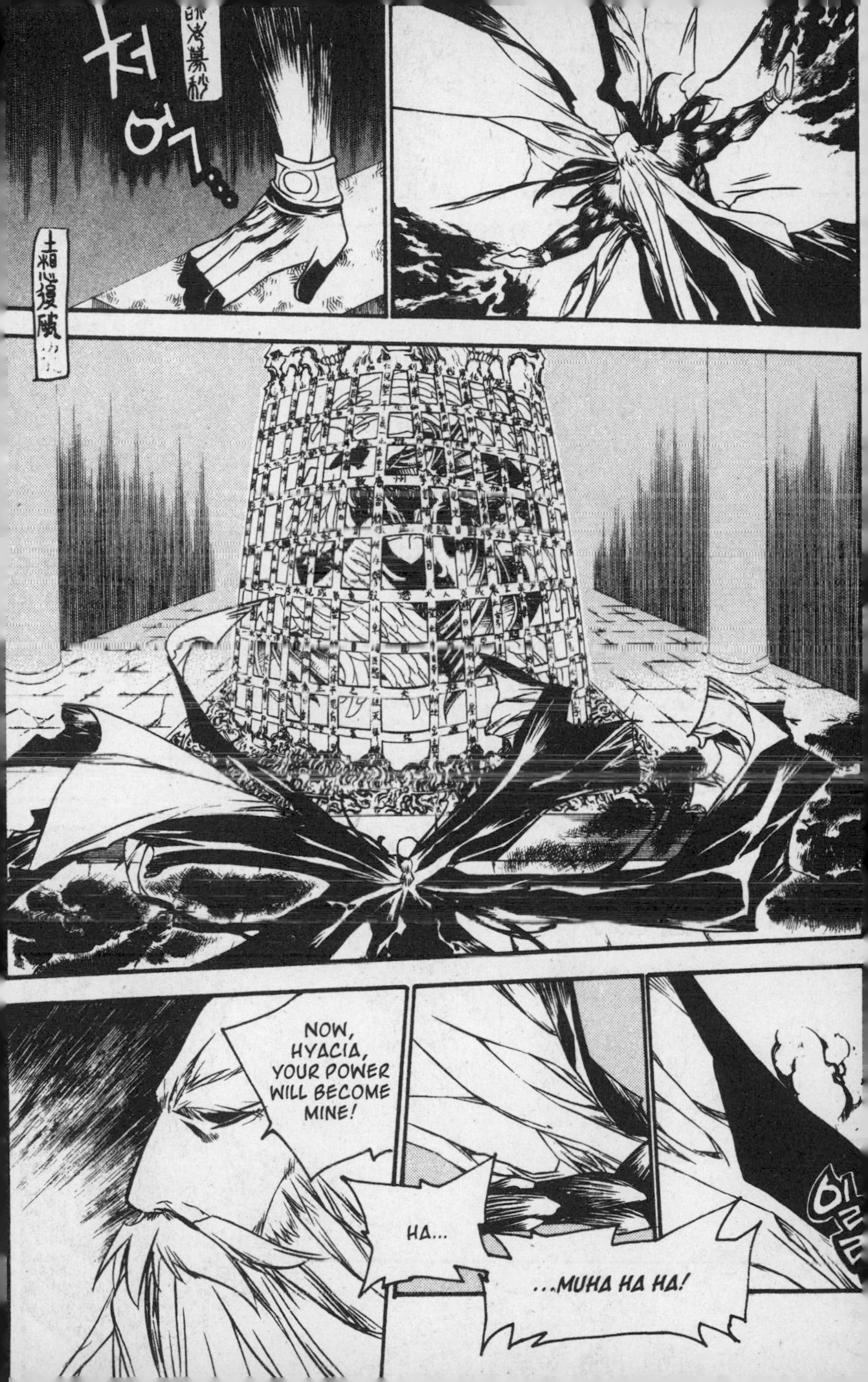
NOW, HYACIA, YOUR POWER WILL BECOME MINE!
HA...
...MUHA HA HA!

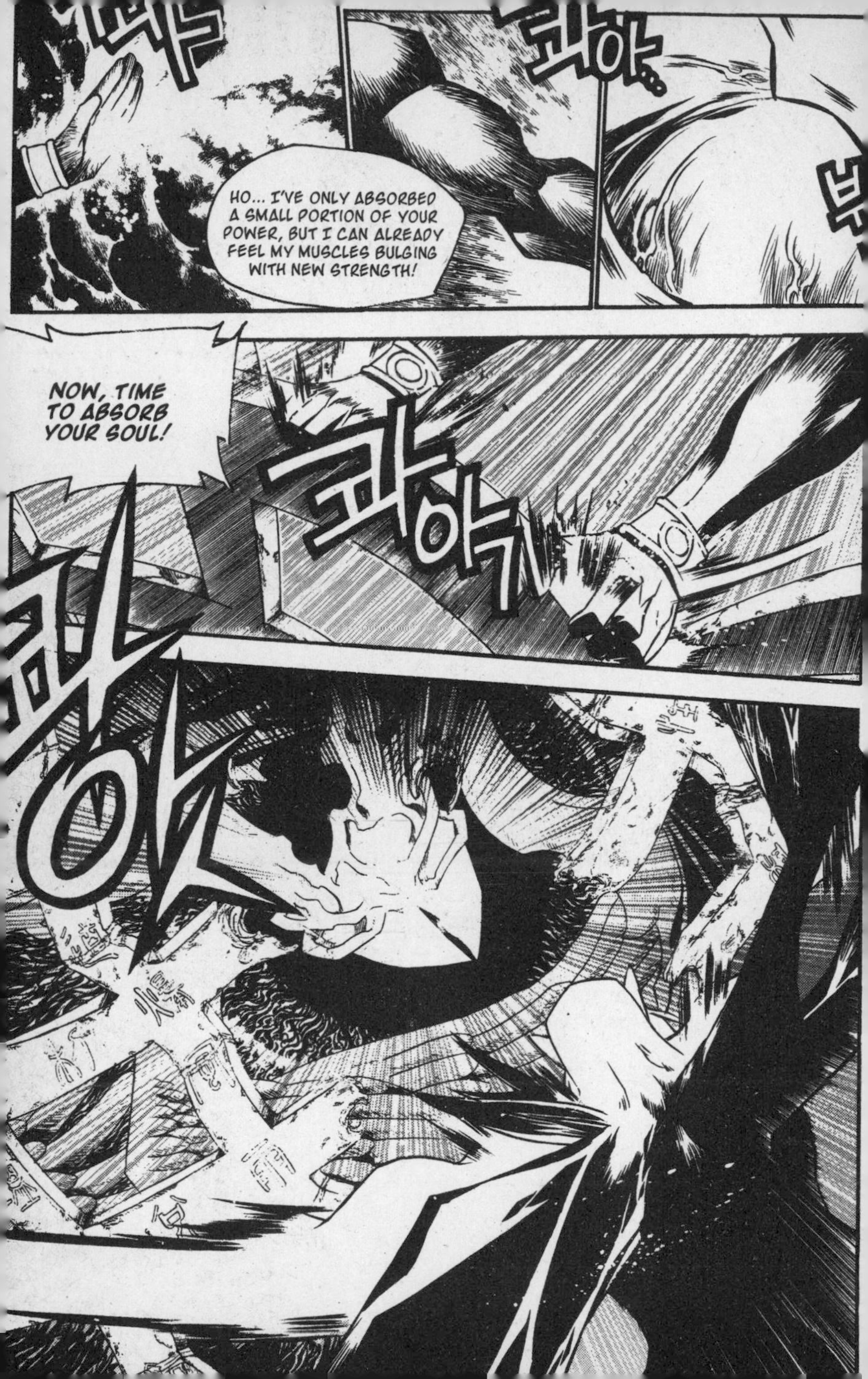
HO... I'VE ONLY ABSORBED A SMALL PORTION OF YOUR POWER, BUT I CAN ALREADY FEEL MY MUSCLES BULGING WITH NEW STRENGTH!
NOW, TIME TO ABSORB YOUR SOUL!

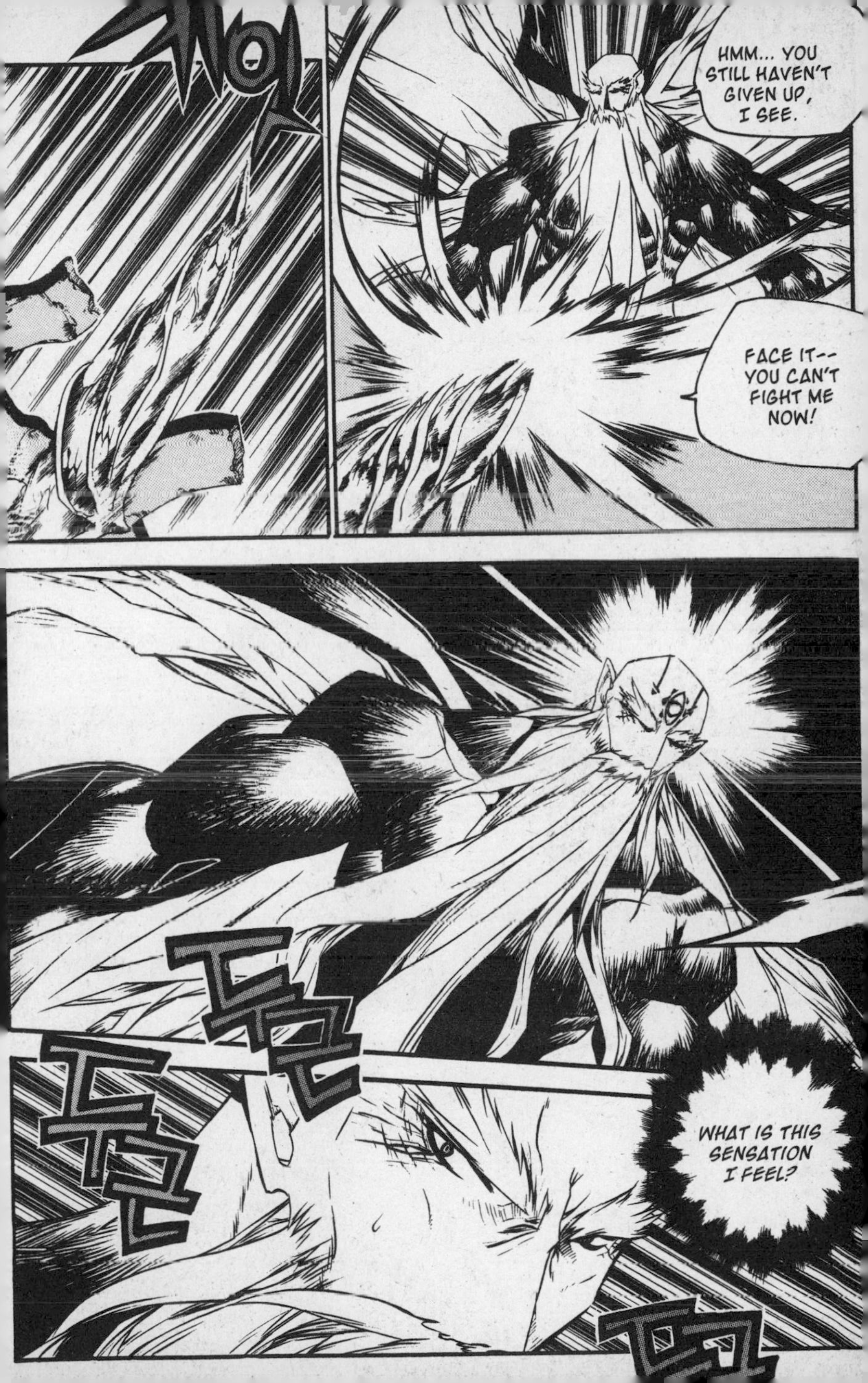
HMM... YOU STILL HAVEN'T GIVEN UP, I SEE.
FACE IT-- YOU CAN'T FIGHT ME NOW!
WHAT IS THIS SENSATION I FEEL?

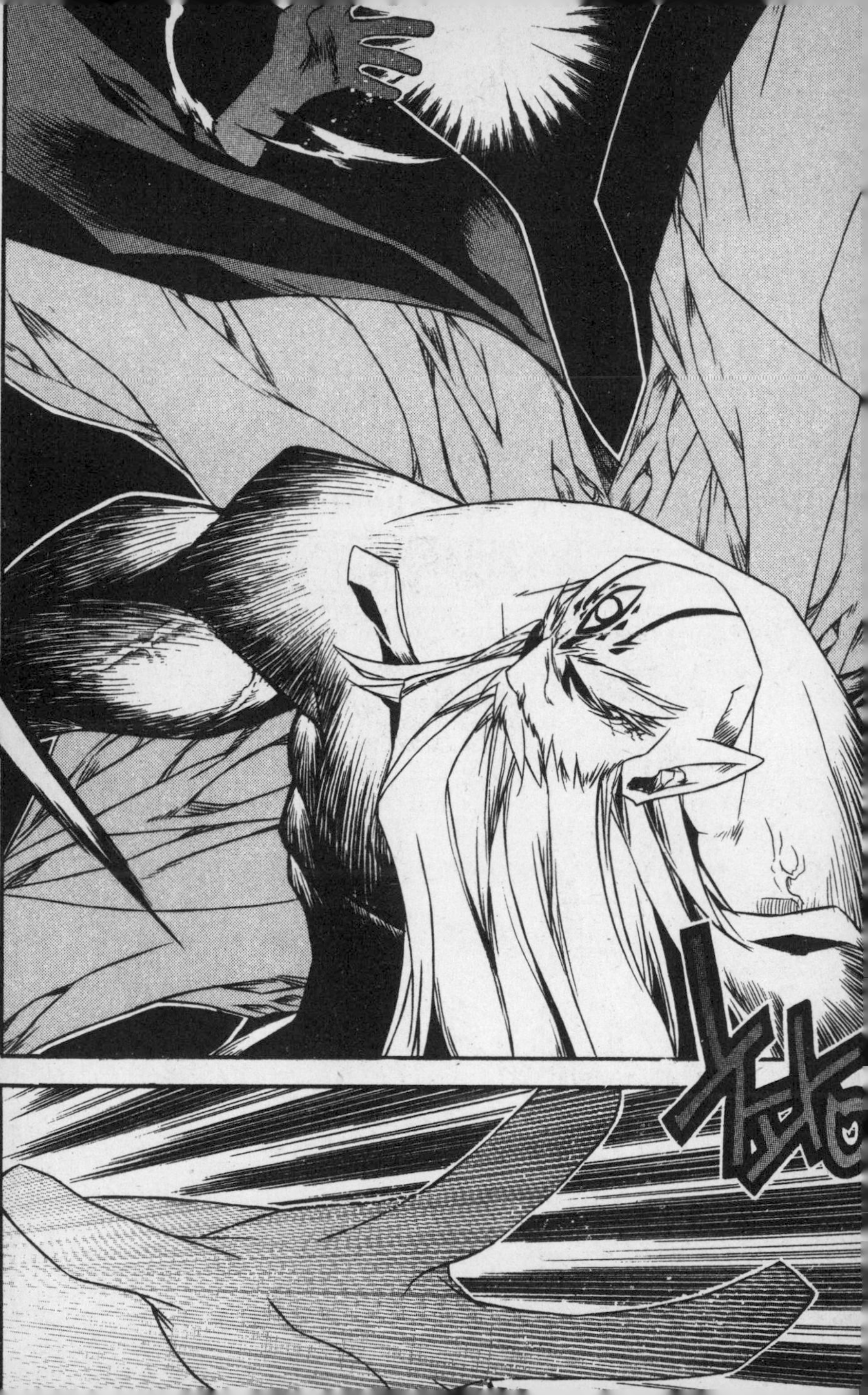

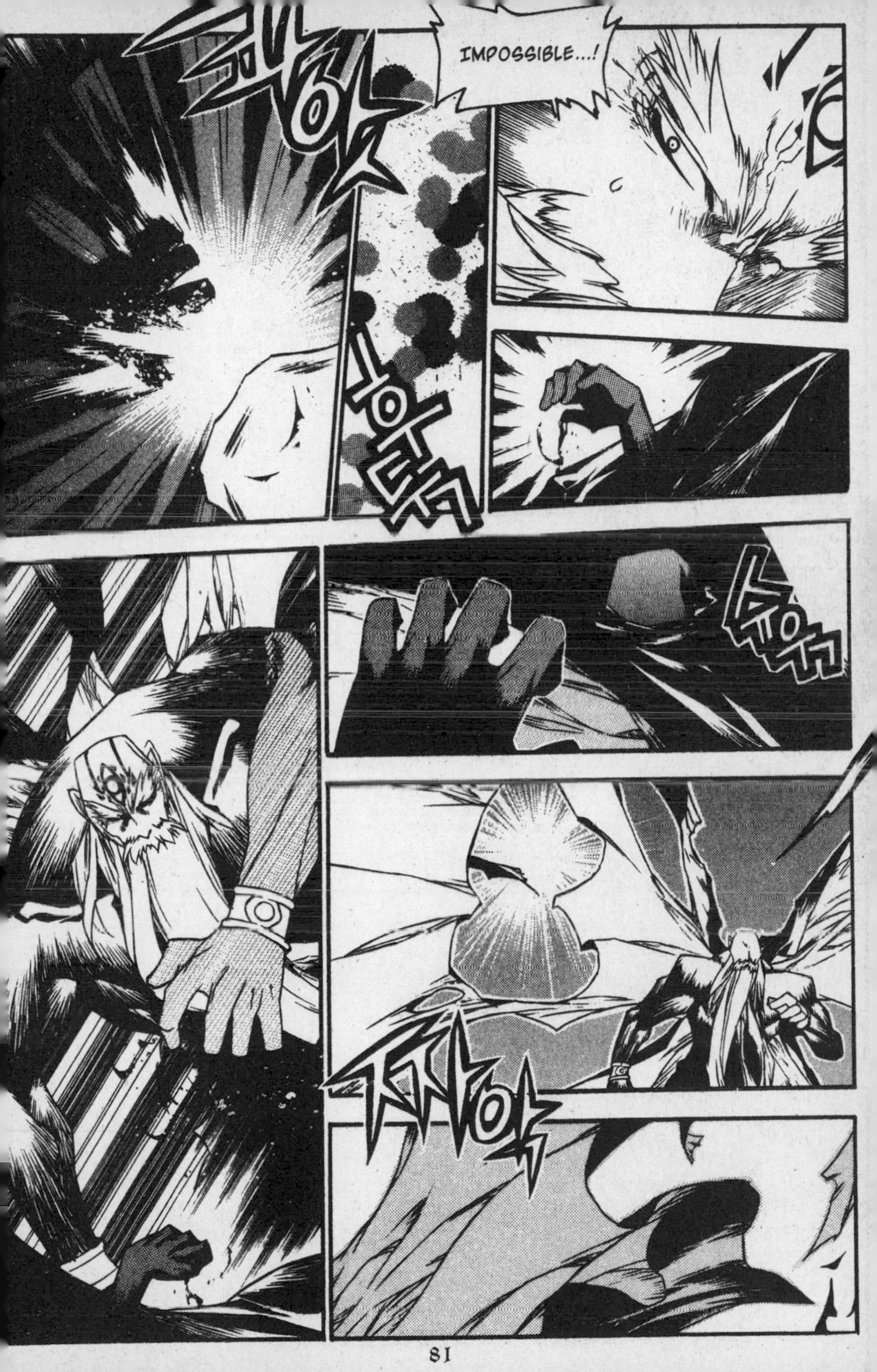
IMPOSSIBLE...!

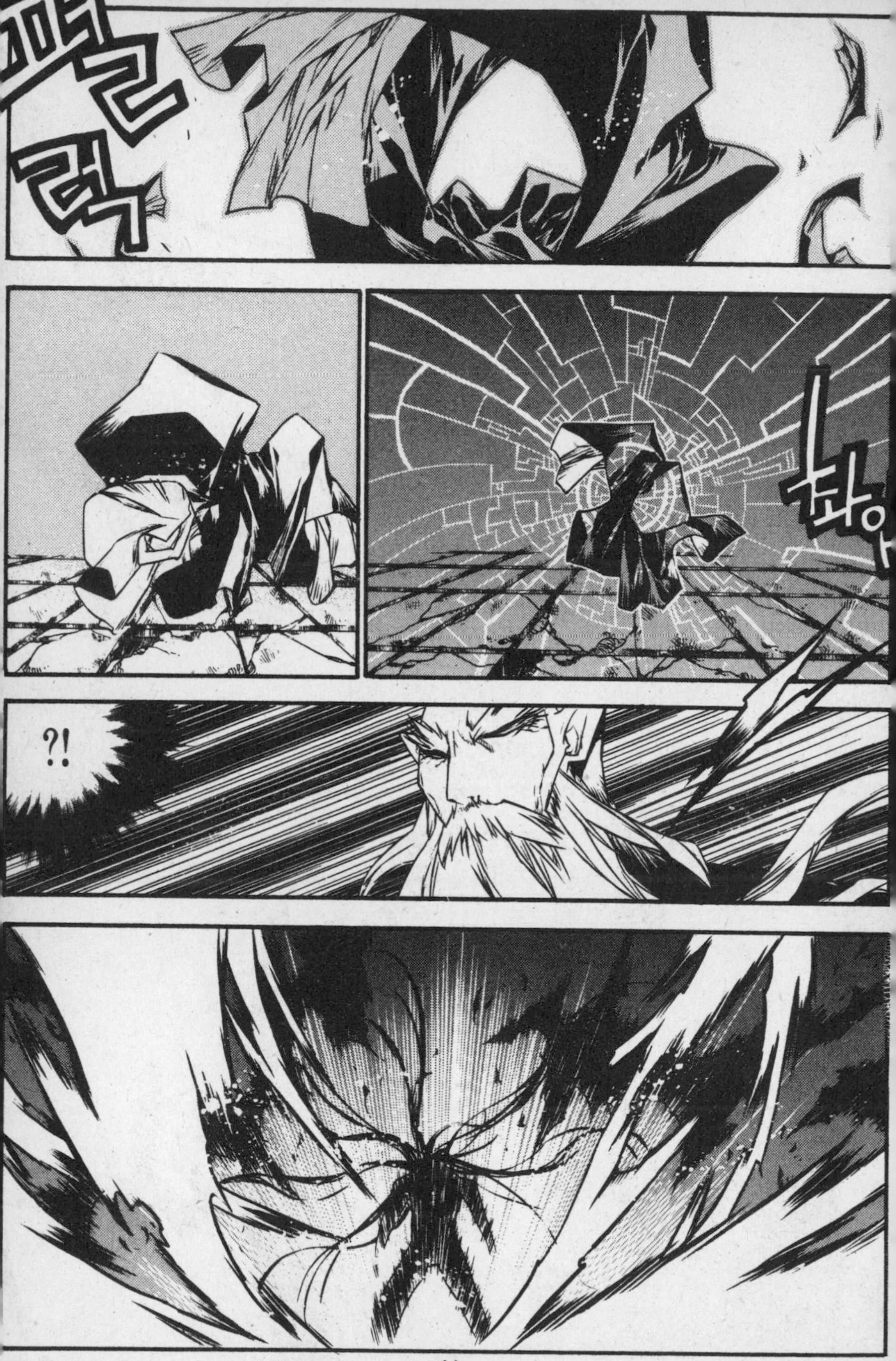
펄럭
?!

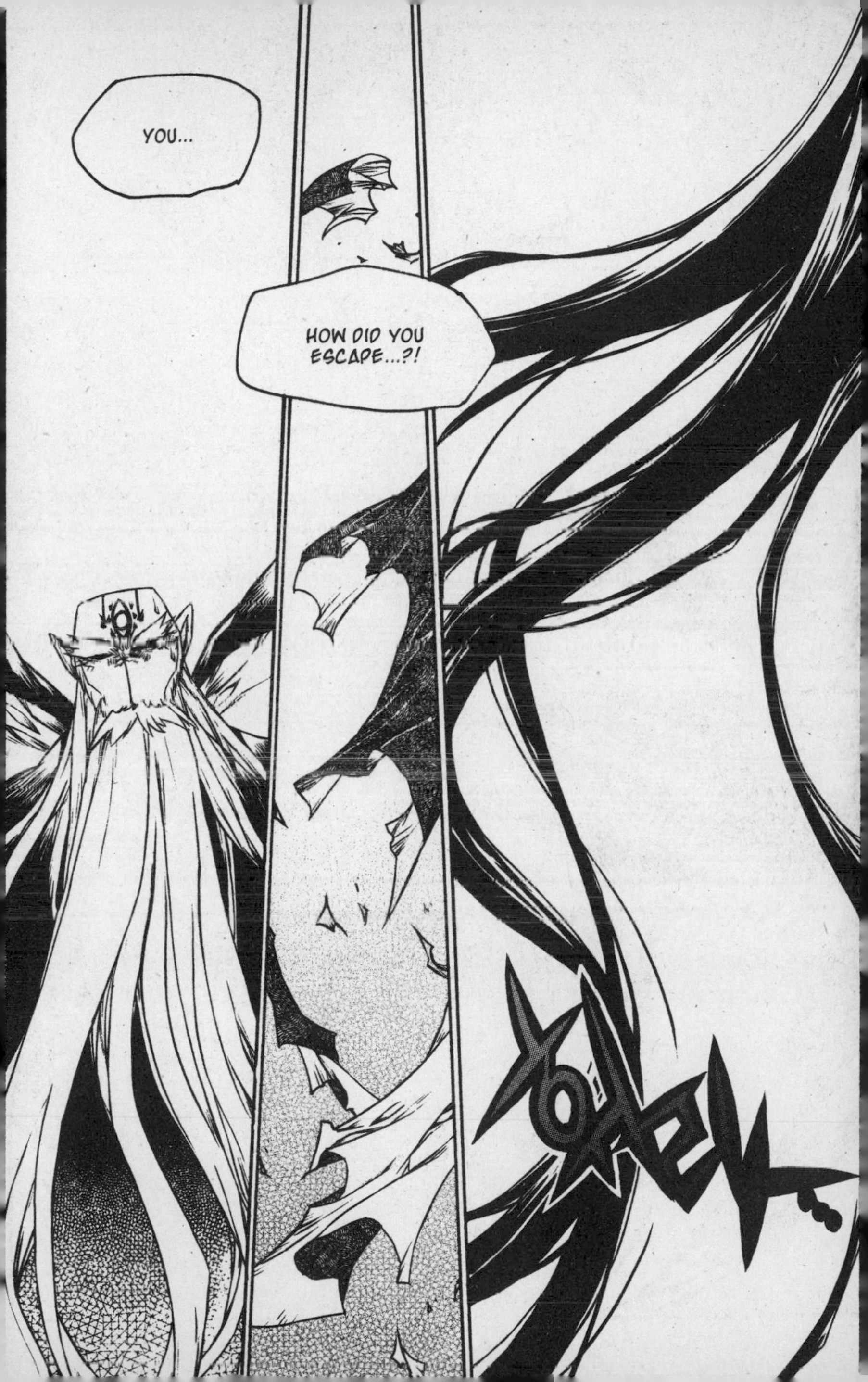
YOU...
HOW DID YOU ESCAPE...?!

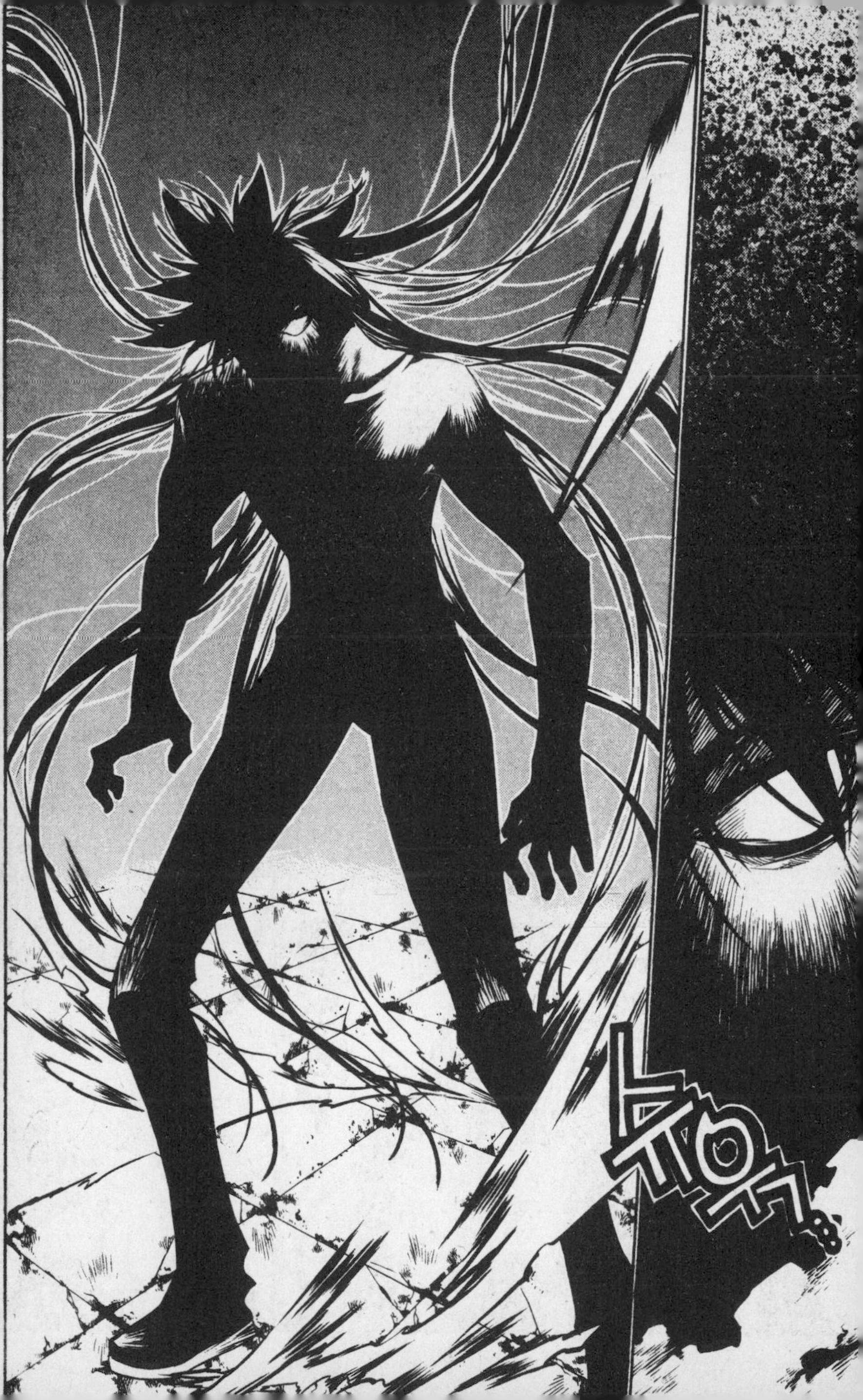

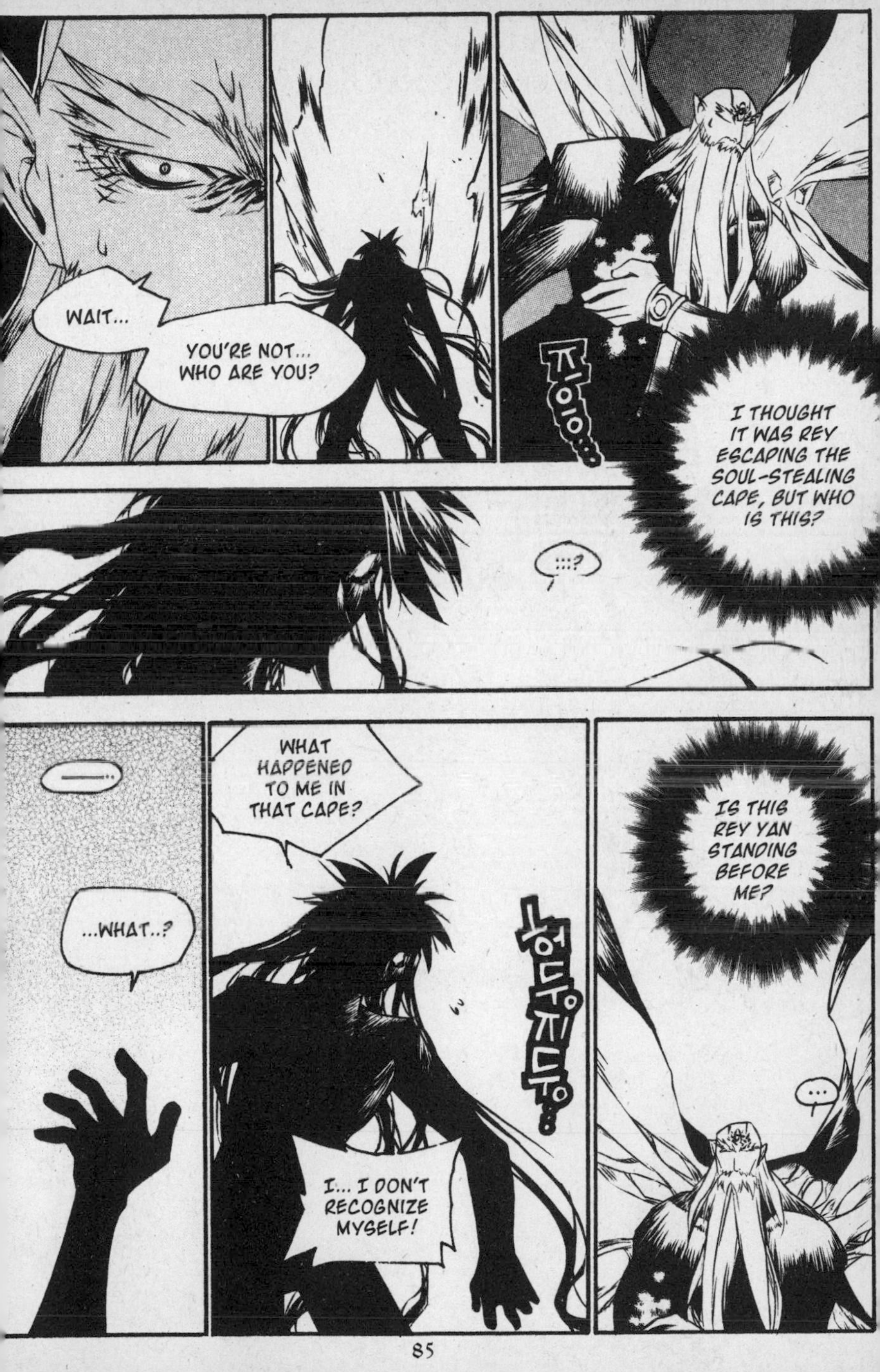
WAIT...
YOU'RE NOT... WHO ARE YOU?
지이이...
I THOUGHT IT WAS REY ESCAPING THE SOUL-STEALING CAPE, BUT WHO IS THIS?
:::?
...WHAT..?
WHAT HAPPENED TO ME IN THAT CAPE?
I... I DON'T RECOGNIZE MYSELF!
IS THIS REY YAN STANDING BEFORE ME?
...

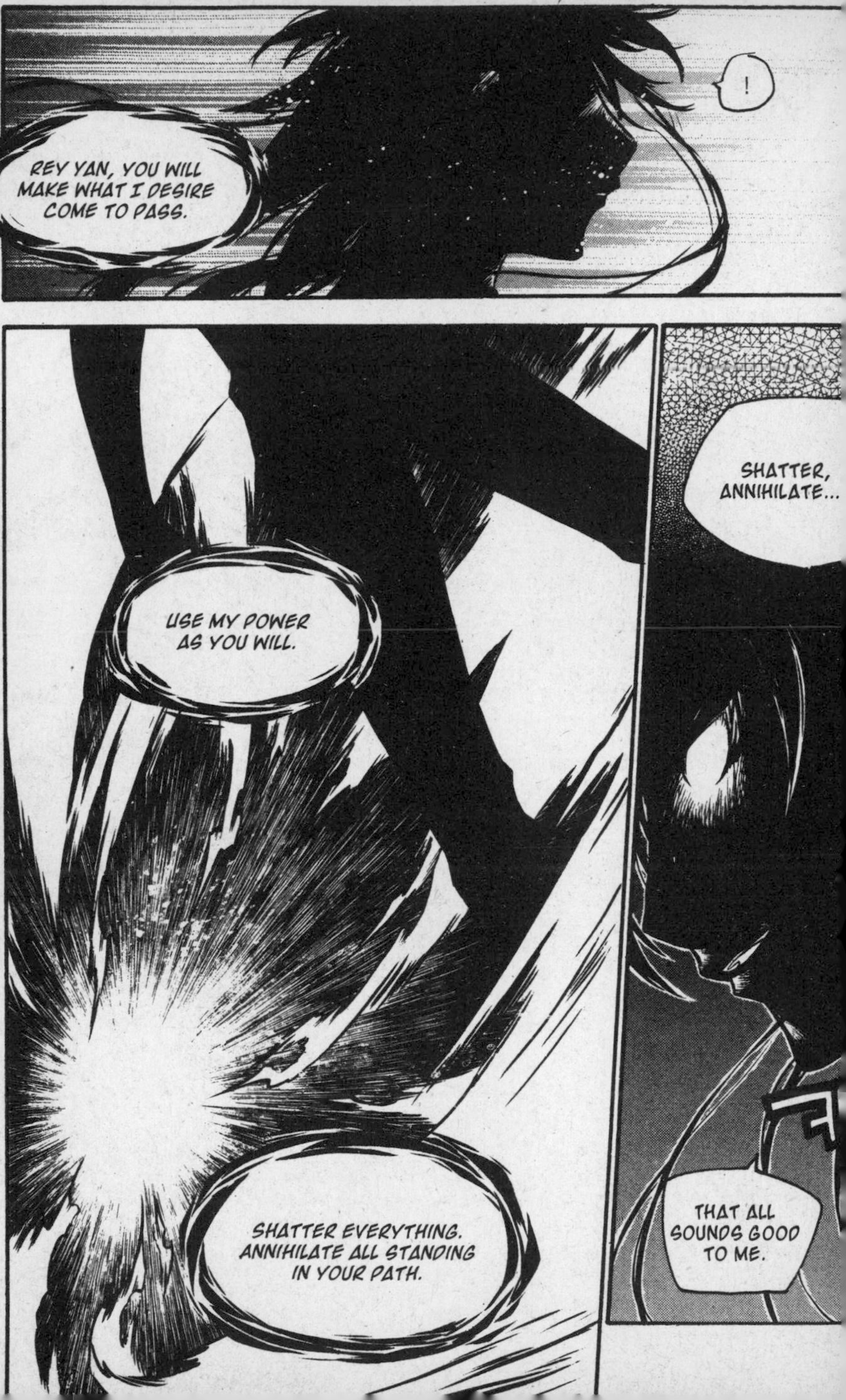
REY YAN, YOU WILL MAKE WHAT I DESIRE COME TO PASS.
!
USE MY POWER AS YOU WILL.
SHATTER EVERYTHING. ANNIHILATE ALL STANDING IN YOUR PATH.
SHATTER, ANNIHILATE...
THAT ALL SOUNDS GOOD TO ME.

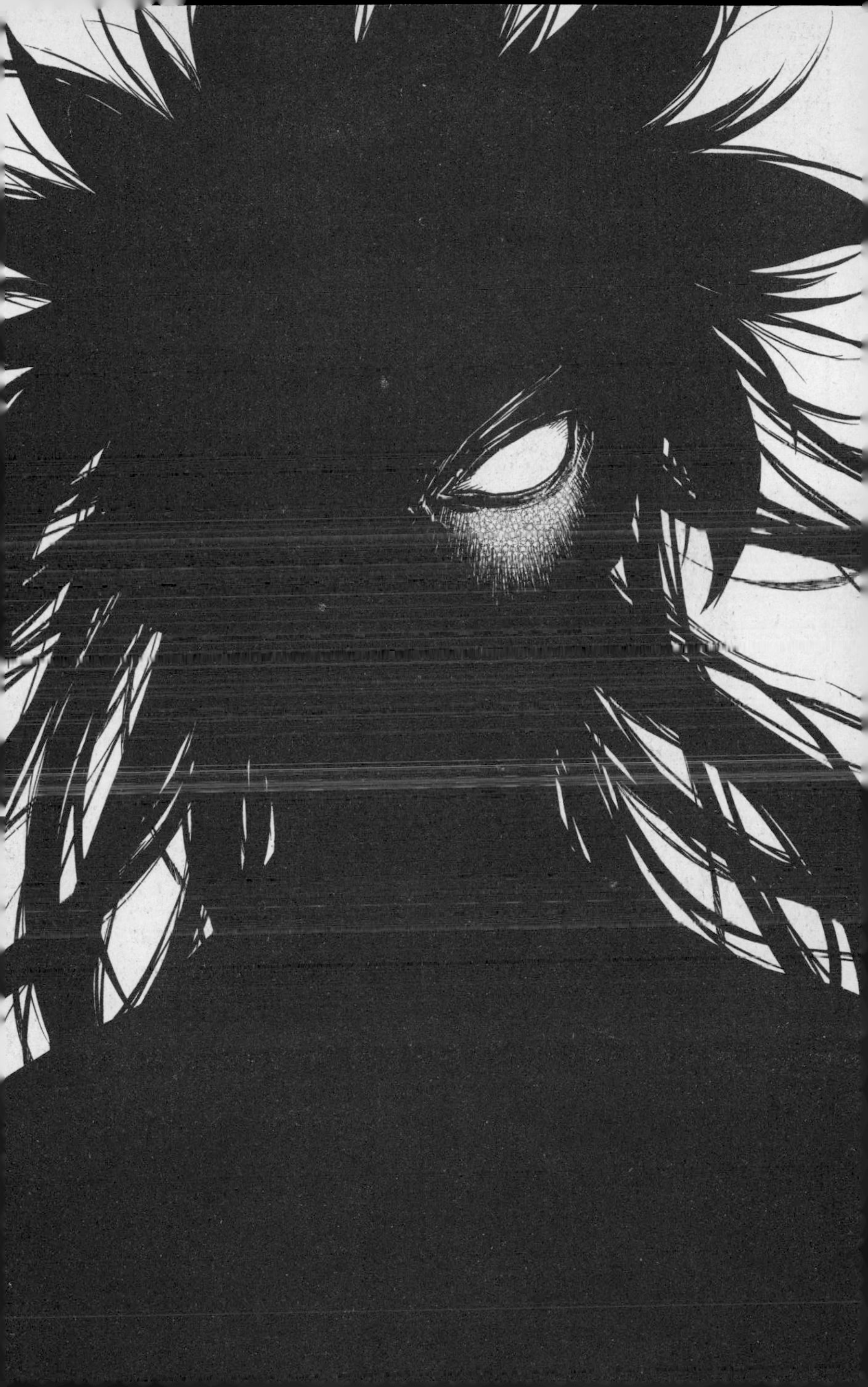

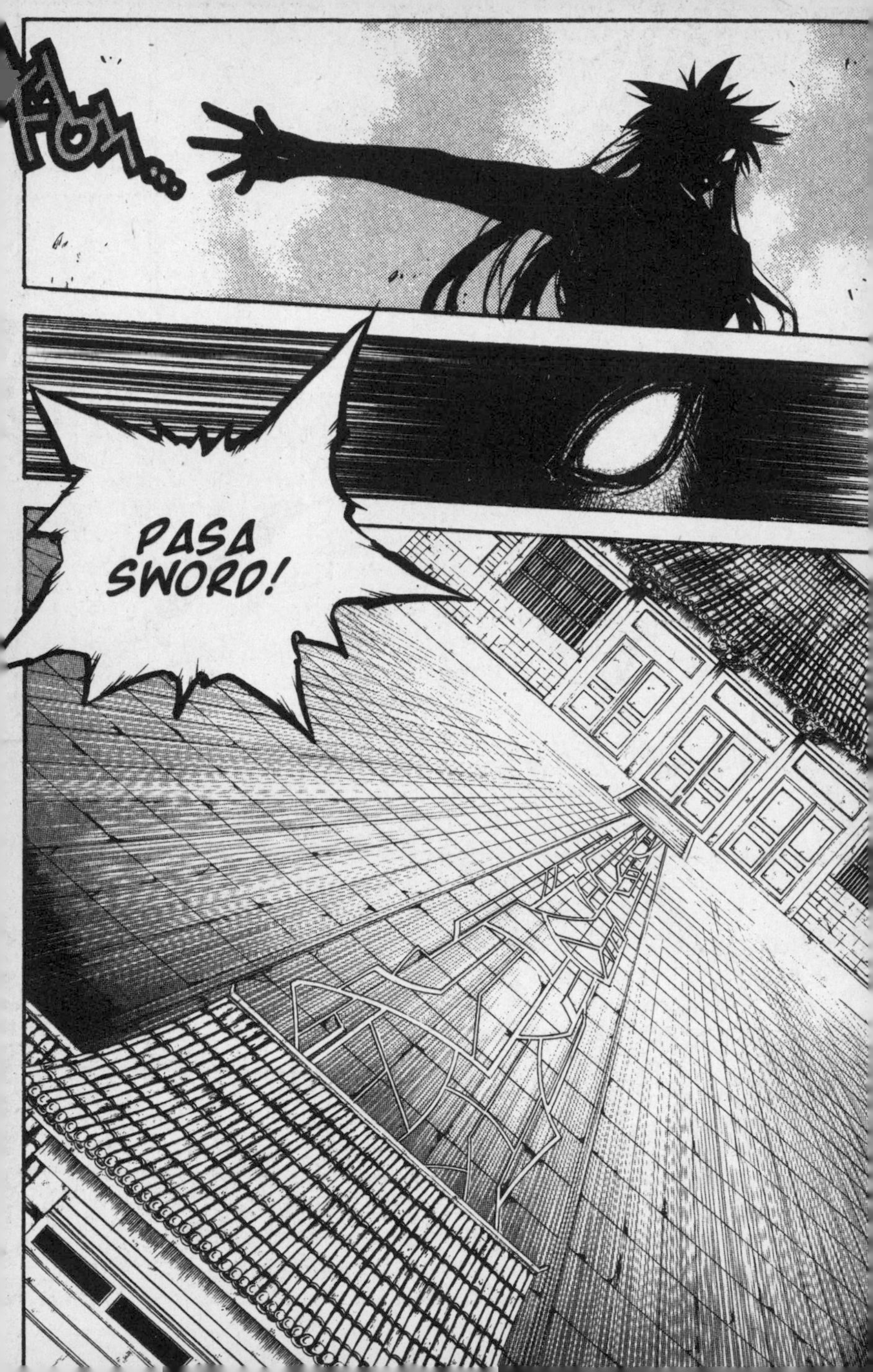
FOM...
PASA SWORD!

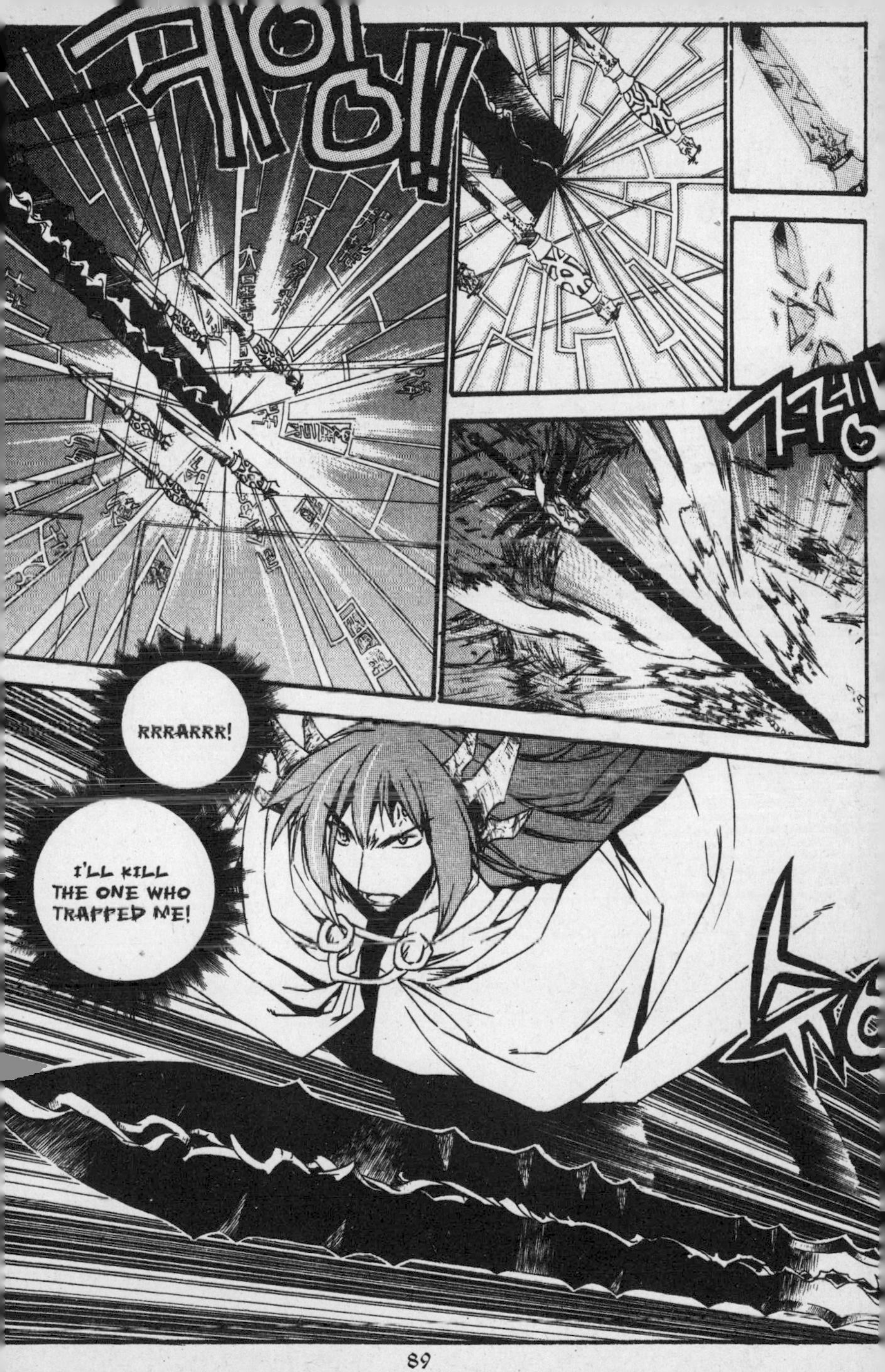
RRRARRR!
I'LL KILL THE ONE WHO TRAPPED ME!

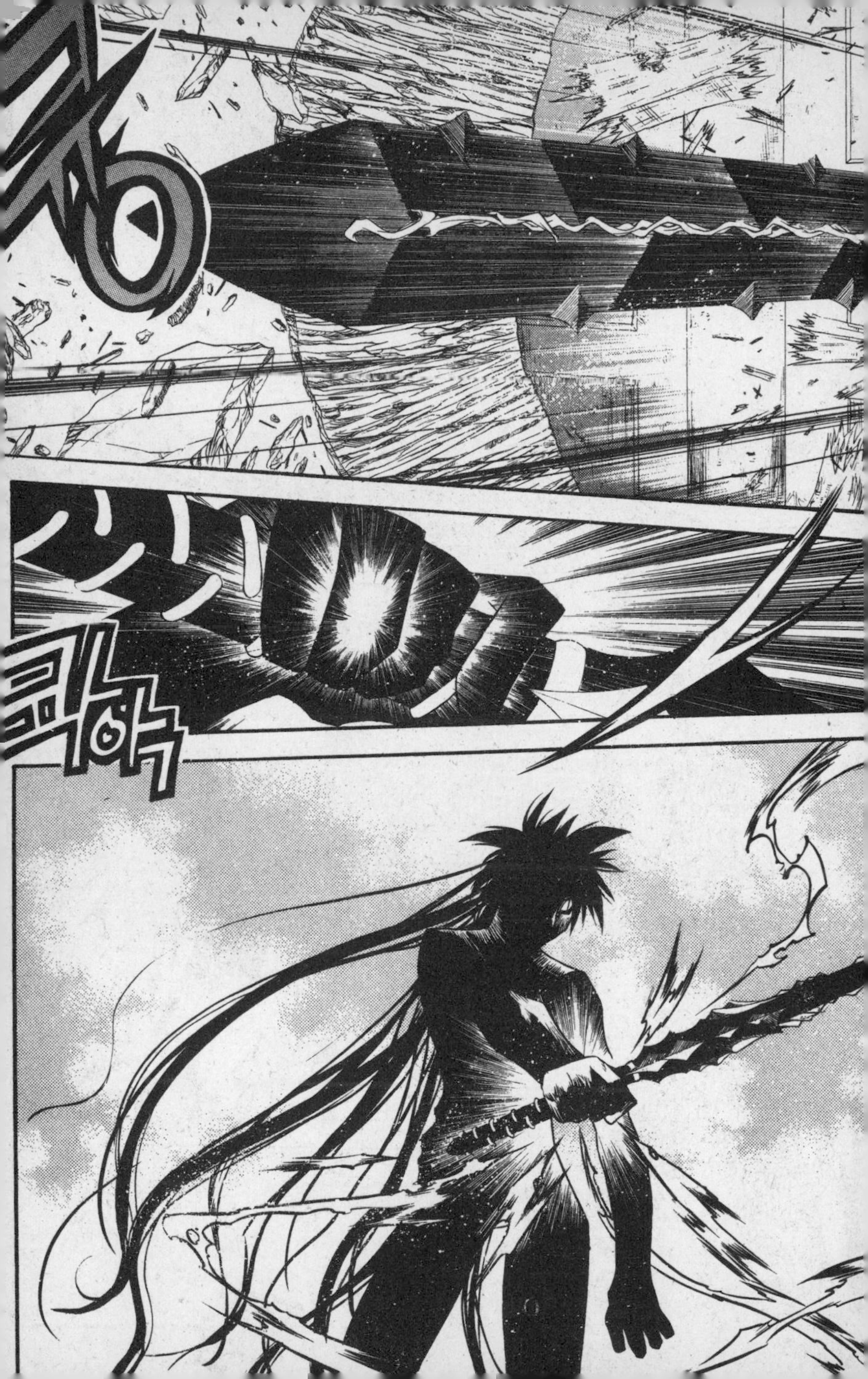

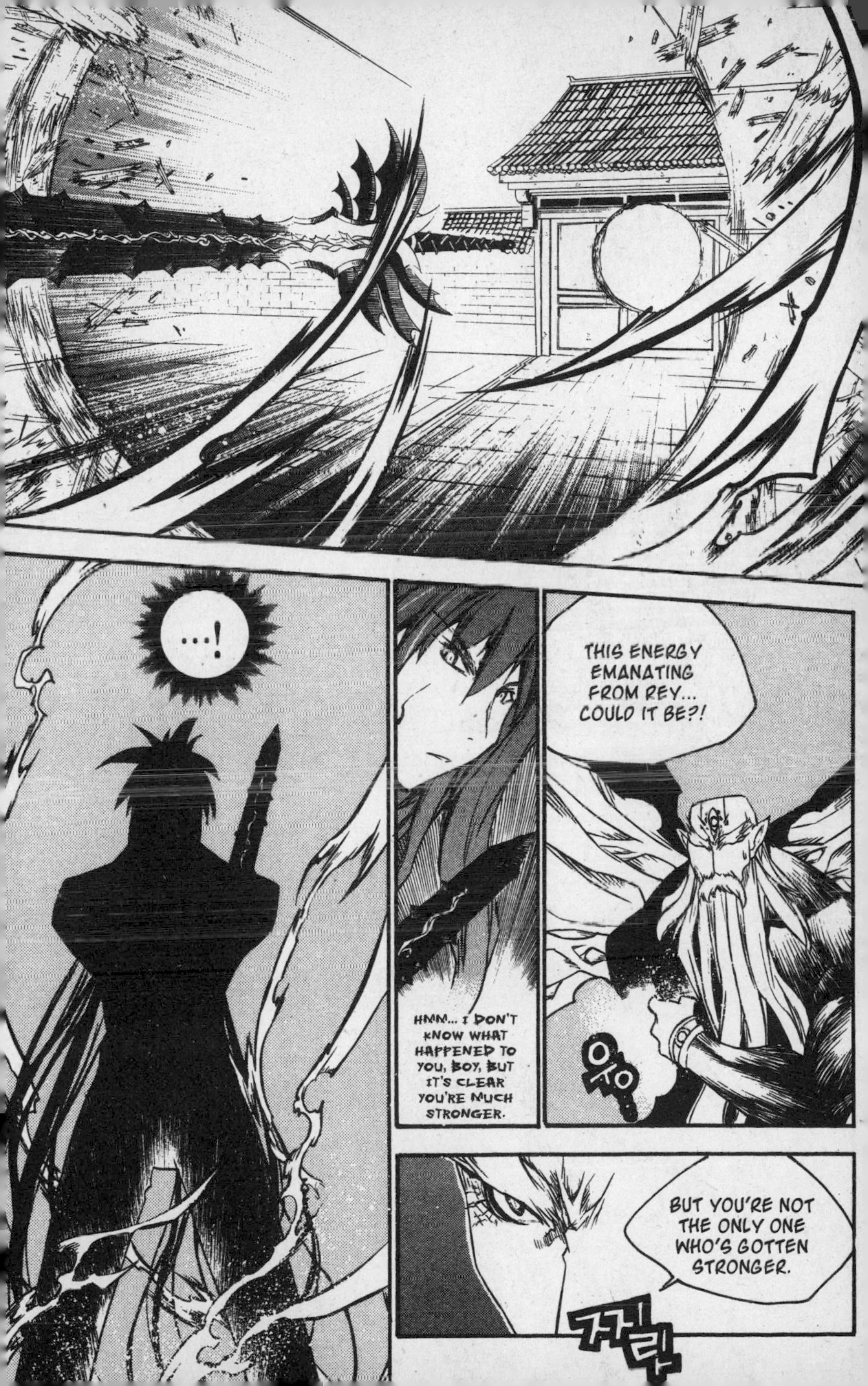
...!
HMM... I DON'T KNOW WHAT HAPPENED TO YOU, BOY, BUT IT'S CLEAR YOU'RE MUCH STRONGER.
THIS ENERGY EMANATING FROM REY... COULD IT BE?!
BUT YOU'RE NOT THE ONLY ONE WHO'S GOTTEN STRONGER.

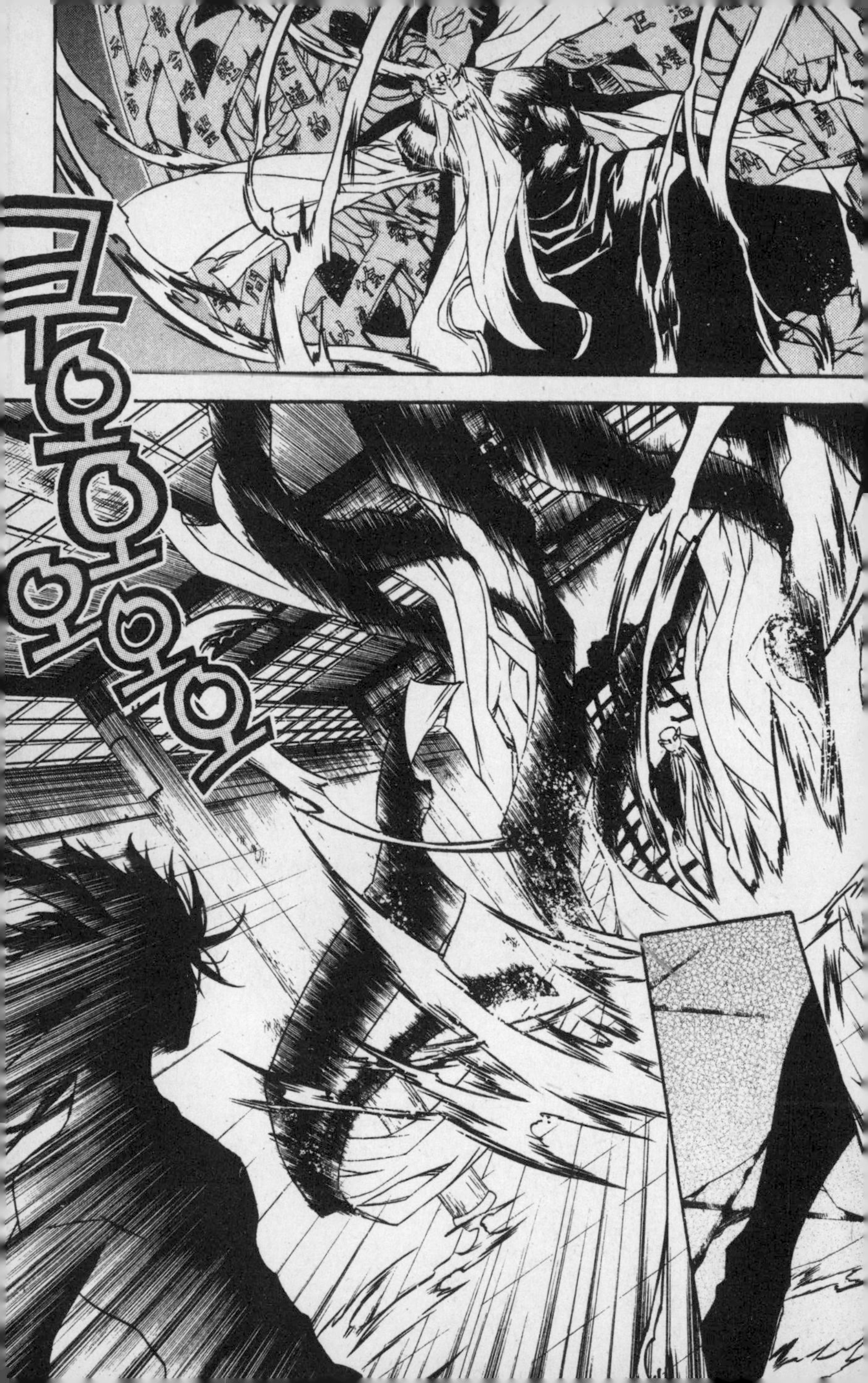
크오오오오오

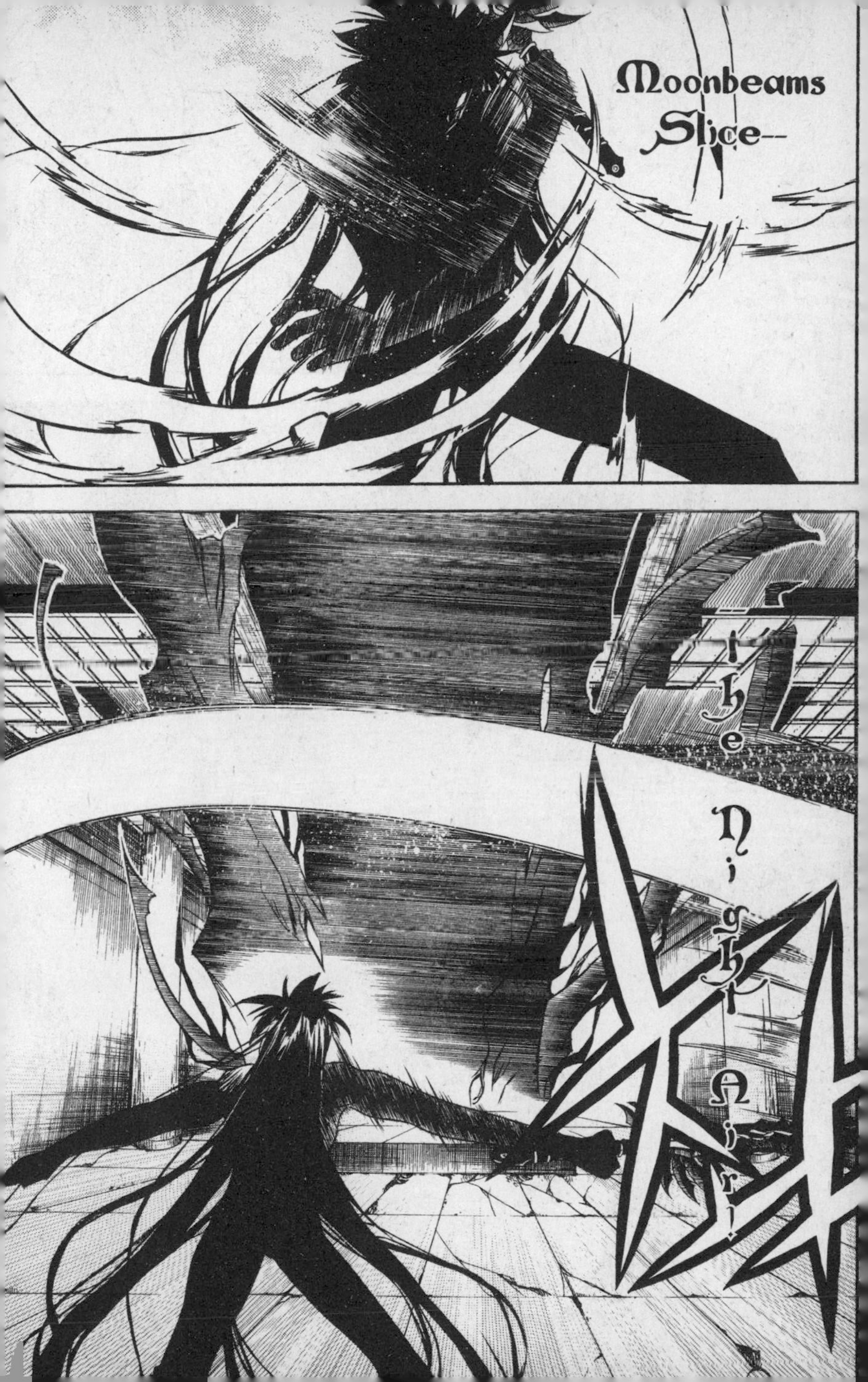
Moonbeams Slice--
The Night Mir!

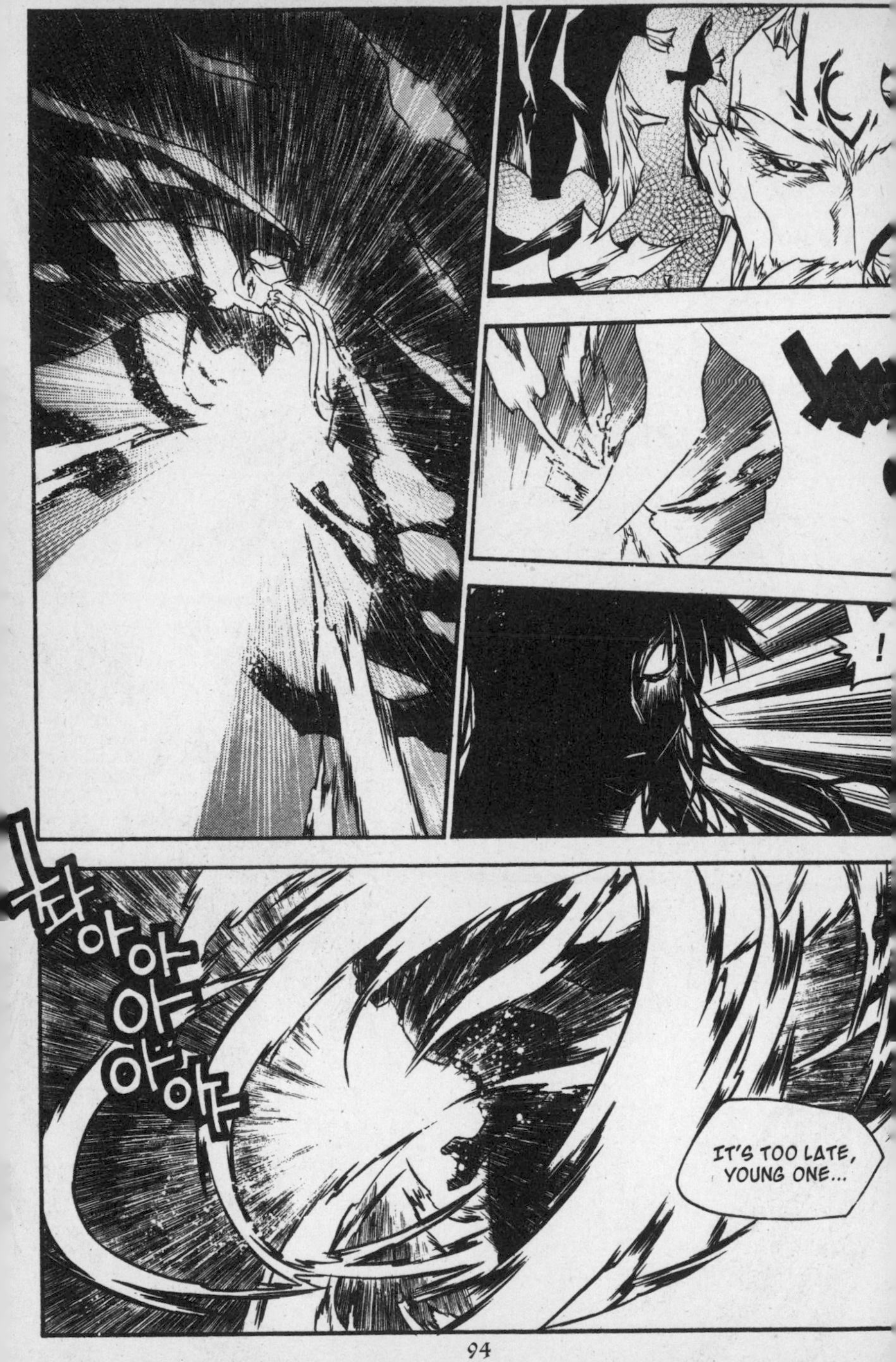
!
촤아아아아아
IT'S TOO LATE, YOUNG ONE...

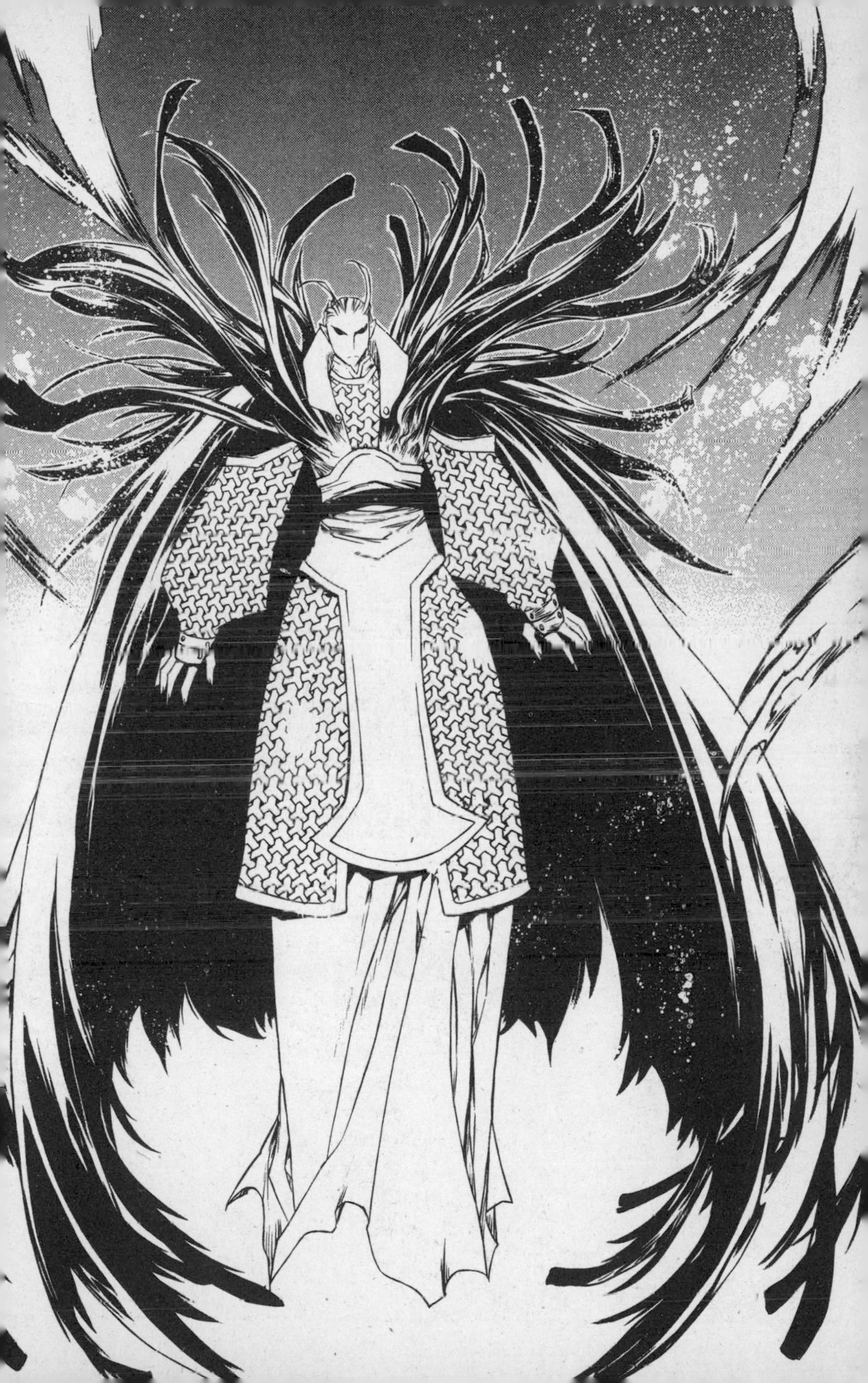

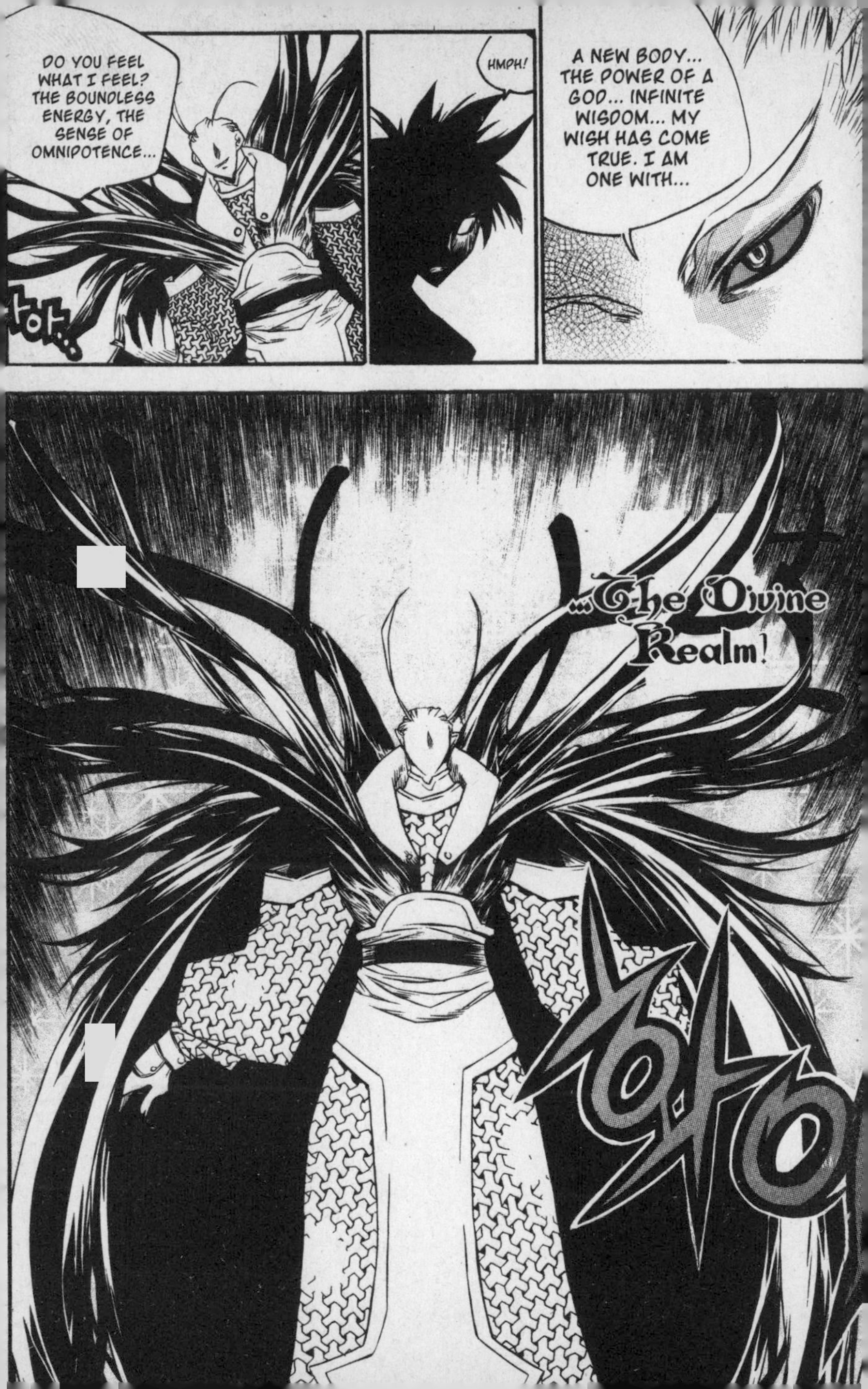
DO YOU FEEL WHAT I FEEL? THE BOUNDLESS ENERGY, THE SENSE OF OMNIPOTENCE...
HMPH!
A NEW BODY... THE POWER OF A GOD... INFINITE WISDOM... MY WISH HAS COME TRUE. I AM ONE WITH...
...The Divine Realm!

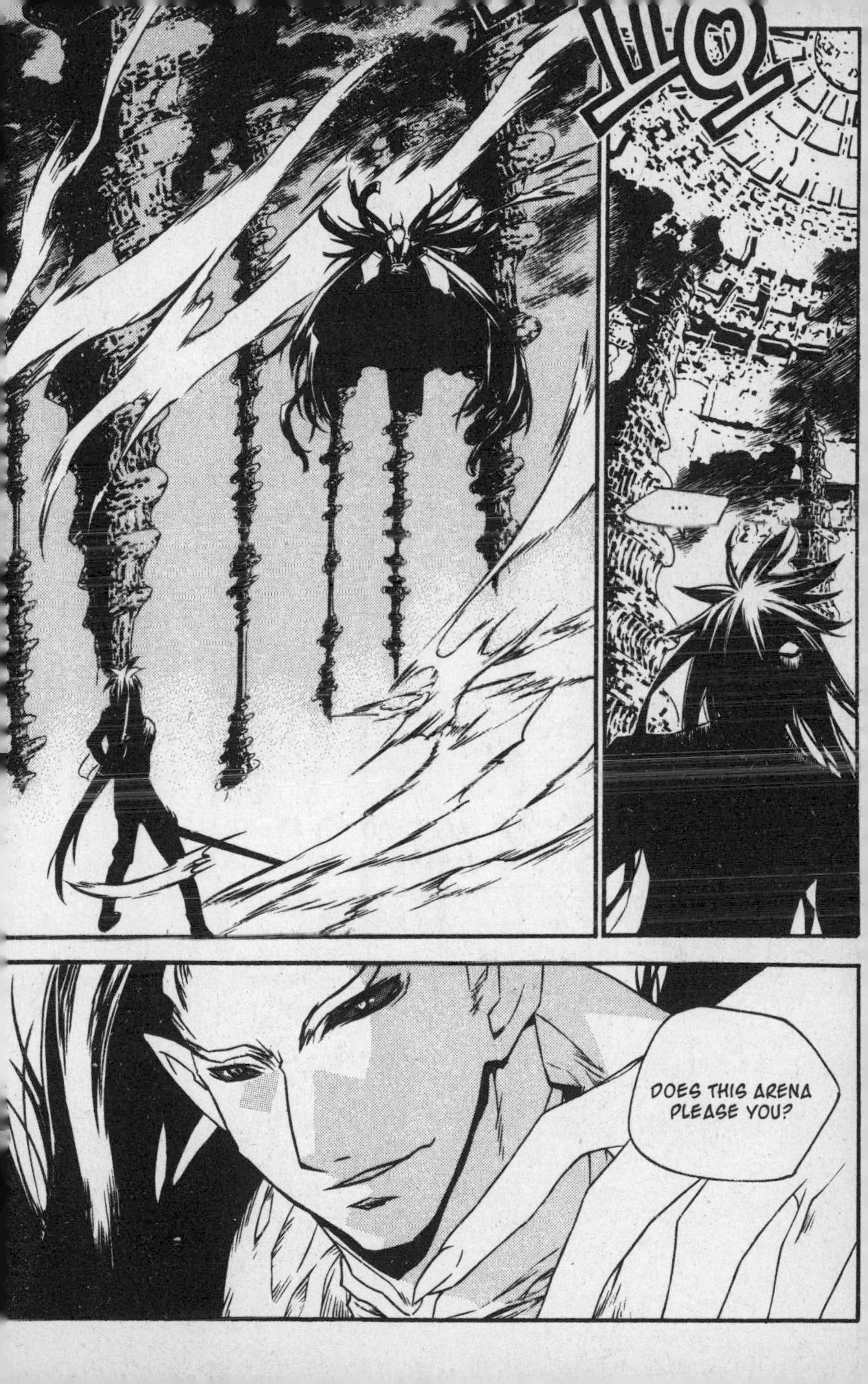
...
DOES THIS ARENA PLEASE YOU?

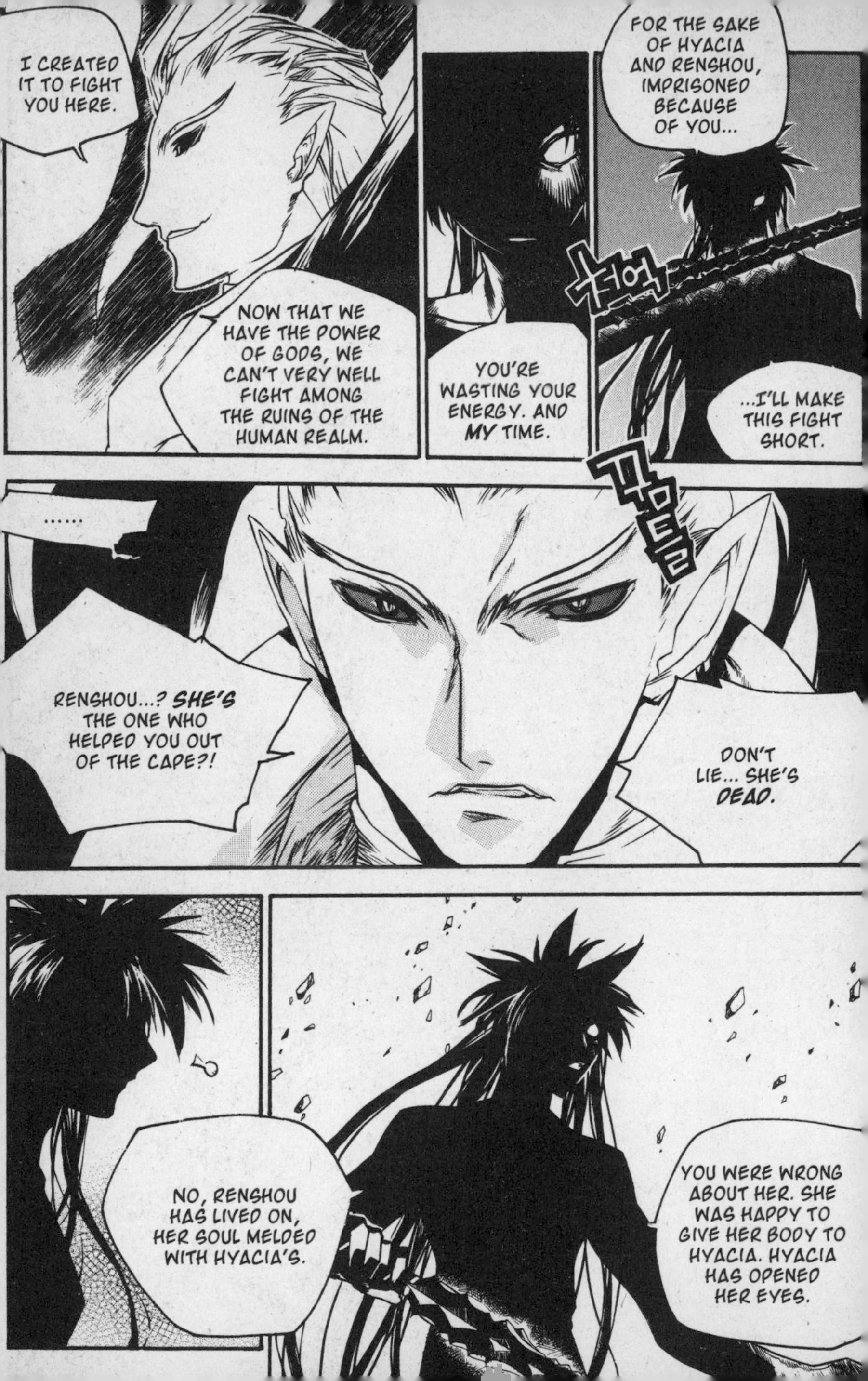
I CREATED IT TO FIGHT YOU HERE.
NOW THAT WE HAVE THE POWER OF GODS, WE CAN'T VERY WELL FIGHT AMONG THE RUINS OF THE HUMAN REALM.
YOU'RE WASTING YOUR ENERGY. AND *MY* TIME.
FOR THE SAKE OF HYACIA AND RENSHOU, IMPRISONED BECAUSE OF YOU...
...I'LL MAKE THIS FIGHT SHORT.
......
RENSHOU...? *SHE'S* THE ONE WHO HELPED YOU OUT OF THE CAPE?!
DON'T LIE... SHE'S *DEAD*.
NO, RENSHOU HAS LIVED ON, HER SOUL MELDED WITH HYACIA'S.
YOU WERE WRONG ABOUT HER. SHE WAS HAPPY TO GIVE HER BODY TO HYACIA. HYACIA HAS OPENED HER EYES.

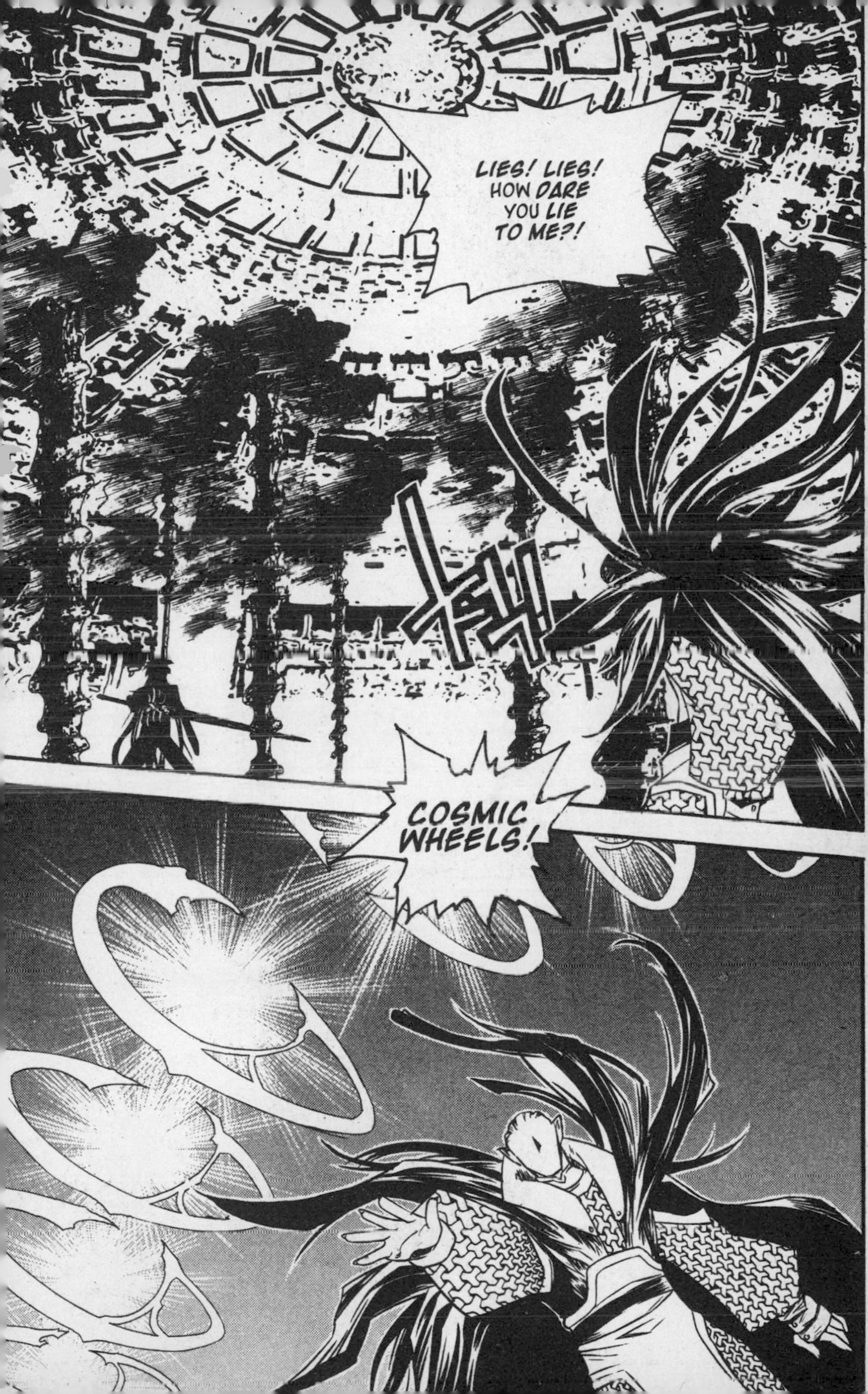
LIES! LIES! HOW DARE YOU LIE TO ME?!
COSMIC WHEELS!

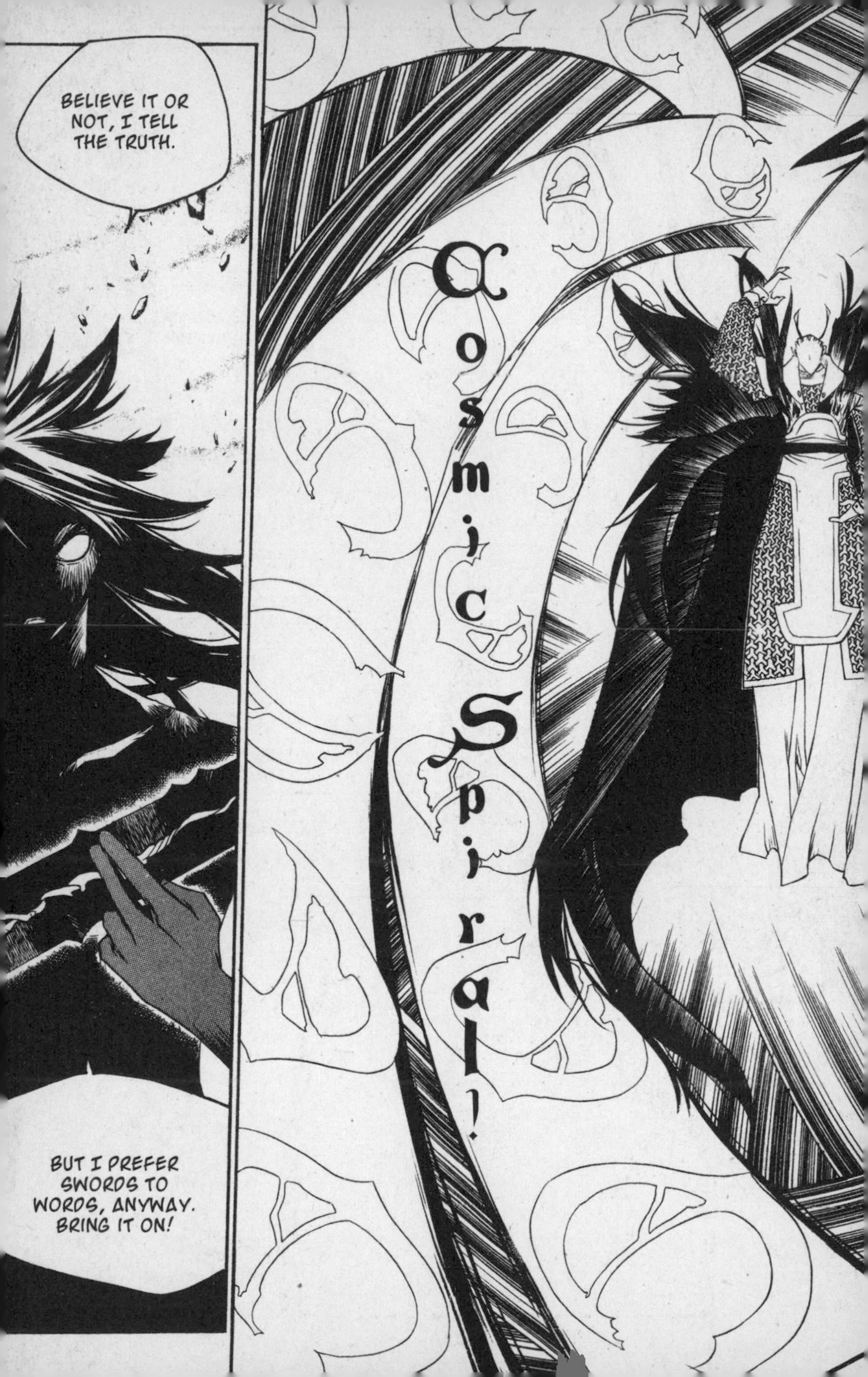
BELIEVE IT OR NOT, I TELL THE TRUTH.
BUT I PREFER SWORDS TO WORDS, ANYWAY. BRING IT ON!
Cosmic Spiral!

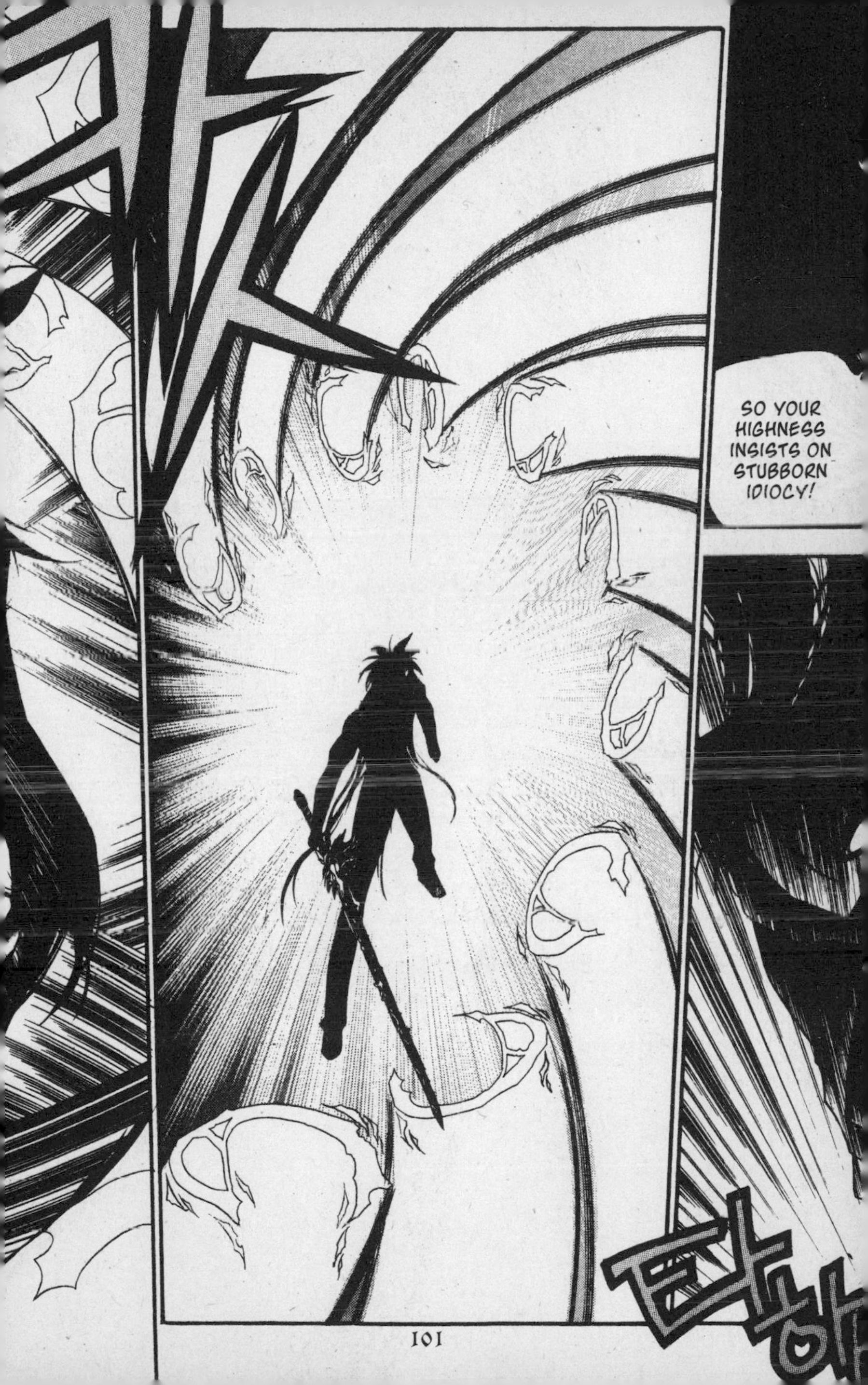
SO YOUR HIGHNESS INSISTS ON STUBBORN IDIOCY!

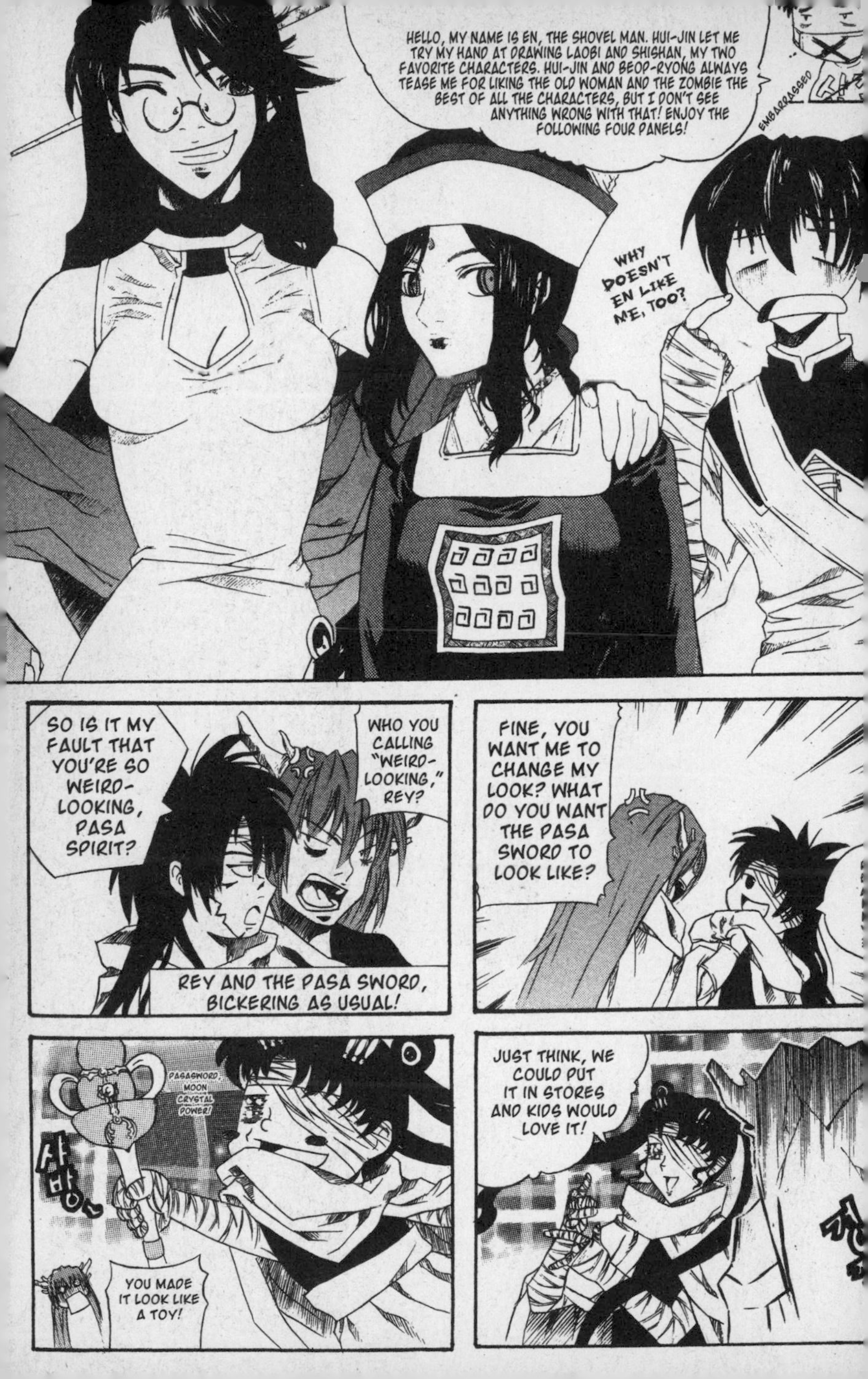
HELLO, MY NAME IS EN, THE SHOVEL MAN. HUI-JIN LET ME TRY MY HAND AT DRAWING LAOBI AND SHISHAN, MY TWO FAVORITE CHARACTERS. HUI-JIN AND BEOP-RYONG ALWAYS TEASE ME FOR LIKING THE OLD WOMAN AND THE ZOMBIE THE BEST OF ALL THE CHARACTERS, BUT I DON'T SEE ANYTHING WRONG WITH THAT! ENJOY THE FOLLOWING FOUR PANELS!
EMBARRASSED
WHY DOESN'T EN LIKE ME, TOO?
SO IS IT MY FAULT THAT YOU'RE SO WEIRD-LOOKING, PASA SPIRIT?
WHO YOU CALLING "WEIRD-LOOKING," REY?
REY AND THE PASA SWORD, BICKERING AS USUAL!
FINE, YOU WANT ME TO CHANGE MY LOOK? WHAT DO YOU WANT THE PASA SWORD TO LOOK LIKE?
PASASWORD, MOON CRYSTAL POWER!
YOU MADE IT LOOK LIKE A TOY!
JUST THINK, WE COULD PUT IT IN STORES AND KIDS WOULD LOVE IT!

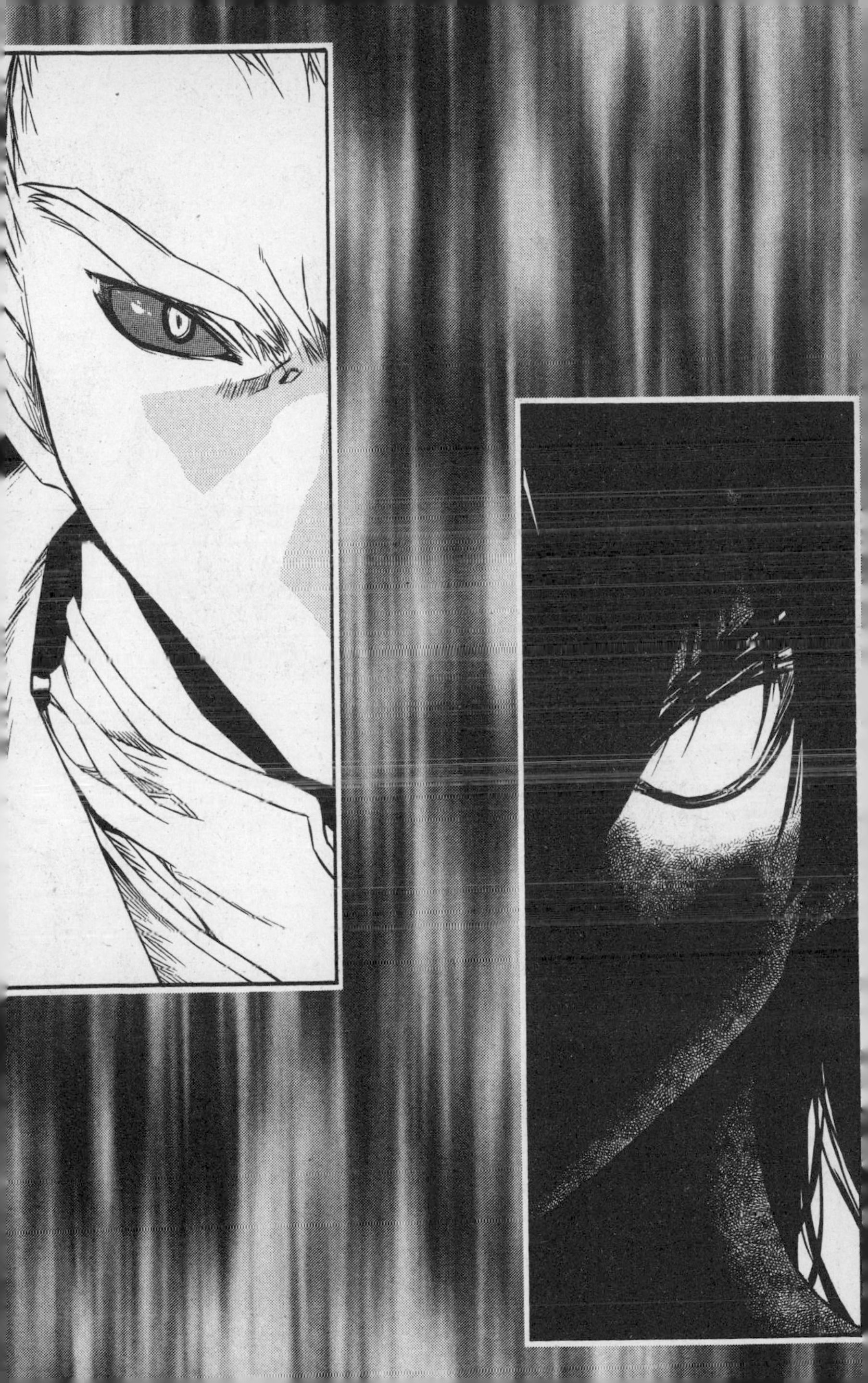

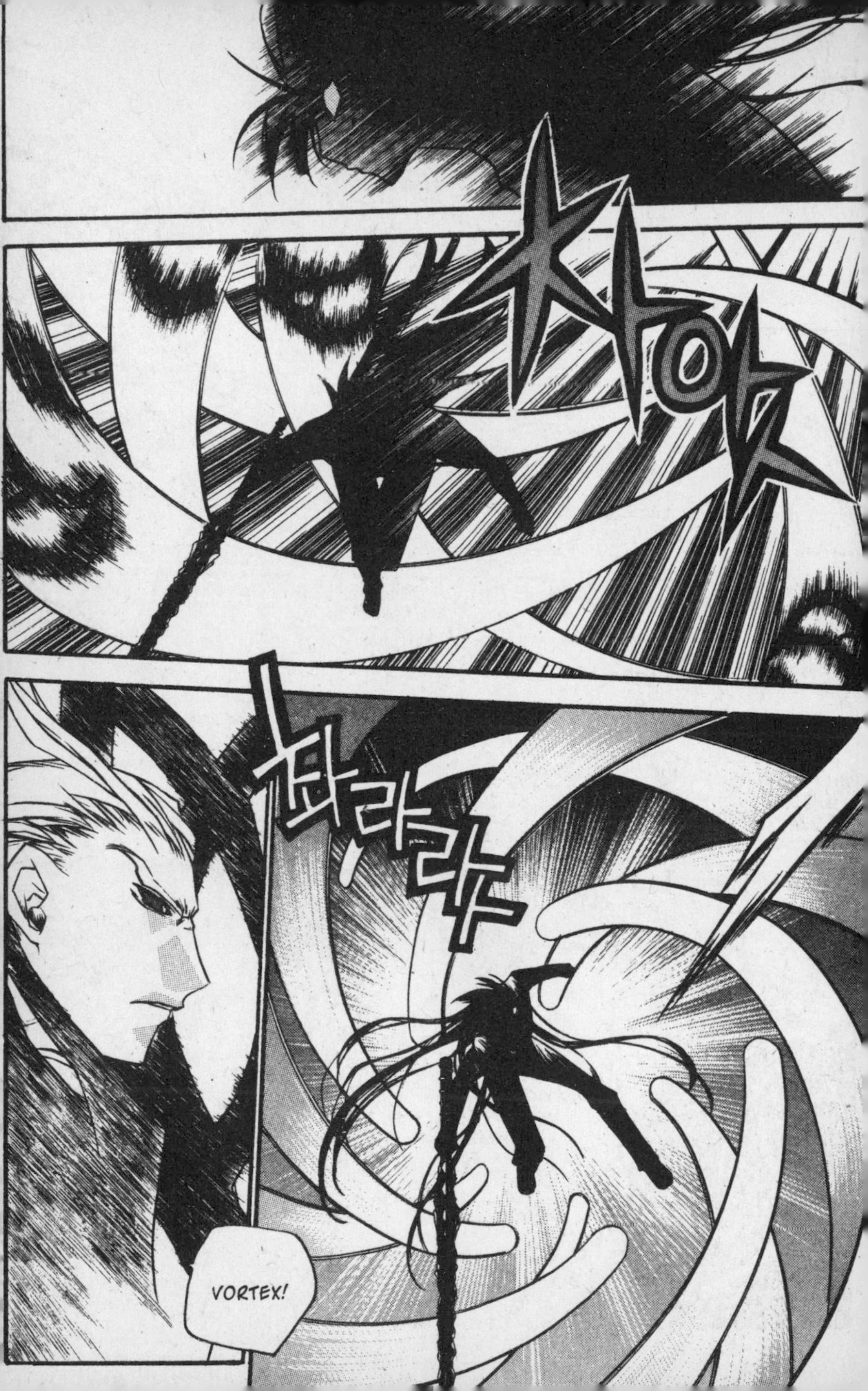
VORTEX!

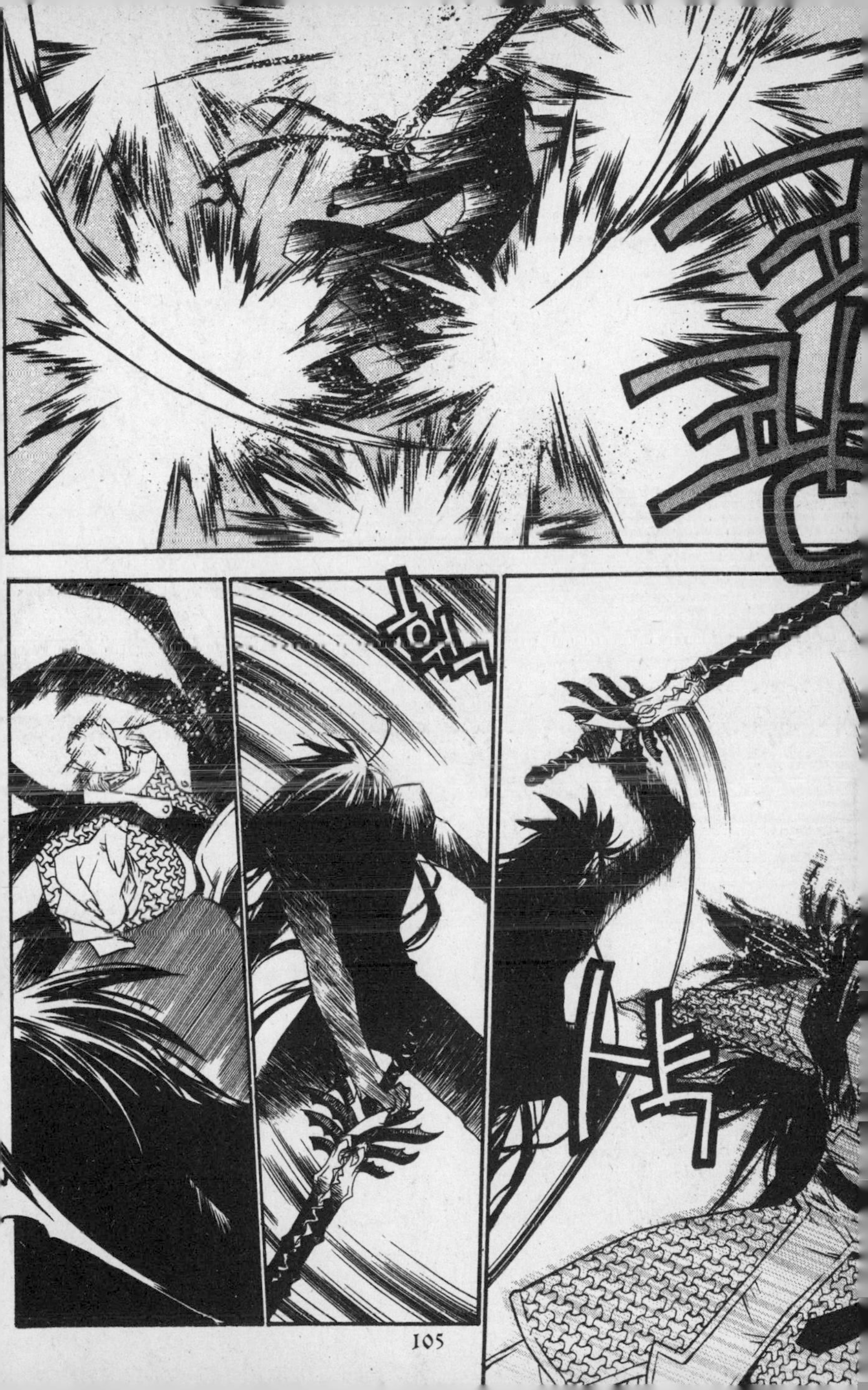

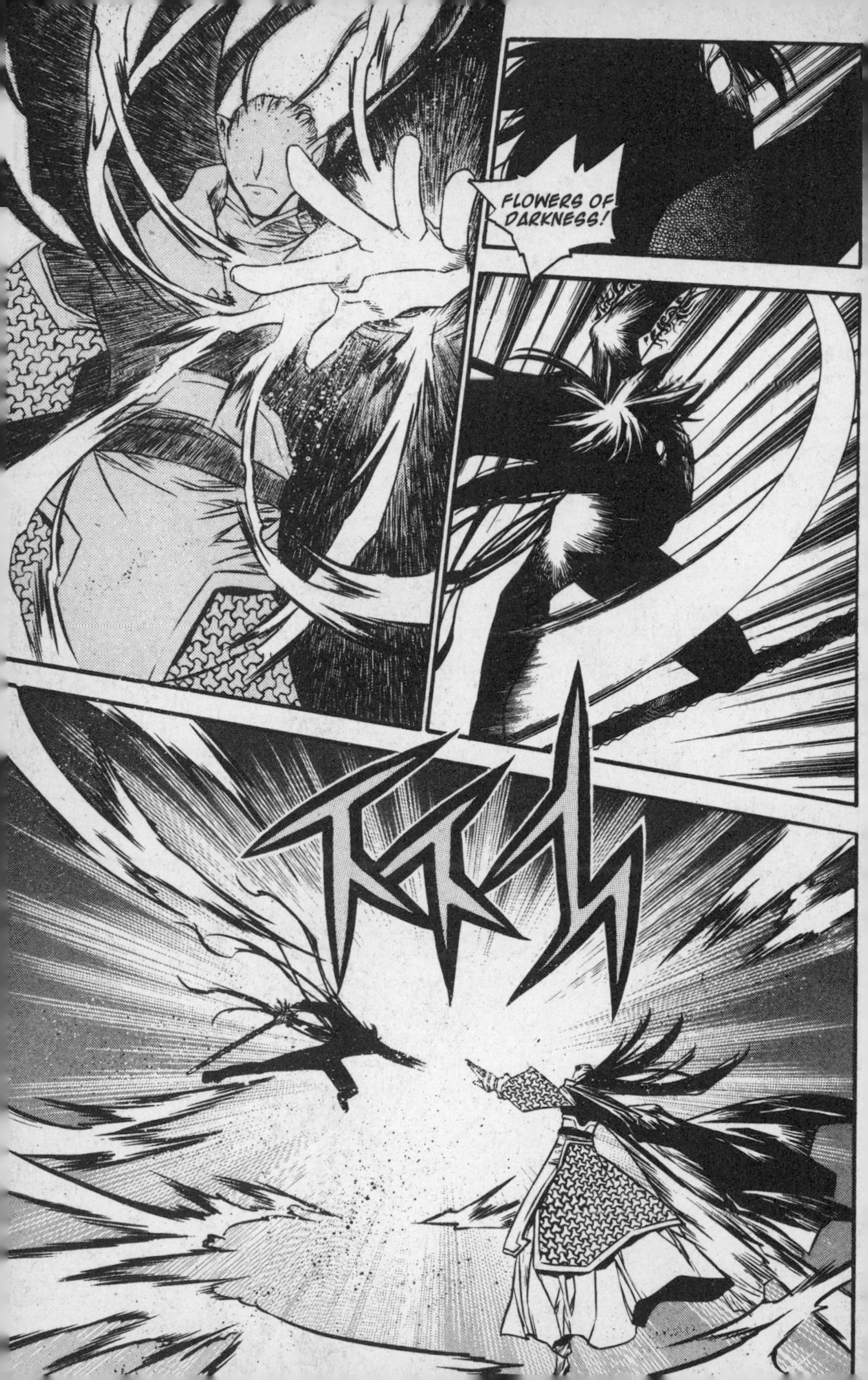
FLOWERS OF DARKNESS!

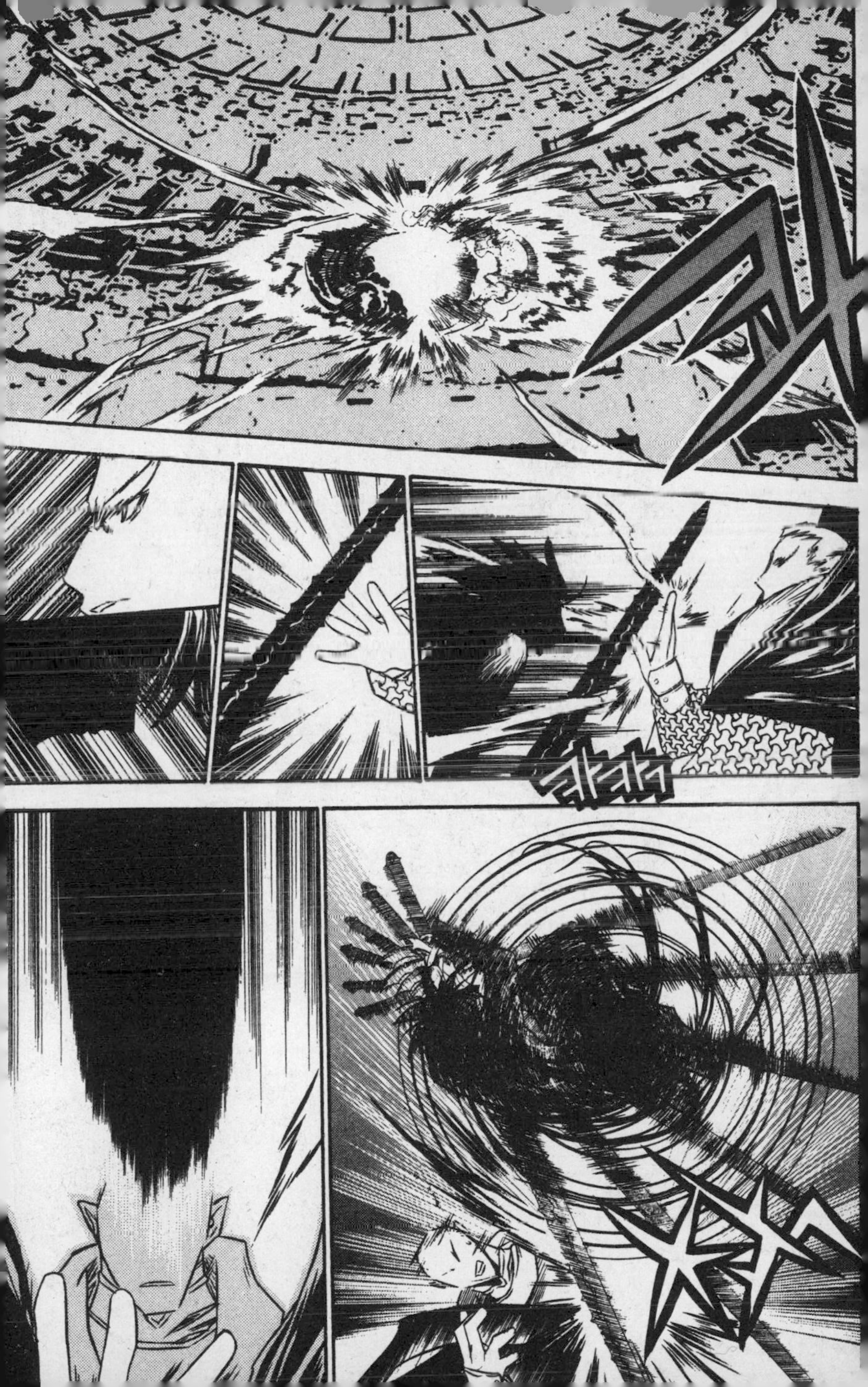

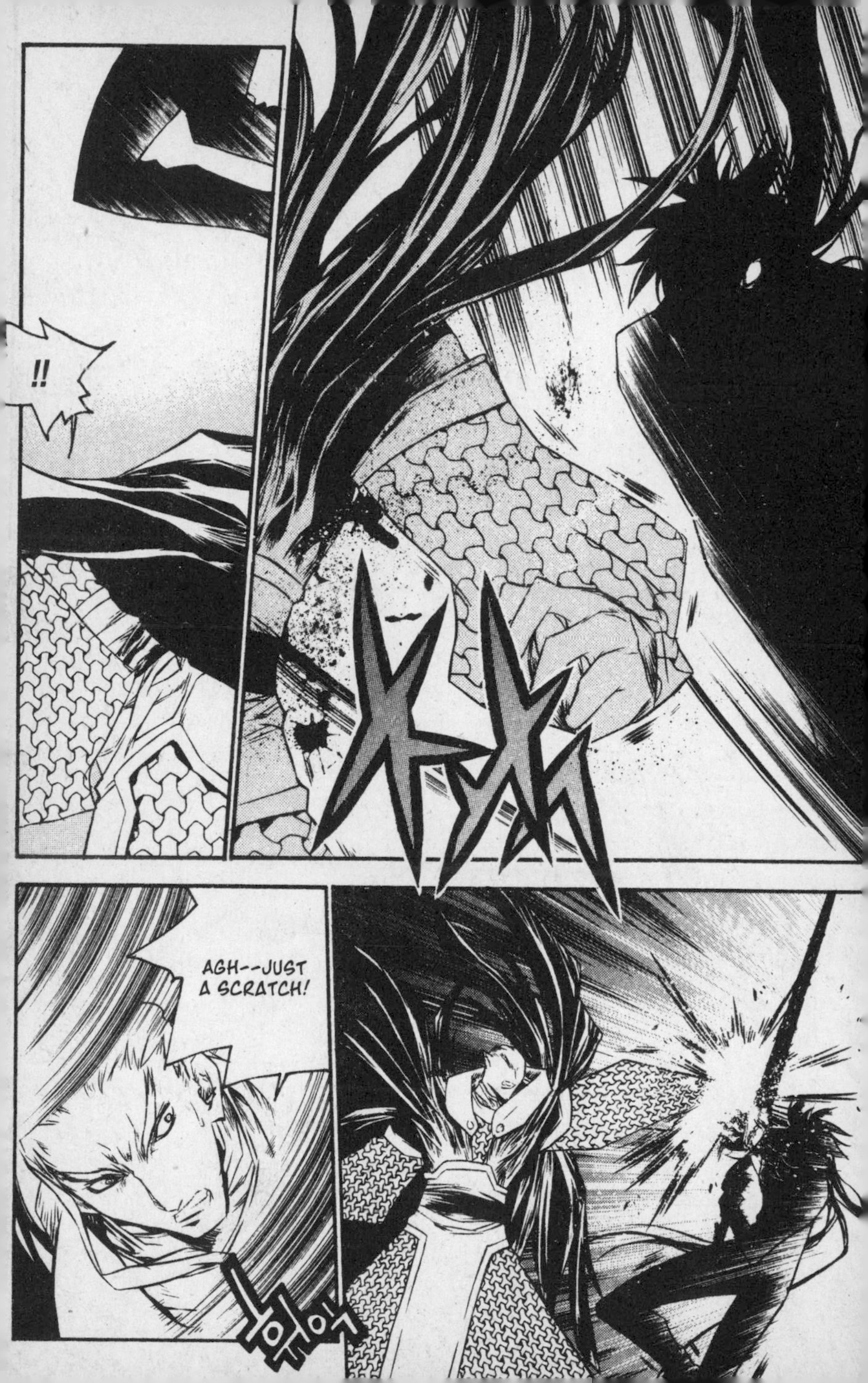
!!
AGH--JUST A SCRATCH!

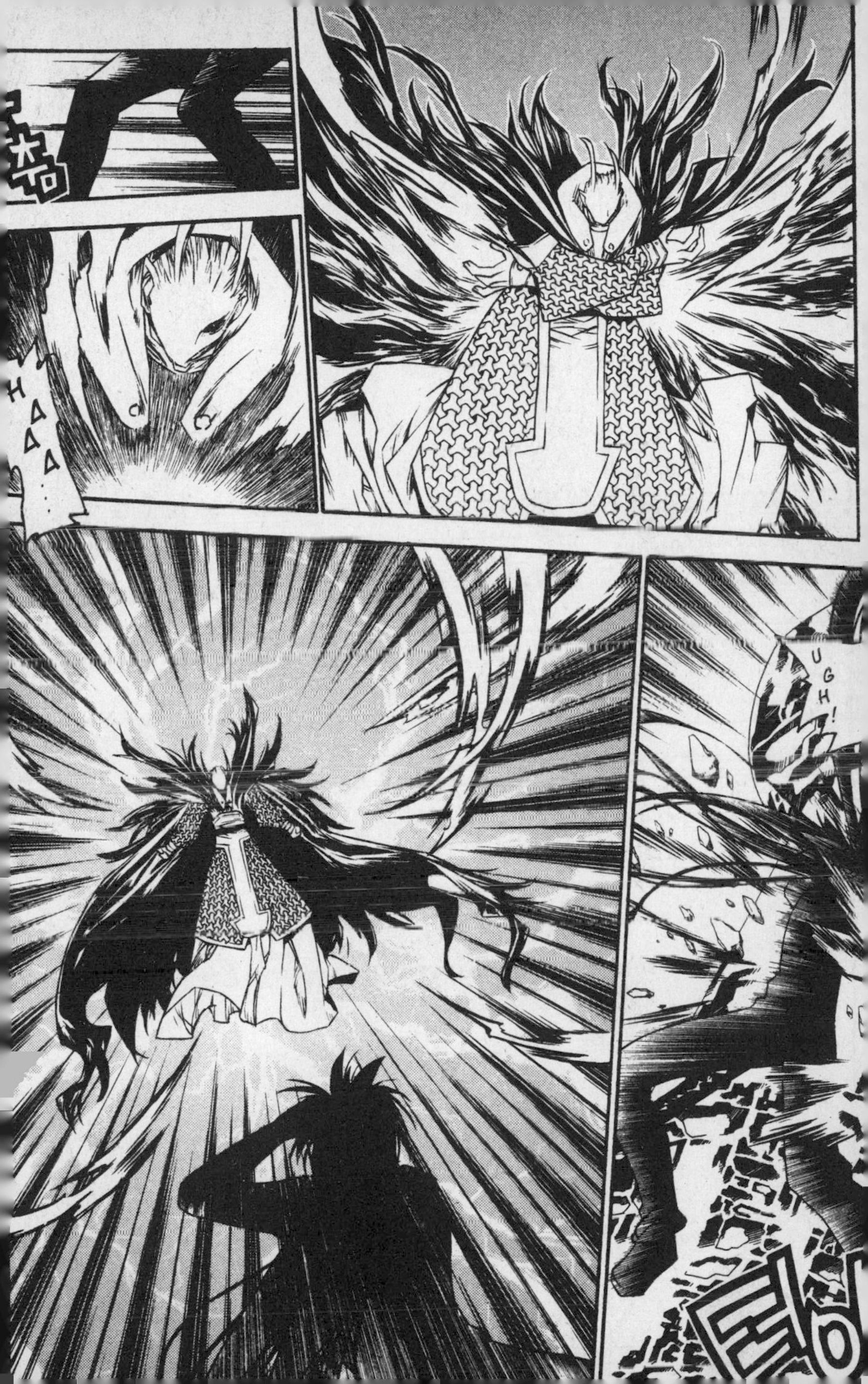
HAAAA...
UGH!

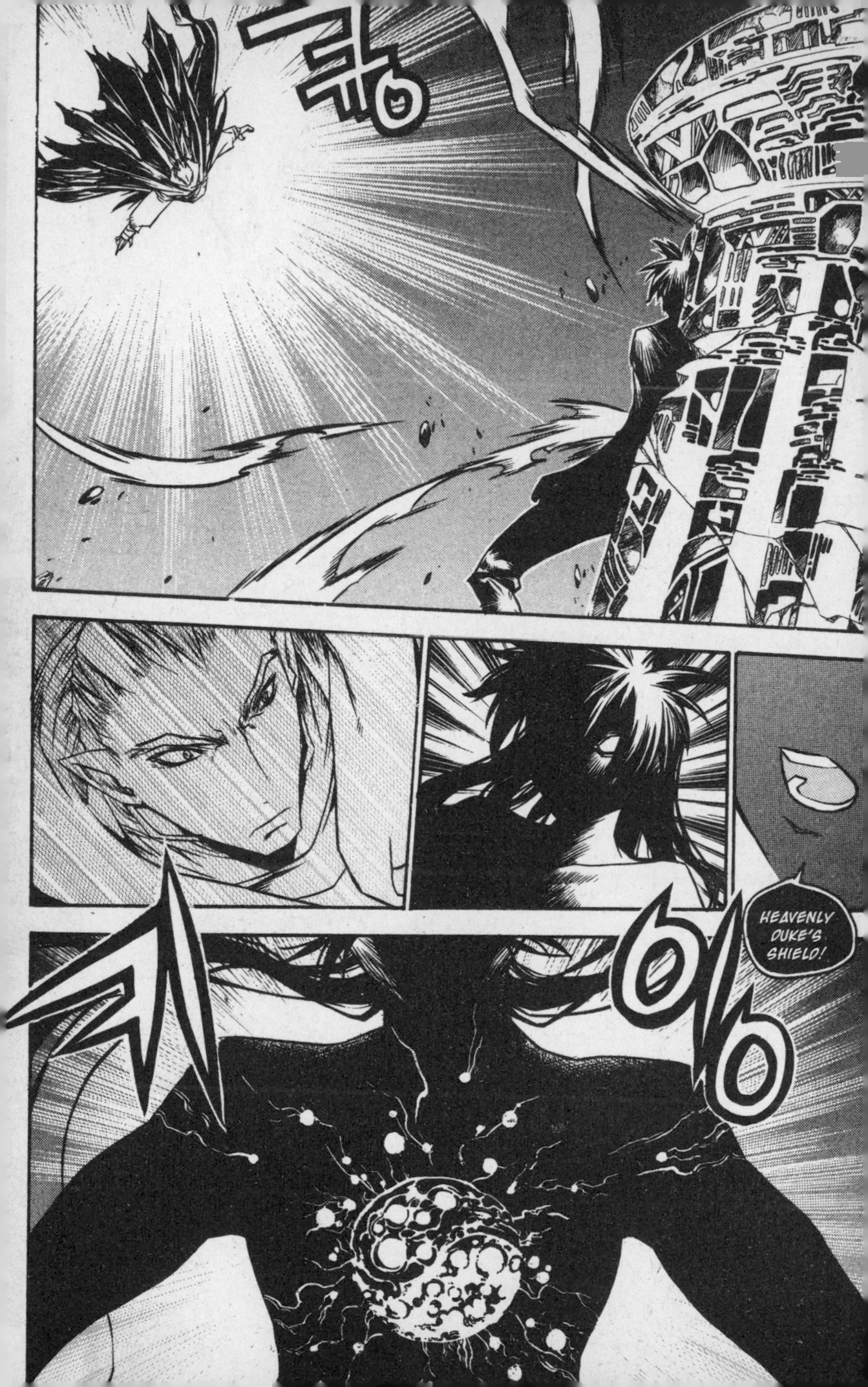
HEAVENLY DUKE'S SHIELD!

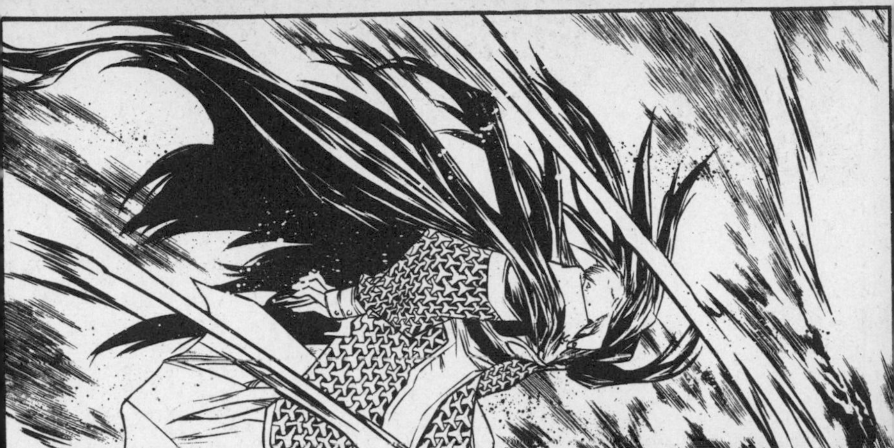

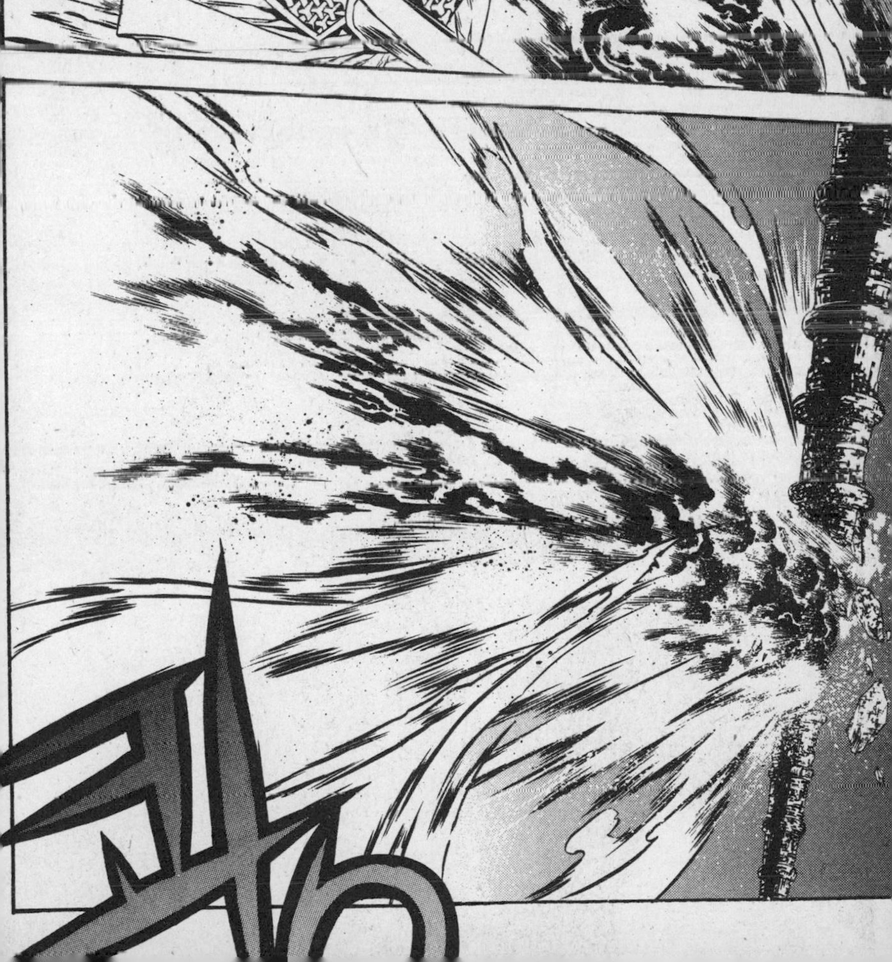

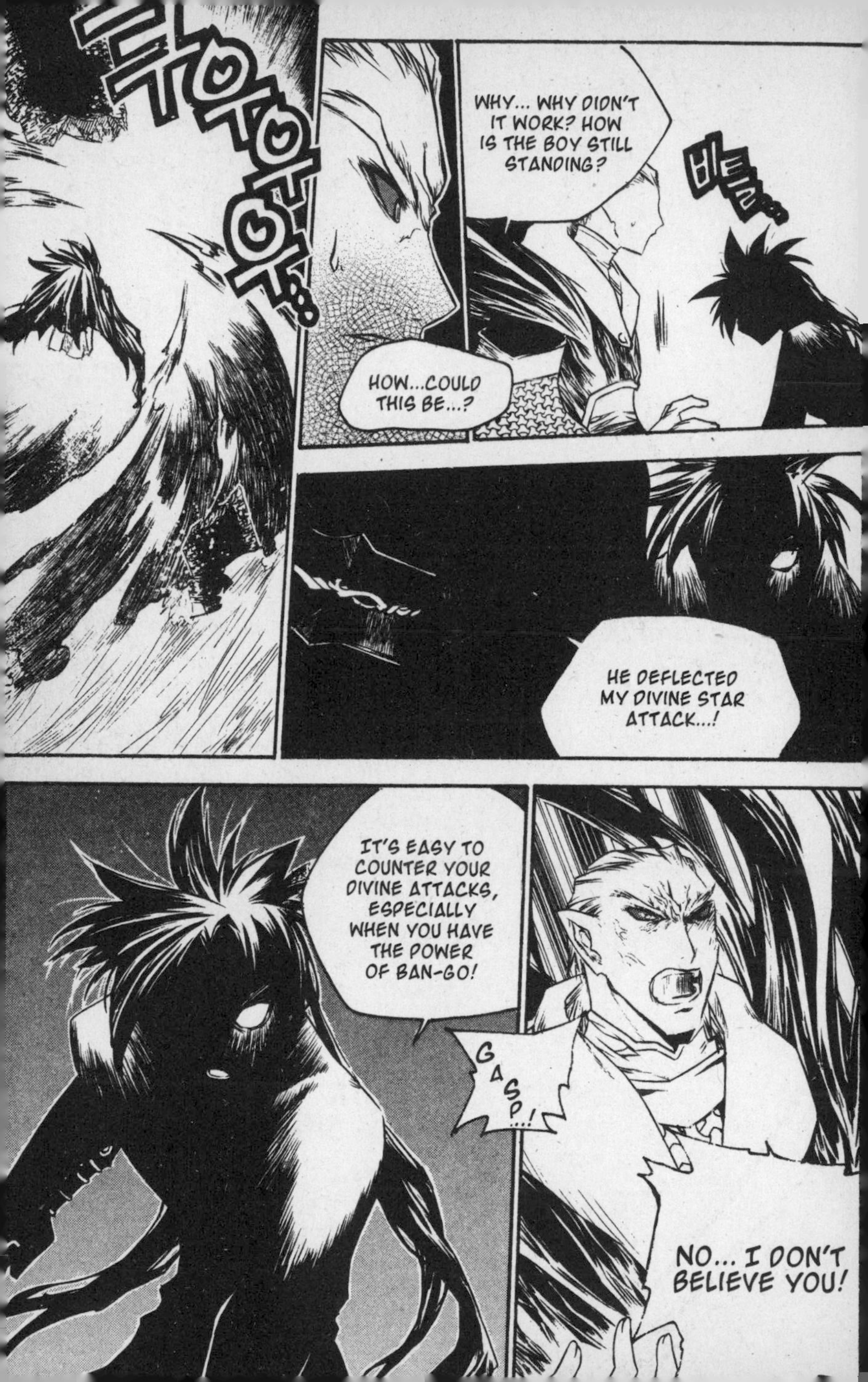
WHY... WHY DIDN'T IT WORK? HOW IS THE BOY STILL STANDING?
비틀...
HOW...COULD THIS BE...?
HE DEFLECTED MY DIVINE STAR ATTACK...!
IT'S EASY TO COUNTER YOUR DIVINE ATTACKS, ESPECIALLY WHEN YOU HAVE THE POWER OF BAN-GO!
GASP...!
NO... I DON'T BELIEVE YOU!

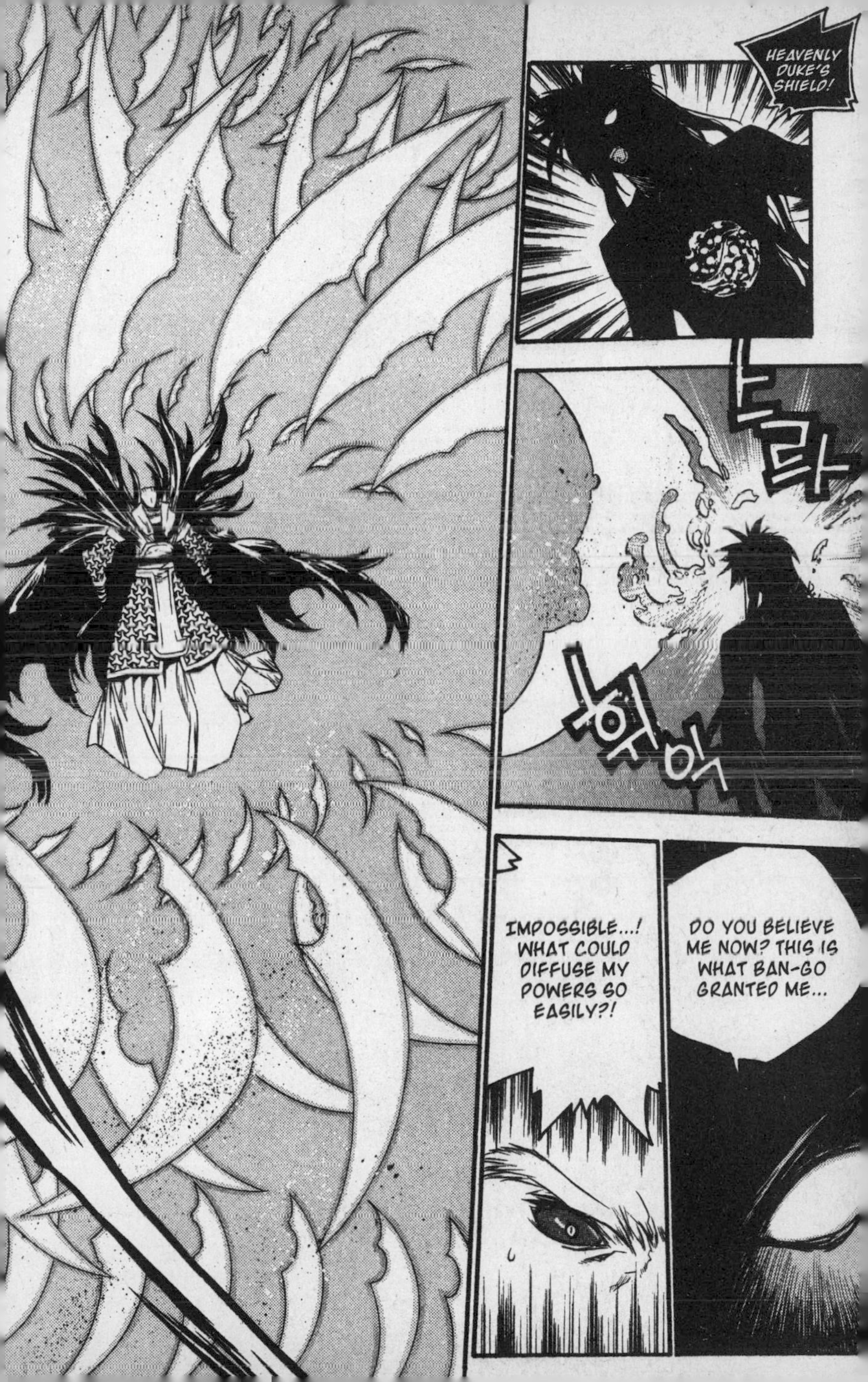
HEAVENLY DUKE'S SHIELD!
IMPOSSIBLE...! WHAT COULD DIFFUSE MY POWERS SO EASILY?!
DO YOU BELIEVE ME NOW? THIS IS WHAT BAN-GO GRANTED ME...

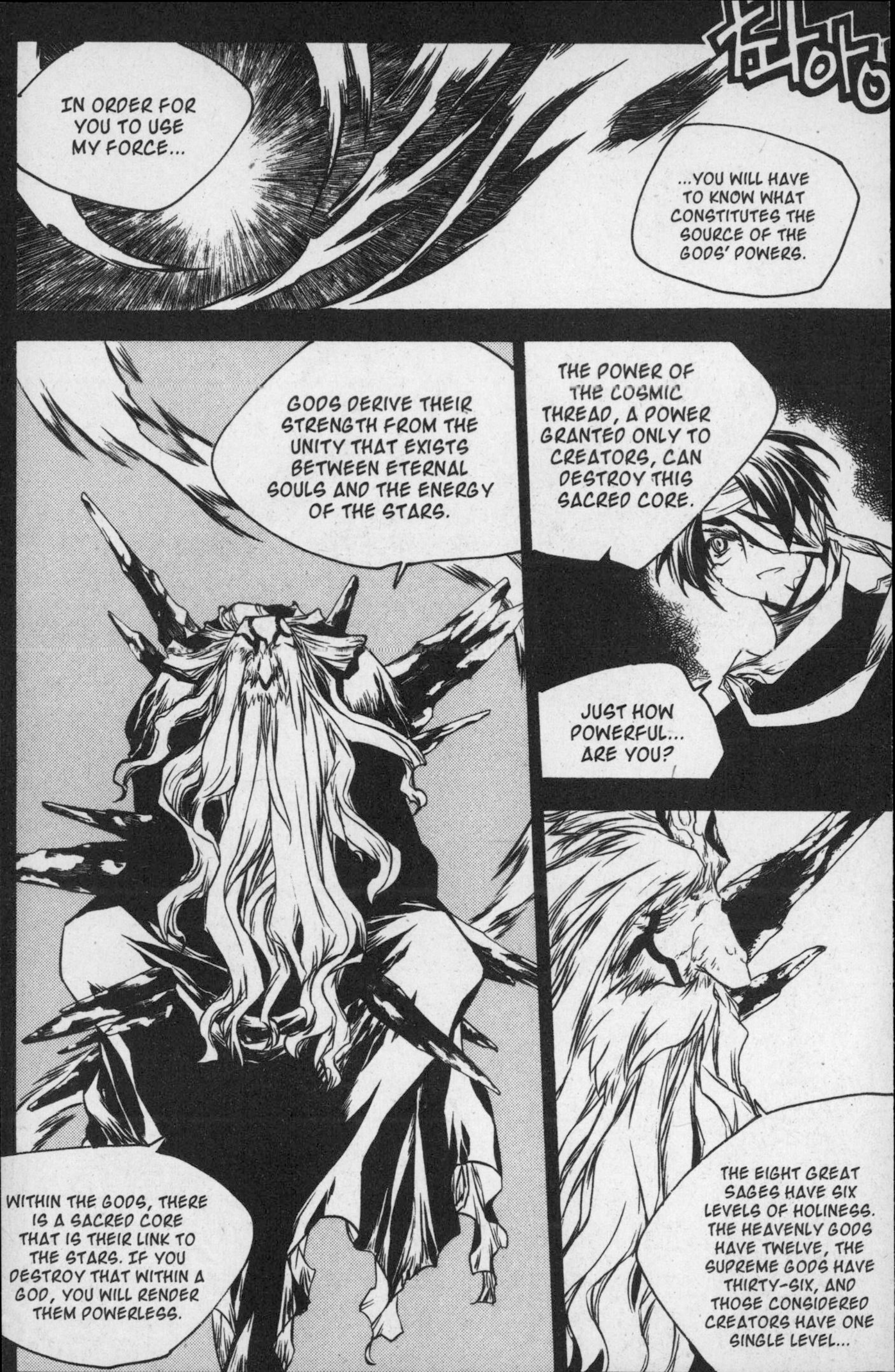
IN ORDER FOR YOU TO USE MY FORCE...
...YOU WILL HAVE TO KNOW WHAT CONSTITUTES THE SOURCE OF THE GODS' POWERS.
GODS DERIVE THEIR STRENGTH FROM THE UNITY THAT EXISTS BETWEEN ETERNAL SOULS AND THE ENERGY OF THE STARS.
WITHIN THE GODS, THERE IS A SACRED CORE THAT IS THEIR LINK TO THE STARS. IF YOU DESTROY THAT WITHIN A GOD, YOU WILL RENDER THEM POWERLESS.
THE POWER OF THE COSMIC THREAD, A POWER GRANTED ONLY TO CREATORS, CAN DESTROY THIS SACRED CORE.
JUST HOW POWERFUL... ARE YOU?
THE EIGHT GREAT SAGES HAVE SIX LEVELS OF HOLINESS. THE HEAVENLY GODS HAVE TWELVE, THE SUPREME GODS HAVE THIRTY-SIX, AND THOSE CONSIDERED CREATORS HAVE ONE SINGLE LEVEL...

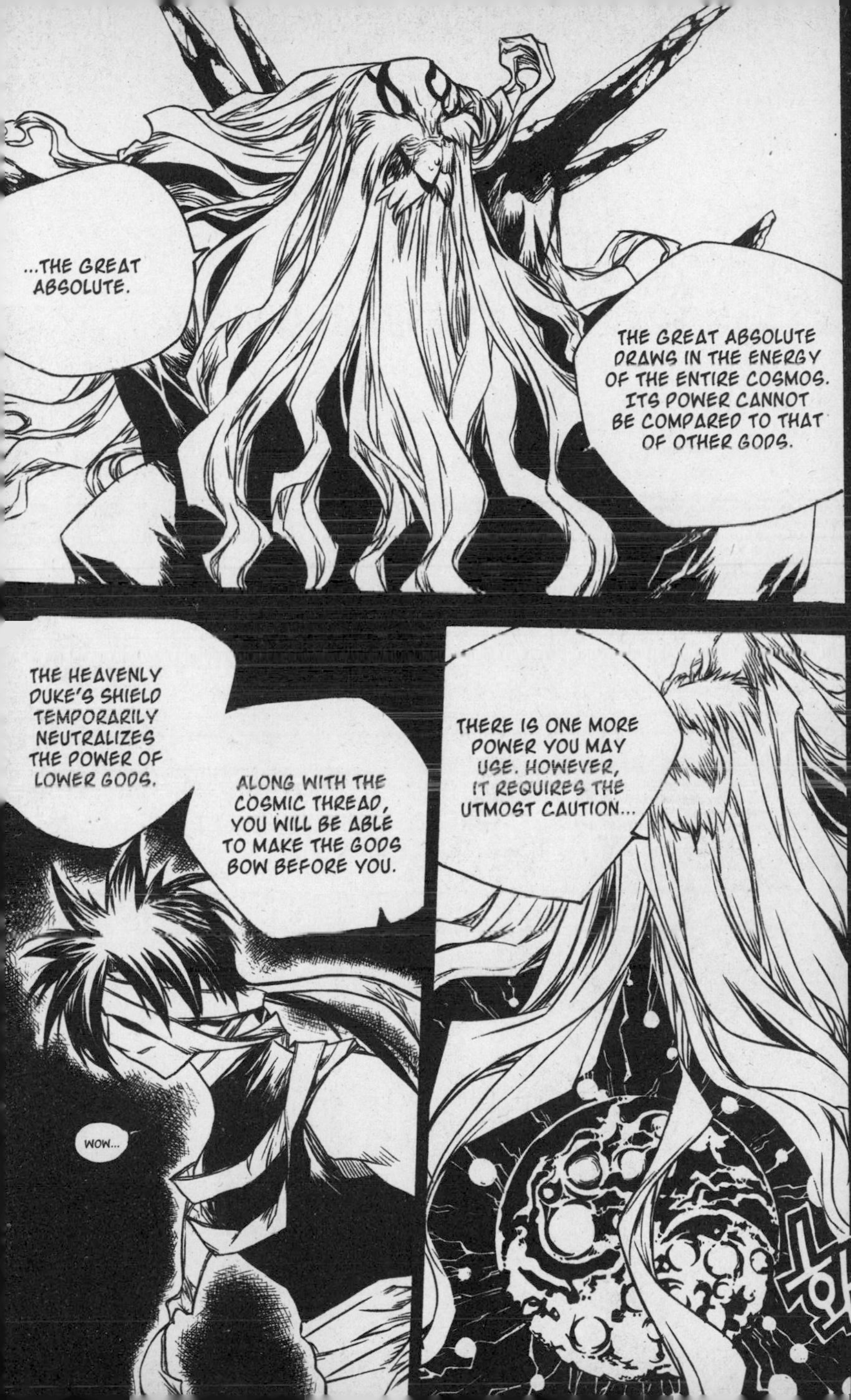
...THE GREAT ABSOLUTE.
THE GREAT ABSOLUTE DRAWS IN THE ENERGY OF THE ENTIRE COSMOS. ITS POWER CANNOT BE COMPARED TO THAT OF OTHER GODS.
THE HEAVENLY DUKE'S SHIELD TEMPORARILY NEUTRALIZES THE POWER OF LOWER GODS.
ALONG WITH THE COSMIC THREAD, YOU WILL BE ABLE TO MAKE THE GODS BOW BEFORE YOU.
WOW...
THERE IS ONE MORE POWER YOU MAY USE. HOWEVER, IT REQUIRES THE UTMOST CAUTION...

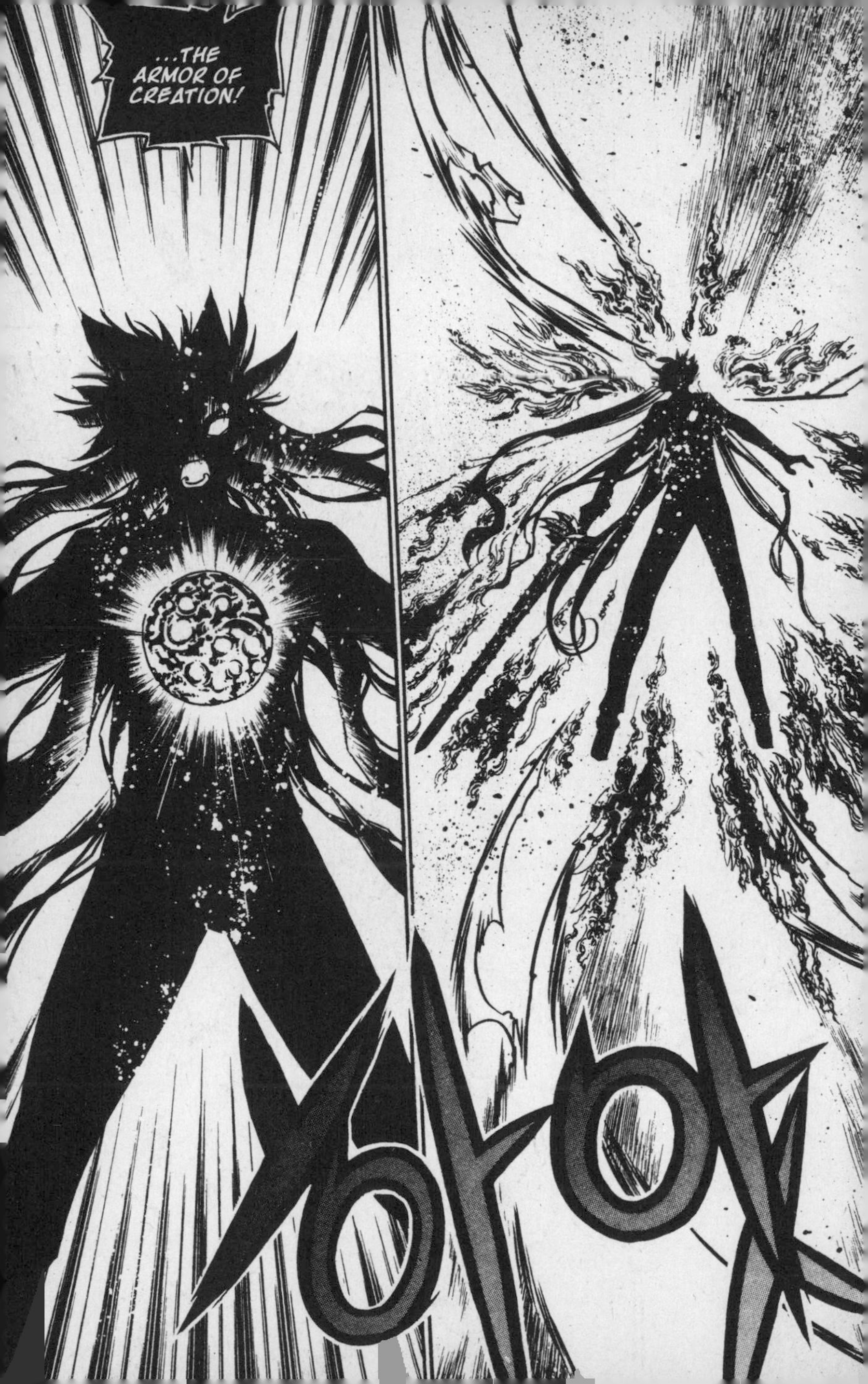
...THE ARMOR OF CREATION!

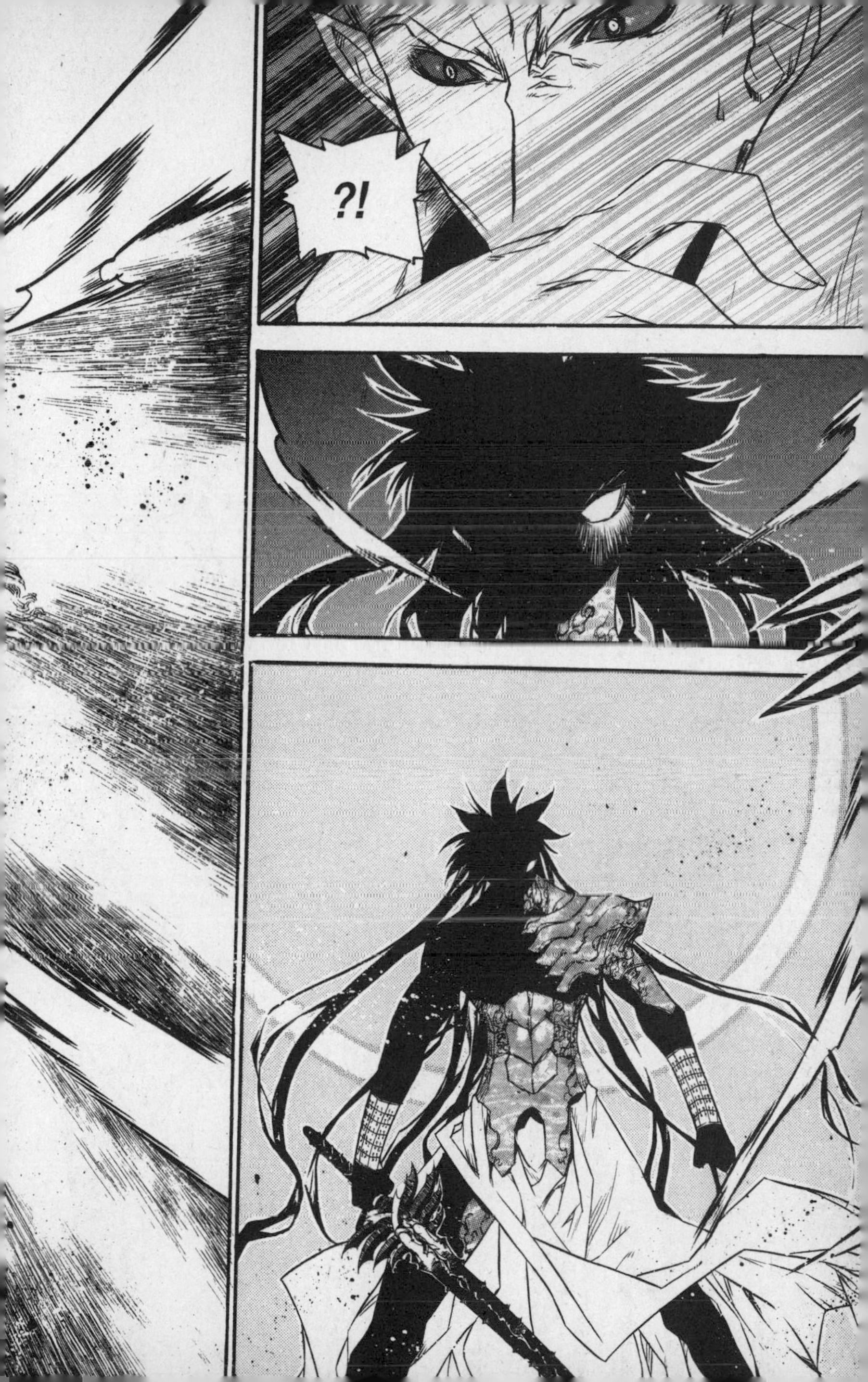
?!

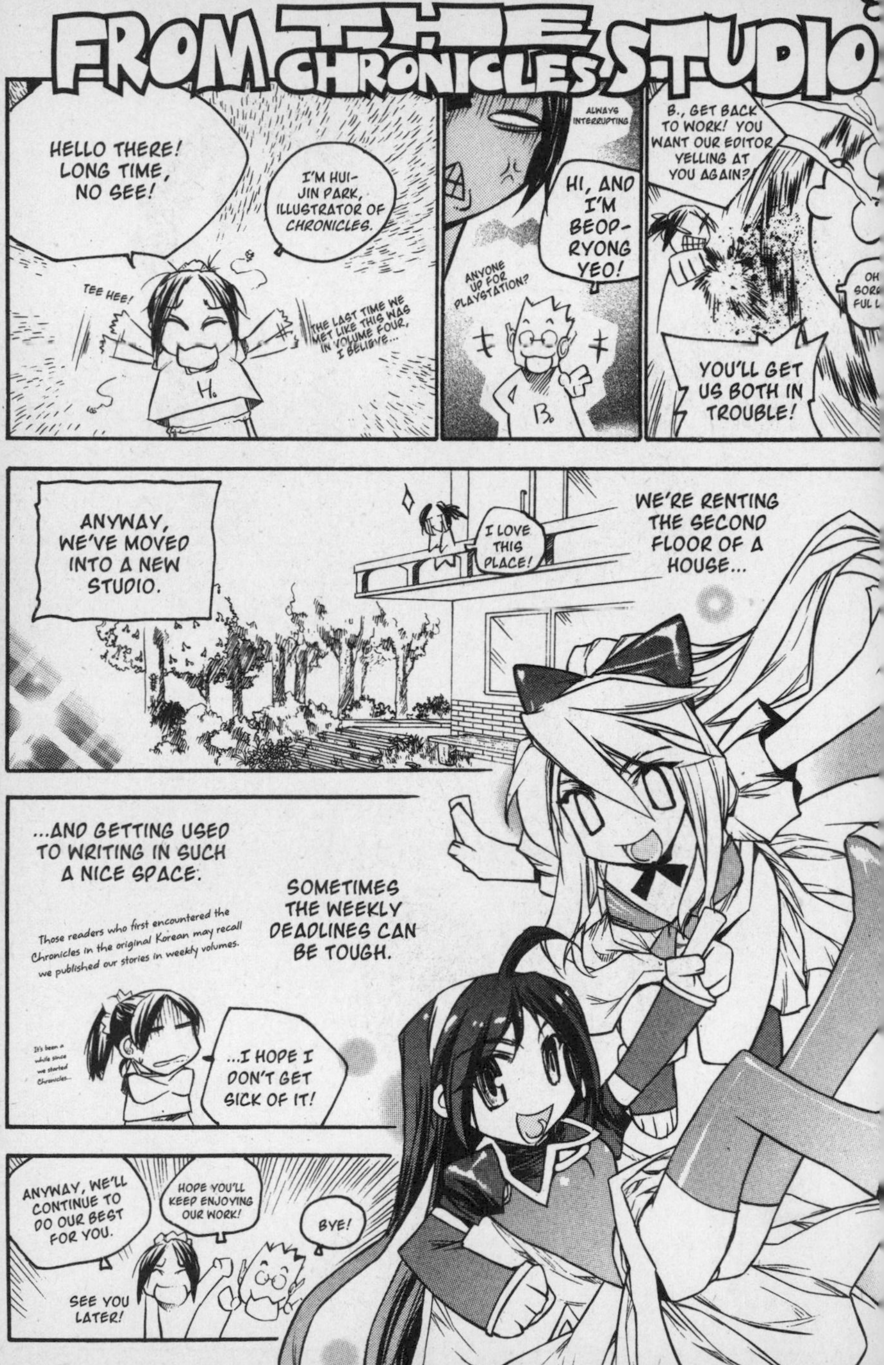
FROM THE CHRONICLES STUDIO
HELLO THERE! LONG TIME, NO SEE!
I'M HUI-JIN PARK, ILLUSTRATOR OF CHRONICLES.
TEE HEE!
THE LAST TIME WE MET LIKE THIS WAS IN VOLUME FOUR, I BELIEVE...
ALWAYS INTERRUPTING
HI, AND I'M BEOP-RYONG YEO!
ANYONE UP FOR PLAYSTATION?
B., GET BACK TO WORK! YOU WANT OUR EDITOR YELLING AT YOU AGAIN?
YOU'LL GET US BOTH IN TROUBLE!
ANYWAY, WE'VE MOVED INTO A NEW STUDIO.
I LOVE THIS PLACE!
WE'RE RENTING THE SECOND FLOOR OF A HOUSE...
...AND GETTING USED TO WRITING IN SUCH A NICE SPACE.
Those readers who first encountered the Chronicles in the original Korean may recall we published our stories in weekly volumes.
SOMETIMES THE WEEKLY DEADLINES CAN BE TOUGH.
It's been a while since we started Chronicles...
...I HOPE I DON'T GET SICK OF IT!
ANYWAY, WE'LL CONTINUE TO DO OUR BEST FOR YOU.
HOPE YOU'LL KEEP ENJOYING OUR WORK!
BYE!
SEE YOU LATER!

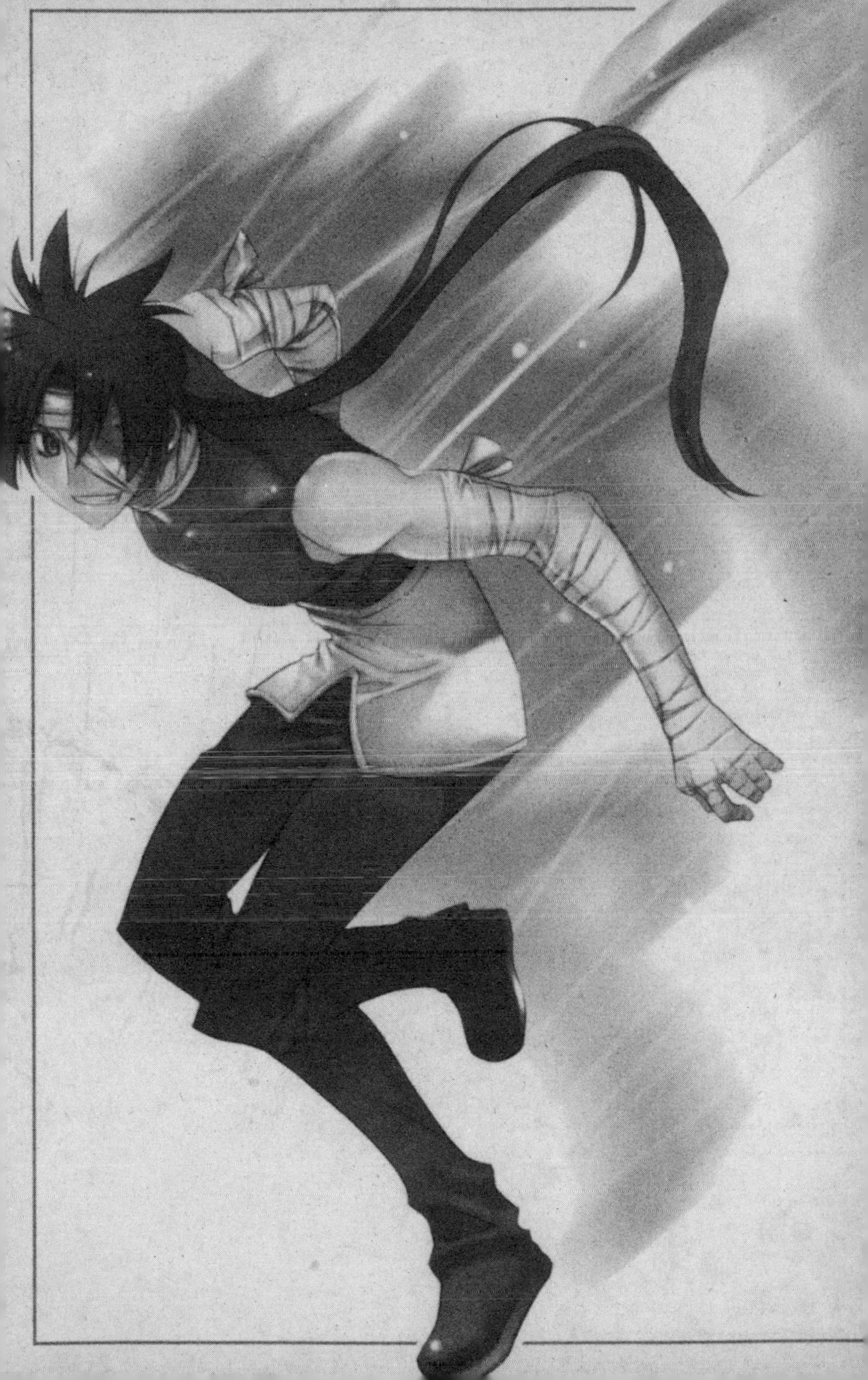

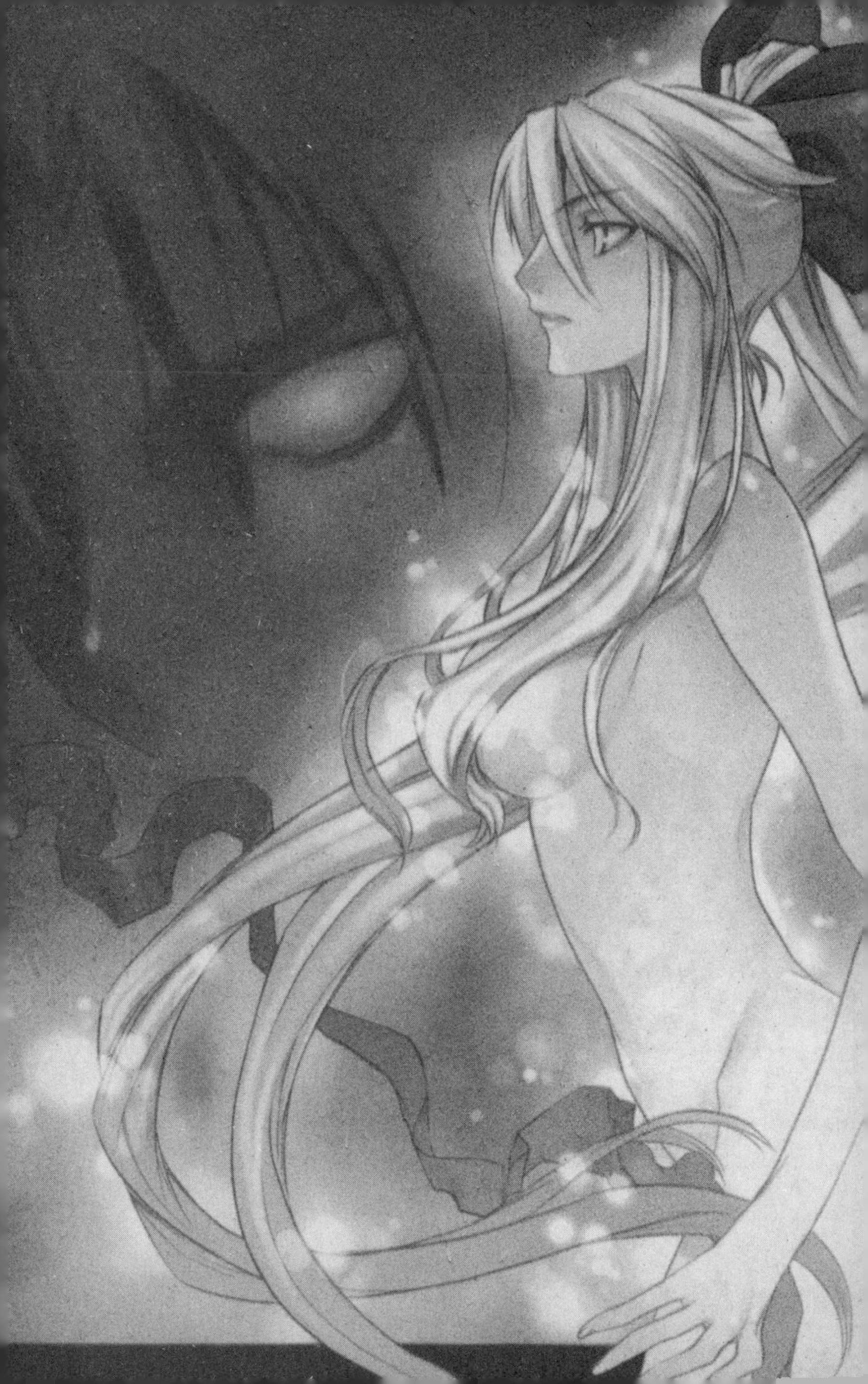

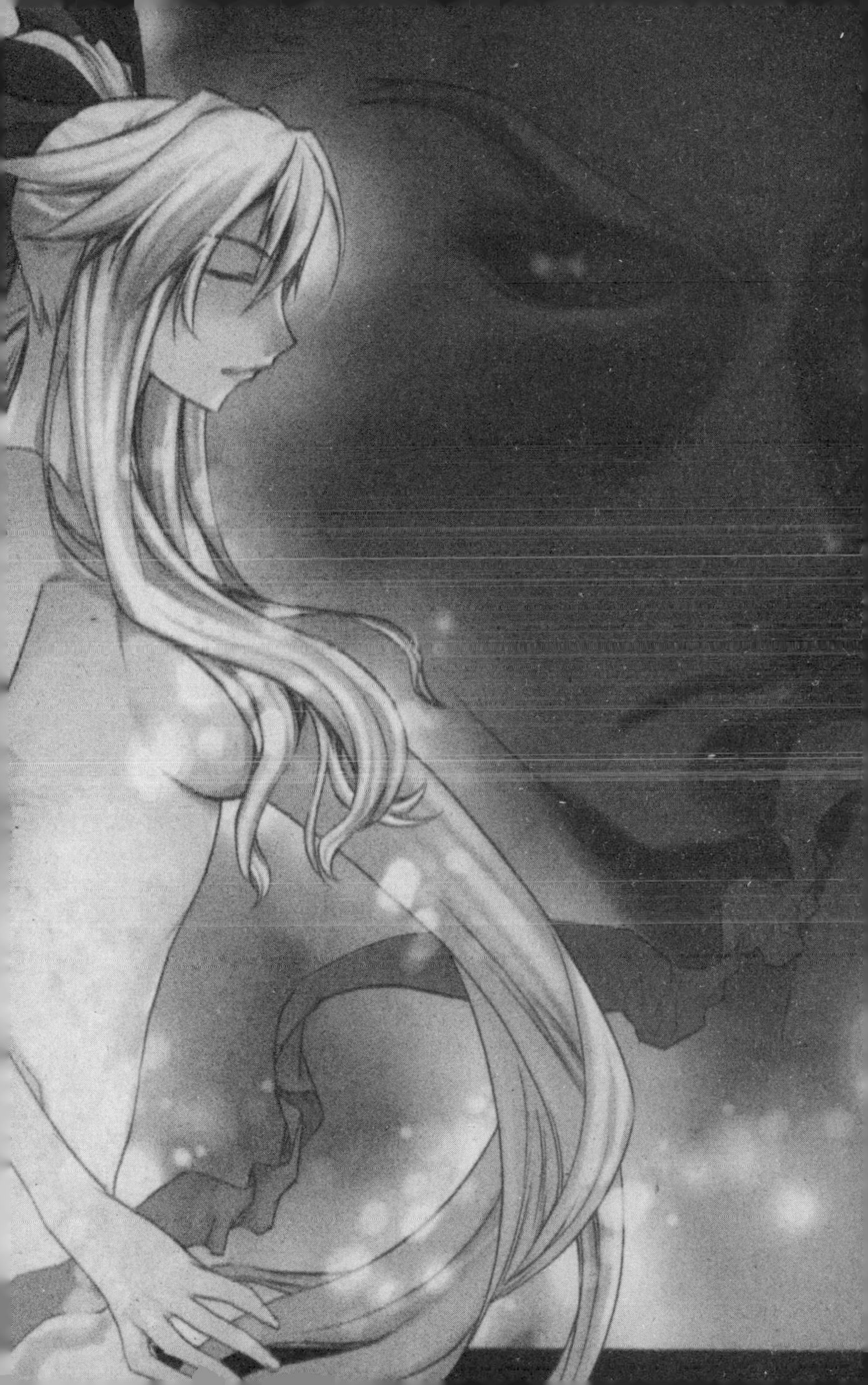

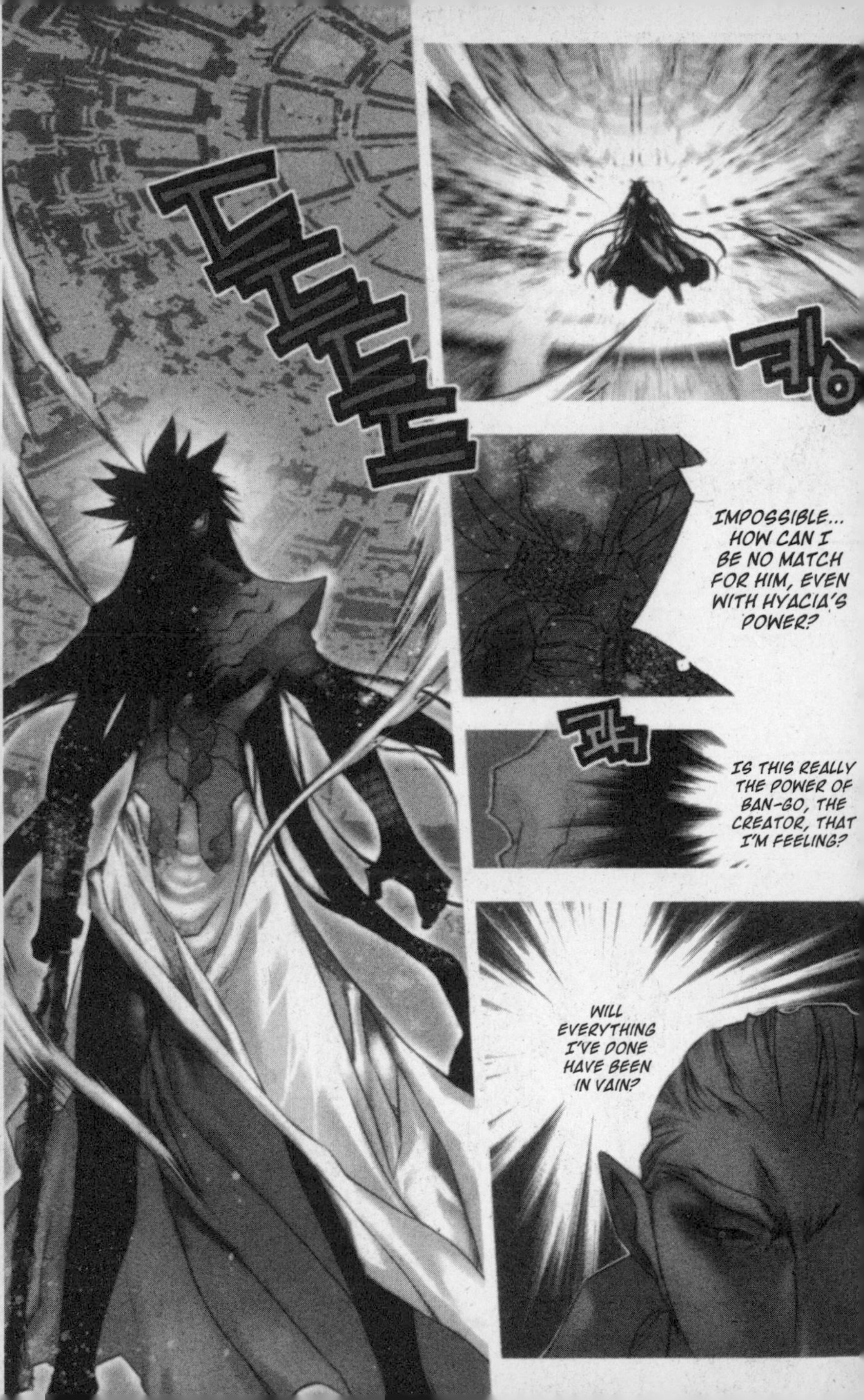
IMPOSSIBLE... HOW CAN I BE NO MATCH FOR HIM, EVEN WITH HYACIA'S POWER?
IS THIS REALLY THE POWER OF BAN-GO, THE CREATOR, THAT I'M FEELING?
WILL EVERYTHING I'VE DONE HAVE BEEN IN VAIN?

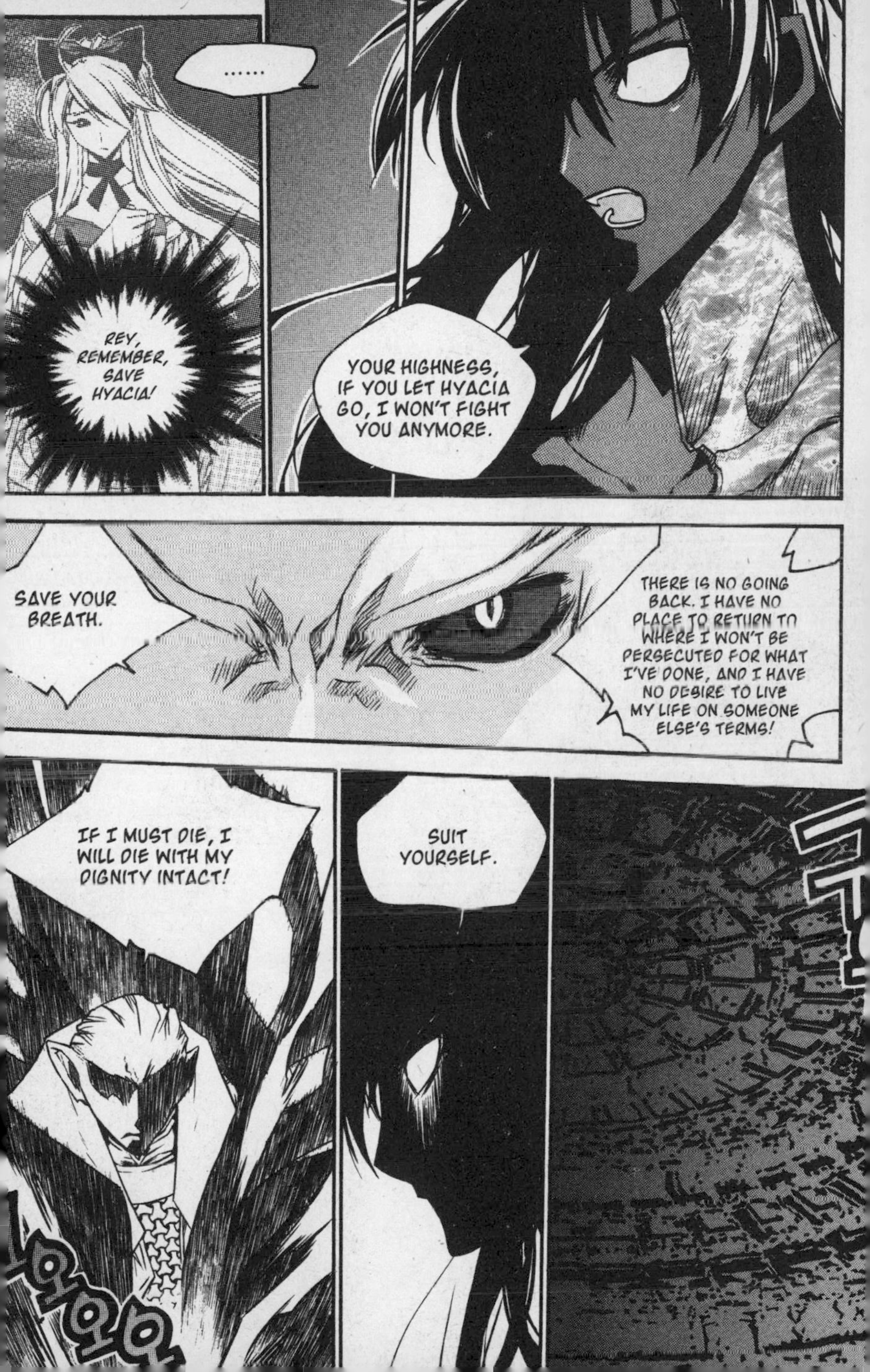
......
REY, REMEMBER, SAVE HYACIA!
YOUR HIGHNESS, IF YOU LET HYACIA GO, I WON'T FIGHT YOU ANYMORE.
SAVE YOUR BREATH.
THERE IS NO GOING BACK. I HAVE NO PLACE TO RETURN TO WHERE I WON'T BE PERSECUTED FOR WHAT I'VE DONE, AND I HAVE NO DESIRE TO LIVE MY LIFE ON SOMEONE ELSE'S TERMS!
IF I MUST DIE, I WILL DIE WITH MY DIGNITY INTACT!
SUIT YOURSELF.

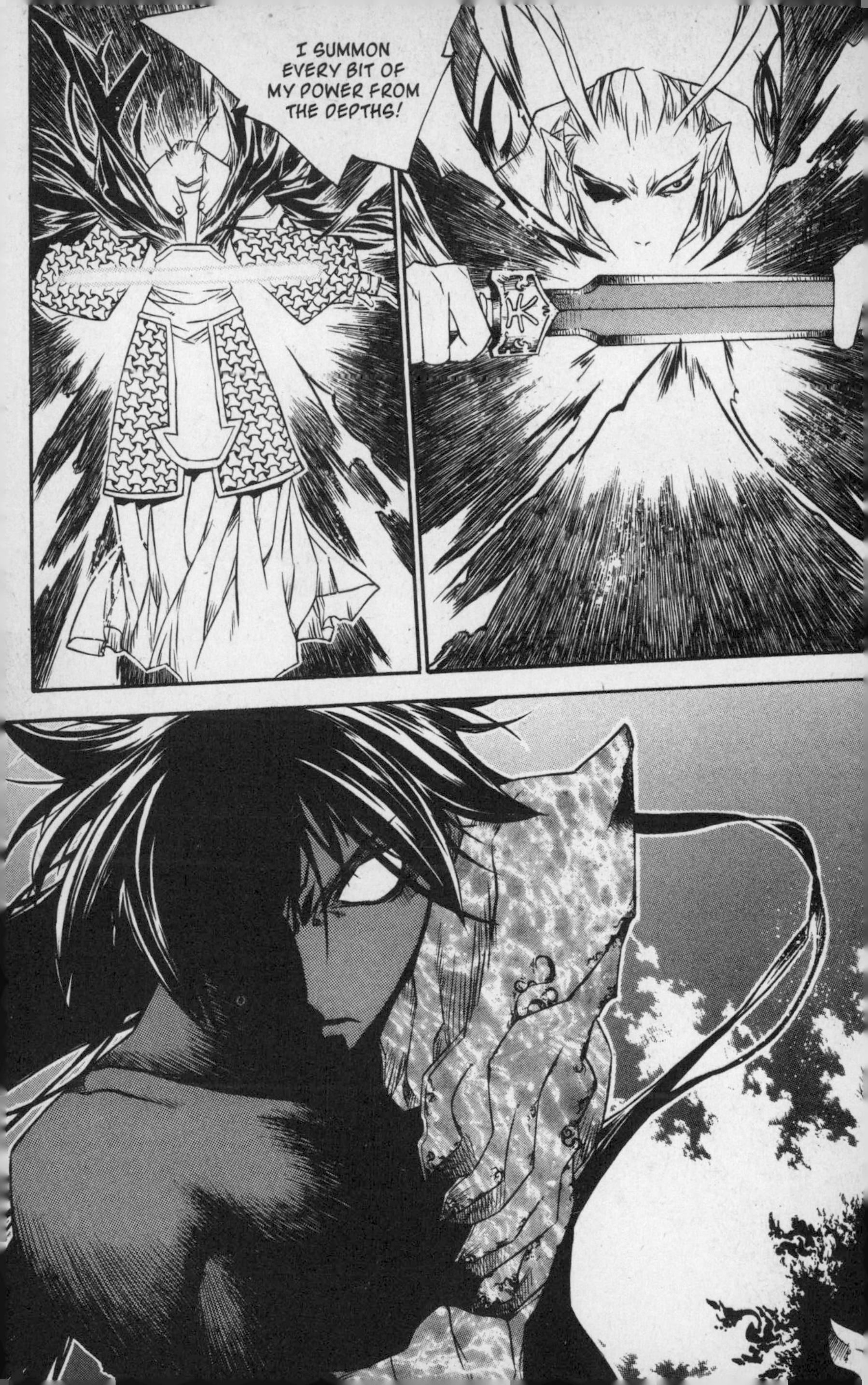
I SUMMON EVERY BIT OF MY POWER FROM THE DEPTHS!

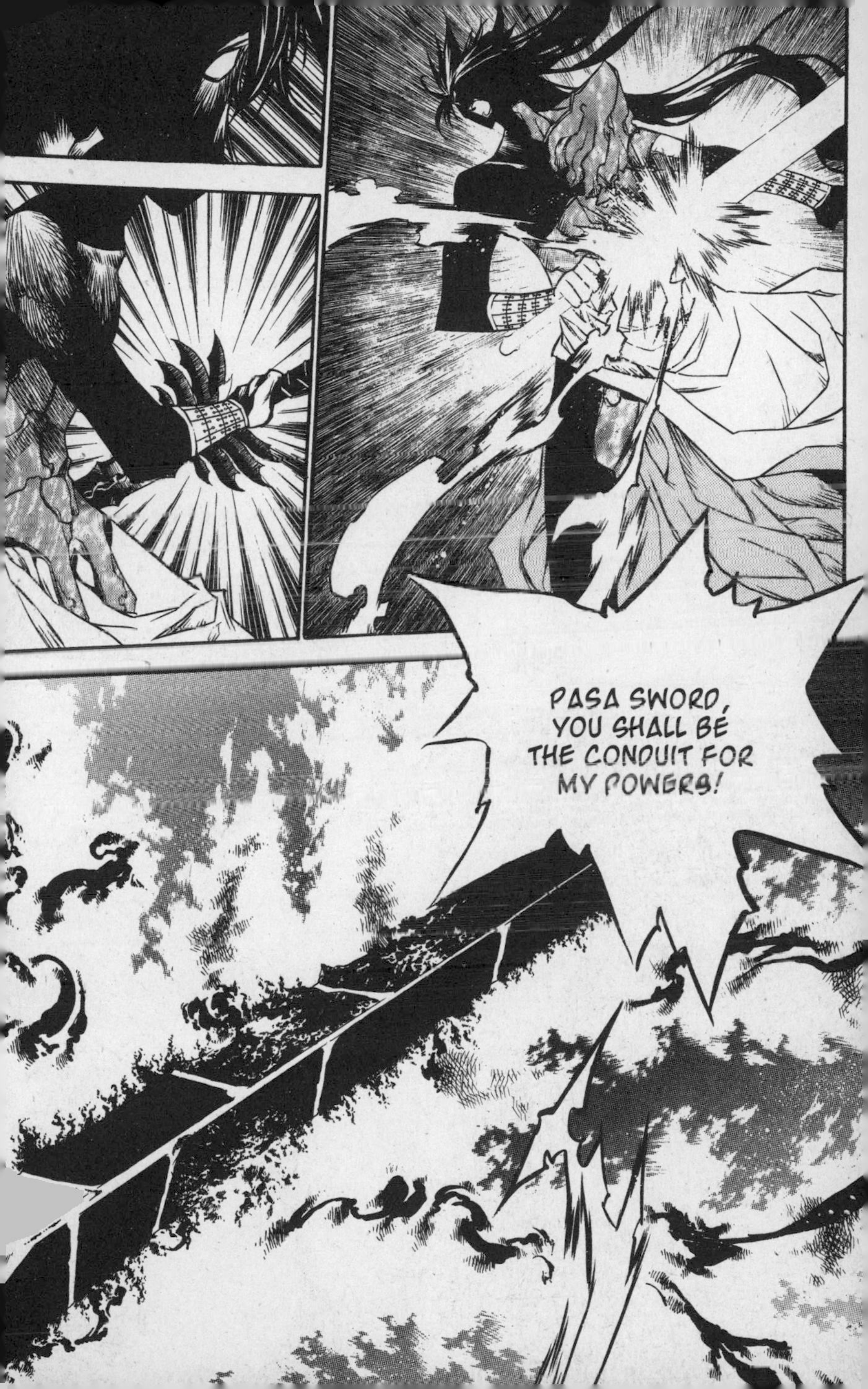
PASA SWORD, YOU SHALL BE THE CONDUIT FOR MY POWERS!

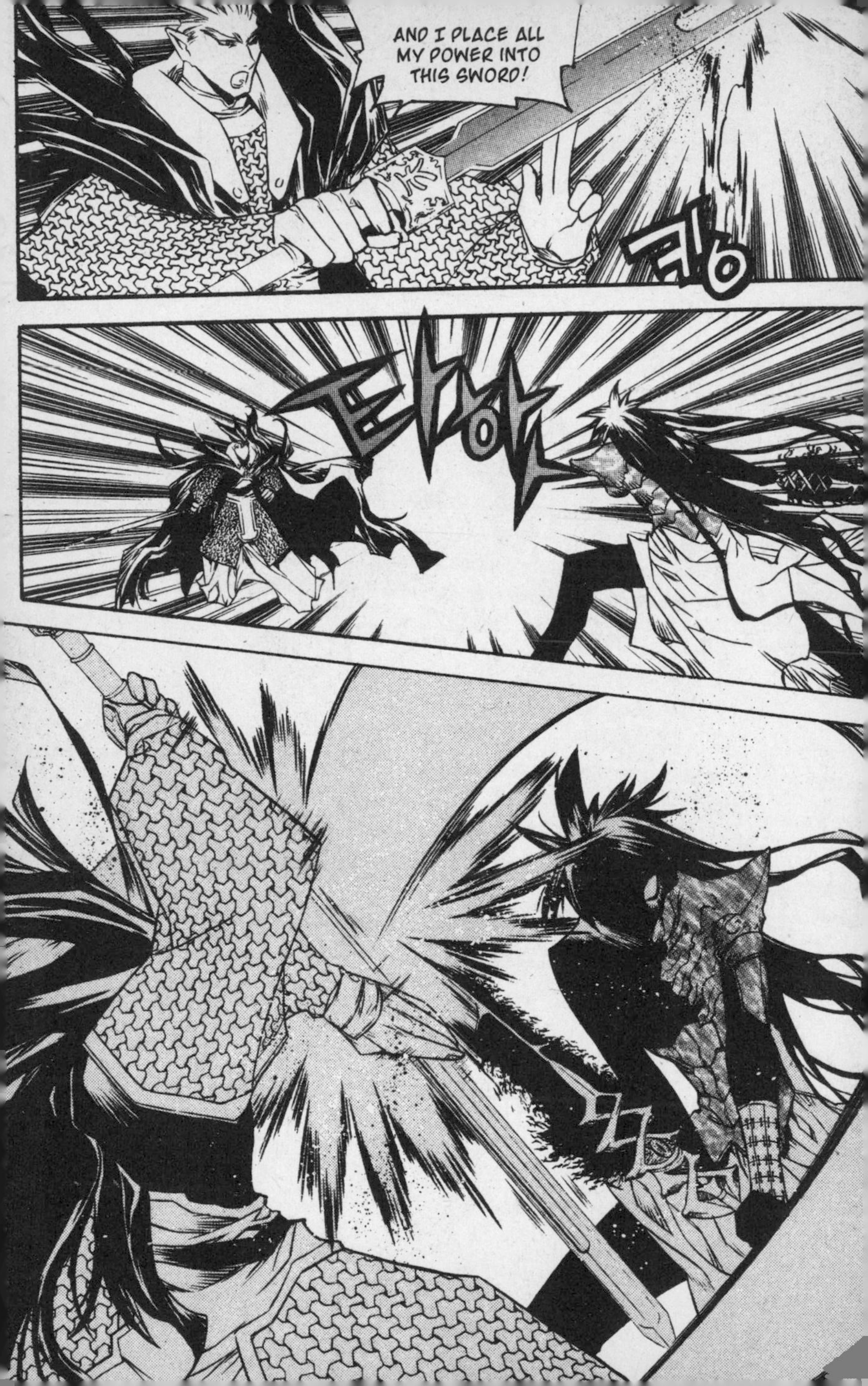
AND I PLACE ALL
MY POWER INTO
THIS SWORD!

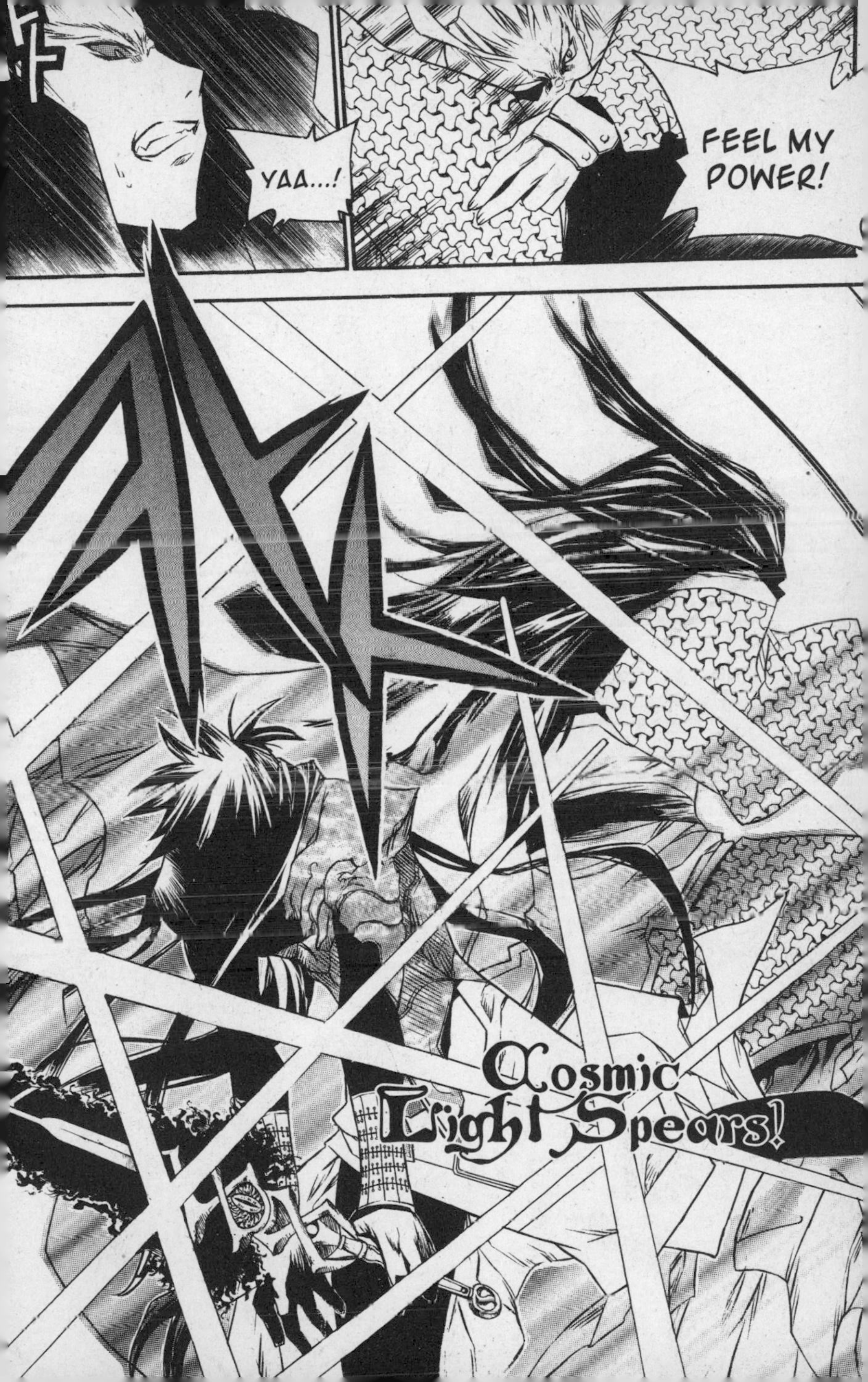
YAA...!
FEEL MY POWER!
Cosmic Light Spears!

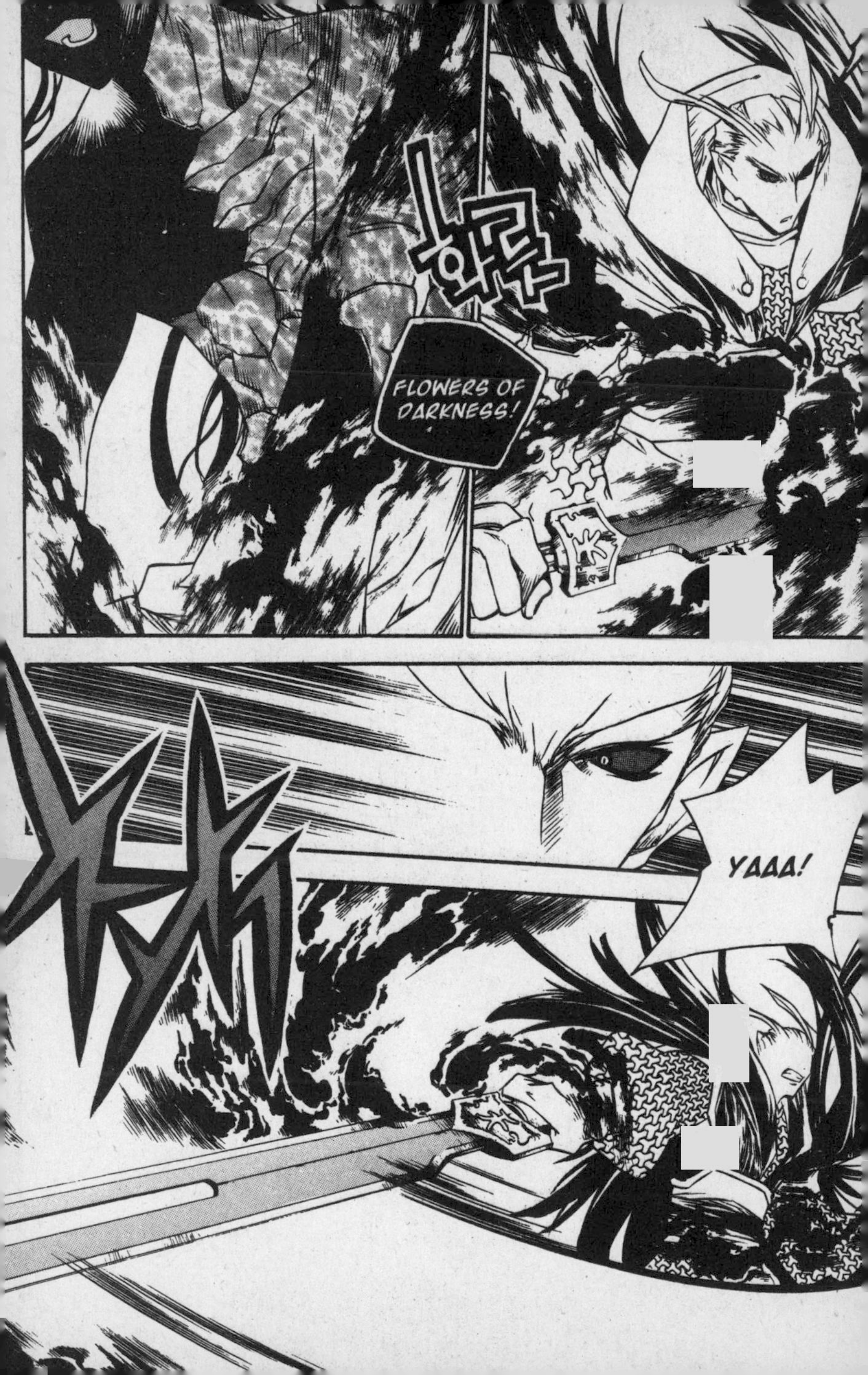
FLOWERS OF DARKNESS!
YAAA!

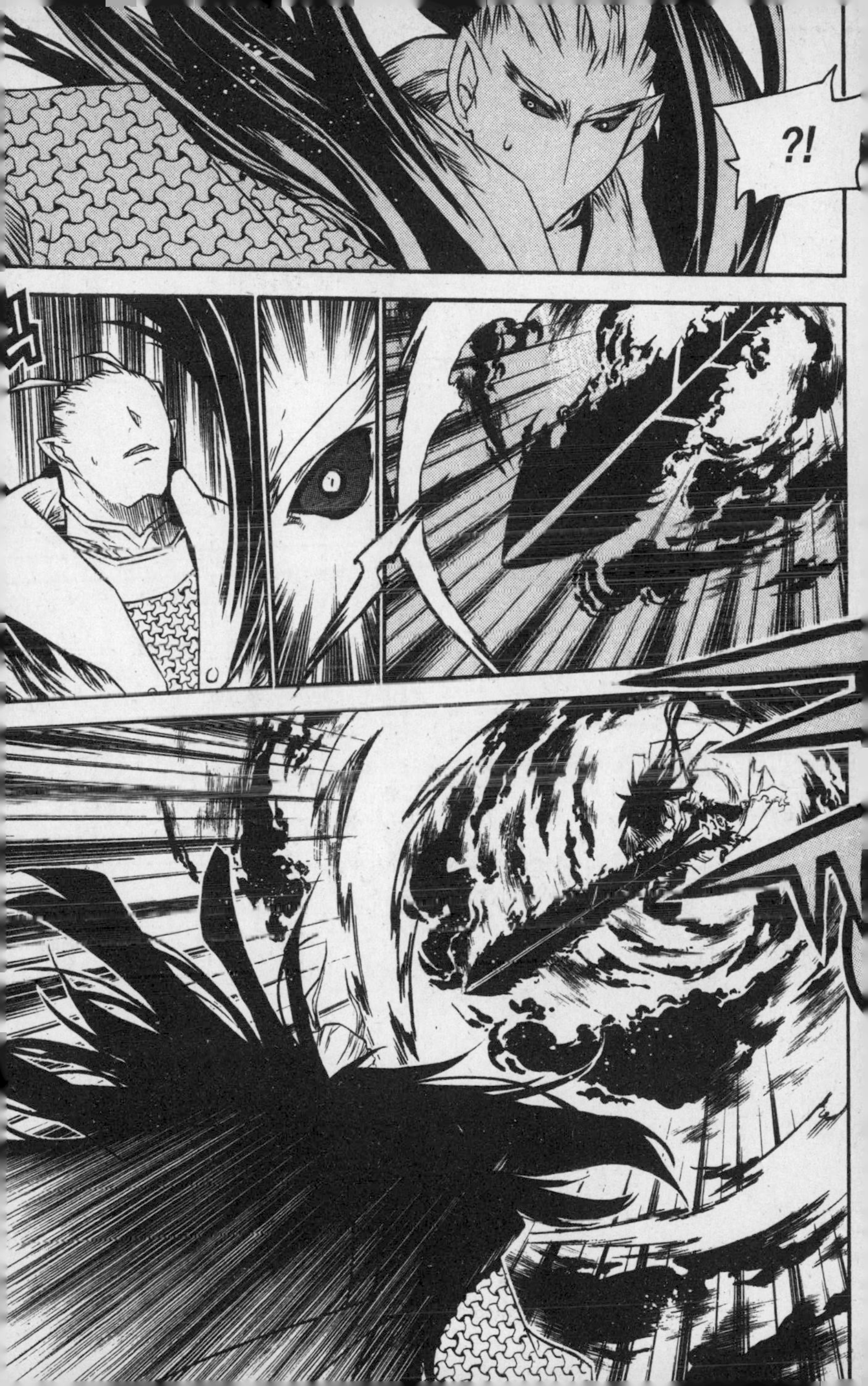
?!

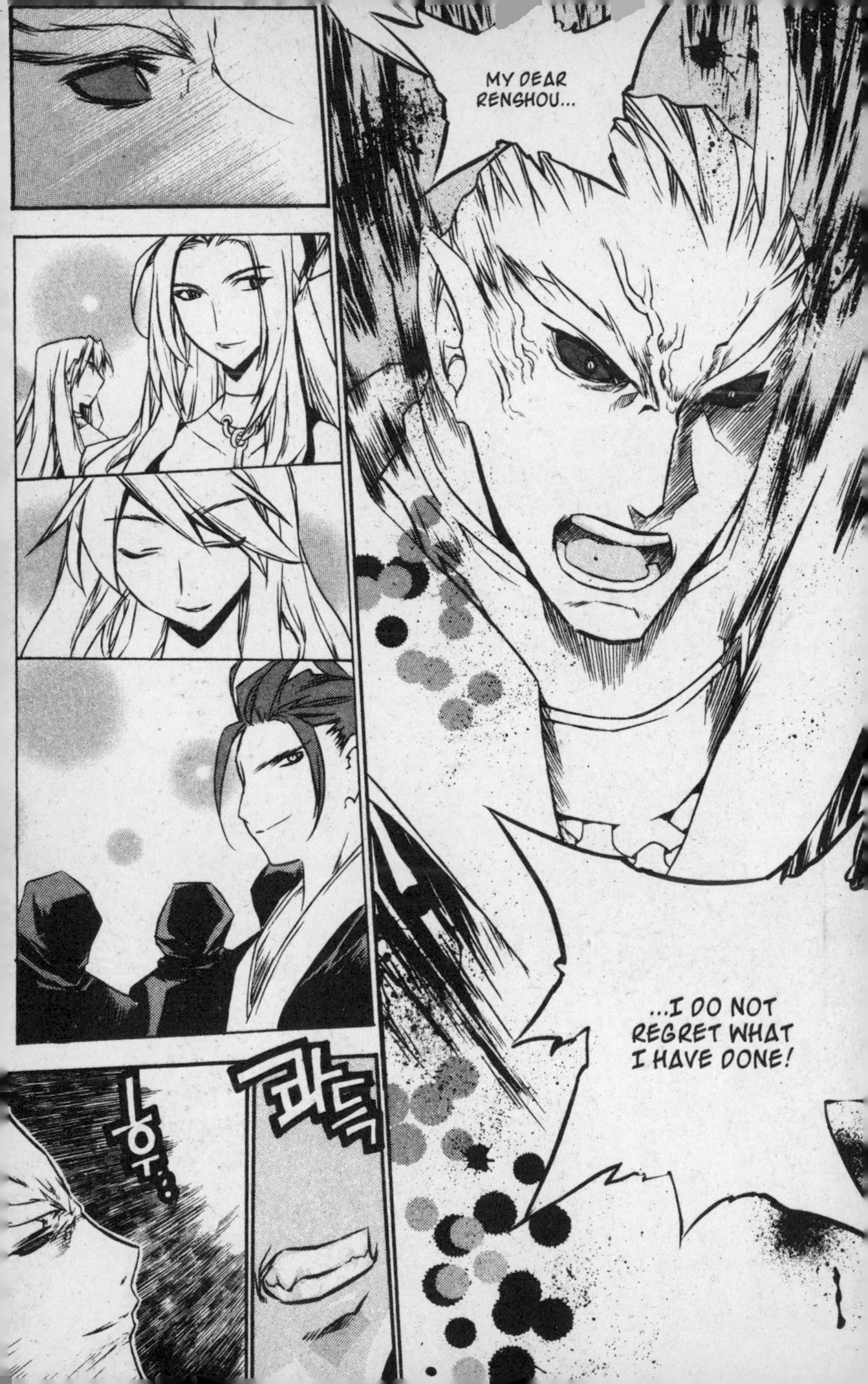
MY DEAR RENSHOU...
후...
파득
...I DO NOT REGRET WHAT I HAVE DONE!

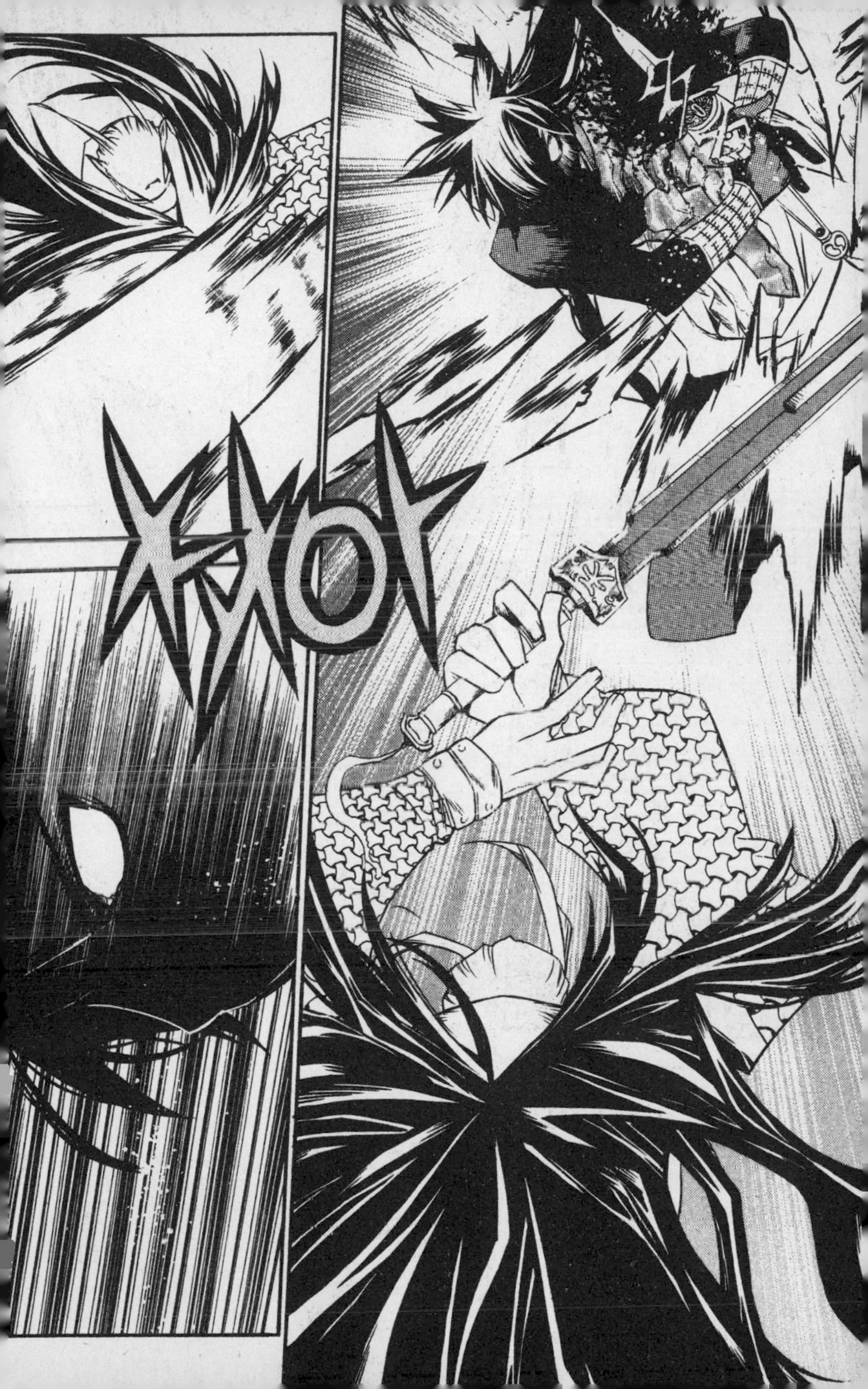

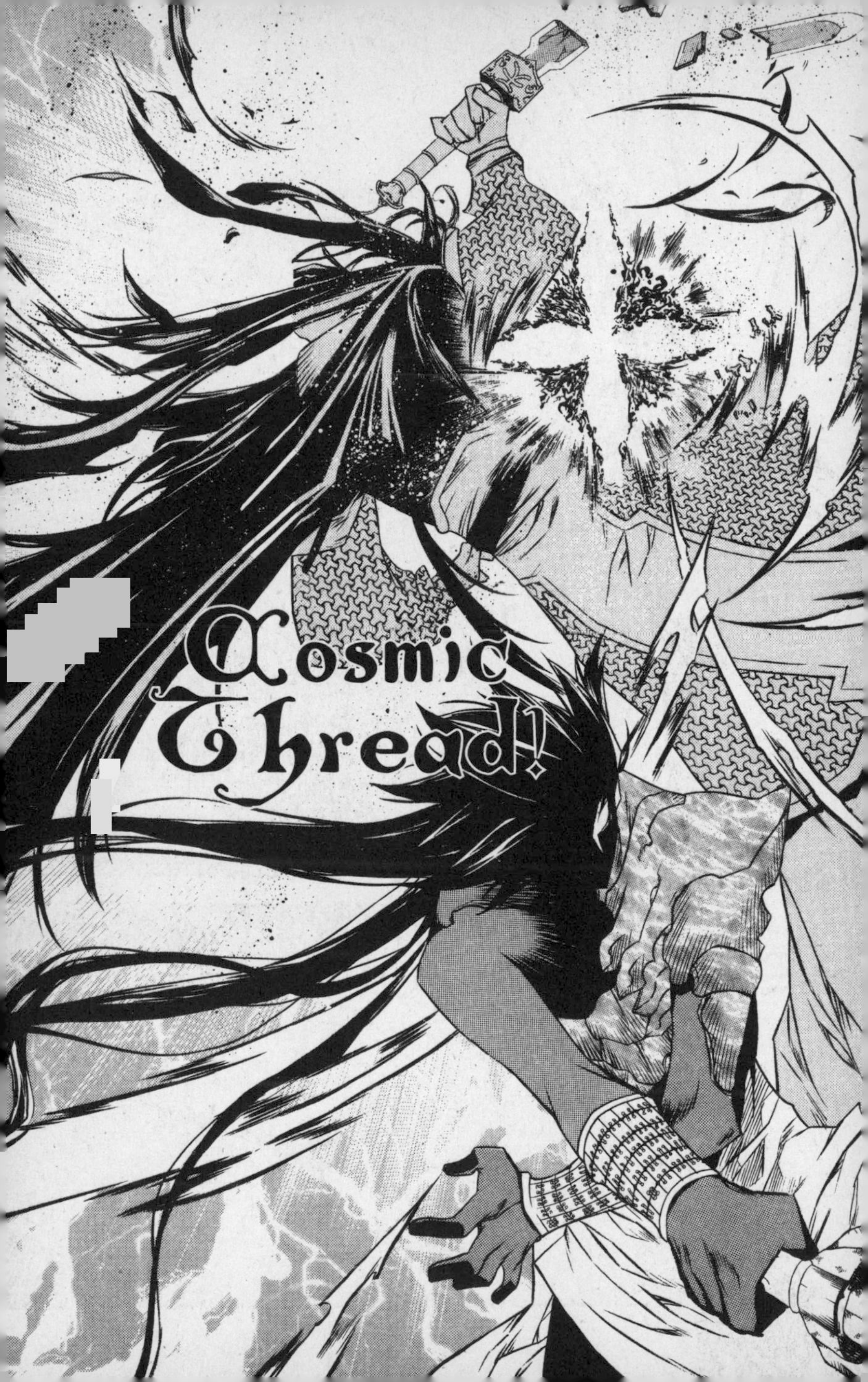
Cosmic Thread!

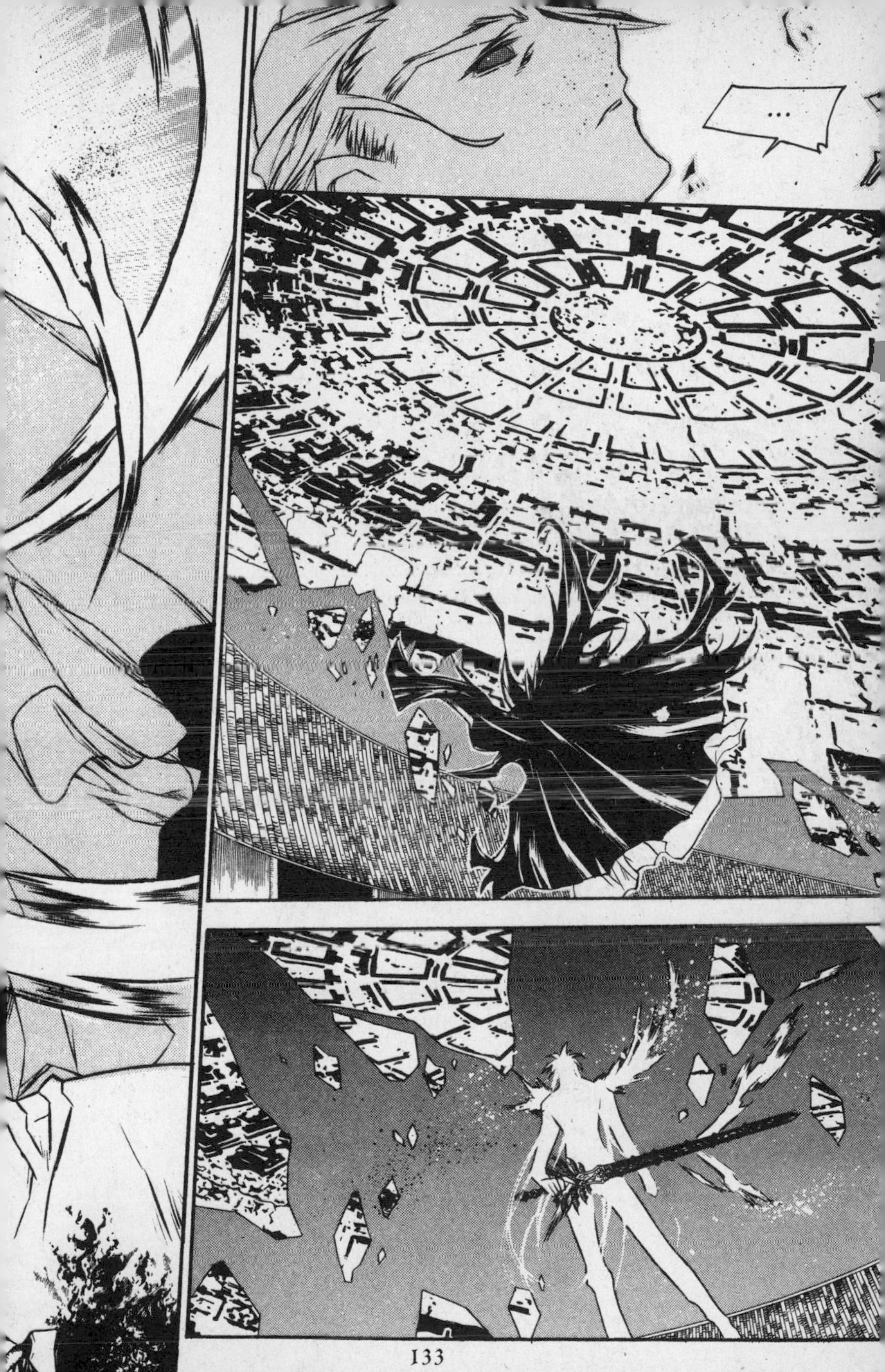
...

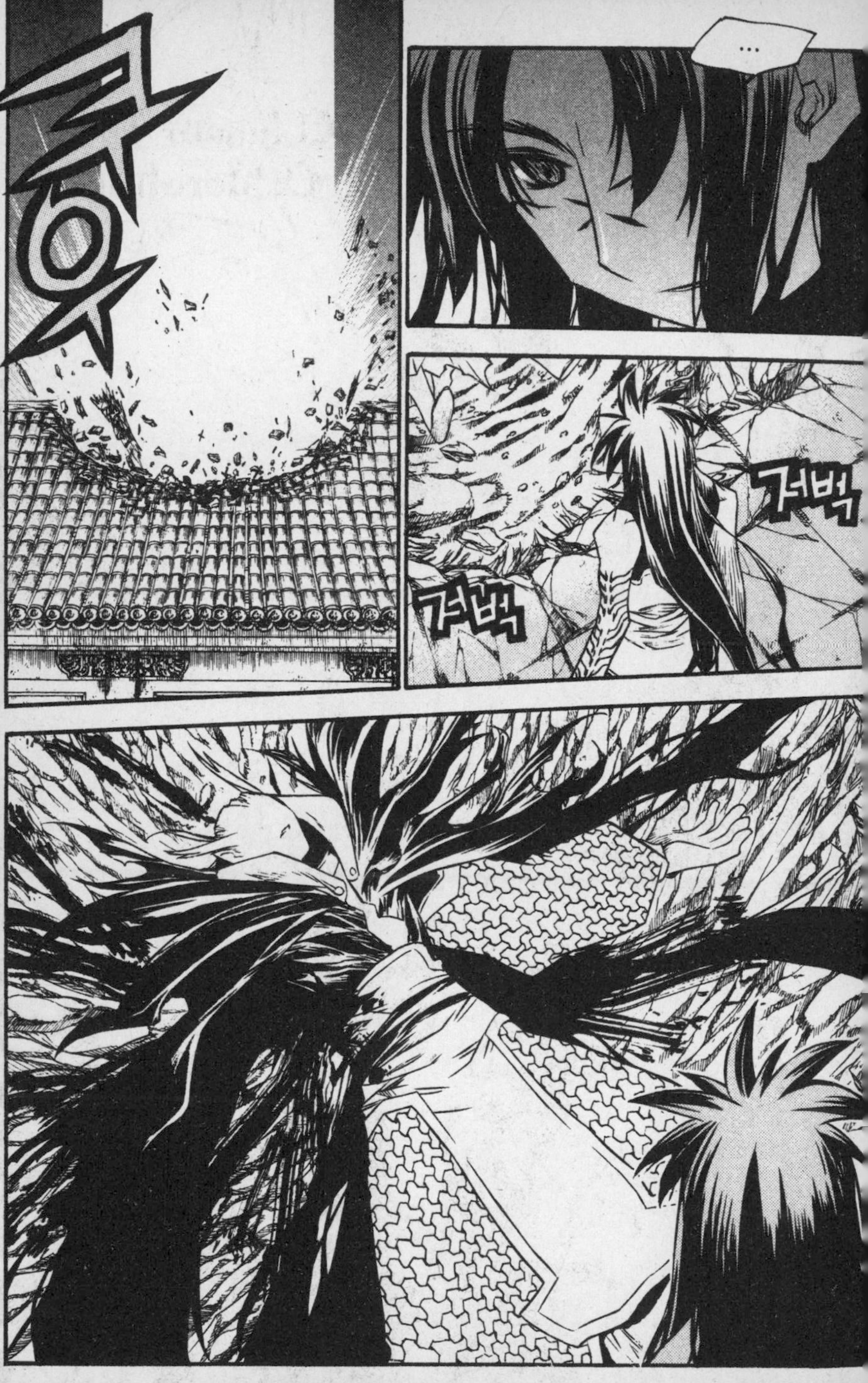
쿵
...
저벅
저벅

Chapter 57
Obliteration

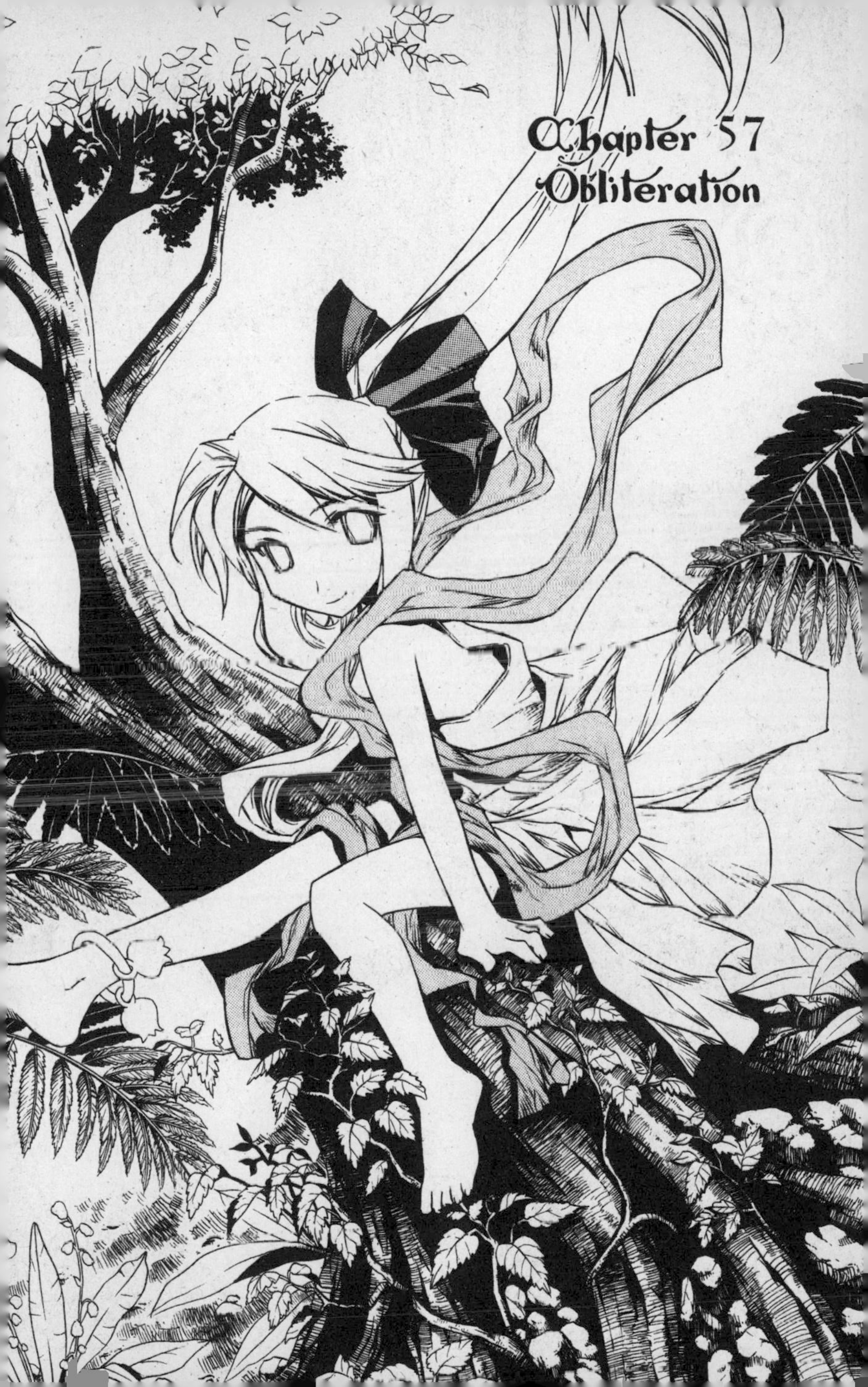

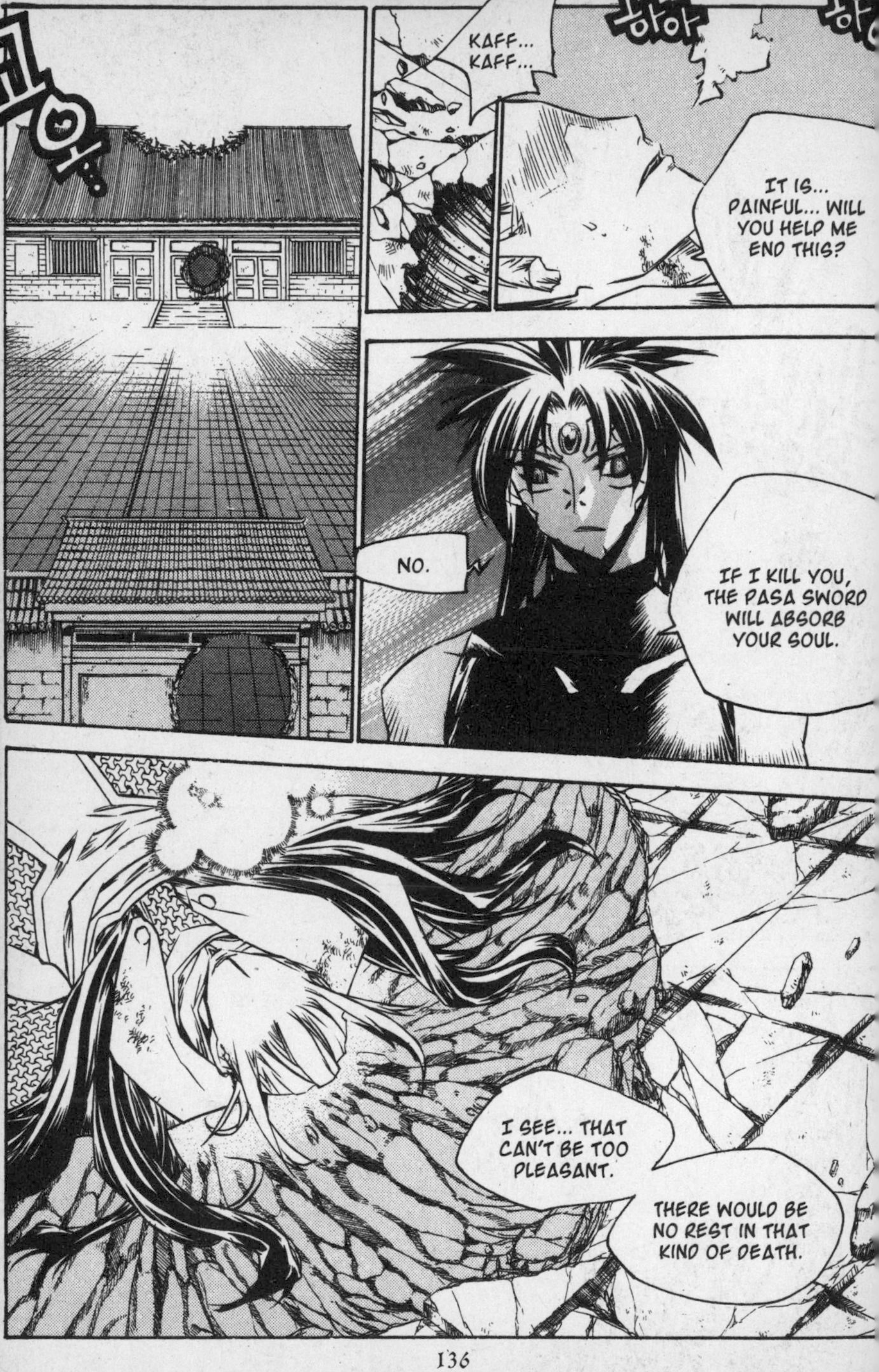
KAFF... KAFF...
IT IS... PAINFUL... WILL YOU HELP ME END THIS?
NO.
IF I KILL YOU, THE PASA SWORD WILL ABSORB YOUR SOUL.
I SEE... THAT CAN'T BE TOO PLEASANT.
THERE WOULD BE NO REST IN THAT KIND OF DEATH.

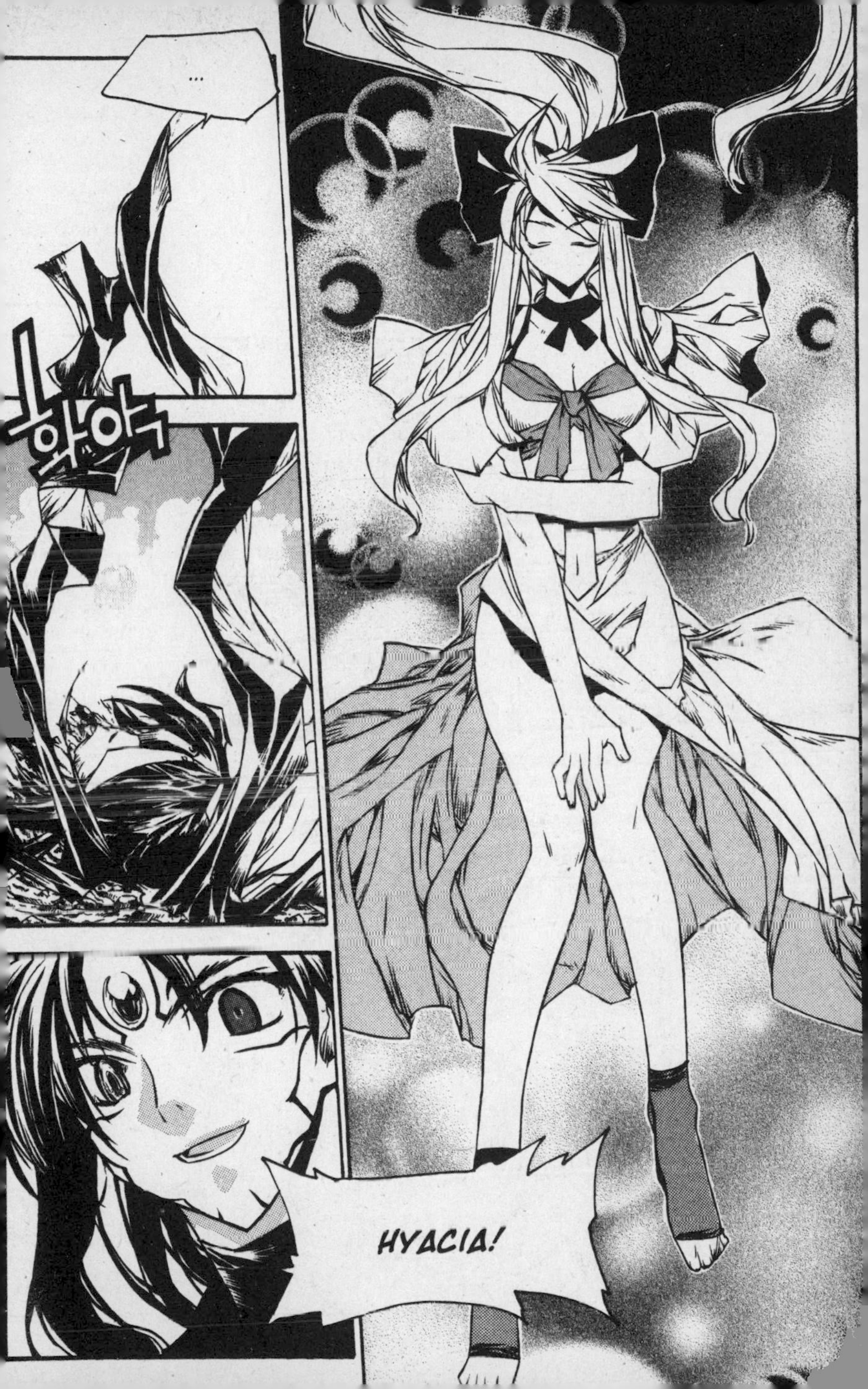
...
화악
HYACIA!

YES, IT'S ME. THANK YOU, REY.

HYACIA? NO...

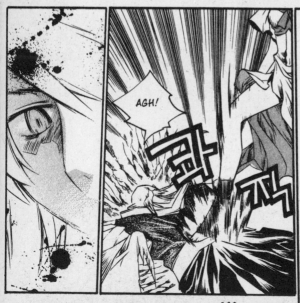

AGH!

POOR FOOL...

!!

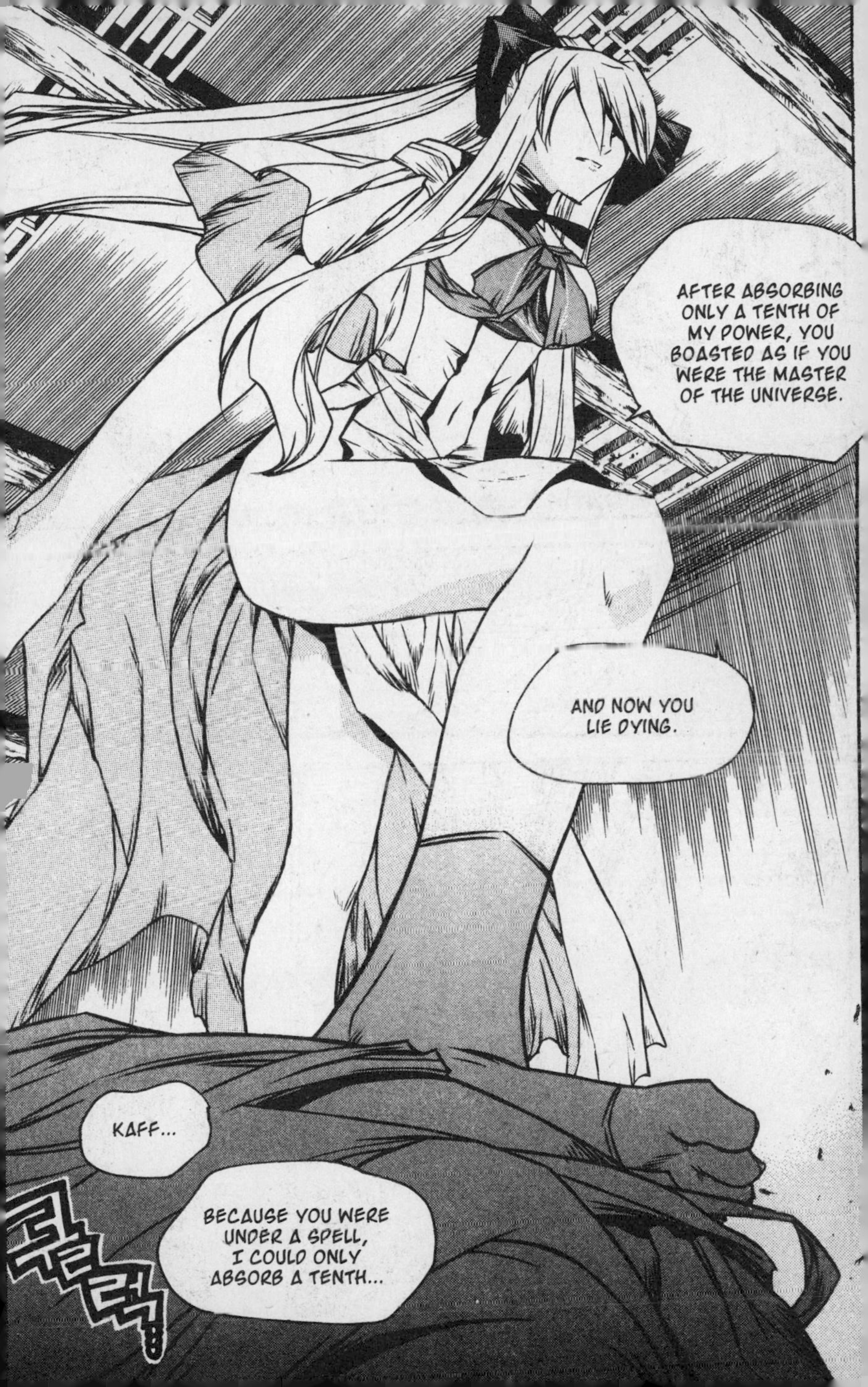
AFTER ABSORBING ONLY A TENTH OF MY POWER, YOU BOASTED AS IF YOU WERE THE MASTER OF THE UNIVERSE.
AND NOW YOU LIE DYING.
KAFF...
BECAUSE YOU WERE UNDER A SPELL, I COULD ONLY ABSORB A TENTH...

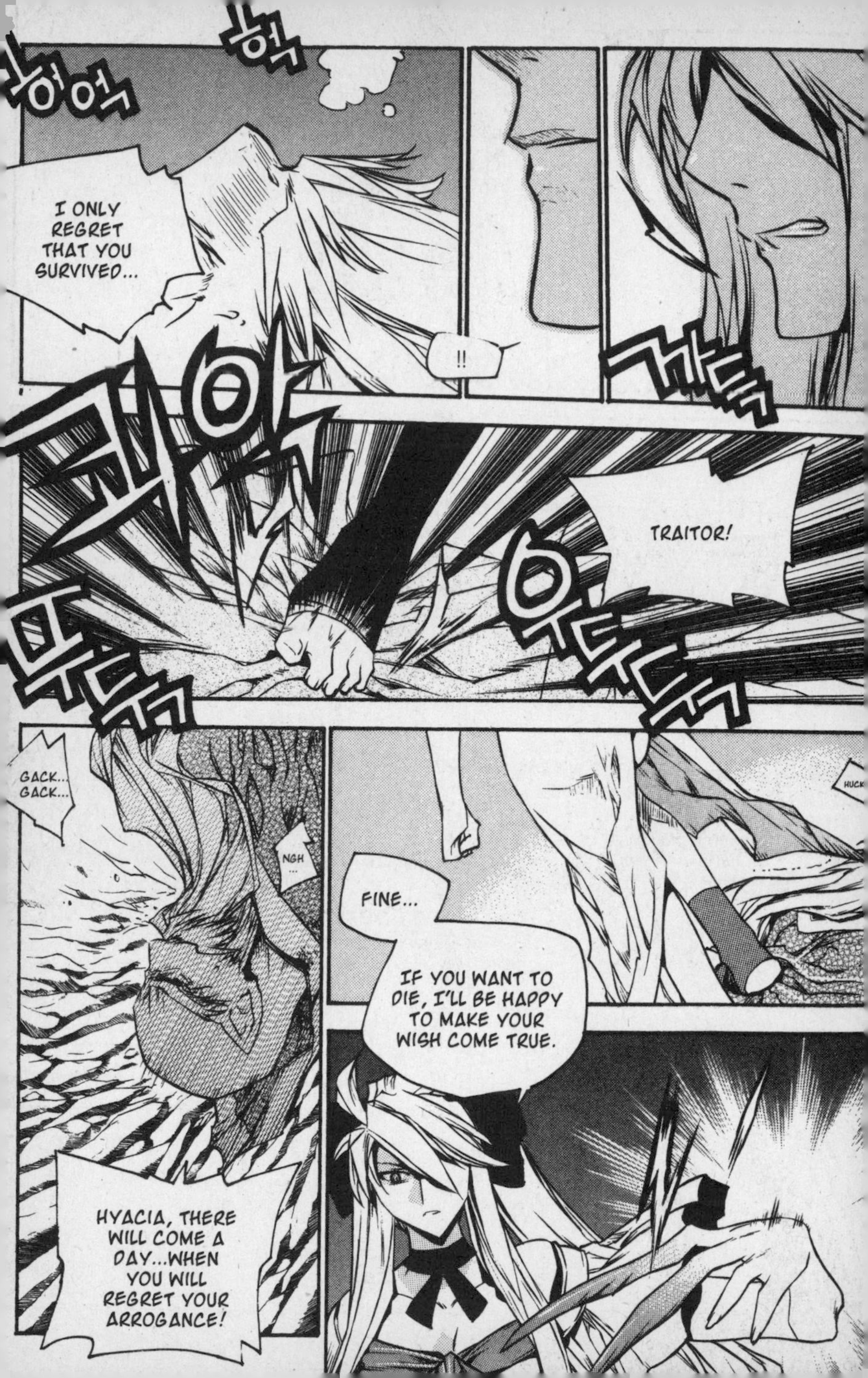
허억
헉
I ONLY REGRET THAT YOU SURVIVED...
!!
까득
콰앙
TRAITOR!
GACK... GACK...
NGH ...
HYACIA, THERE WILL COME A DAY...WHEN YOU WILL REGRET YOUR ARROGANCE!
HUCK
FINE...
IF YOU WANT TO DIE, I'LL BE HAPPY TO MAKE YOUR WISH COME TRUE.

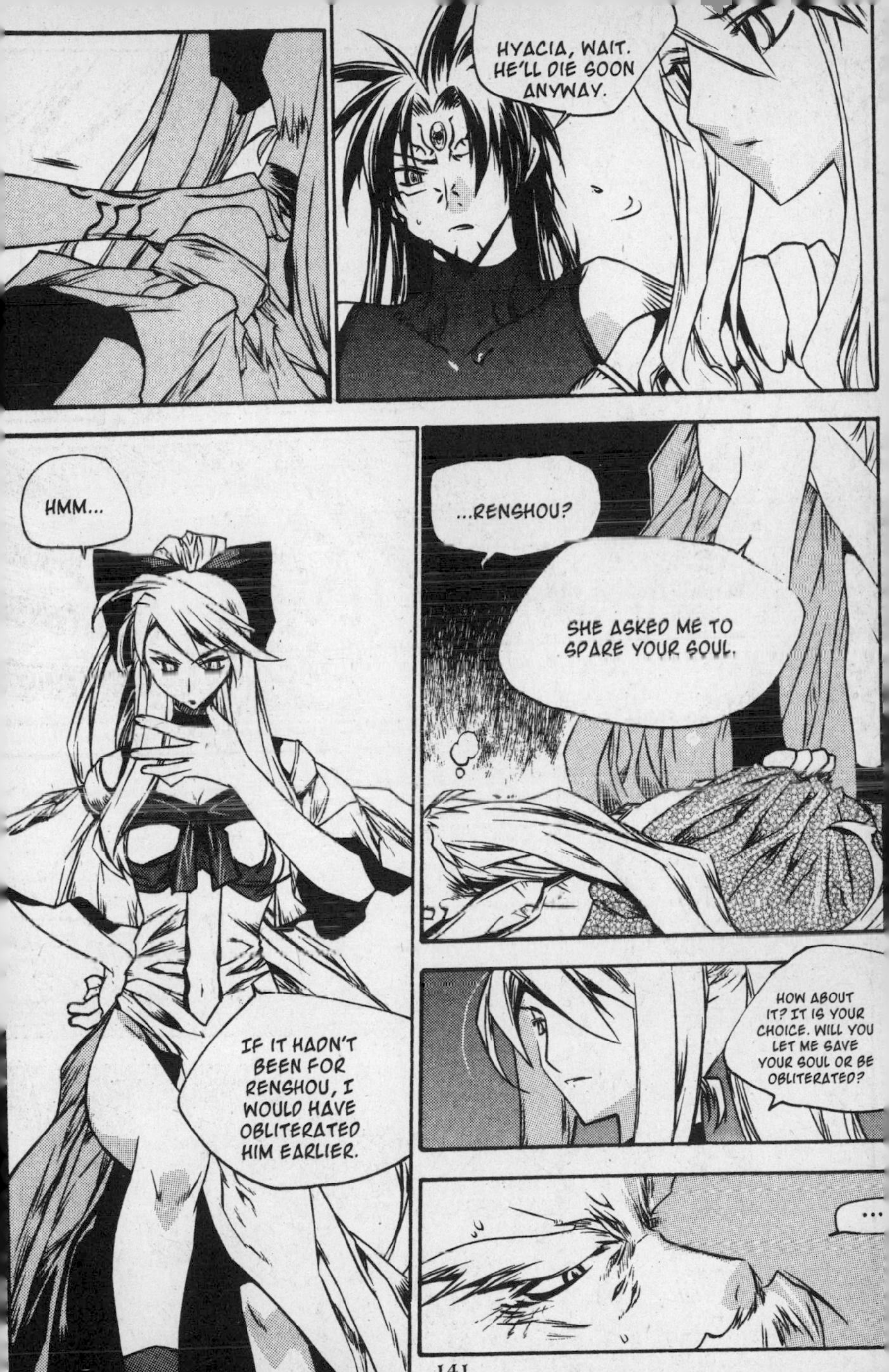
HYACIA, WAIT. HE'LL DIE SOON ANYWAY.
HMM...
IF IT HADN'T BEEN FOR RENSHOU, I WOULD HAVE OBLITERATED HIM EARLIER.
...RENSHOU?
SHE ASKED ME TO SPARE YOUR SOUL.
HOW ABOUT IT? IT IS YOUR CHOICE. WILL YOU LET ME SAVE YOUR SOUL OR BE OBLITERATED?
...

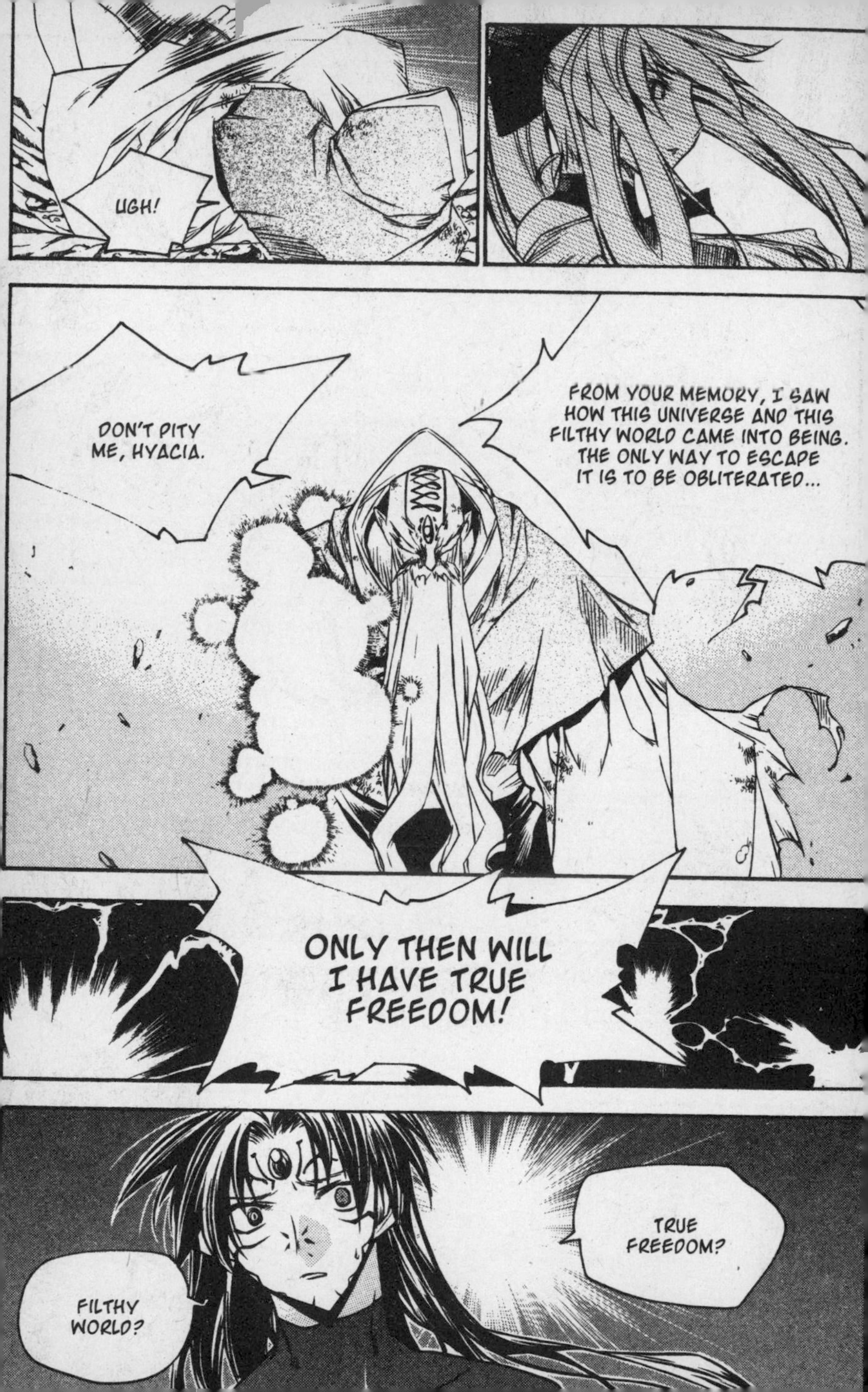
UGH!
DON'T PITY ME, HYACIA.
FROM YOUR MEMORY, I SAW HOW THIS UNIVERSE AND THIS FILTHY WORLD CAME INTO BEING. THE ONLY WAY TO ESCAPE IT IS TO BE OBLITERATED...
ONLY THEN WILL I HAVE TRUE FREEDOM!
FILTHY WORLD?
TRUE FREEDOM?

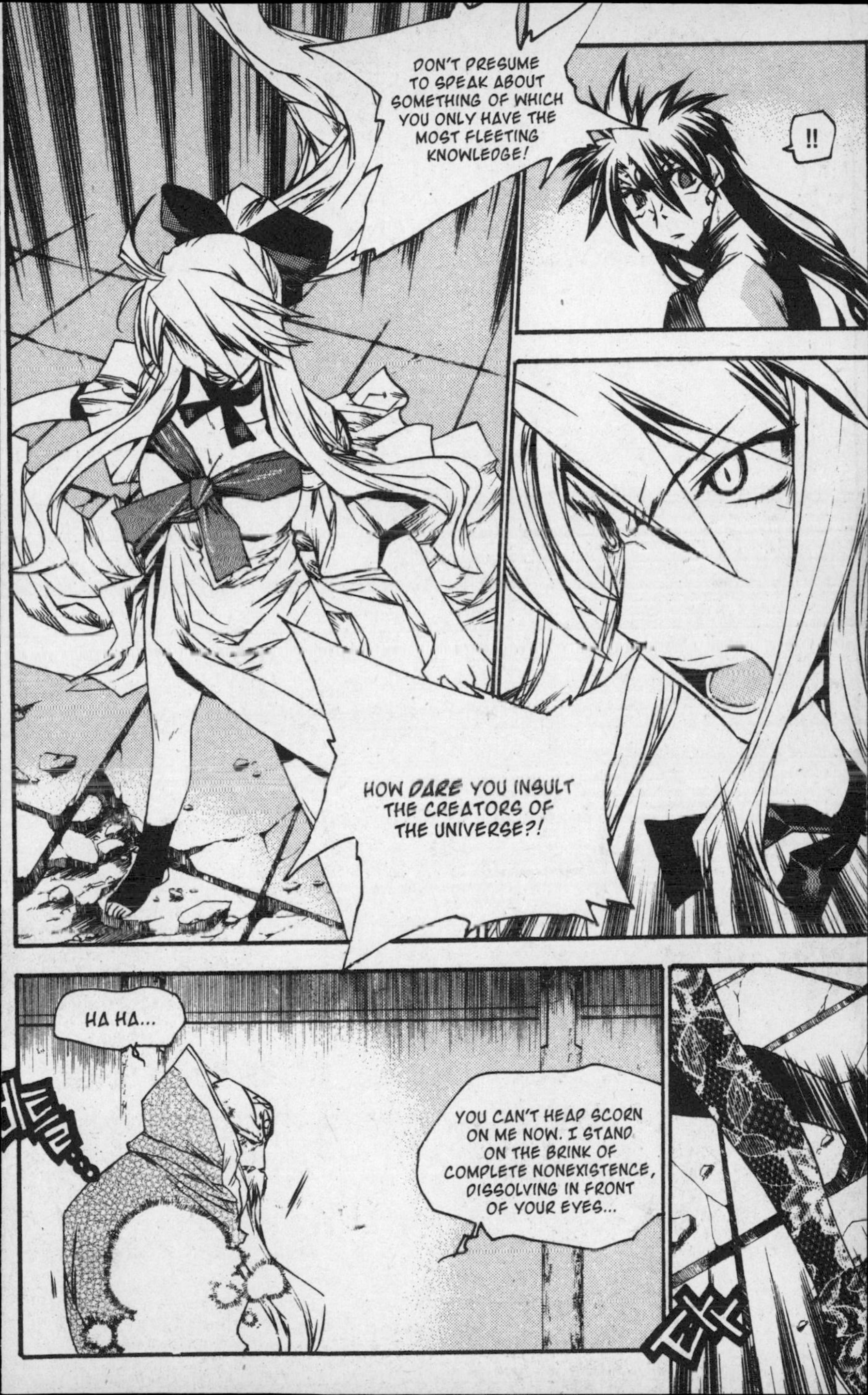
DON'T PRESUME TO SPEAK ABOUT SOMETHING OF WHICH YOU ONLY HAVE THE MOST FLEETING KNOWLEDGE!
!!
HOW DARE YOU INSULT THE CREATORS OF THE UNIVERSE?!
HA HA...
YOU CAN'T HEAP SCORN ON ME NOW. I STAND ON THE BRINK OF COMPLETE NONEXISTENCE, DISSOLVING IN FRONT OF YOUR EYES...

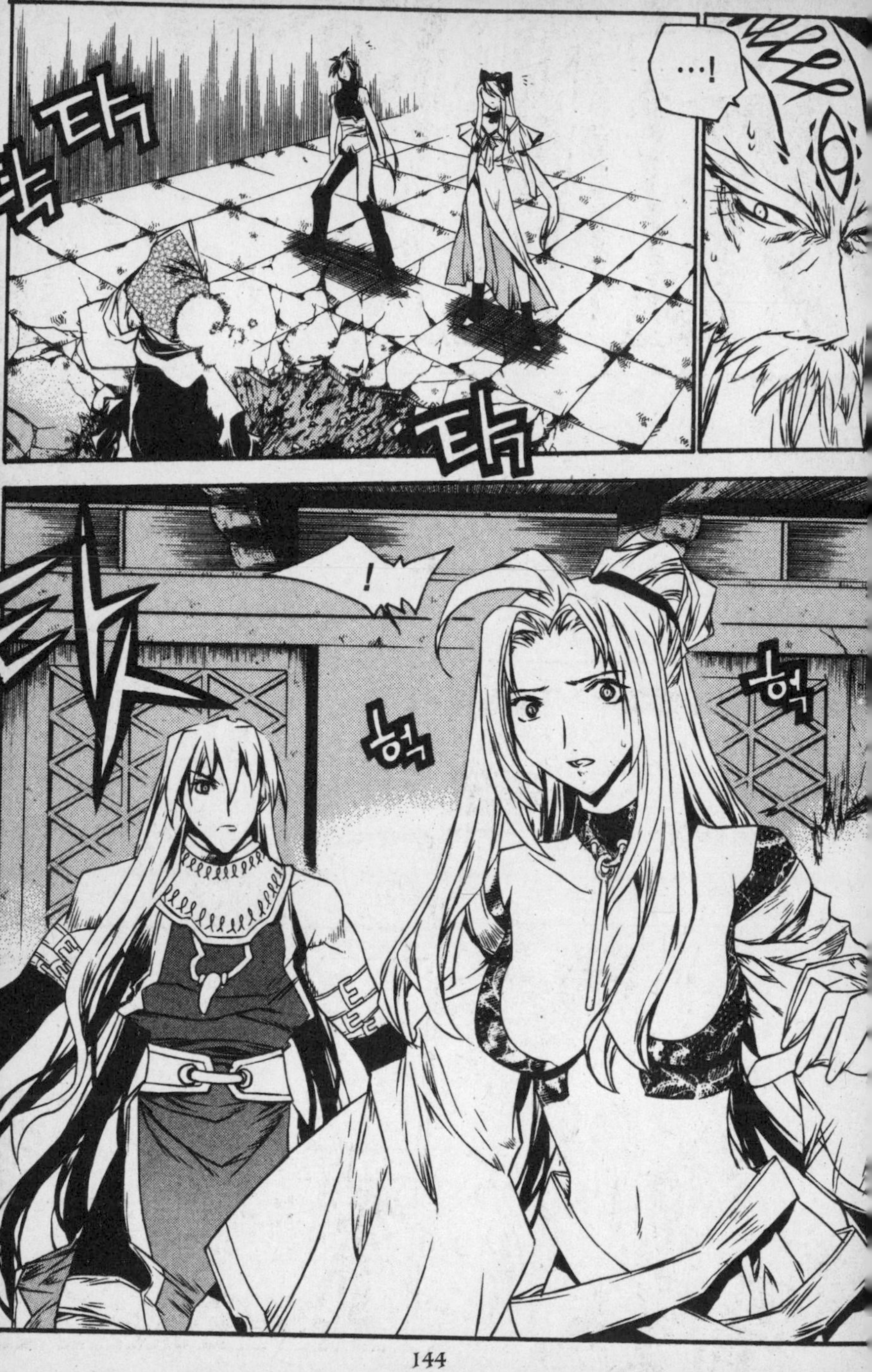
탁
탁
...!
탁
!
헉
헉

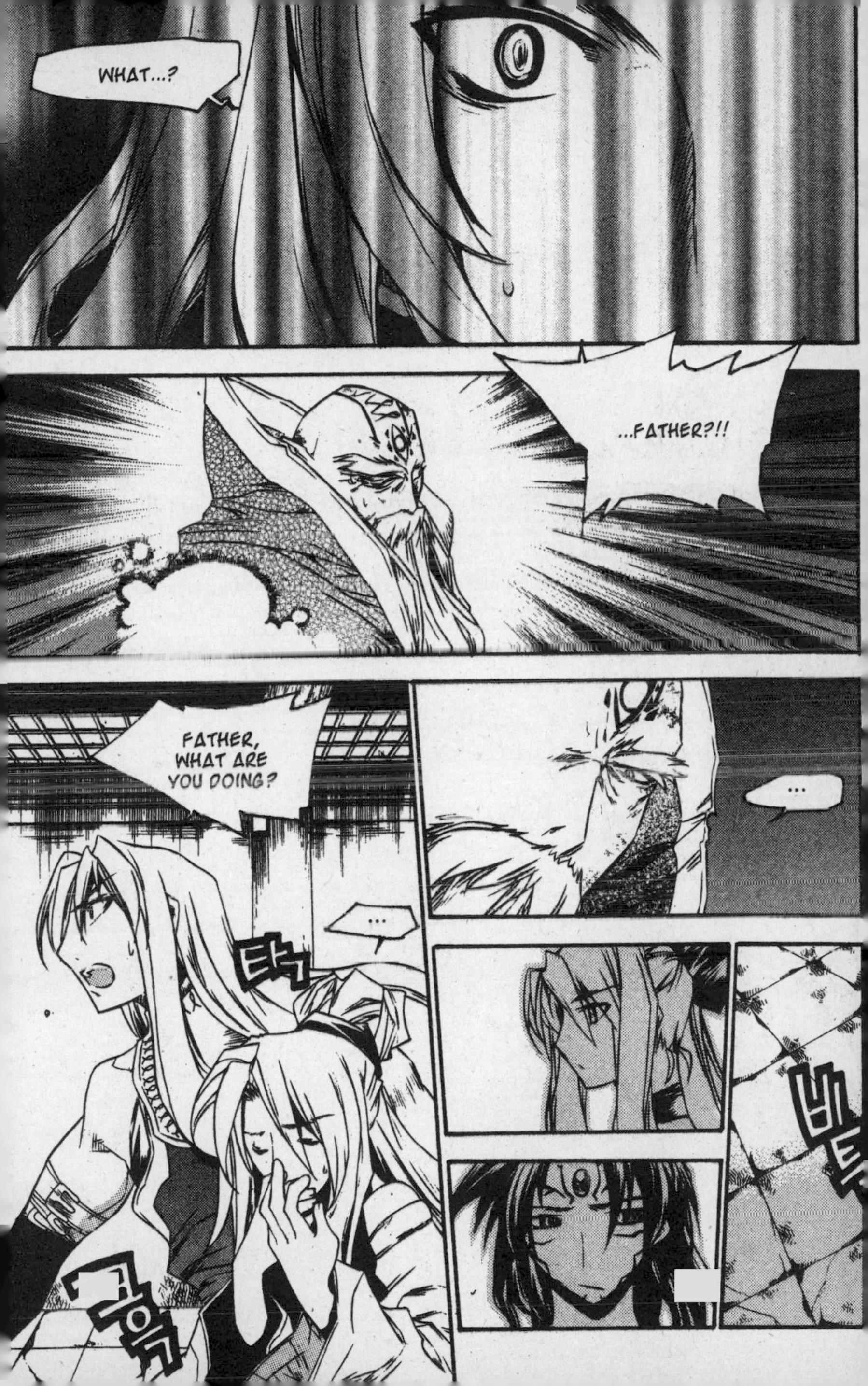
WHAT...?
...FATHER?!!
FATHER, WHAT ARE YOU DOING?
...
...

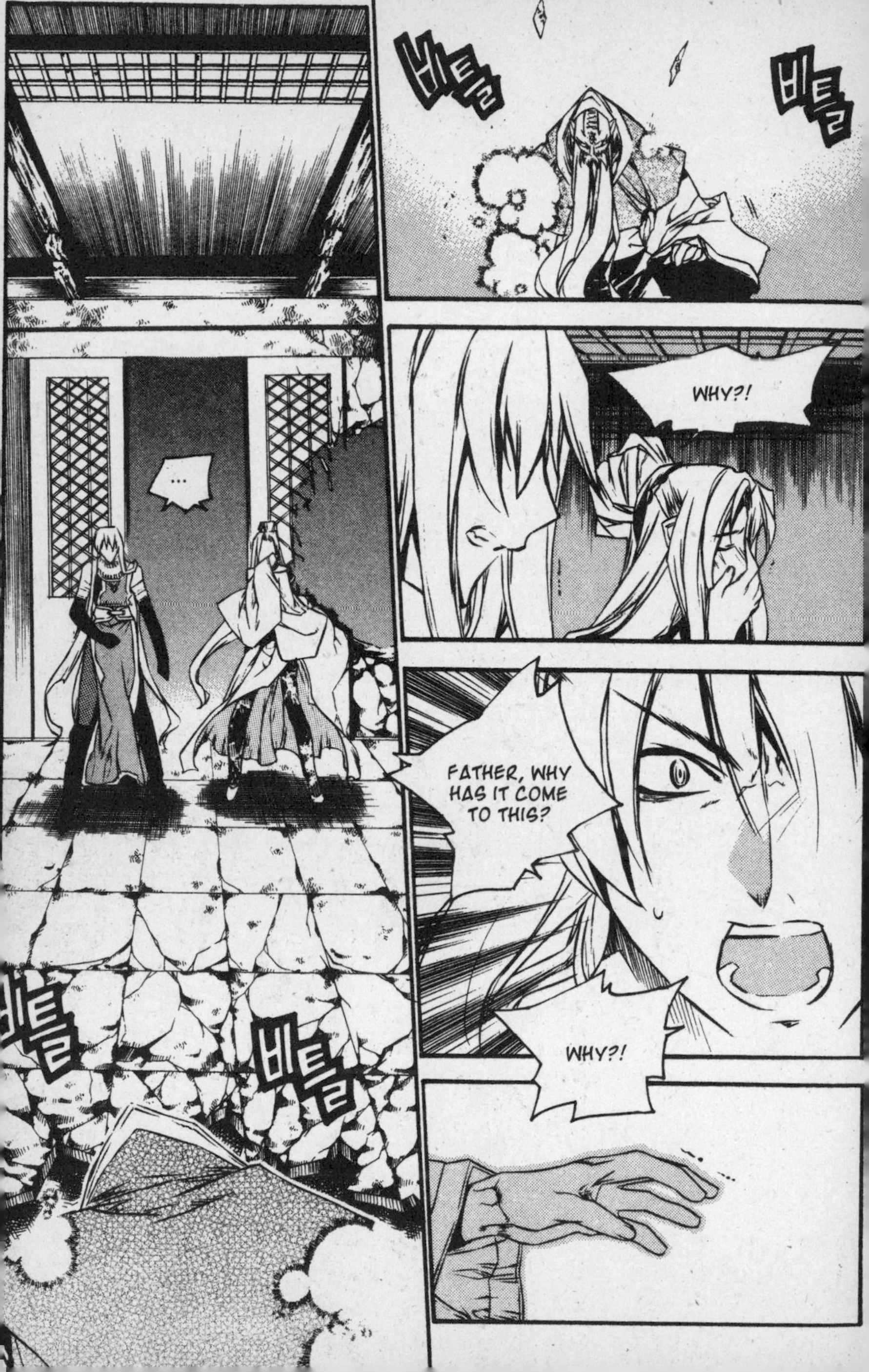
...
비틀
비틀
비틀
비틀
WHY?!
FATHER, WHY HAS IT COME TO THIS?
WHY?!

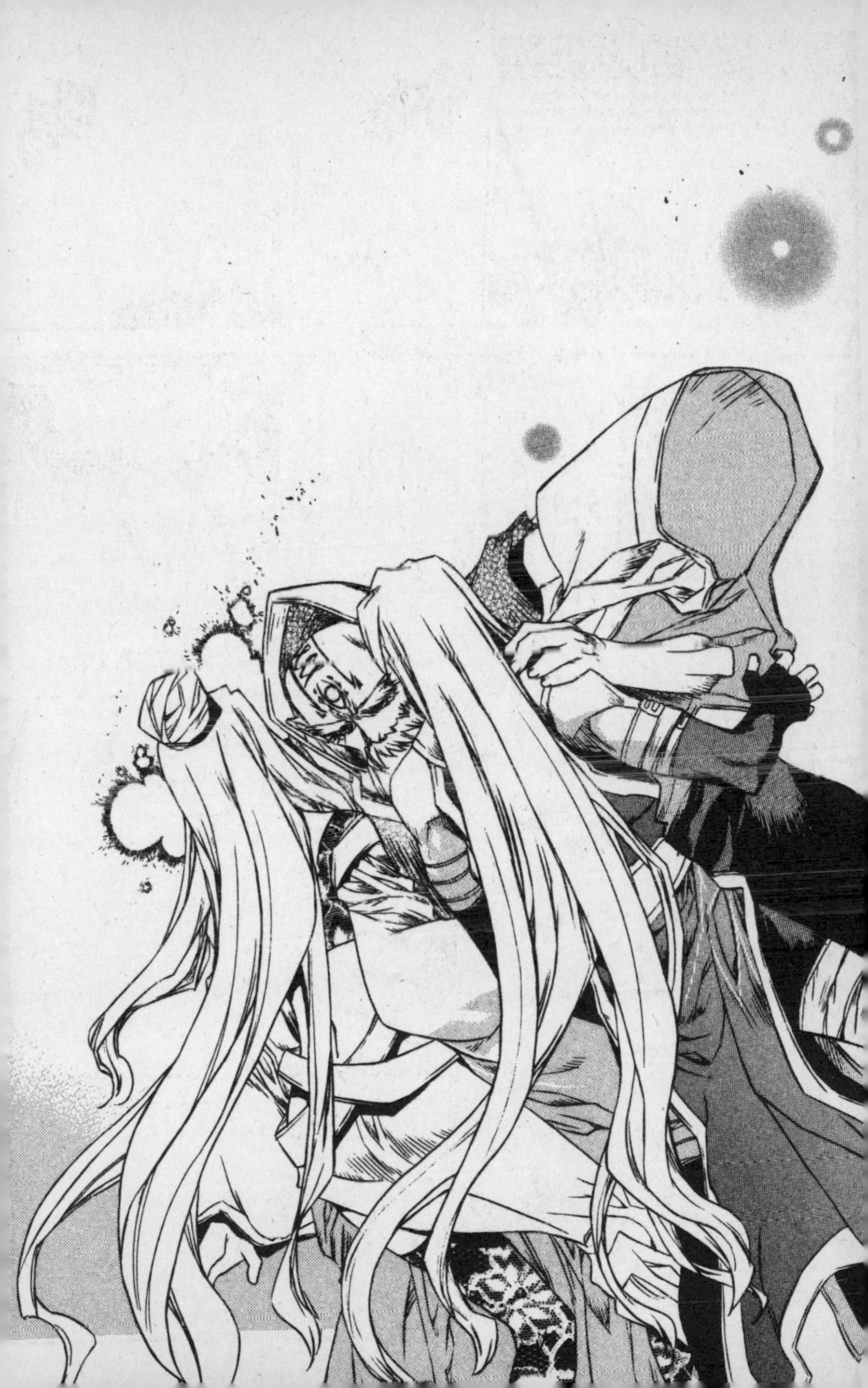

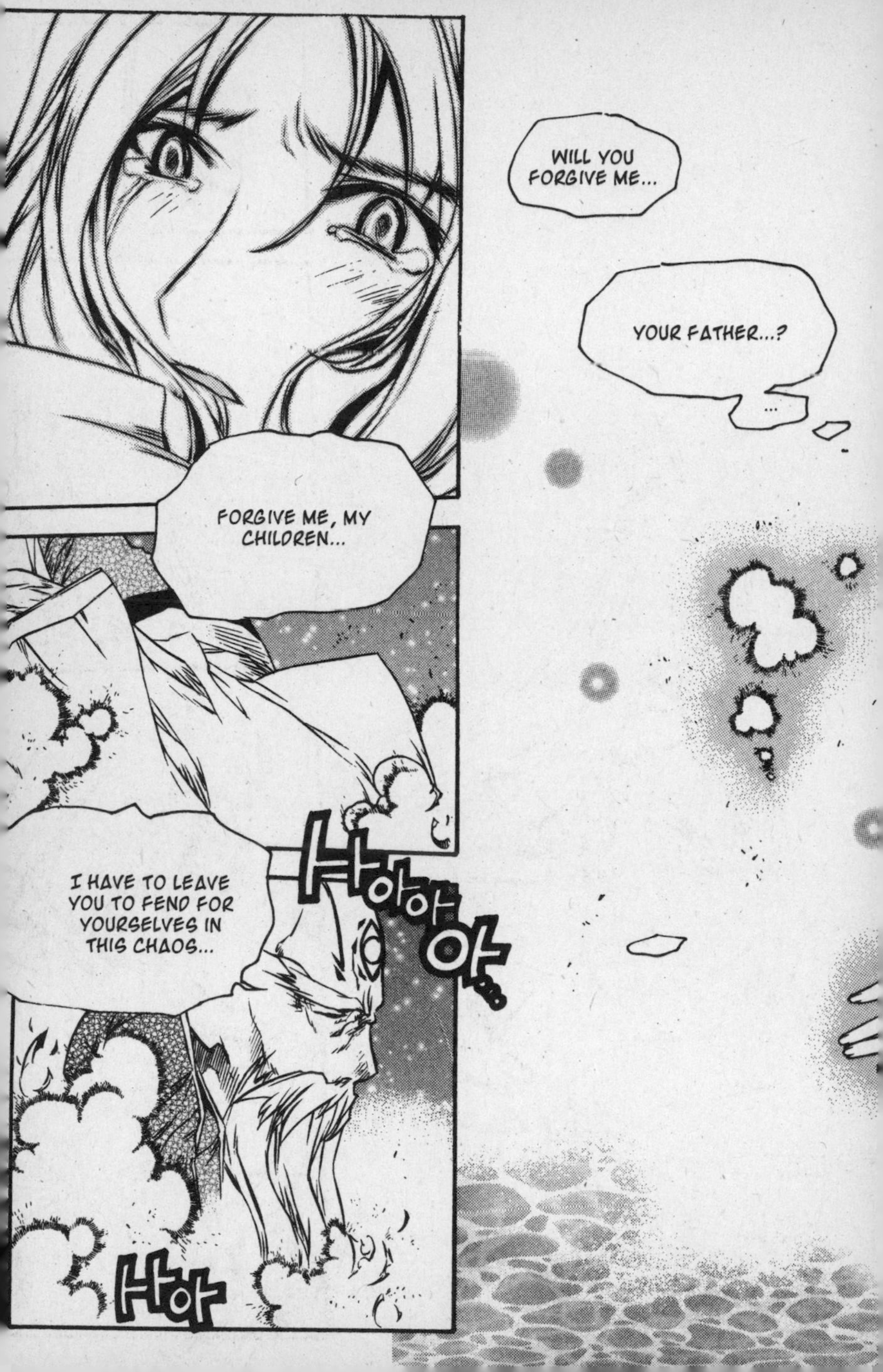
FORGIVE ME, MY CHILDREN...
I HAVE TO LEAVE YOU TO FEND FOR YOURSELVES IN THIS CHAOS...
WILL YOU FORGIVE ME...
YOUR FATHER...?
...

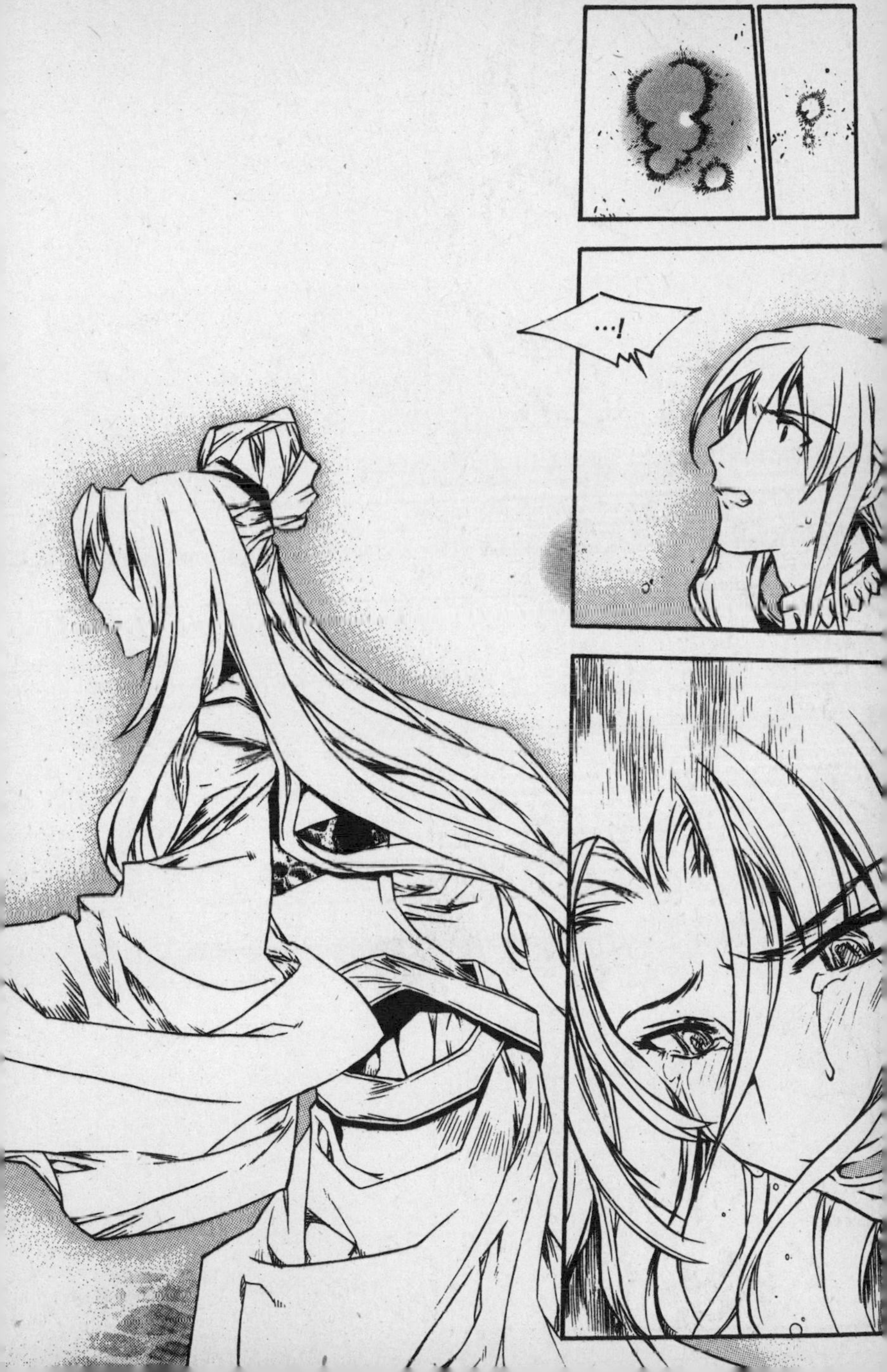

...!

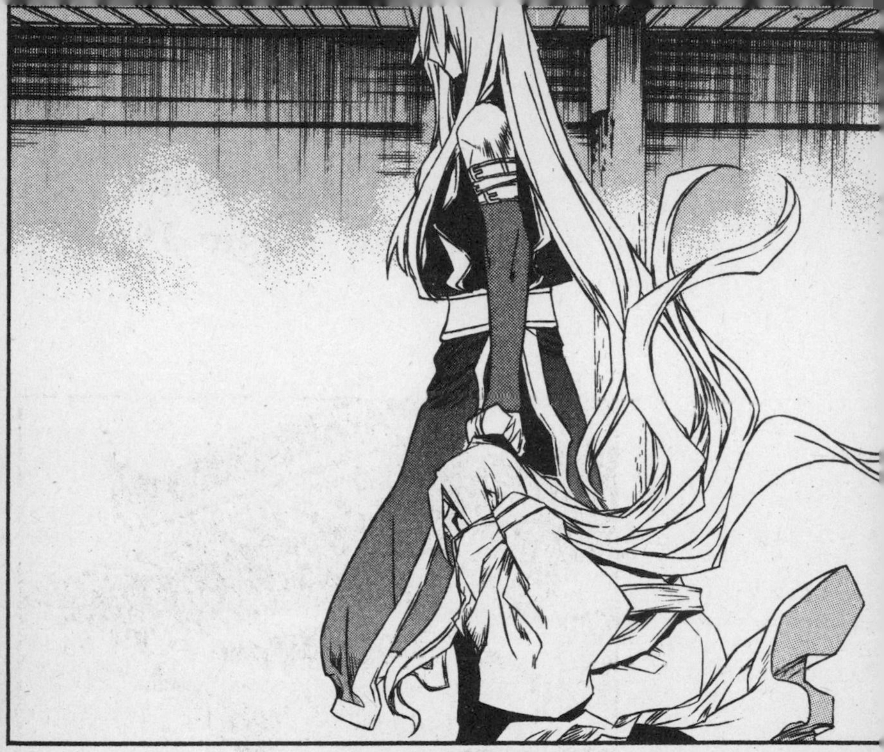

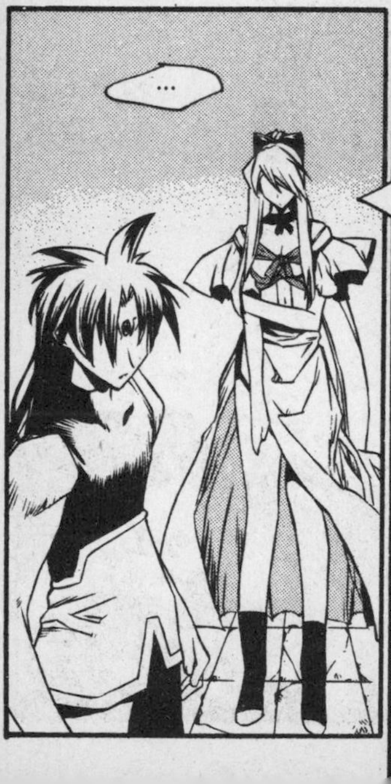
...

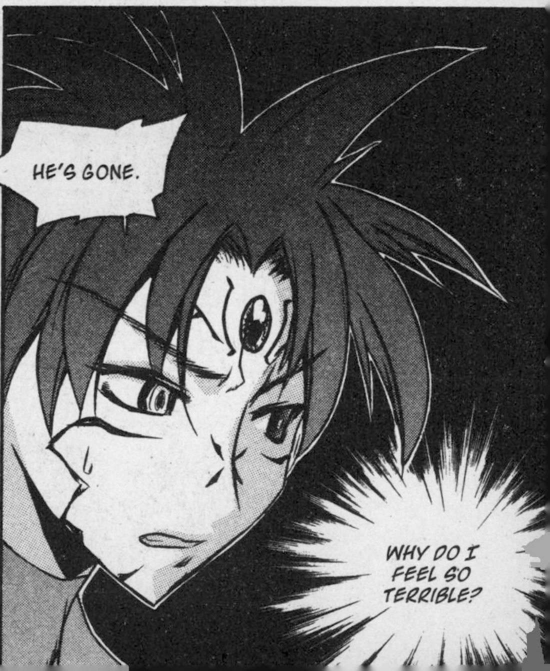
HE'S GONE.
WHY DO I FEEL SO TERRIBLE?

Chapter 58
The Return

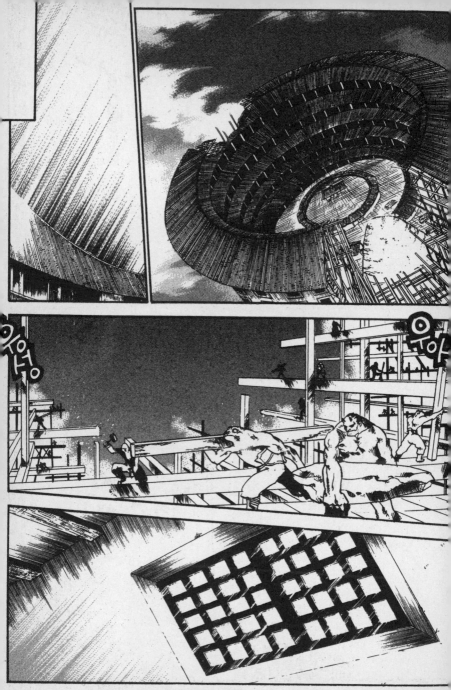

152

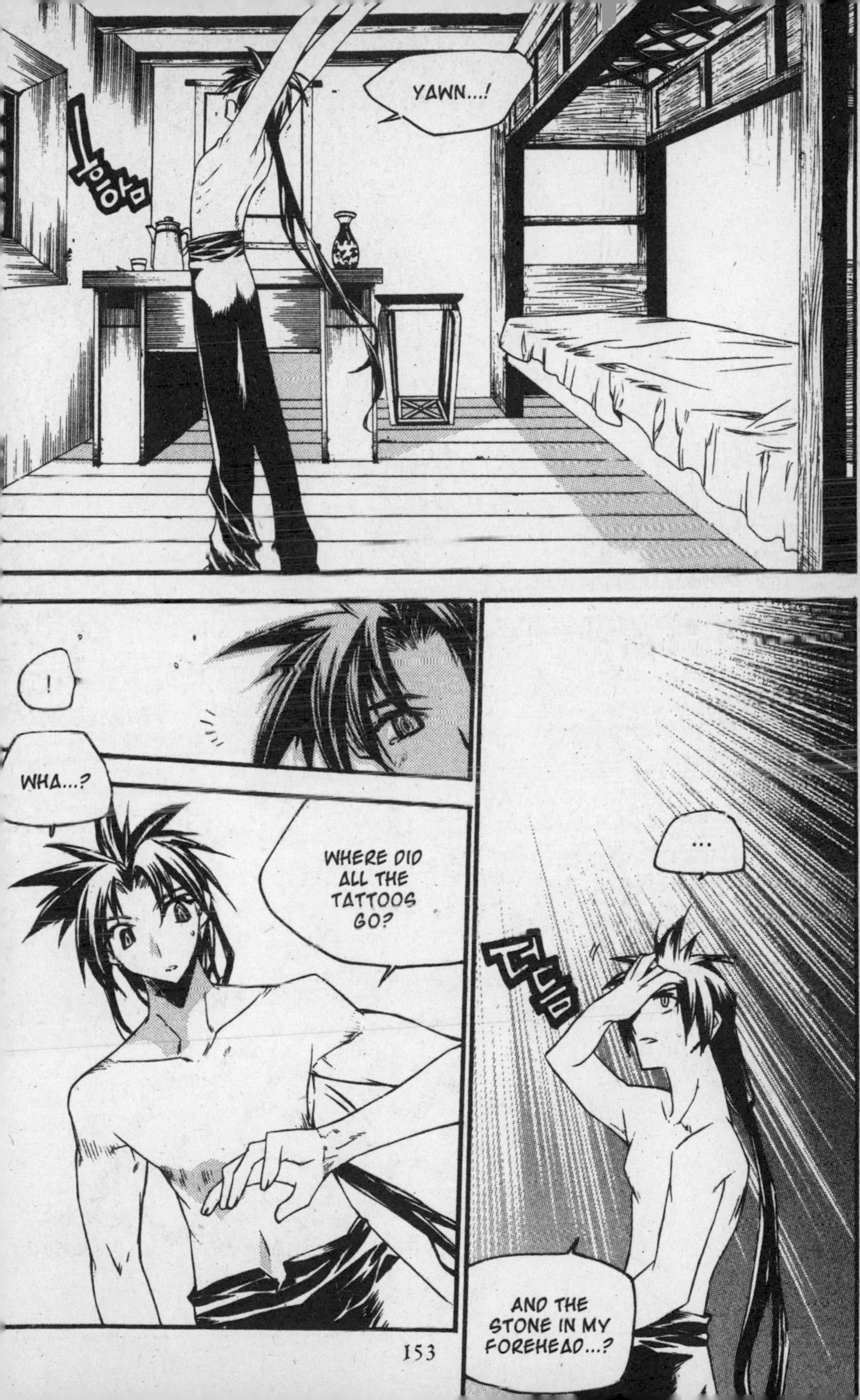
YAWN...!
!
WHA...?
WHERE DID ALL THE TATTOOS GO?
...
AND THE STONE IN MY FOREHEAD...?

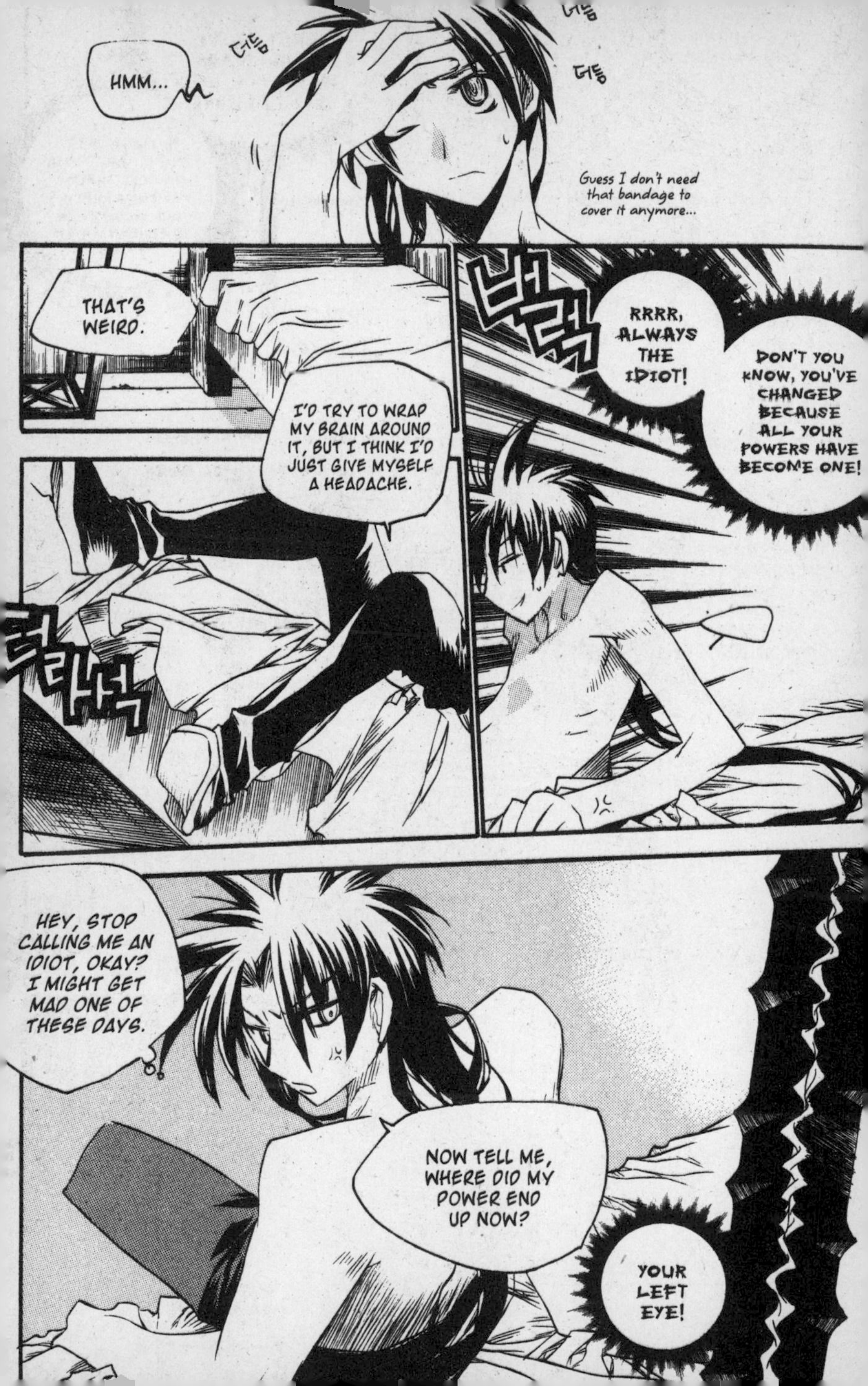
HMM...
Guess I don't need that bandage to cover it anymore...
THAT'S WEIRD.
I'D TRY TO WRAP MY BRAIN AROUND IT, BUT I THINK I'D JUST GIVE MYSELF A HEADACHE.
RRRR, ALWAYS THE IDIOT!
DON'T YOU KNOW, YOU'VE CHANGED BECAUSE ALL YOUR POWERS HAVE BECOME ONE!
HEY, STOP CALLING ME AN IDIOT, OKAY? I MIGHT GET MAD ONE OF THESE DAYS.
NOW TELL ME, WHERE DID MY POWER END UP NOW?
YOUR LEFT EYE!

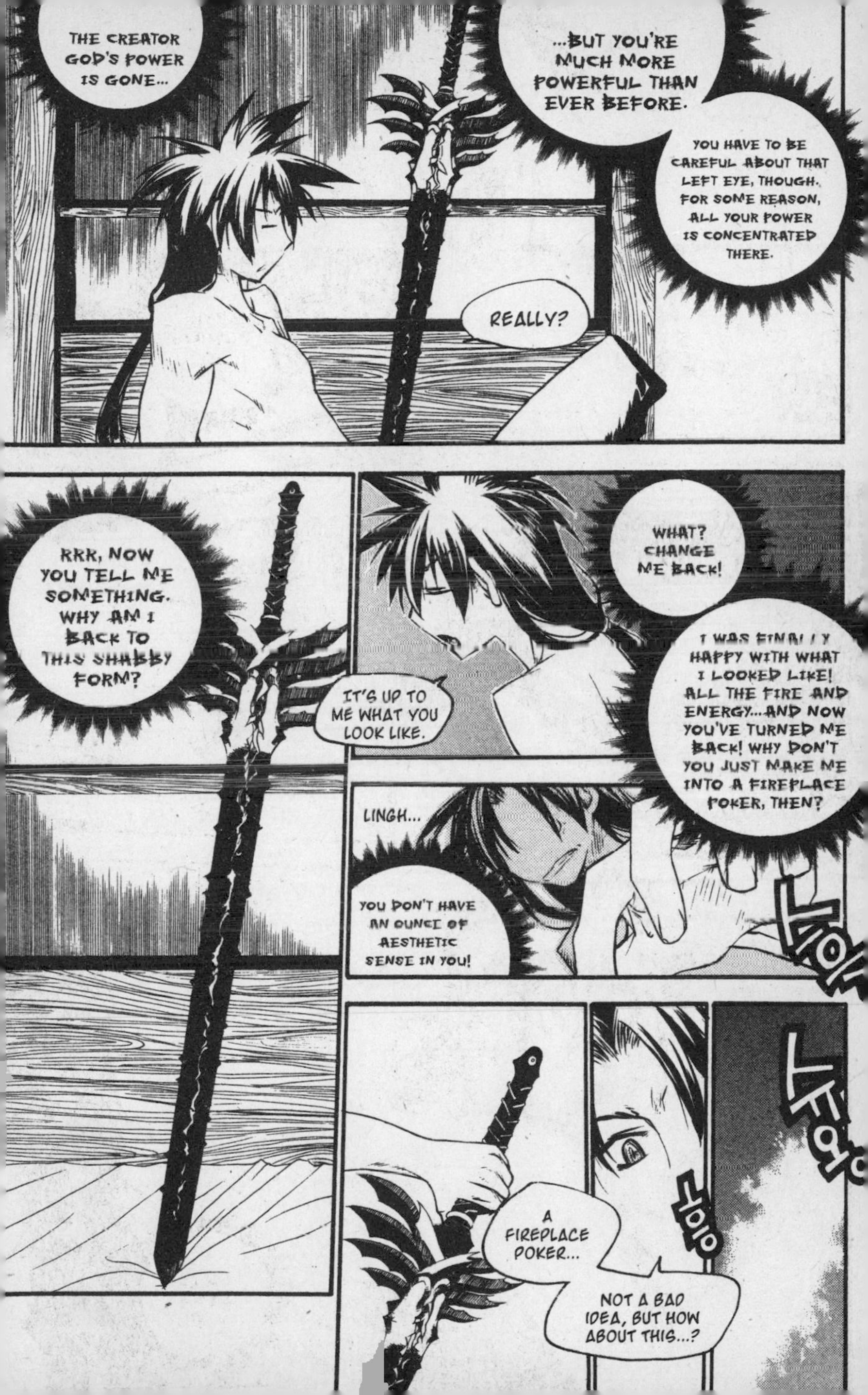
THE CREATOR GOD'S POWER IS GONE...
...BUT YOU'RE MUCH MORE POWERFUL THAN EVER BEFORE.
YOU HAVE TO BE CAREFUL ABOUT THAT LEFT EYE, THOUGH. FOR SOME REASON, ALL YOUR POWER IS CONCENTRATED THERE.
REALLY?
RRR, NOW YOU TELL ME SOMETHING. WHY AM I BACK TO THIS SHABBY FORM?
IT'S UP TO ME WHAT YOU LOOK LIKE.
WHAT? CHANGE ME BACK!
I WAS FINALLY HAPPY WITH WHAT I LOOKED LIKE! ALL THE FIRE AND ENERGY...AND NOW YOU'VE TURNED ME BACK! WHY DON'T YOU JUST MAKE ME INTO A FIREPLACE POKER, THEN?
LINGH...
YOU DON'T HAVE AN OUNCE OF AESTHETIC SENSE IN YOU!
A FIREPLACE POKER...
NOT A BAD IDEA, BUT HOW ABOUT THIS...?

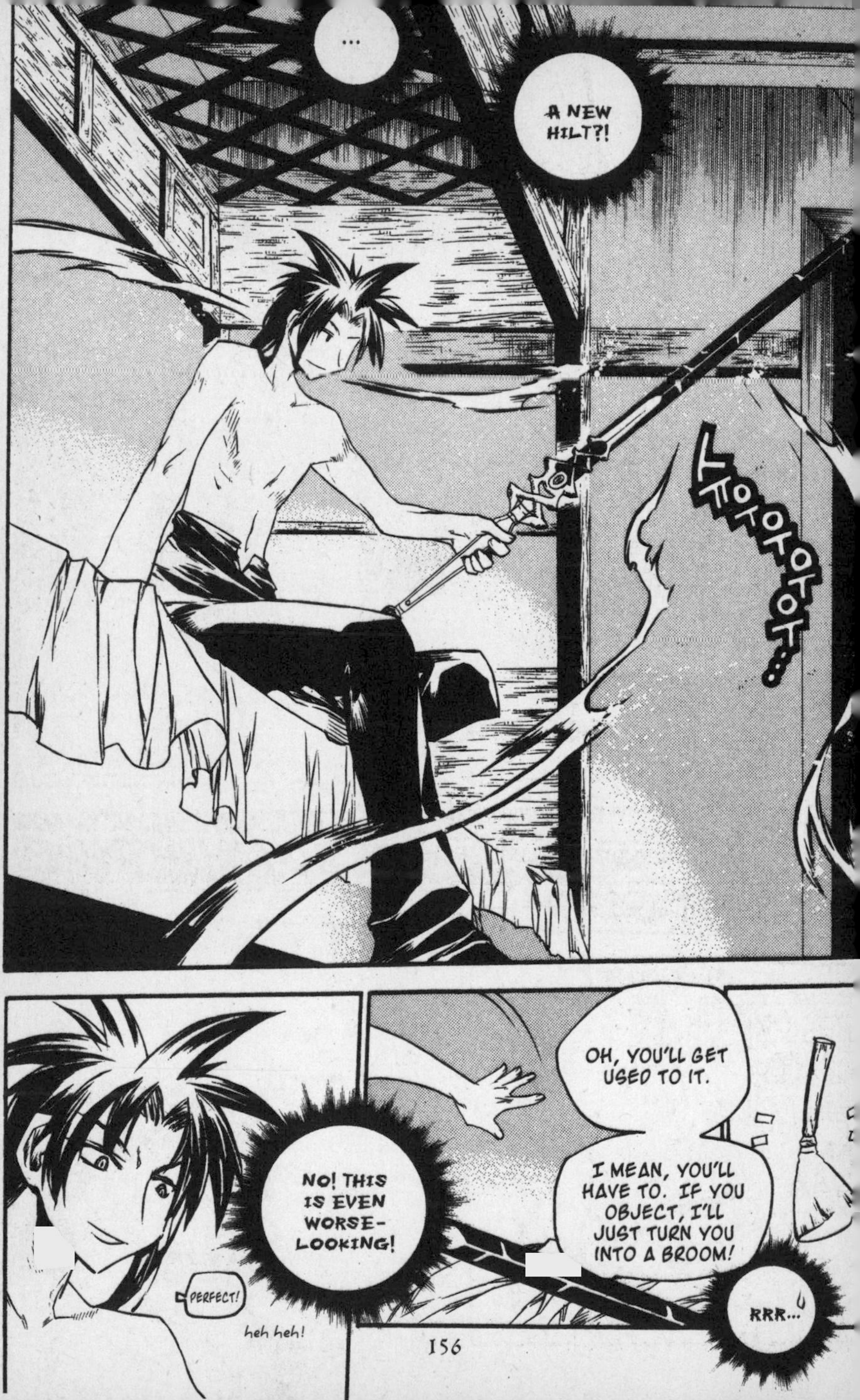
...
A NEW HILT?!
TOTOTOTOT..
NO! THIS IS EVEN WORSE-LOOKING!
PERFECT!
heh heh!
OH, YOU'LL GET USED TO IT.
I MEAN, YOU'LL HAVE TO. IF YOU OBJECT, I'LL JUST TURN YOU INTO A BROOM!
RRR...

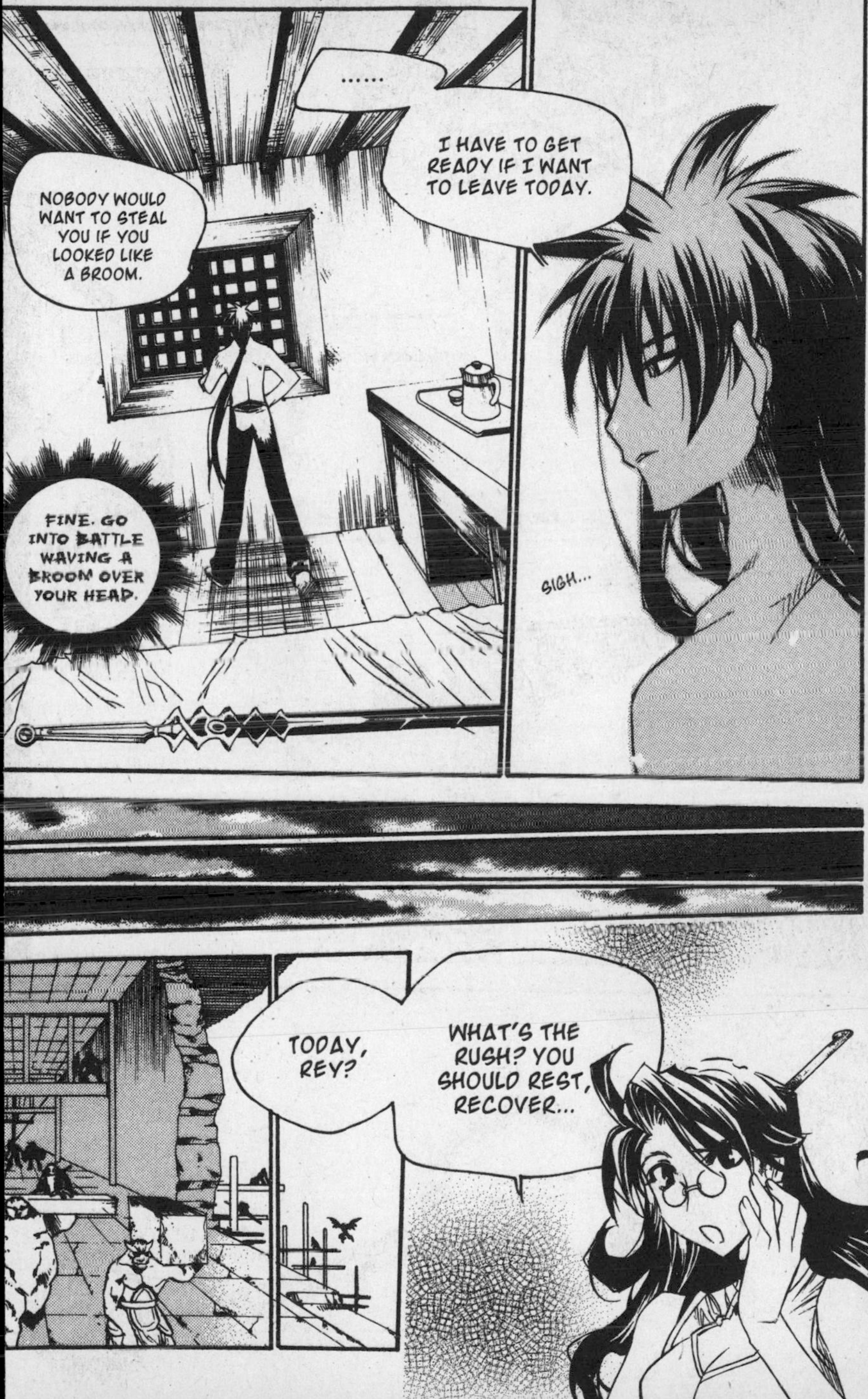
......
NOBODY WOULD WANT TO STEAL YOU IF YOU LOOKED LIKE A BROOM.
FINE. GO INTO BATTLE WAVING A BROOM OVER YOUR HEAD.
I HAVE TO GET READY IF I WANT TO LEAVE TODAY.
SIGH...
TODAY, REY?
WHAT'S THE RUSH? YOU SHOULD REST, RECOVER...

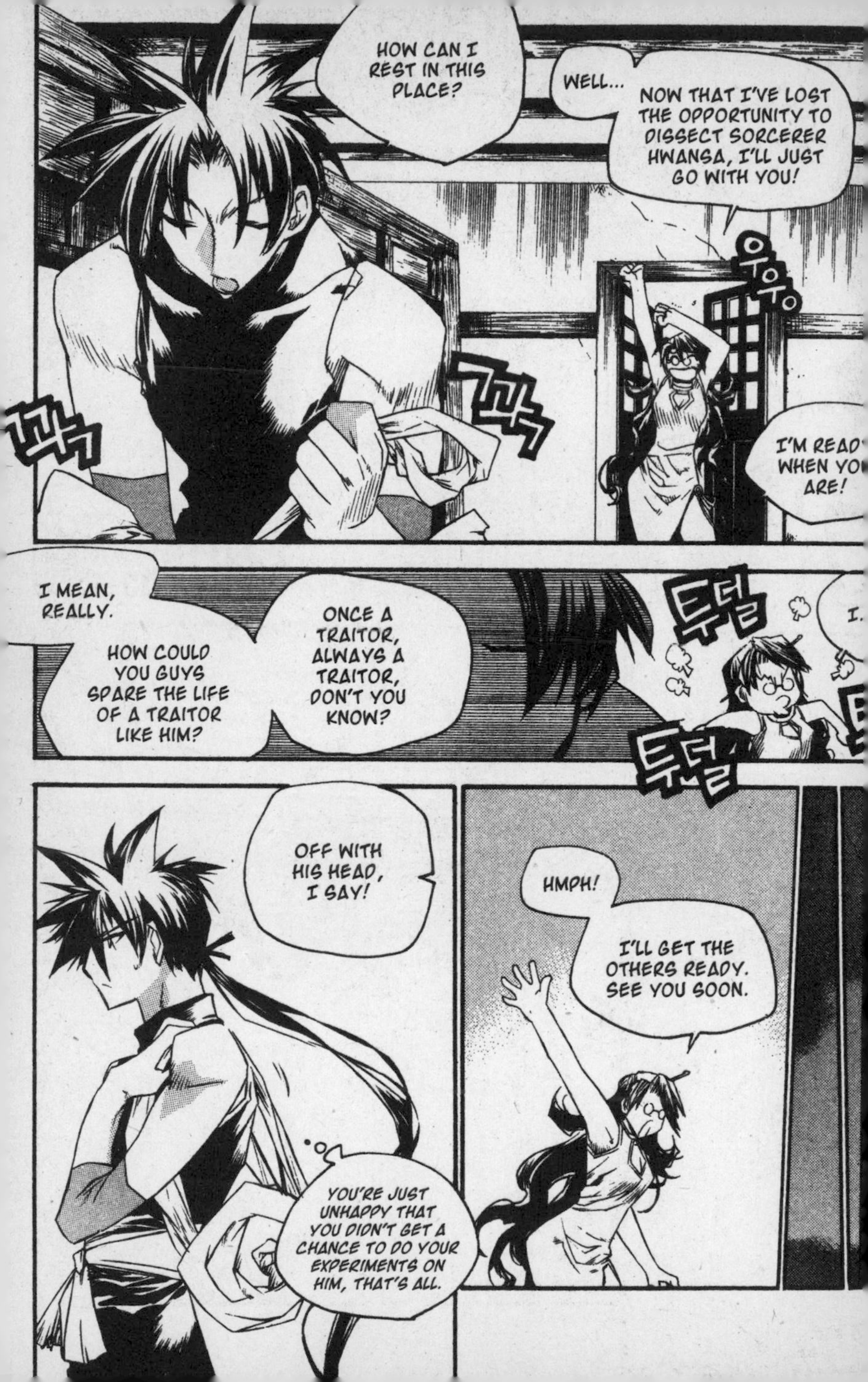
HOW CAN I REST IN THIS PLACE?
꽉
꽉
WELL...
NOW THAT I'VE LOST THE OPPORTUNITY TO DISSECT SORCERER HWANSA, I'LL JUST GO WITH YOU!
I'M READ WHEN YO ARE!
I MEAN, REALLY.
HOW COULD YOU GUYS SPARE THE LIFE OF A TRAITOR LIKE HIM?
ONCE A TRAITOR, ALWAYS A TRAITOR, DON'T YOU KNOW?
투덜
I.
투덜
OFF WITH HIS HEAD, I SAY!
YOU'RE JUST UNHAPPY THAT YOU DIDN'T GET A CHANCE TO DO YOUR EXPERIMENTS ON HIM, THAT'S ALL.
HMPH!
I'LL GET THE OTHERS READY. SEE YOU SOON.

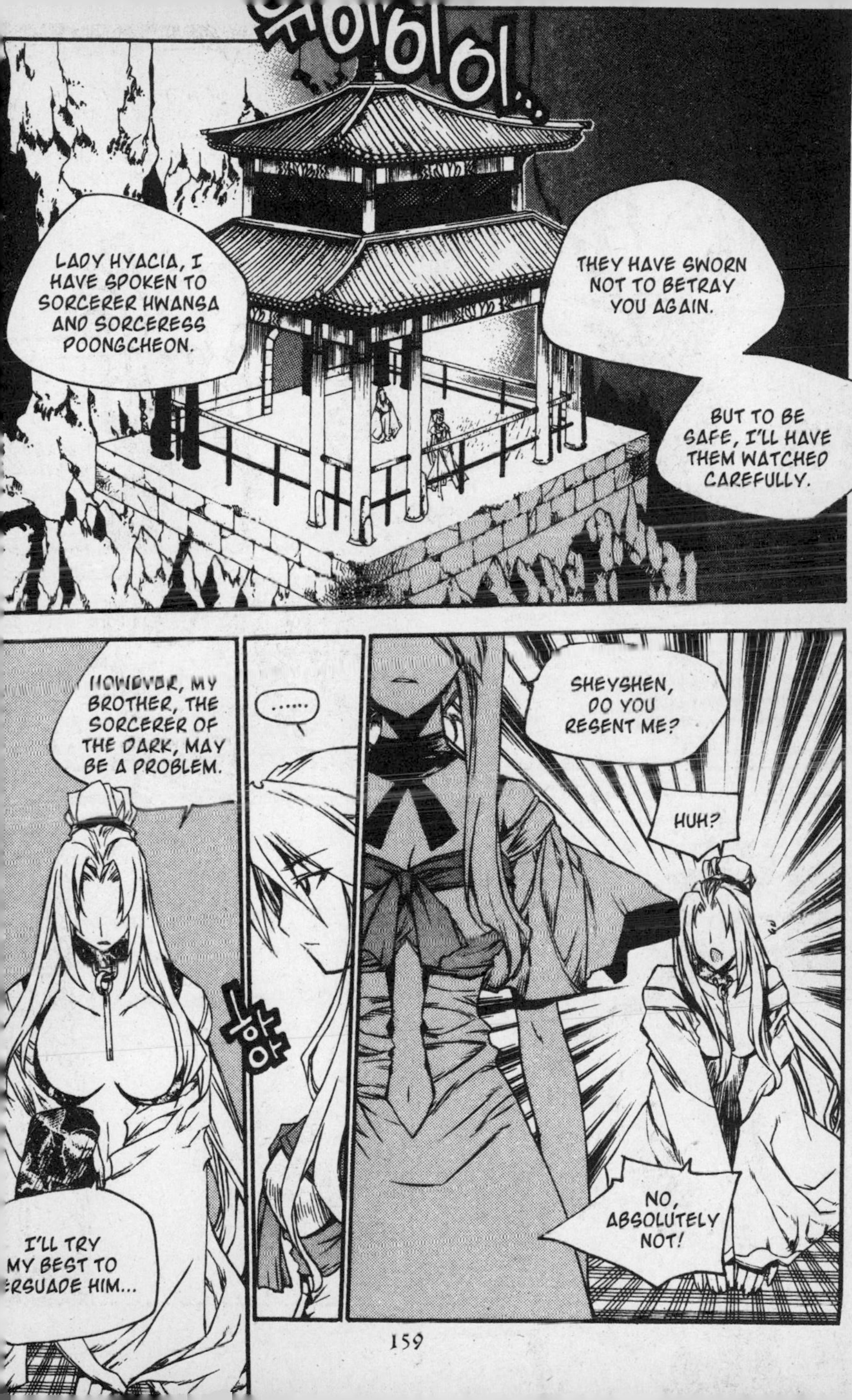

LADY HYACIA, I HAVE SPOKEN TO SORCERER HWANSA AND SORCERESS POONGCHEON.
THEY HAVE SWORN NOT TO BETRAY YOU AGAIN.
BUT TO BE SAFE, I'LL HAVE THEM WATCHED CAREFULLY.
HOWEVER, MY BROTHER, THE SORCERER OF THE DARK, MAY BE A PROBLEM.
I'LL TRY MY BEST TO ERSUADE HIM...
......
SHEYSHEN, DO YOU RESENT ME?
HUH?
NO, ABSOLUTELY NOT!

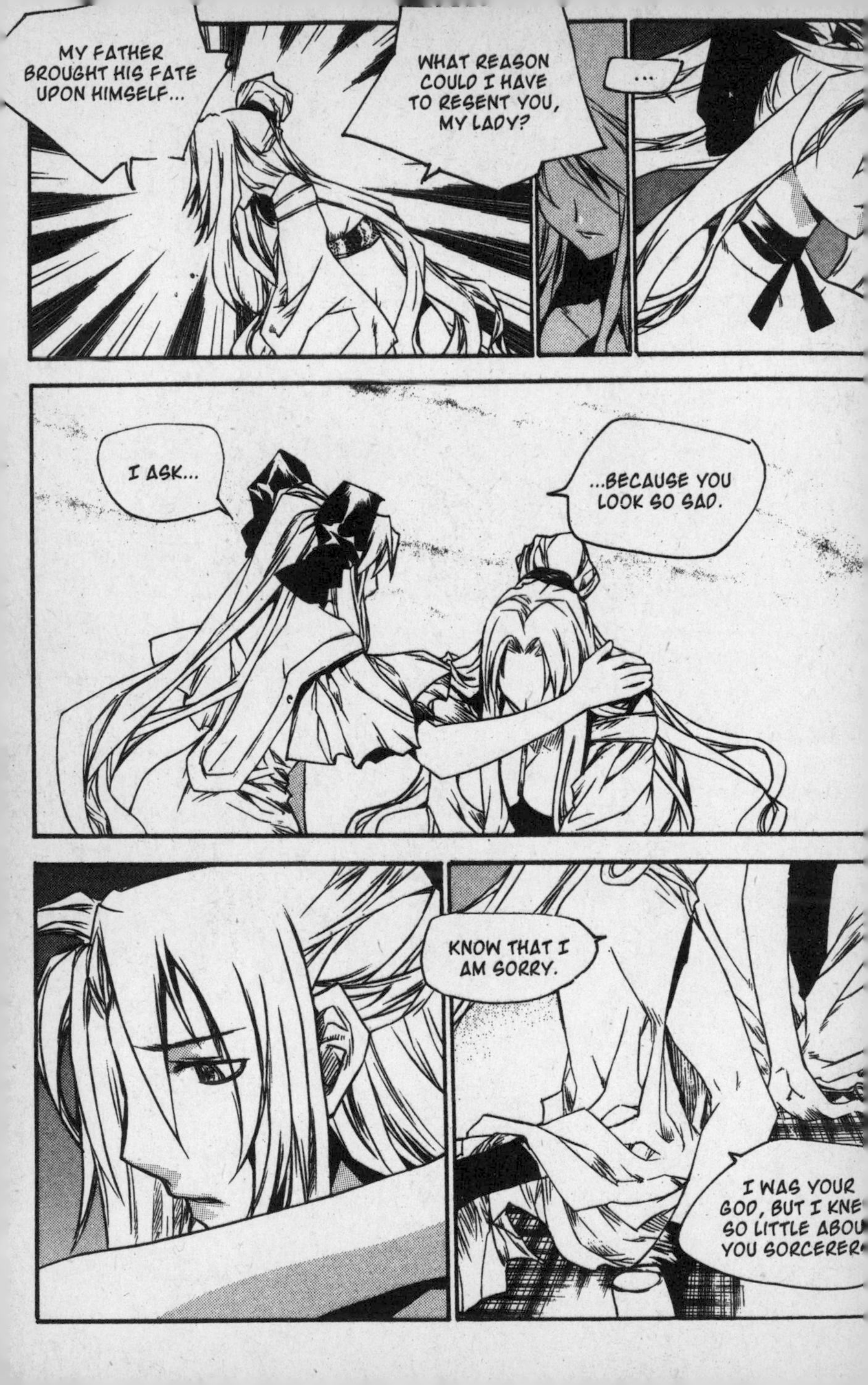
MY FATHER BROUGHT HIS FATE UPON HIMSELF...
WHAT REASON COULD I HAVE TO RESENT YOU, MY LADY?
...
I ASK...
...BECAUSE YOU LOOK SO SAD.
KNOW THAT I AM SORRY.
I WAS YOUR GOD, BUT I KNE
SO LITTLE ABOU
YOU SORCERER

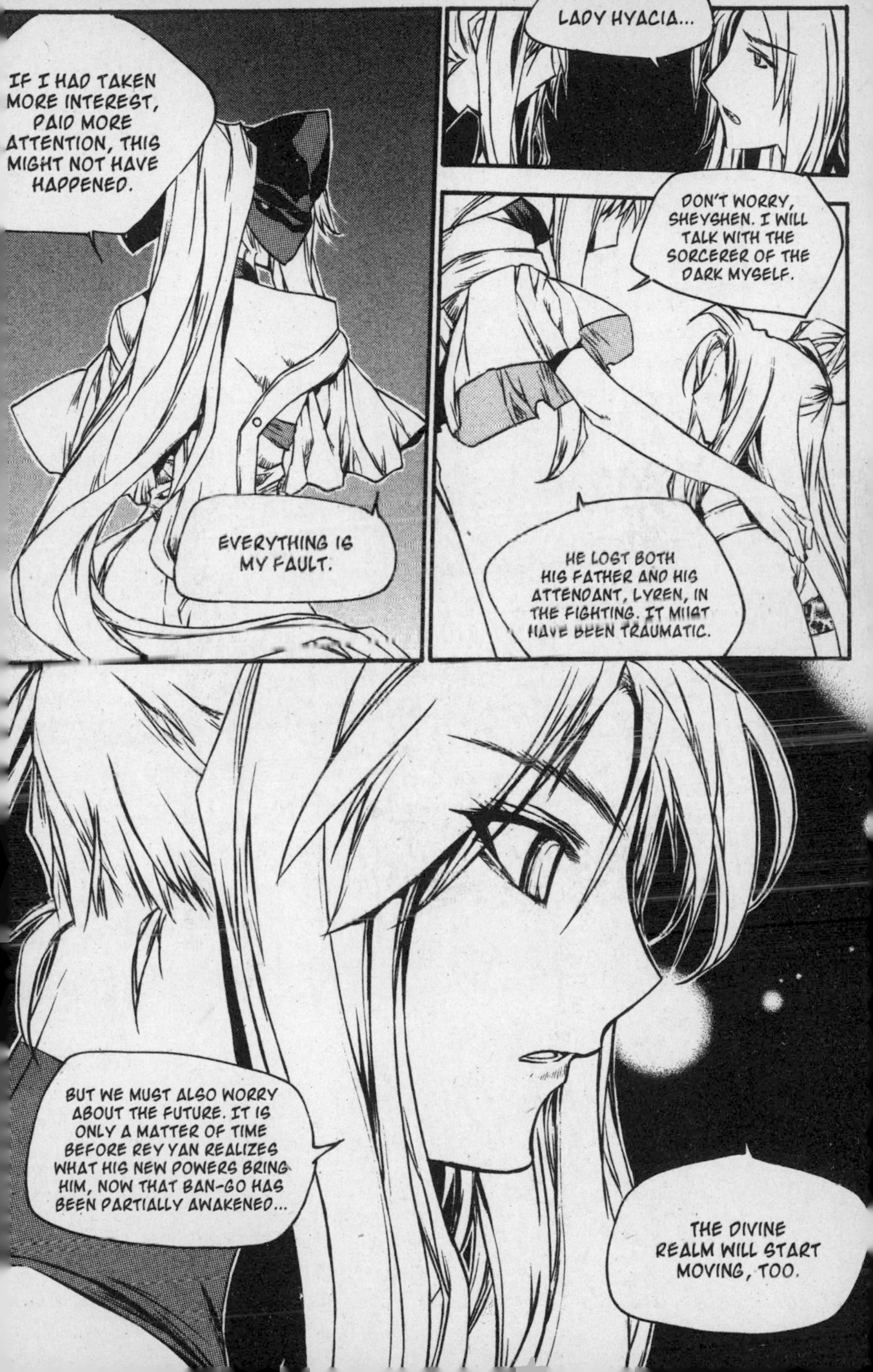
IF I HAD TAKEN MORE INTEREST, PAID MORE ATTENTION, THIS MIGHT NOT HAVE HAPPENED.
EVERYTHING IS MY FAULT.
LADY HYACIA...
DON'T WORRY, SHEYSHEN. I WILL TALK WITH THE SORCERER OF THE DARK MYSELF.
HE LOST BOTH HIS FATHER AND HIS ATTENDANT, LYREN, IN THE FIGHTING. IT MUST HAVE BEEN TRAUMATIC.
BUT WE MUST ALSO WORRY ABOUT THE FUTURE. IT IS ONLY A MATTER OF TIME BEFORE REY YAN REALIZES WHAT HIS NEW POWERS BRING HIM, NOW THAT BAN-GO HAS BEEN PARTIALLY AWAKENED...
THE DIVINE REALM WILL START MOVING, TOO.

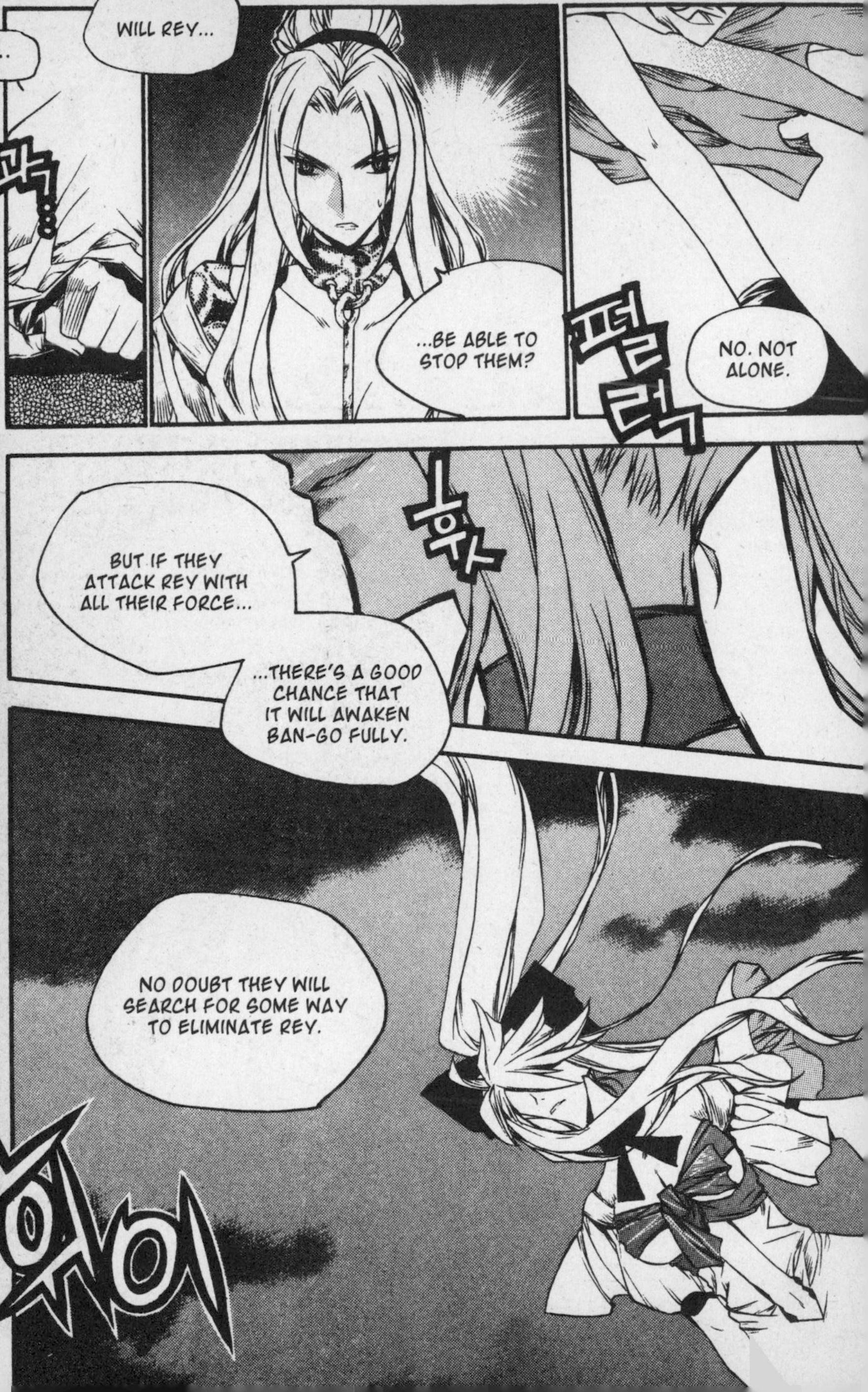
...
WILL REY...
...BE ABLE TO STOP THEM?
펄럭
NO. NOT ALONE.
BUT IF THEY ATTACK REY WITH ALL THEIR FORCE...
...THERE'S A GOOD CHANCE THAT IT WILL AWAKEN BAN-GO FULLY.
NO DOUBT THEY WILL SEARCH FOR SOME WAY TO ELIMINATE REY.

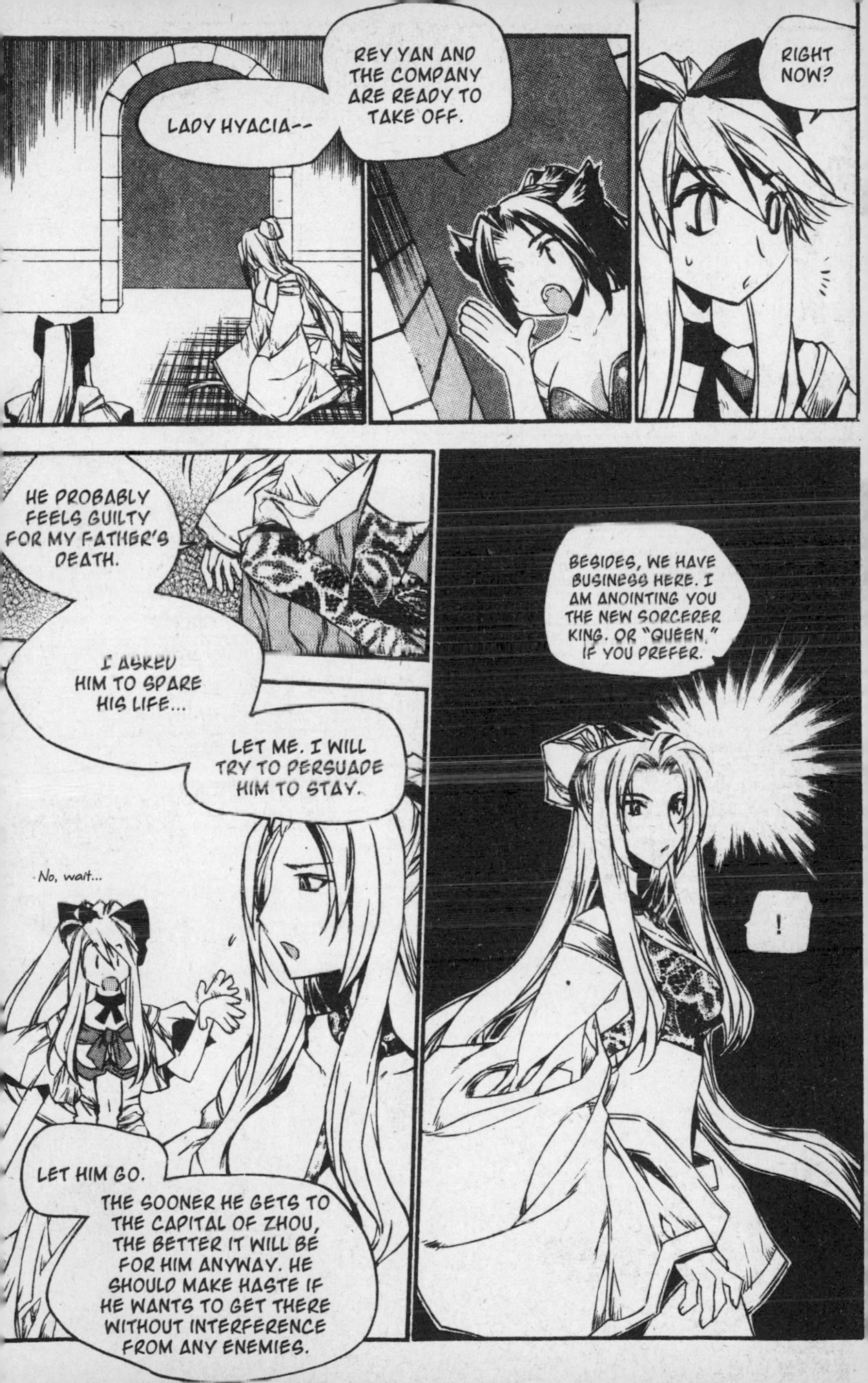
LADY HYACIA--
REY YAN AND THE COMPANY ARE READY TO TAKE OFF.
RIGHT NOW?
HE PROBABLY FEELS GUILTY FOR MY FATHER'S DEATH.
I ASKED HIM TO SPARE HIS LIFE...
LET ME. I WILL TRY TO PERSUADE HIM TO STAY.
No, wait...
LET HIM GO.
THE SOONER HE GETS TO THE CAPITAL OF ZHOU, THE BETTER IT WILL BE FOR HIM ANYWAY. HE SHOULD MAKE HASTE IF HE WANTS TO GET THERE WITHOUT INTERFERENCE FROM ANY ENEMIES.
BESIDES, WE HAVE BUSINESS HERE. I AM ANOINTING YOU THE NEW SORCERER KING. OR "QUEEN," IF YOU PREFER.
!

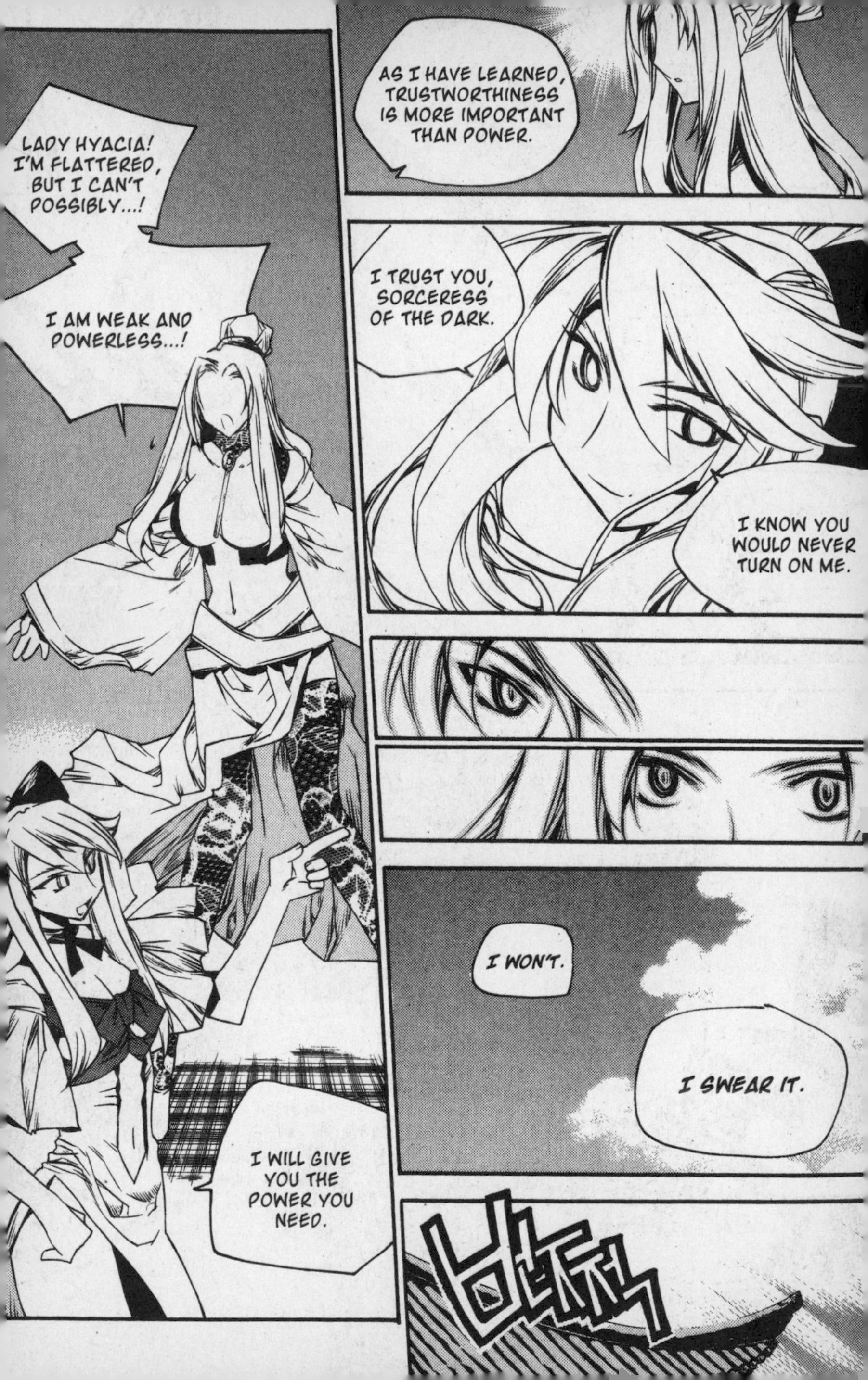
LADY HYACIA! I'M FLATTERED, BUT I CAN'T POSSIBLY...!
I AM WEAK AND POWERLESS...!
I WILL GIVE YOU THE POWER YOU NEED.
AS I HAVE LEARNED, TRUSTWORTHINESS IS MORE IMPORTANT THAN POWER.
I TRUST YOU, SORCERESS OF THE DARK.
I KNOW YOU WOULD NEVER TURN ON ME.
I WON'T.
I SWEAR IT.

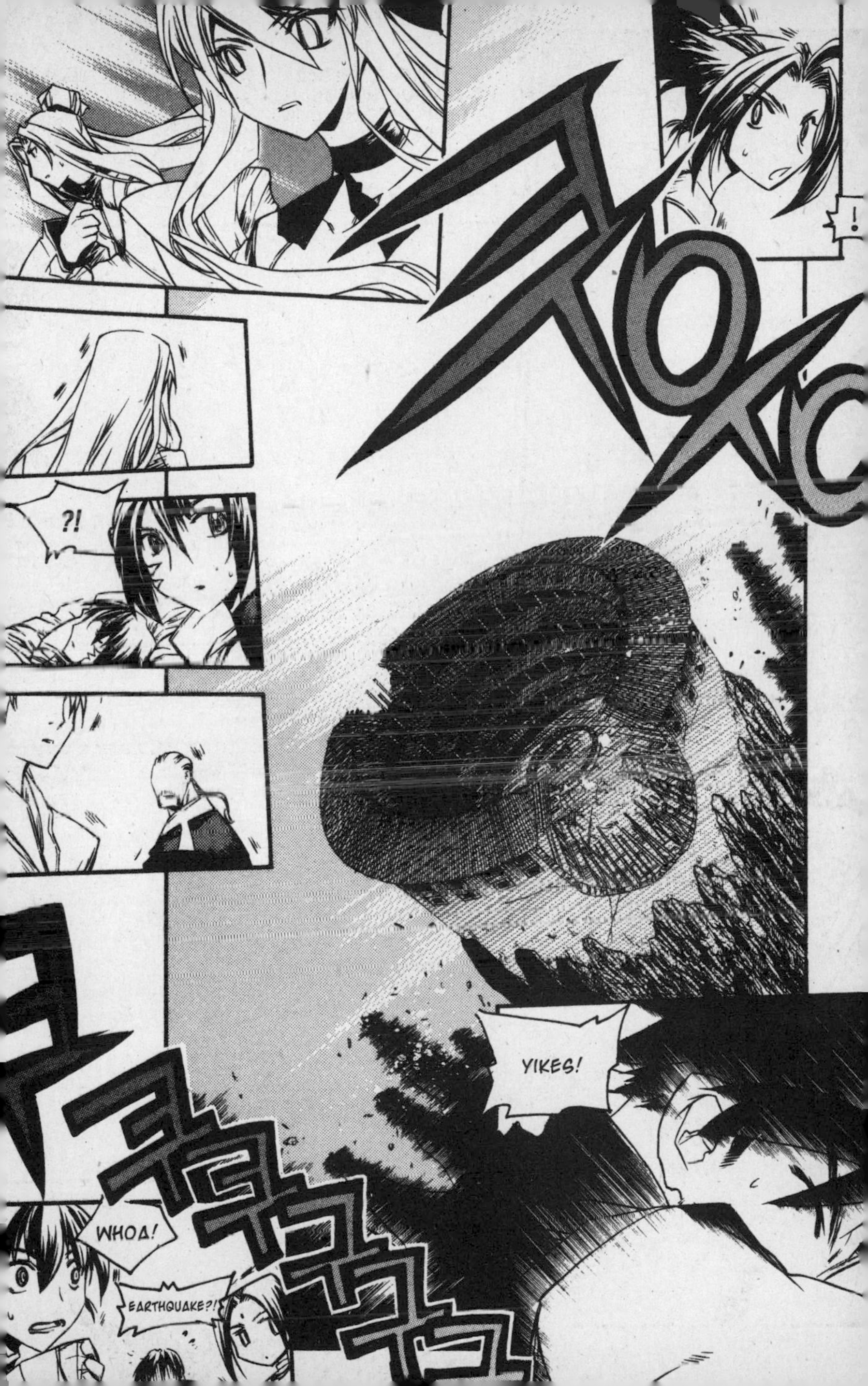
!
?!
YIKES!
WHOA!
EARTHQUAKE?!

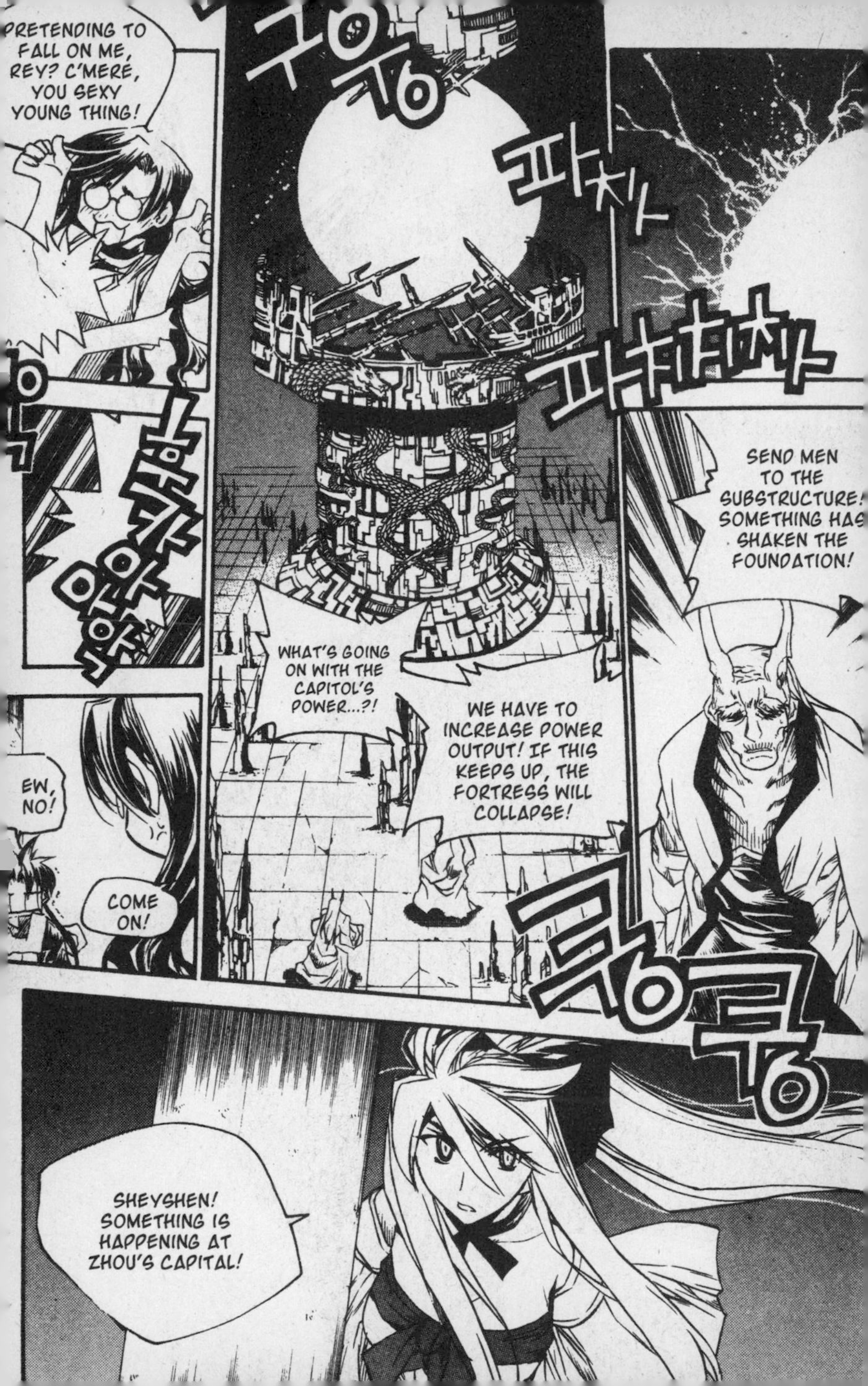
PRETENDING TO FALL ON ME, REY? C'MERE, YOU SEXY YOUNG THING!
EW, NO!
COME ON!
WHAT'S GOING ON WITH THE CAPITOL'S POWER...?!
WE HAVE TO INCREASE POWER OUTPUT! IF THIS KEEPS UP, THE FORTRESS WILL COLLAPSE!
SEND MEN TO THE SUBSTRUCTURE! SOMETHING HAS SHAKEN THE FOUNDATION!
SHEYSHEN! SOMETHING IS HAPPENING AT ZHOU'S CAPITAL!

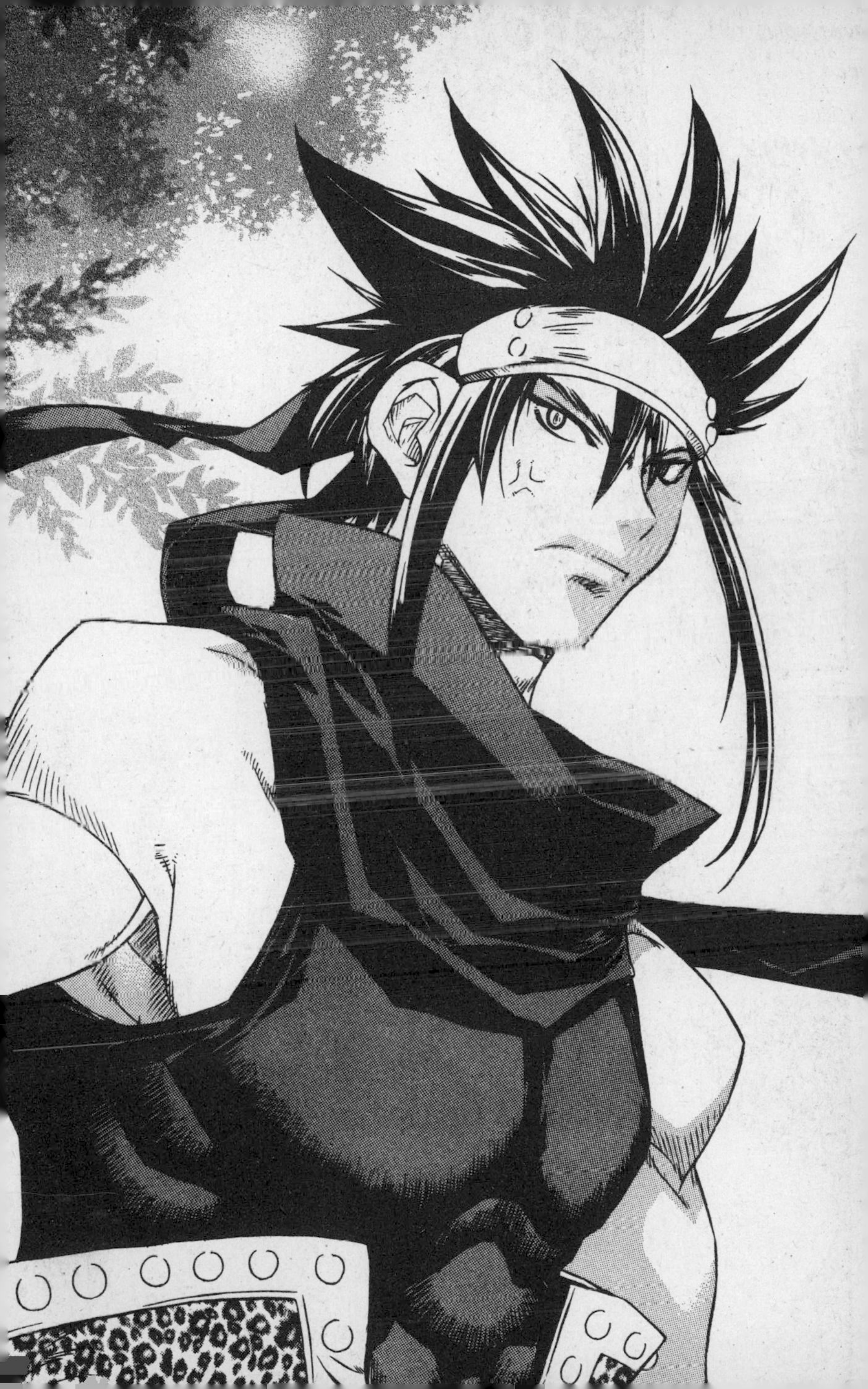

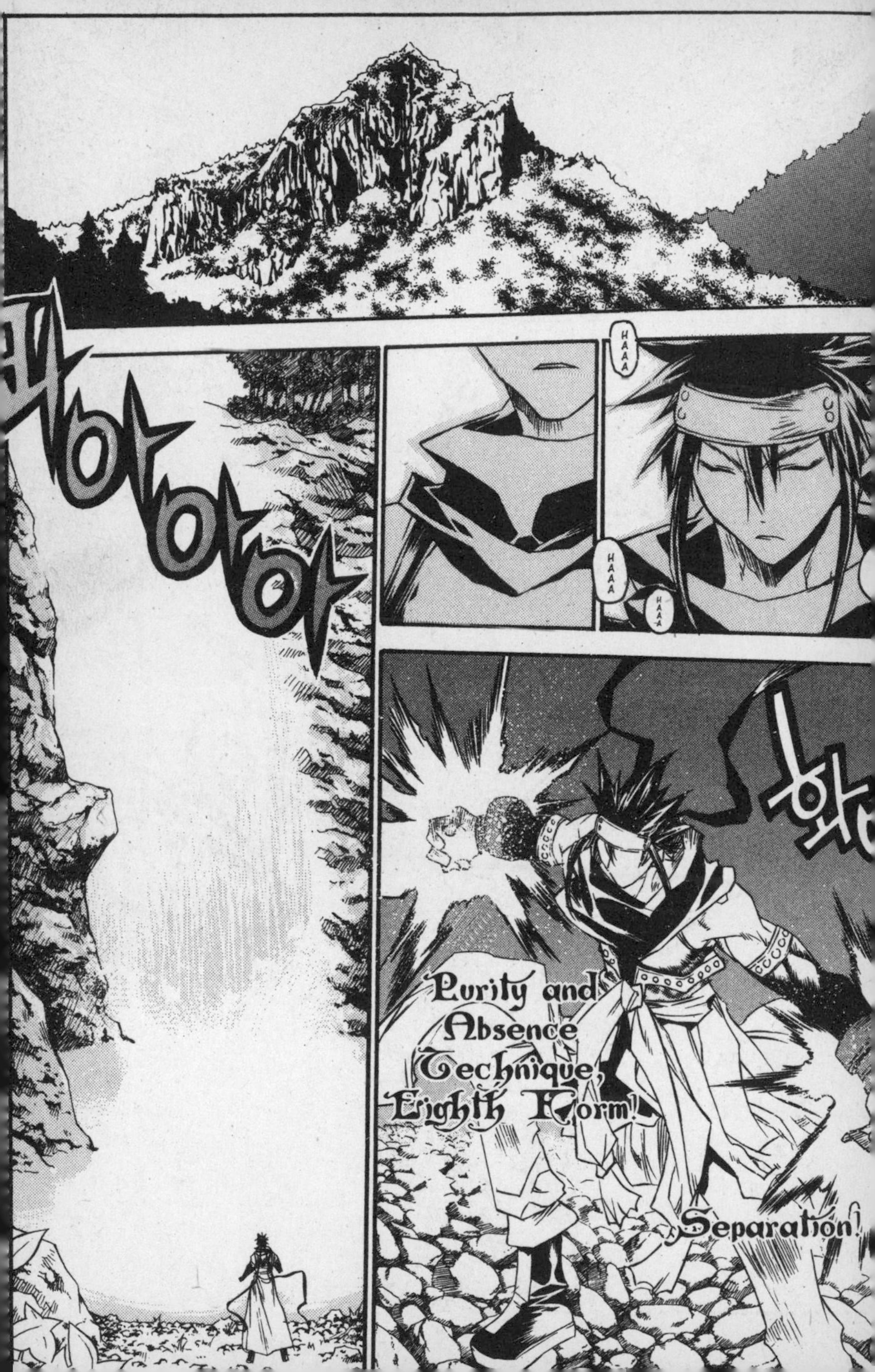
HAAA
HAAA
HAAA
Purity and Absence Technique, Eighth Form!
Separation!

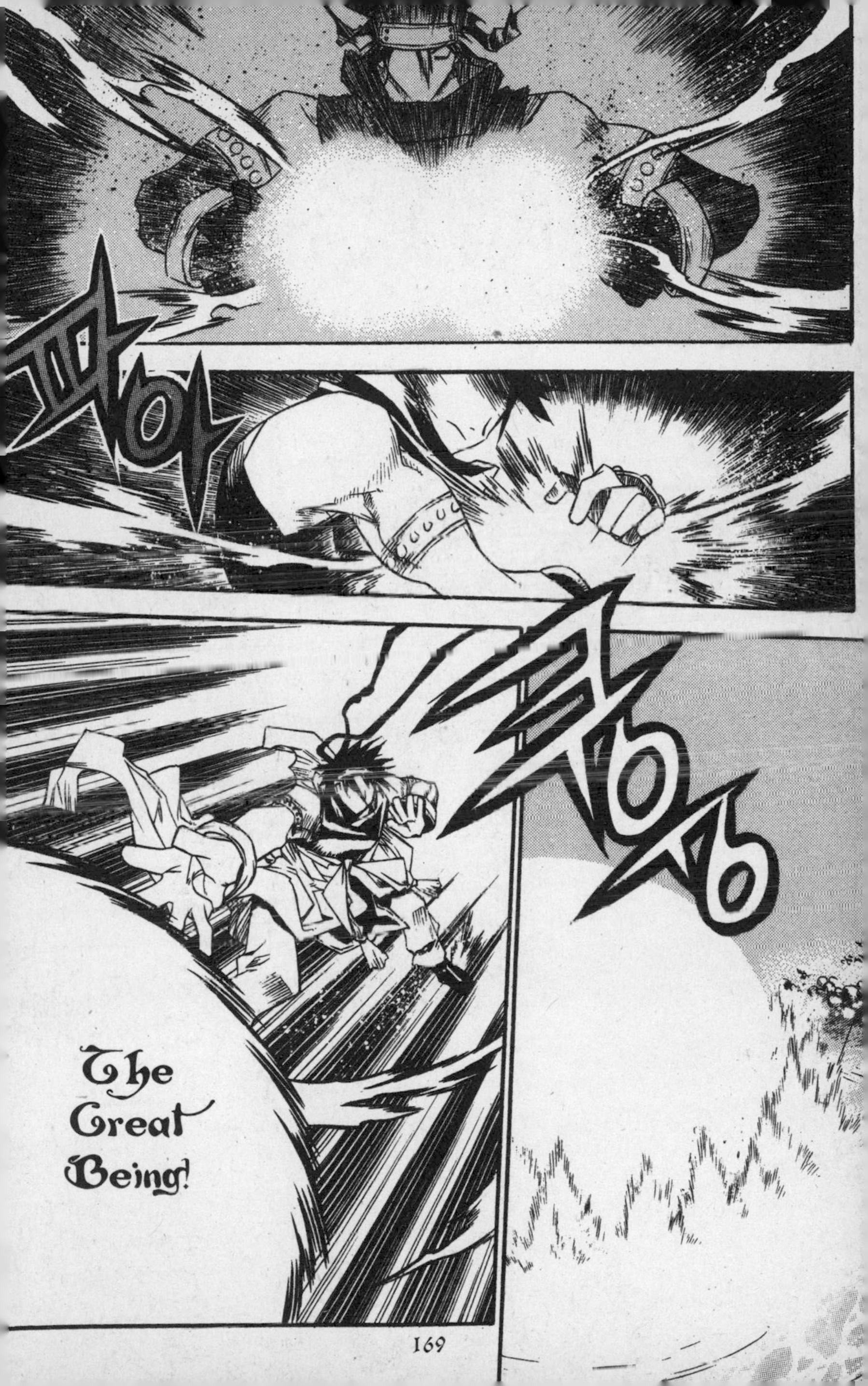
The Great Being!

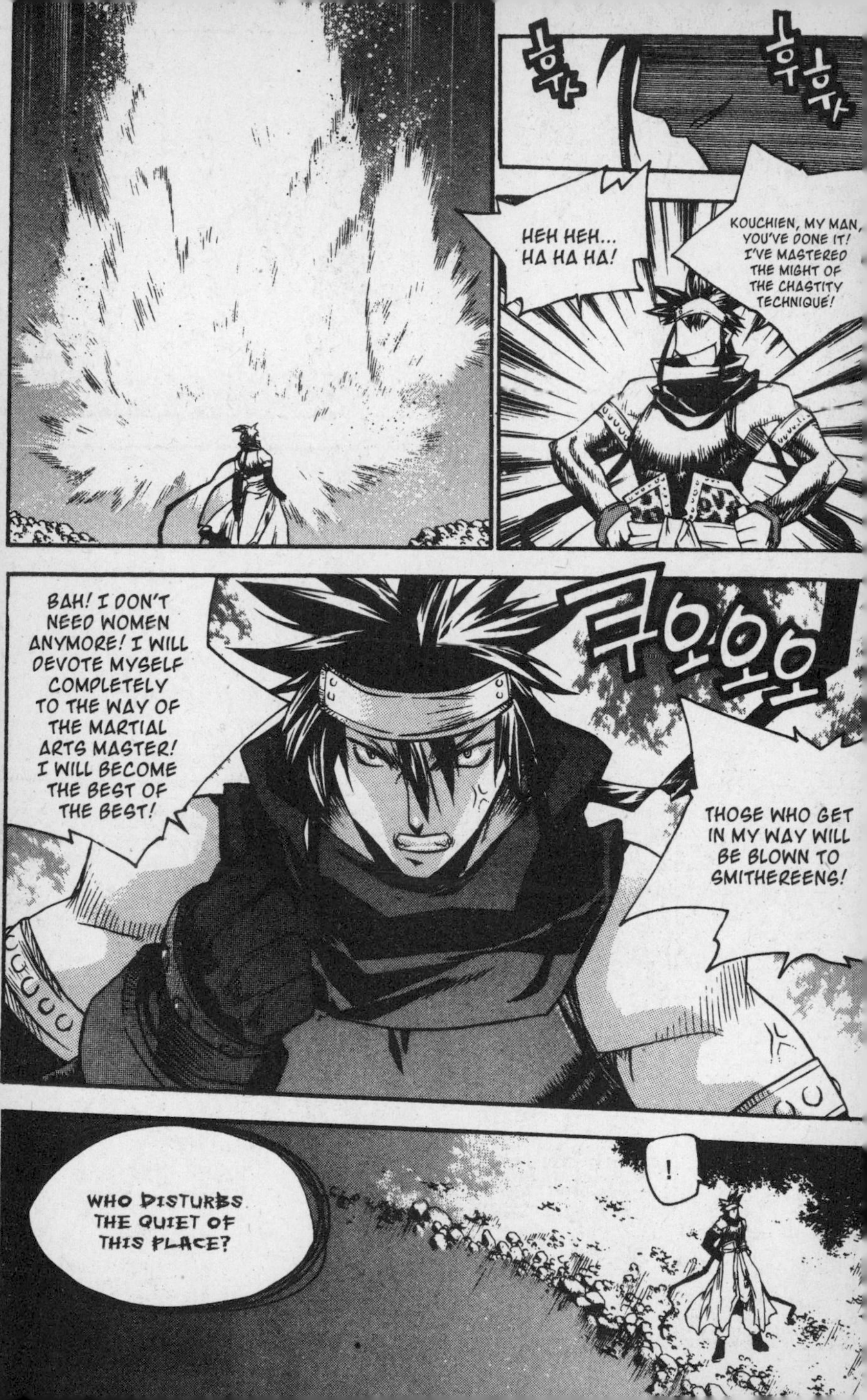
후앗
후후앗
HEH HEH... HA HA HA!
KOUCHIEN, MY MAN, YOU'VE DONE IT! I'VE MASTERED THE MIGHT OF THE CHASTITY TECHNIQUE!
BAH! I DON'T NEED WOMEN ANYMORE! I WILL DEVOTE MYSELF COMPLETELY TO THE WAY OF THE MARTIAL ARTS MASTER! I WILL BECOME THE BEST OF THE BEST!
쿠오오오
THOSE WHO GET IN MY WAY WILL BE BLOWN TO SMITHEREENS!
WHO DISTURBS THE QUIET OF THIS PLACE?
!

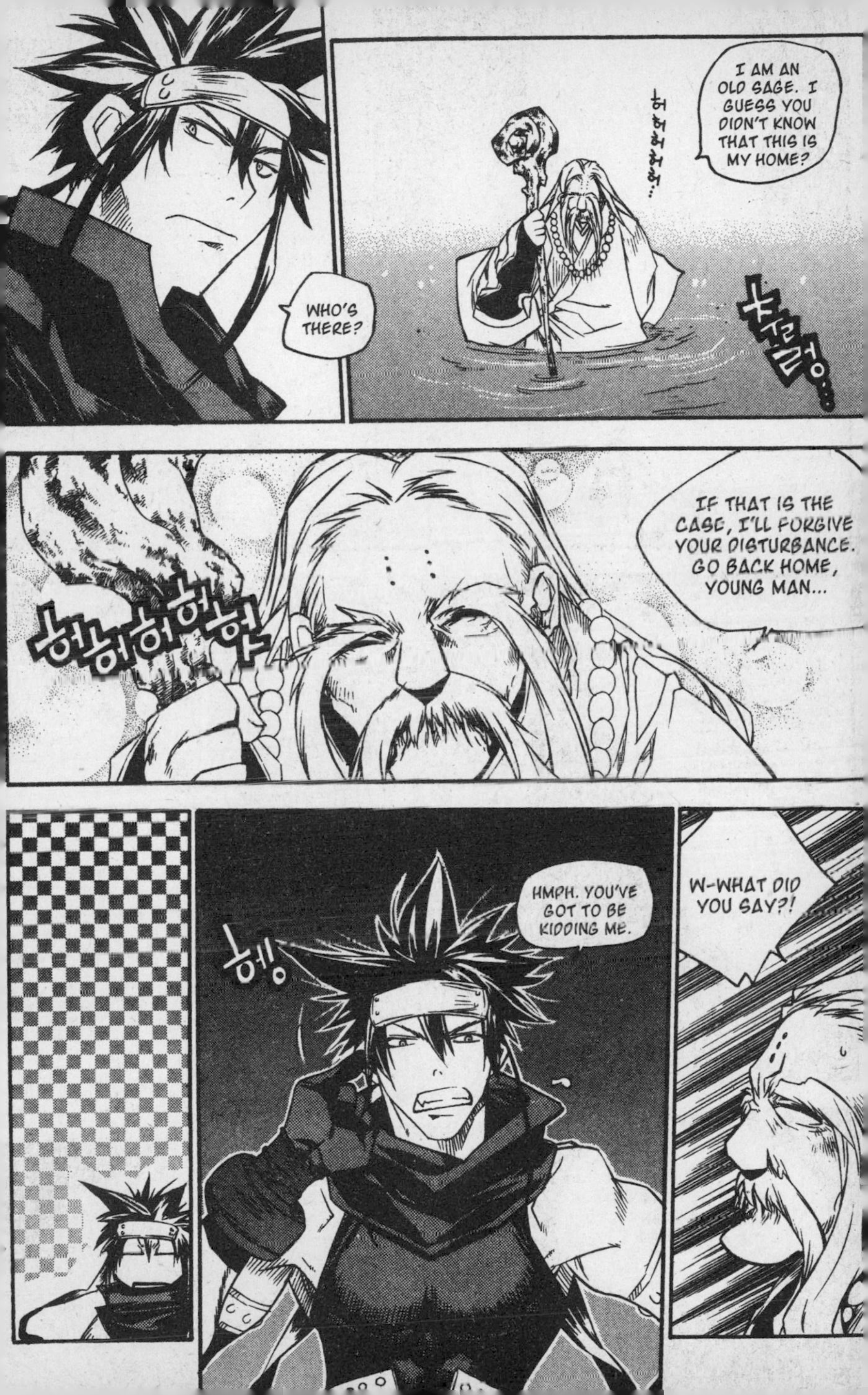
WHO'S THERE?
I AM AN OLD SAGE. I GUESS YOU DIDN'T KNOW THAT THIS IS MY HOME?
출렁...
IF THAT IS THE CASE, I'LL FORGIVE YOUR DISTURBANCE. GO BACK HOME, YOUNG MAN...
헹
HMPH. YOU'VE GOT TO BE KIDDING ME.
W-WHAT DID YOU SAY?!

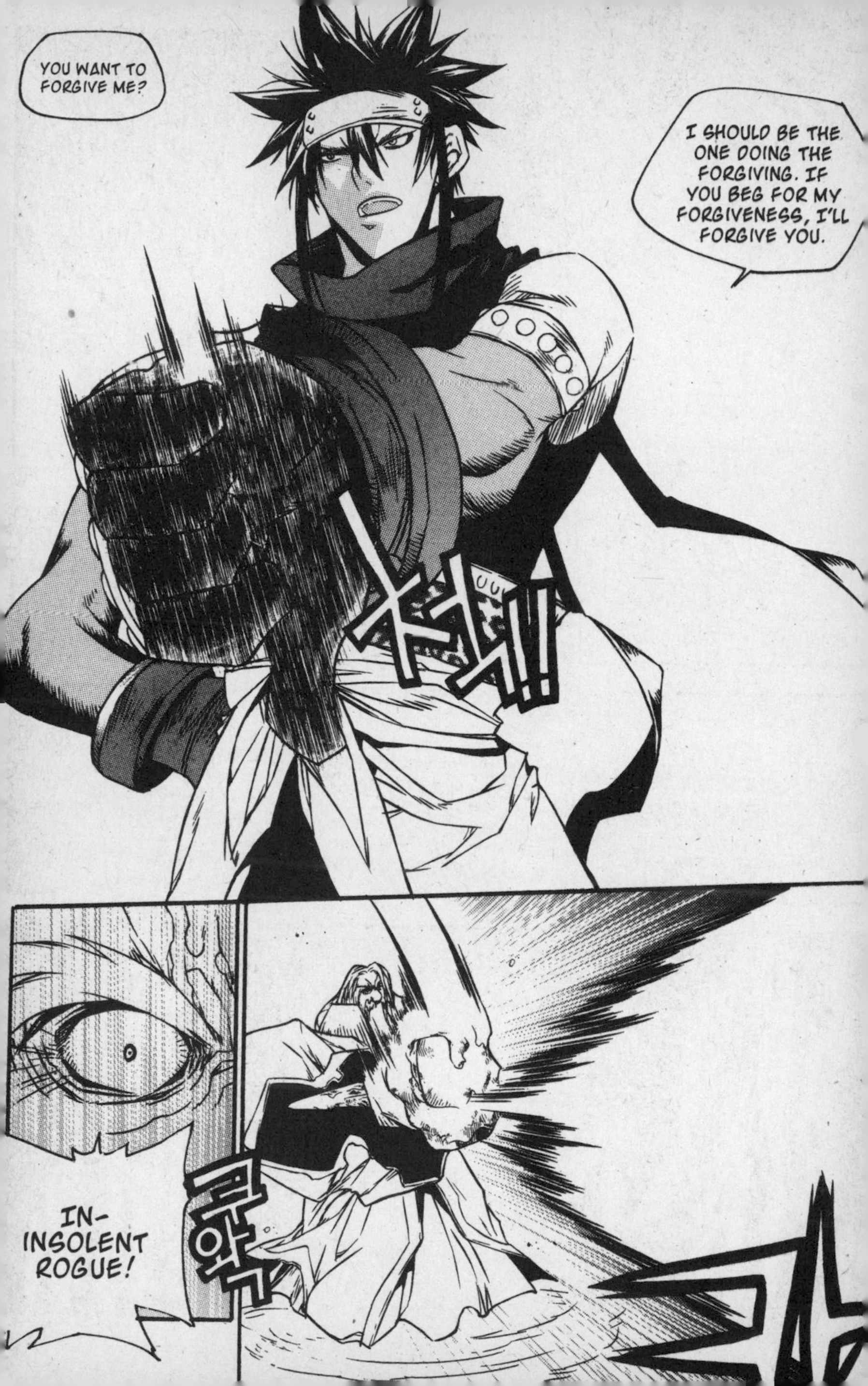
YOU WANT TO FORGIVE ME?
I SHOULD BE THE ONE DOING THE FORGIVING. IF YOU BEG FOR MY FORGIVENESS, I'LL FORGIVE YOU.
IN- INSOLENT ROGUE!

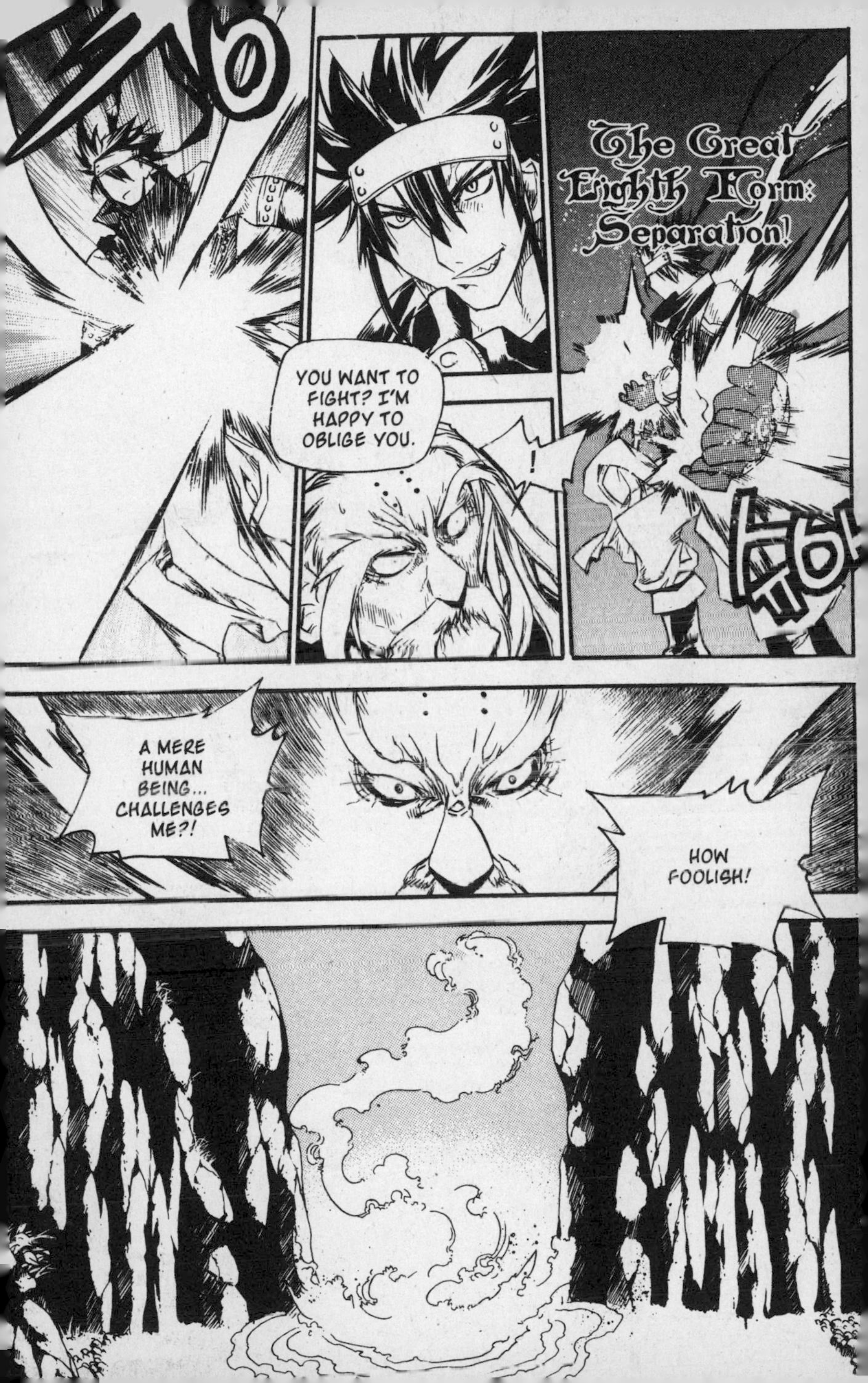
The Great Eighth Form: Separation!
YOU WANT TO FIGHT? I'M HAPPY TO OBLIGE YOU.
!
A MERE HUMAN BEING... CHALLENGES ME?!
HOW FOOLISH!

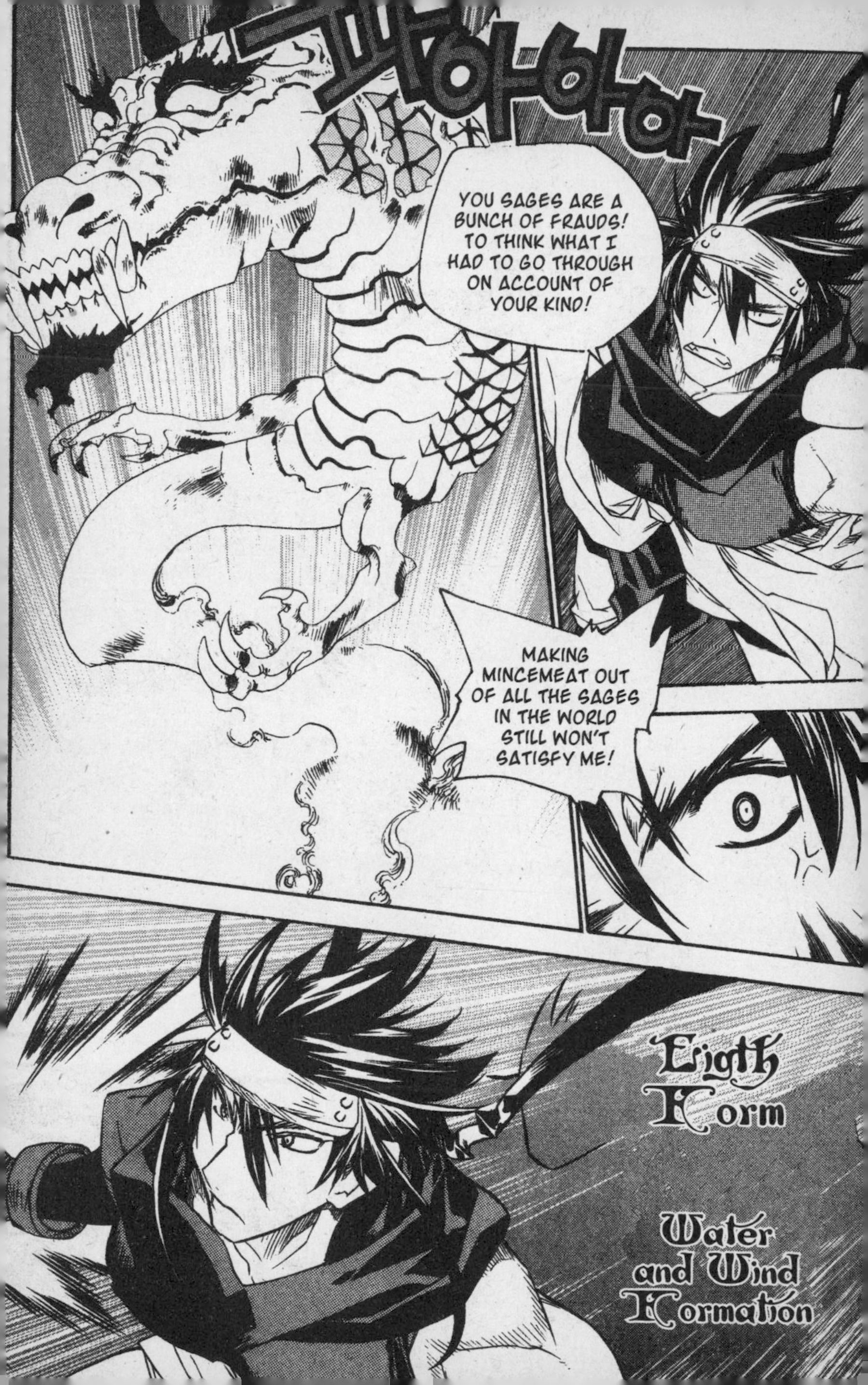
YOU SAGES ARE A BUNCH OF FRAUDS! TO THINK WHAT I HAD TO GO THROUGH ON ACCOUNT OF YOUR KIND!
MAKING MINCEMEAT OUT OF ALL THE SAGES IN THE WORLD STILL WON'T SATISFY ME!
Eigth Form
Water and Wind Formation

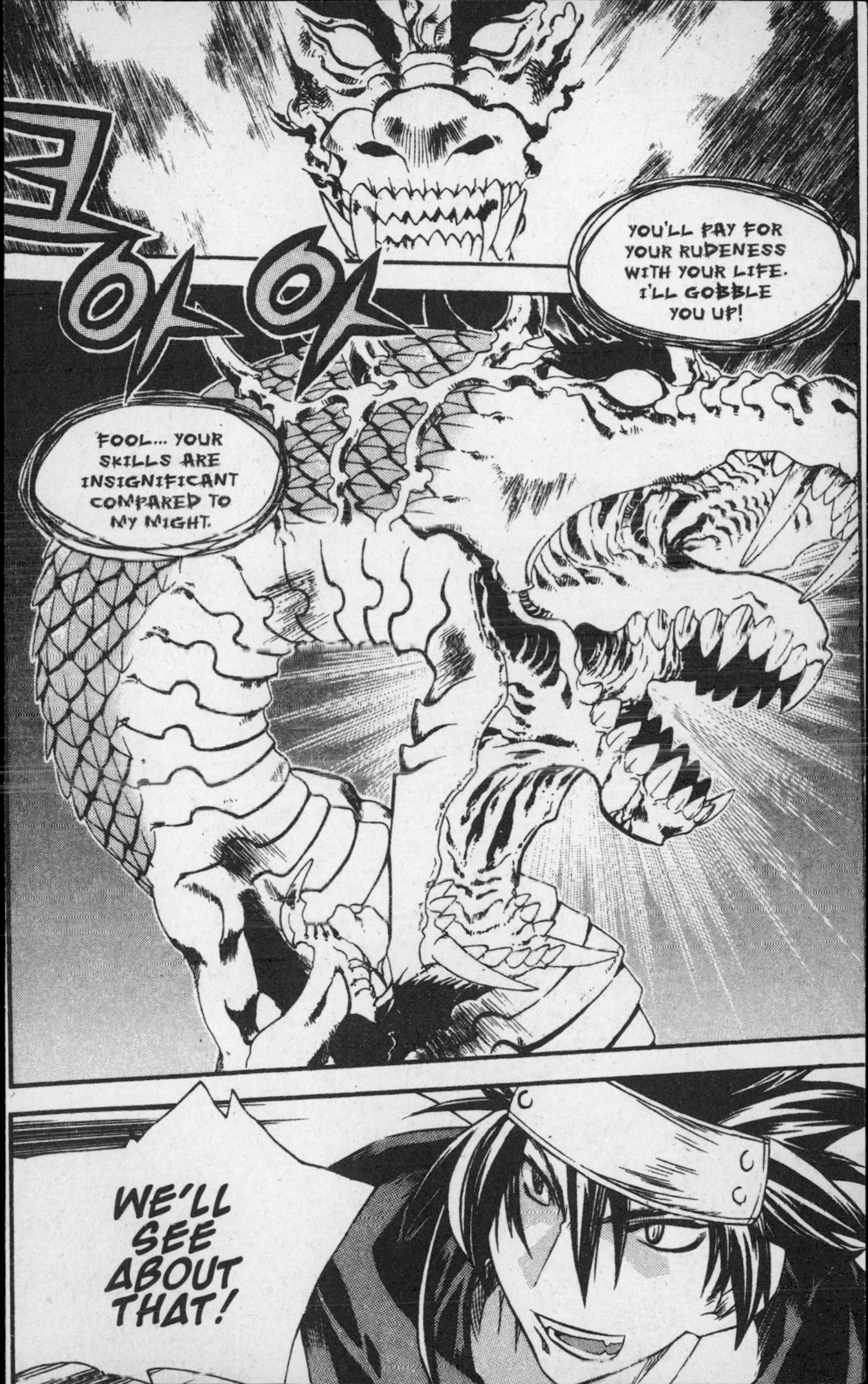
YOU'LL PAY FOR YOUR RUDENESS WITH YOUR LIFE. I'LL GOBBLE YOU UP!
FOOL... YOUR SKILLS ARE INSIGNIFICANT COMPARED TO MY MIGHT.
WE'LL SEE ABOUT THAT!

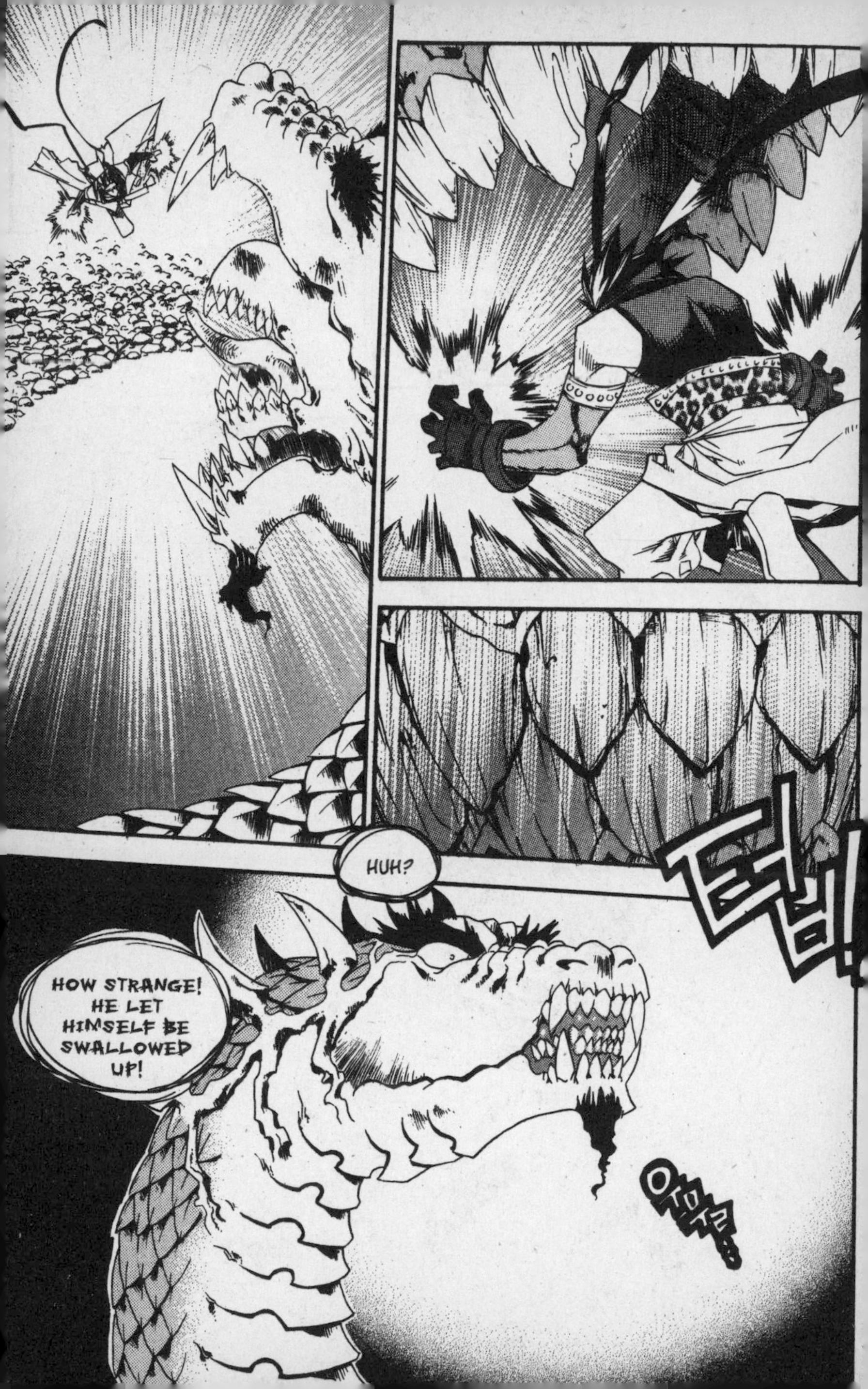
HUH?
HOW STRANGE! HE LET HIMSELF BE SWALLOWED UP!

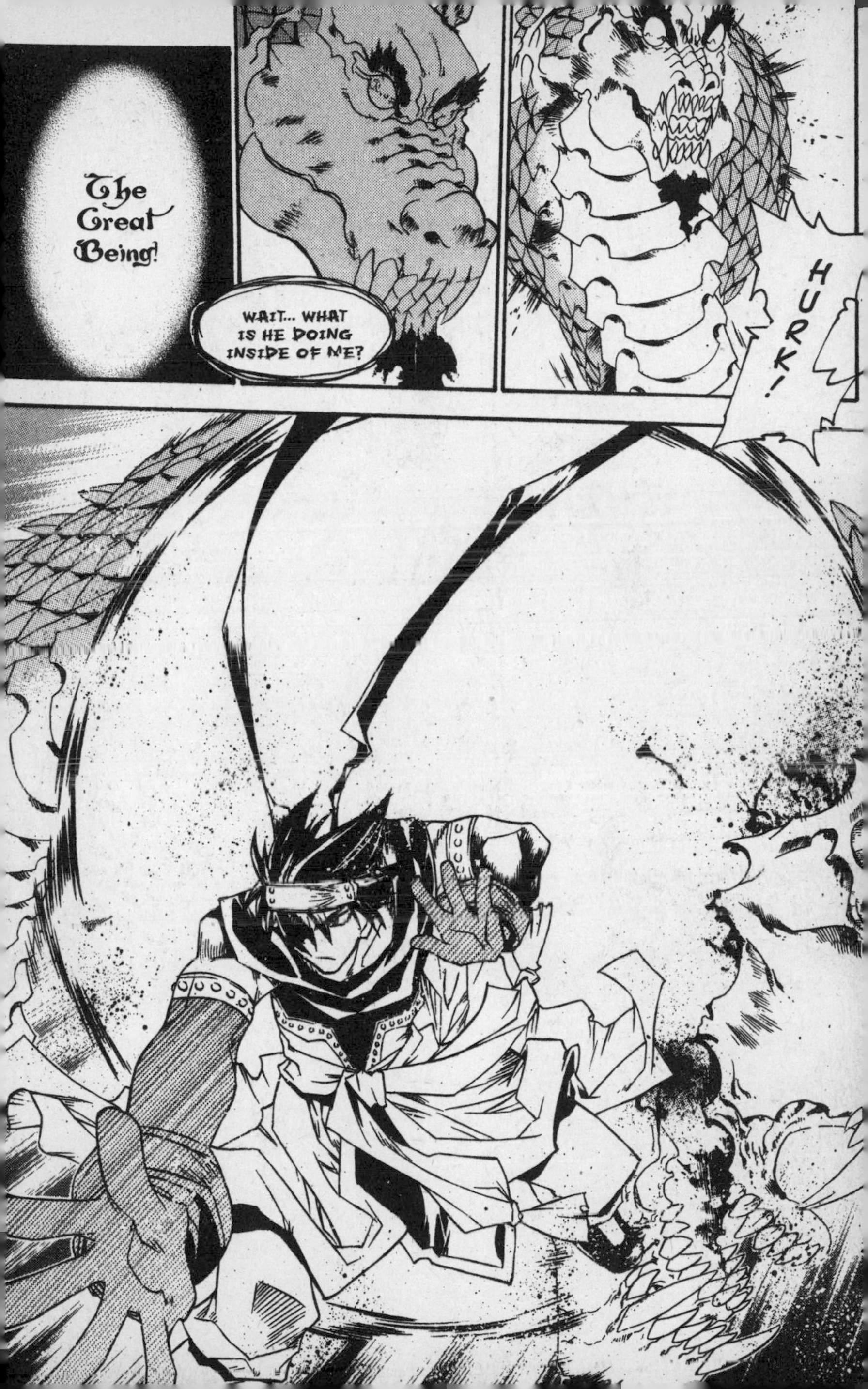
The Great Being!
WAIT... WHAT IS HE DOING INSIDE OF ME?
HURK!

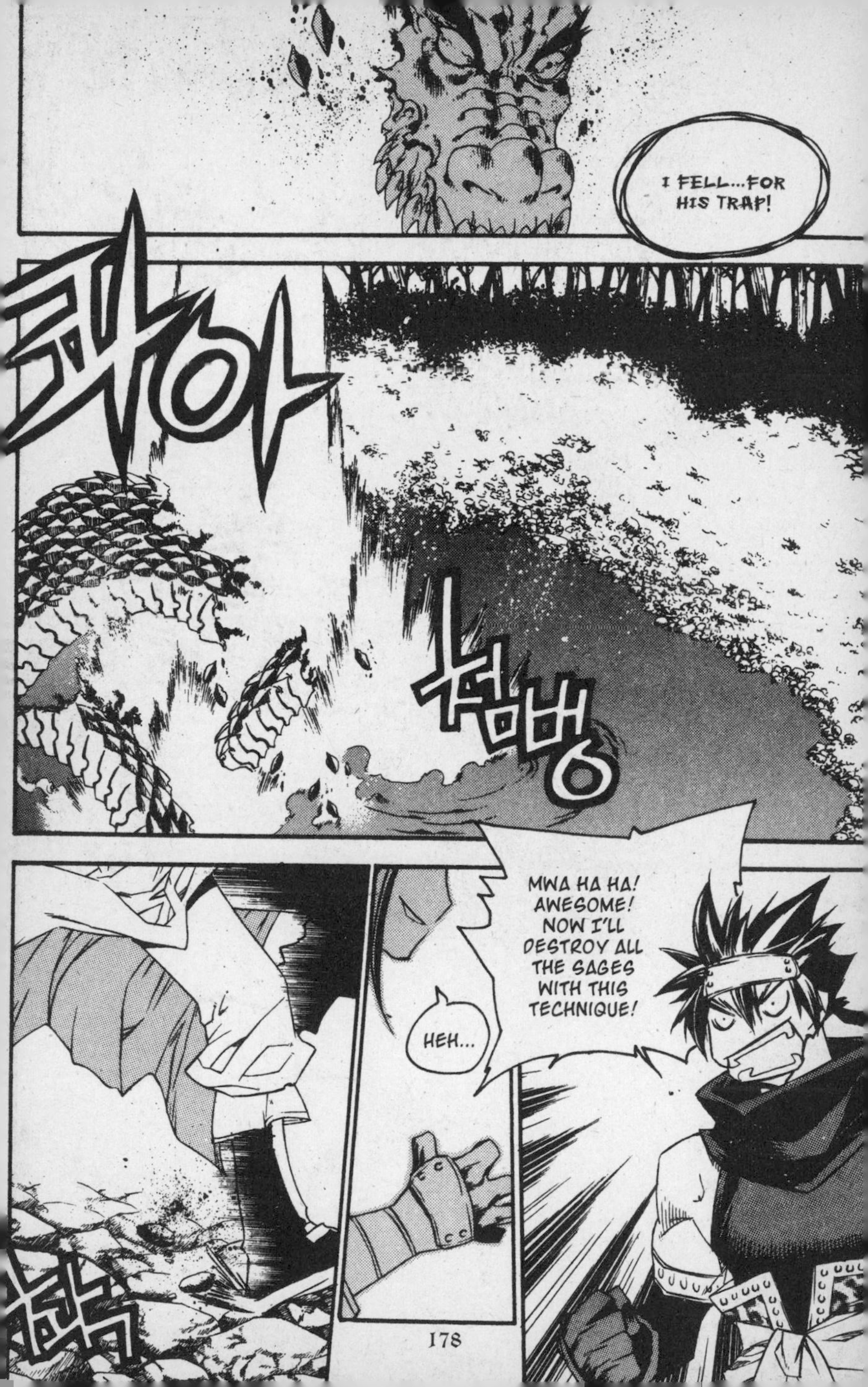
I FELL...FOR HIS TRAP!
HEH...
MWA HA HA! AWESOME! NOW I'LL DESTROY ALL THE SAGES WITH THIS TECHNIQUE!

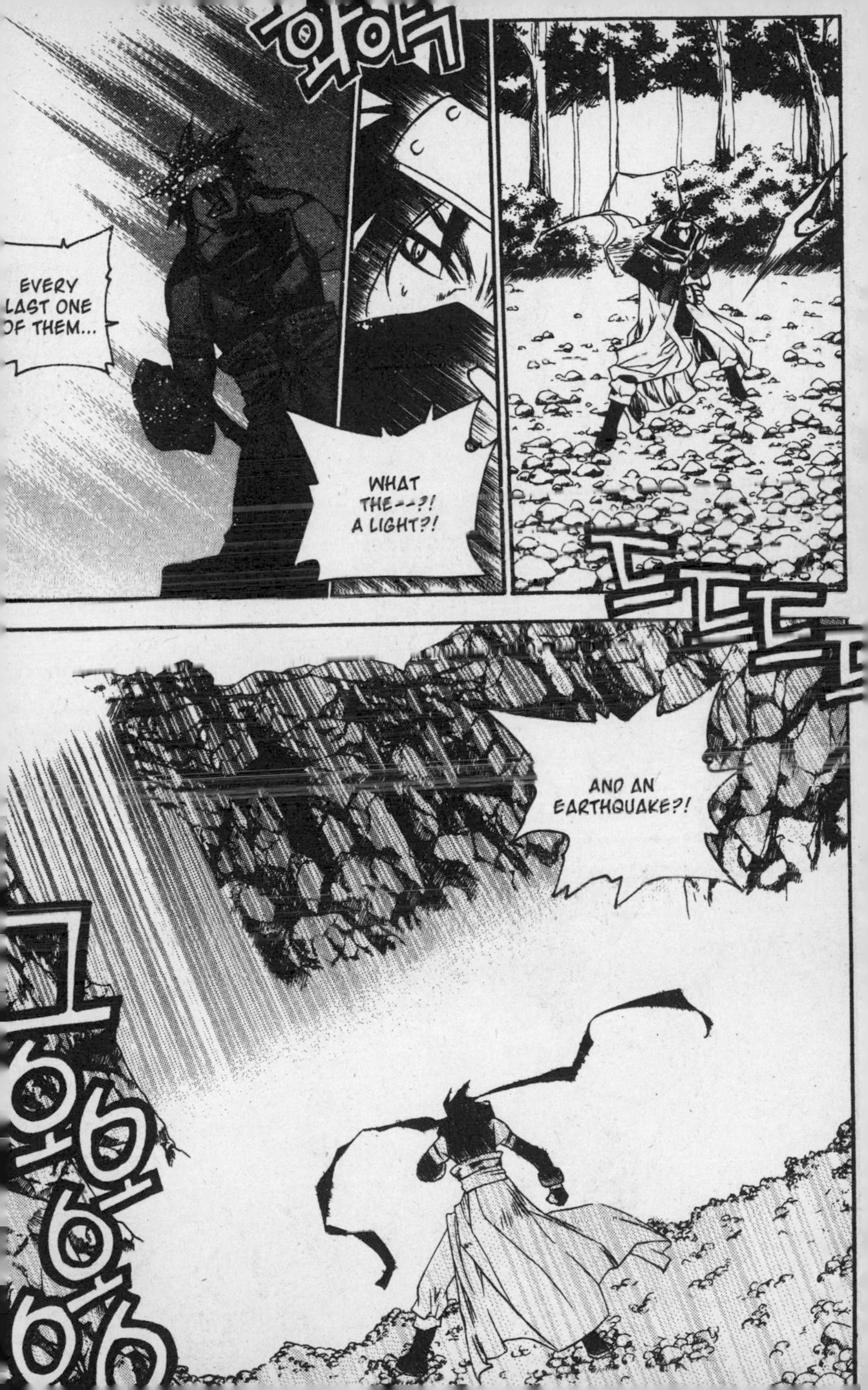
EVERY LAST ONE OF THEM...
WHAT THE--?! A LIGHT?!
AND AN EARTHQUAKE?!

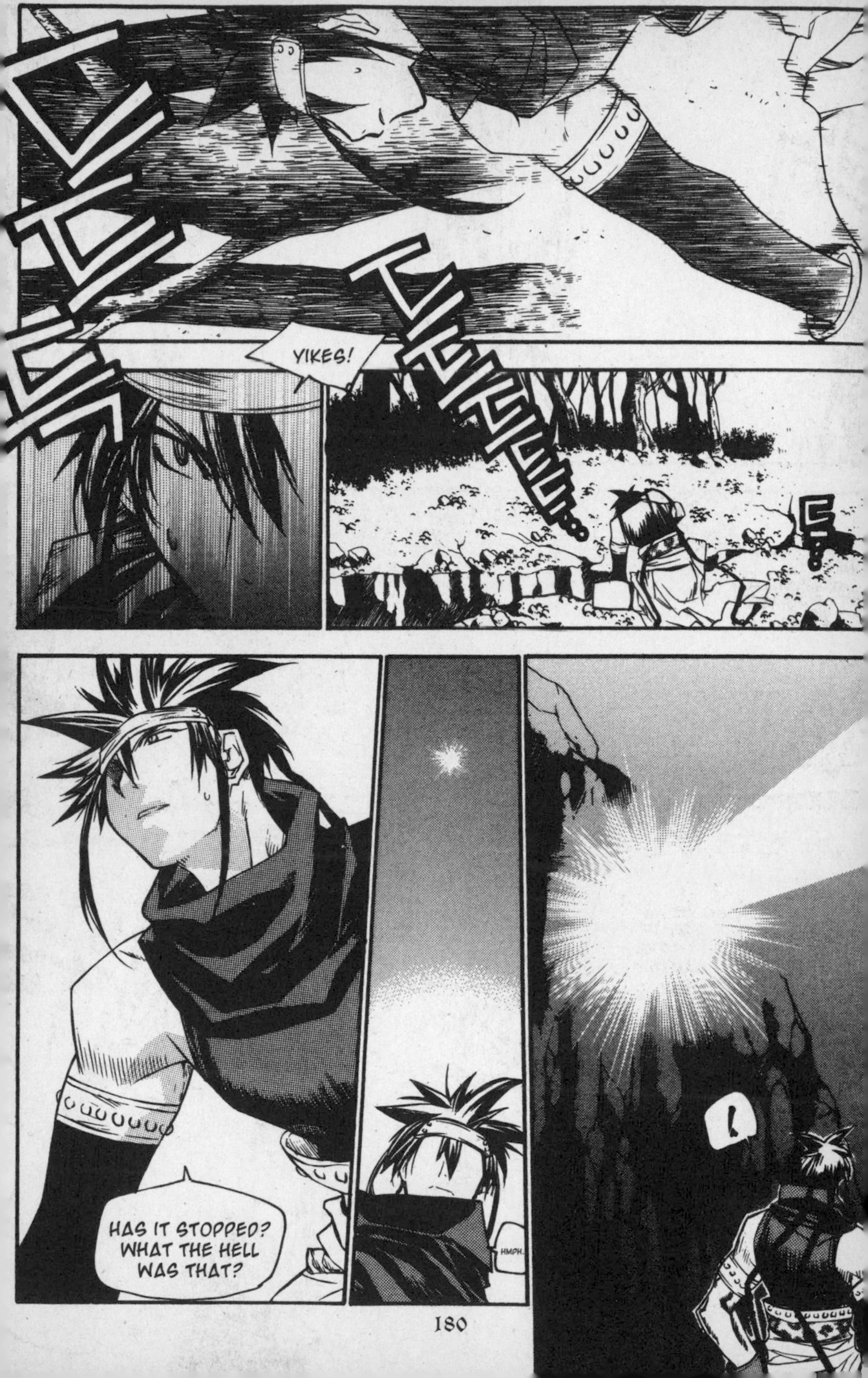
YIKES!
HAS IT STOPPED? WHAT THE HELL WAS THAT?
HMPH.

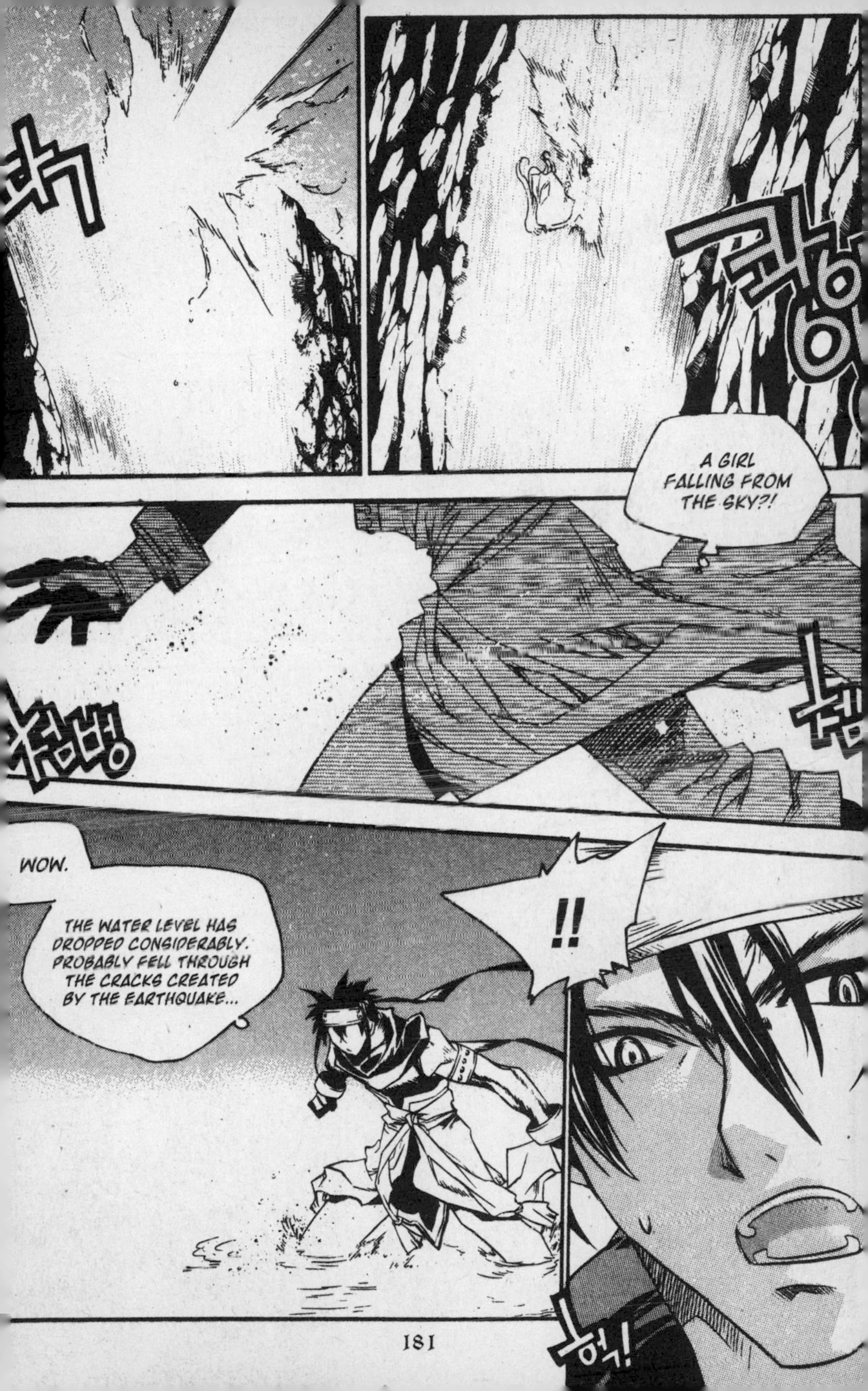
A GIRL FALLING FROM THE SKY?!
WOW.
THE WATER LEVEL HAS DROPPED CONSIDERABLY. PROBABLY FELL THROUGH THE CRACKS CREATED BY THE EARTHQUAKE...
!!
헉!

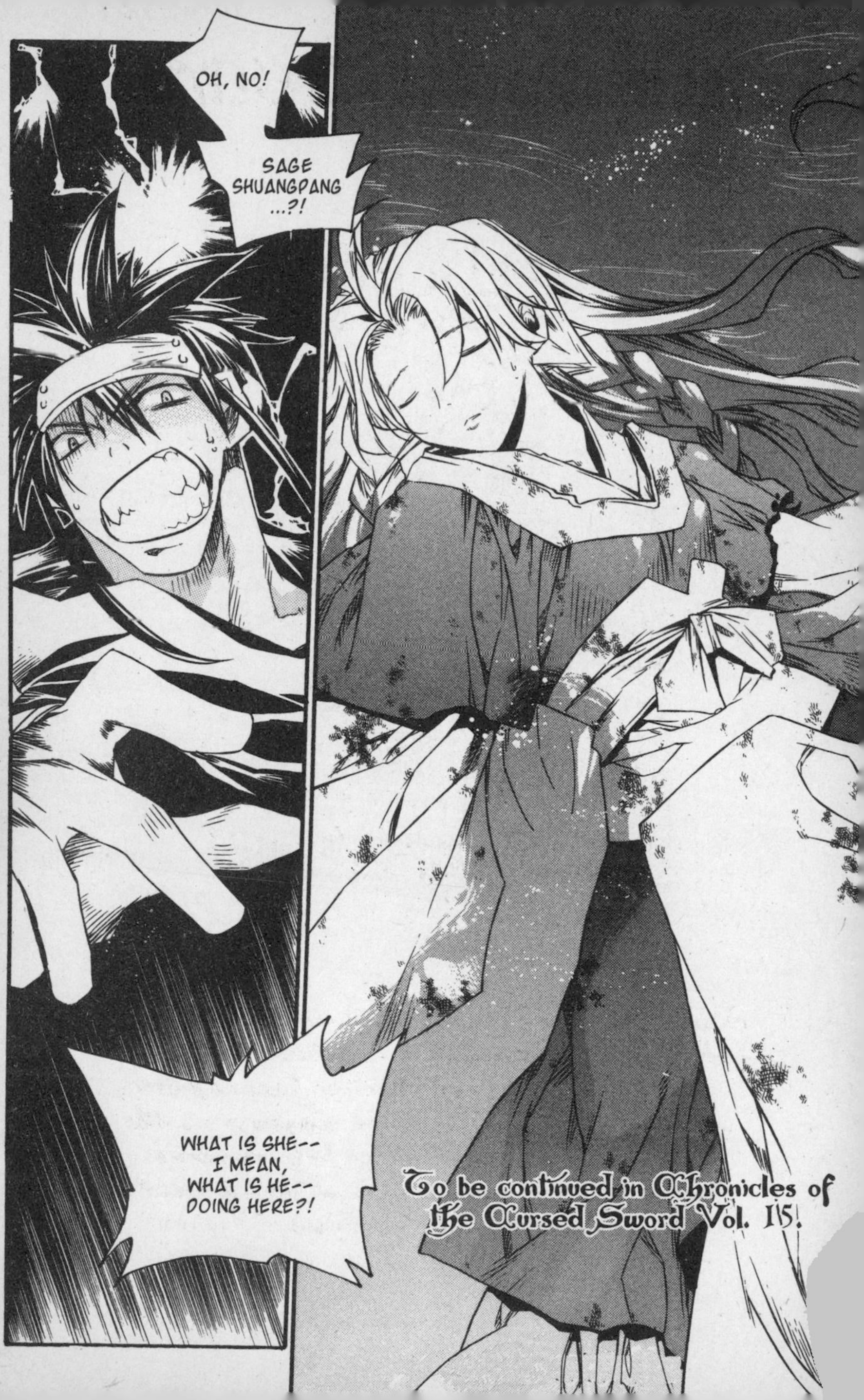
OH, NO!
SAGE SHUANGPANG ...?!
WHAT IS SHE-- I MEAN, WHAT IS HE-- DOING HERE?!
To be continued in Chronicles of the Cursed Sword Vol. 15.

NEXT VOLUME

TOKYOPOP
CHRONICLES OF THE
CURSED SWORD
AUTHOR: YEO BEOP-RYONG
ILLUSTRATOR: PARK HUI-JIN
15

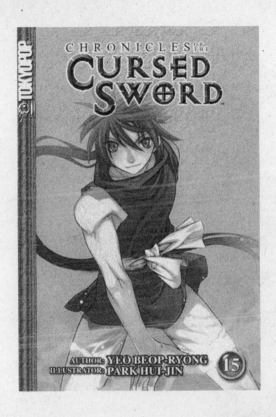

Ravenously hungry for power and completely without mercy, Jaryoon returns to his homeland only to find it in ruins. Amongst the destruction, Jaryoon comes across an unconscious Shyao and engages in a battle to the death with Sage Heian! Who will survive this clash of the titans? And what stunning secret will be revealed by Guae, a disciple of Taorun?

TOKYOPOP PRESENTS
MANGA 漫画
THE NEW SIZZLING HOT
FREE
MAGAZINE
ZELDA AND FRIEND FROM
WAR ON FLESH
© Justin Boring, Greg Hildebrandt and TOKYOPOP Inc.
SIGN UP FOR FREE WWW.TOKYOPOP.COM

TOKYOPOP SHOP

Music...mystery...and Murder!

RoadSong

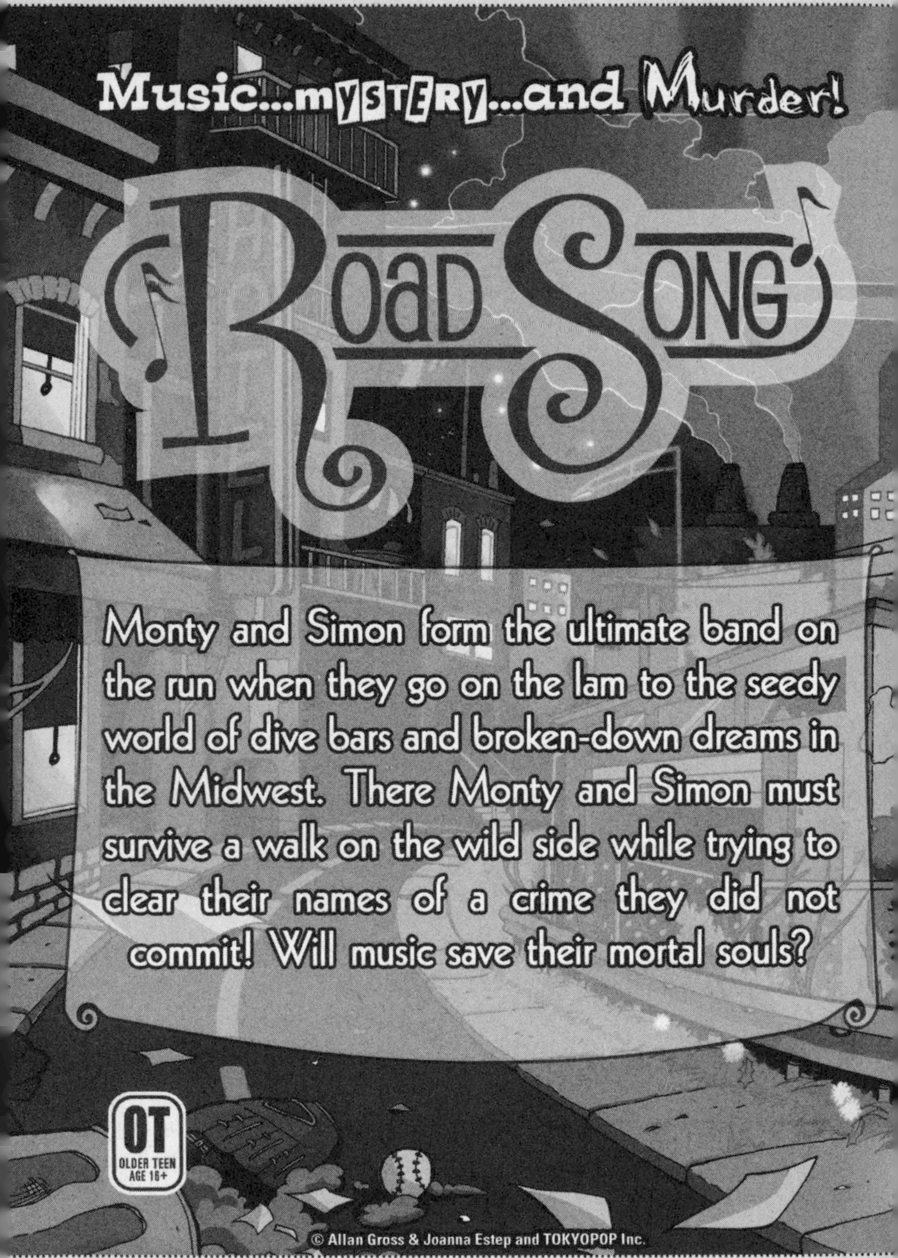

Monty and Simon form the ultimate band on the run when they go on the lam to the seedy world of dive bars and broken-down dreams in the Midwest. There Monty and Simon must survive a walk on the wild side while trying to clear their names of a crime they did not commit! Will music save their mortal souls?

OT
OLDER TEEN
AGE 16+

READ A CHAPTER OF THE MANGA ONLINE FOR FREE:

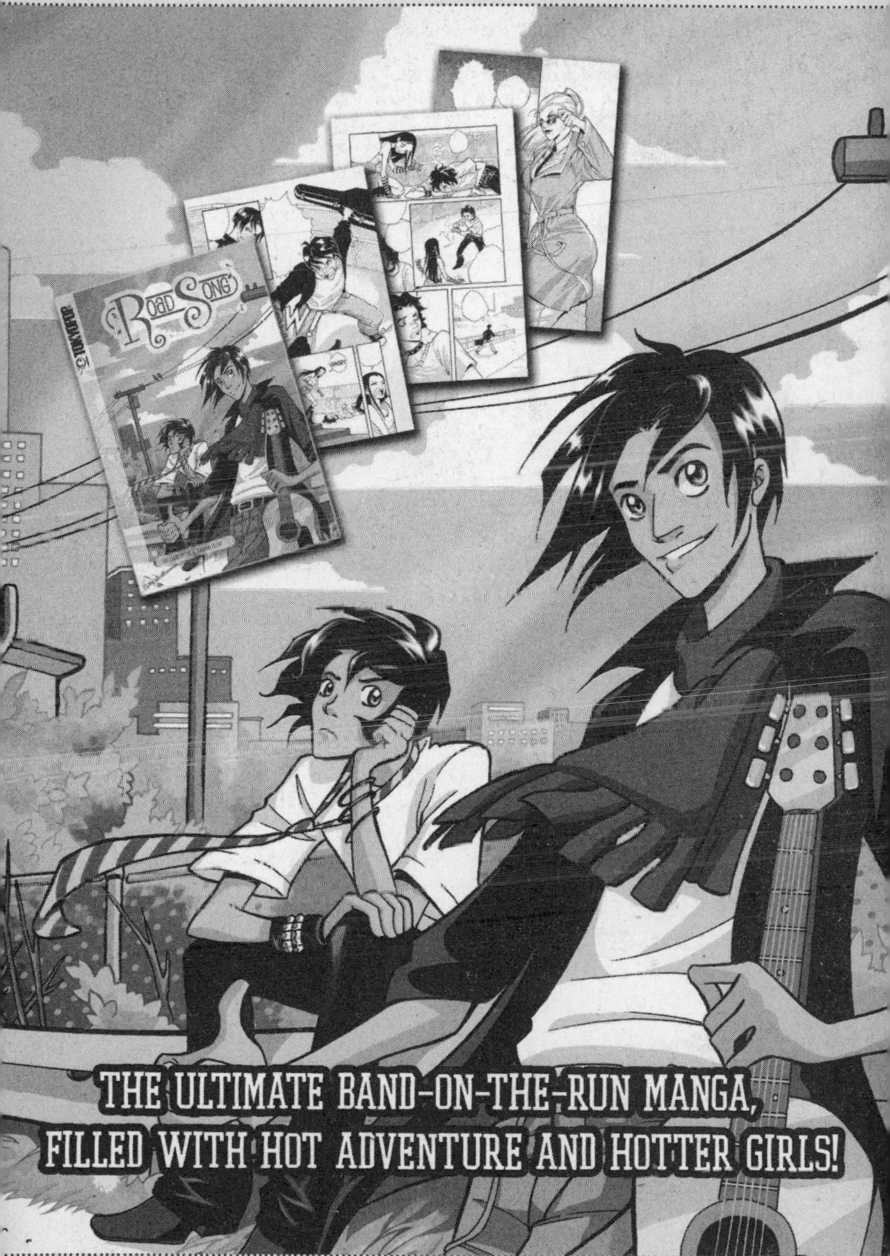
ROAD SONG
THE ULTIMATE BAND-ON-THE-RUN MANGA,
FILLED WITH HOT ADVENTURE AND HOTTER GIRLS!

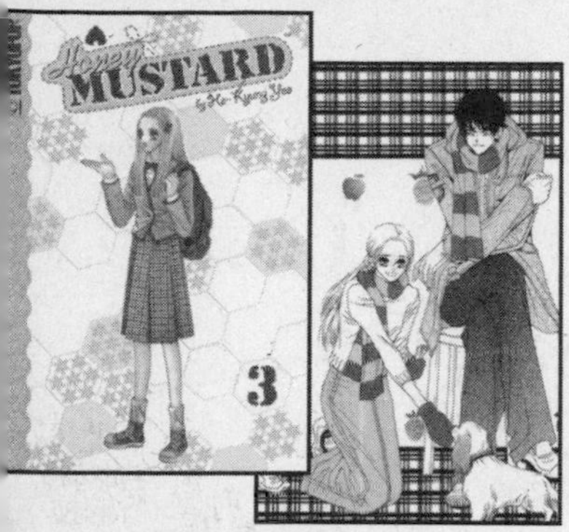
Honey MUSTARD
3

BY HO-KYUNG YEO

HONEY MUSTARD

I'm often asked about the title of *Honey Mustard*. What does a condiment have to do with romance and teen angst? One might ask the same thing about a basket of fruits, but I digress. Honey mustard is sweet with a good dose of bite, and I'd say that sums up this series pretty darn well, too. Ho-Kyung Yeo does a marvelous job of balancing the painful situations of adolescence with plenty of whacked-out humor to keep the mood from getting *too* heavy. It's a good, solid romantic comedy...and come to think of it, it'd go great with that sandwich.

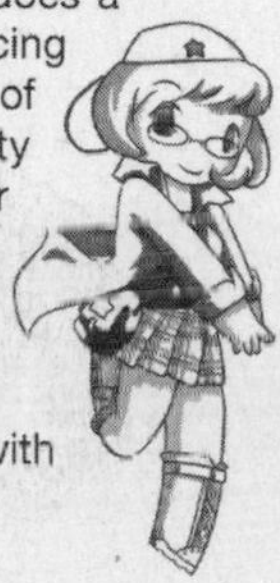

~Carol Fox, Editor

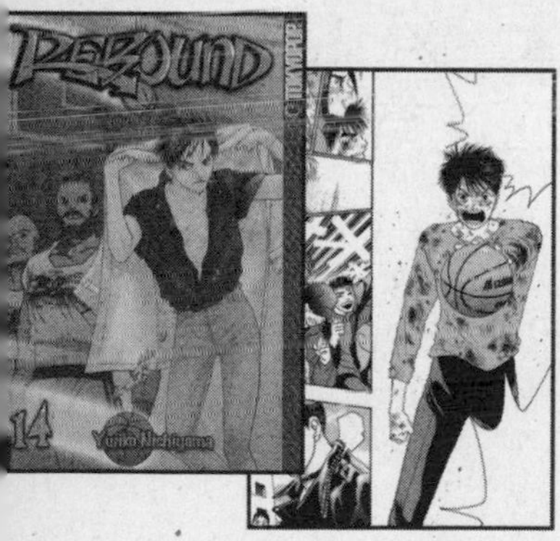
REBOUND
14
Yuriko Nishiyama

BY YURIKO NISHIYAMA

REBOUND

At first glance, *Rebound* may seem like a simple sports manga. But on closer inspection, you'll find that the real drama takes place off the court. While the kids of the Johnan basketball team play and grow as a team, they learn valuable life lessons as well. By fusing the raw energy of basketball with the apple pie earnestness of an afterschool special, Yuriko Nishiyama has created a unique and heartfelt manga that appeals to all readers, male and female.

~Troy Lewter, Editor

© Minari Endoh/ICHIJINSHA

DAZZLE
BY MINARI ENDOH

When a young girl named Rahzel sets out to see the world, she meets Alzeid, a mysterious loner on a mission to find his father's killer. Although the two share similar magical abilities, they don't exactly see eye-to-eye...but they will need each other to survive their journey!

An epic coming-of-age story from an accomplished manga artist!

© CHIHO SAITOU and IKUNI & Be-PaPas

THE WORLD EXISTS FOR ME
BY BE-PAPAS AND CHIHO SAITOU

Once upon a time, the source of the devil R's invincible powers was *The Book of S & M*. But one day, a young man stole the book without knowing what it was, cut it into strips and used it to create a girl doll named "S" and a boy doll named "M." With that act, the unimaginable power that the devil held from the book was unleashed upon the world!

From the creators of the manga classic *Revolutionary Girl Utena!*

© Keitaro Arima

TSUKUYOMI: MOON PHASE
BY KEITARO ARIMA

Cameraman Kouhei Midou is researching Schwarz Quelle Castle. When he steps inside the castle's great walls, he discovers a mysterious little girl, Hazuki, who's been trapped there for years. Utilizing her controlling charm, Hazuki tries to get Kouhei to set her free. But this sweet little girl isn't everything she appears to be...

The manga that launched the popular anime!

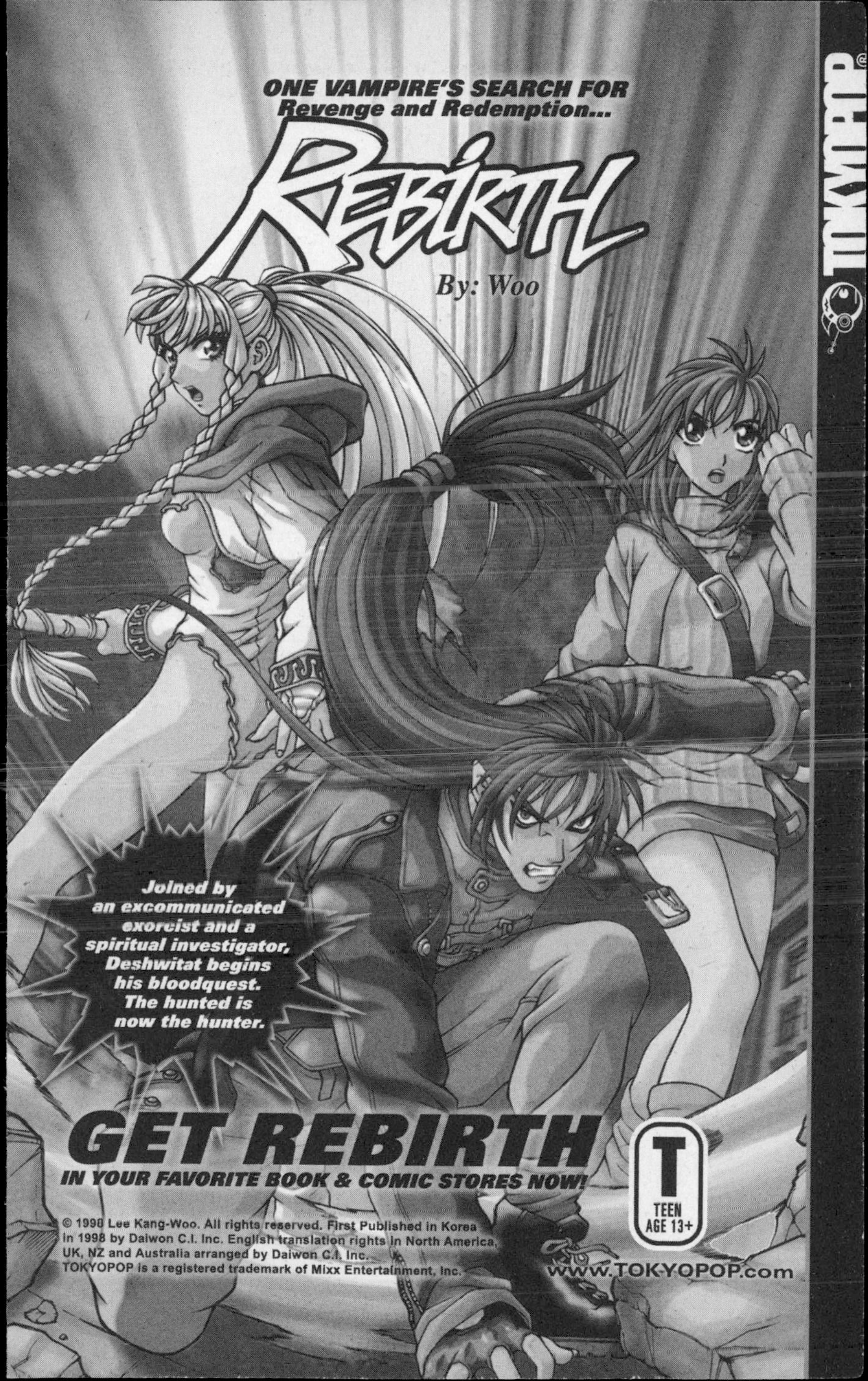
ONE VAMPIRE'S SEARCH FOR
Revenge and Redemption...
REBIRTH
By: Woo
Joined by an excommunicated exorcist and a spiritual investigator, Deshwitat begins his bloodquest. The hunted is now the hunter.
GET REBIRTH
IN YOUR FAVORITE BOOK & COMIC STORES NOW!
T
TEEN
AGE 13+
© 1998 Lee Kang-Woo. All rights reserved. First Published in Korea in 1998 by Daiwon C.I. Inc. English translation rights in North America, UK, NZ and Australia arranged by Daiwon C.I. Inc.
TOKYOPOP is a registered trademark of Mixx Entertainment, Inc.
www.TOKYOPOP.com
TOKYOPOP®